THE I TATTI
RENAISSANCE LIBRARY

James Hankins, General Editor

BOCCACCIO
FAMOUS WOMEN

ITRL I

GIOVANNI BOCCACCIO
✦ ✦ ✦
FAMOUS WOMEN

EDITED AND TRANSLATED BY

VIRGINIA BROWN

THE I TATTI RENAISSANCE LIBRARY
HARVARD UNIVERSITY PRESS
CAMBRIDGE, MASSACHUSETTS
LONDON, ENGLAND

Series design by Dean Bornstein

Library of Congress Cataloging-in-Publication Data

Boccaccio, Giovanni, 1313–1375
[De mulieribus claris. English & Latin]
Famous women / Giovanni Boccaccio;
edited and translated by Virginia Brown.
p.   cm. — (ITRL; 1)
Includes bibliographical references and index.
ISBN 0-674-00347-0 (alk. paper)
1. Women — Biography.   I. Brown, Virginia, 1940–
II. Title   III. I Tatti Renaissance library; 1.
PQ4274.D5 E5 2001
920.72 — dc21
[B]   00-053492

Second printing, 2001

Contents

ॐ॰ॐ

Introduction   xi

FAMOUS WOMEN

Dedication   2
Preface   8

· CONTENTS ·

· CONTENTS ·

· CONTENTS ·

Introduction

✥✥✥

It is a surprise to many modern readers to learn that Giovanni Boccaccio's most popular work, the collection of one hundred stories known as the *Decameron*, is by no means typical of his writings. In fact, the *Decameron* is almost an *unicum* among Boccaccio's works. Despite his unmatched skill as a storyteller, a skill that has delighted many generations of readers, the *novella* was not a genre that the Florentine writer cultivated over long periods of his career. As a glance at the dates and titles of his numerous works will show,[1] Boccaccio (1313–1375) consumed the earlier part of his literary career composing, in Italian, a series of elegant poems and prose romances that may be broadly classed as courtly literature. After the composition of the *Decameron* (1348–1351), Boccaccio devoted the last decades of his life, dominated by the influence of Petrarch's humanism, to compiling, in Latin, several large and learned tomes, including a mythological encyclopedia, a compendium of the lives of great men, a geographical encyclopedia, and the biographical compendium of famous women translated here. Yet while Boccaccio's vernacular works continue to be read and studied by students of Italian literature and his *Decameron* enjoys undiminished popularity, the Latin prose works of his later years, written in a stilted and diffuse style, have mostly gathered dust on the shelves. But at least one of them, the compendium of *Famous Women*, deserves to be better known.

Boccaccio's *Famous Women* (*De mulieribus claris*) is the first collection of biographies in Western literature devoted exclusively to women. The nucleus of this innovative work, consisting in its final form of 104 chapters,[2] was written at Certaldo between the summer of 1361 and the summer of 1362. It was dedicated to Andrea

Acciaiuoli, Countess of Altavilla, a Tuscan noblewoman living in southern Italy. Andrea was the sister of Niccolò Acciaiuoli, an old friend of Boccaccio who was a member of an eminent Florentine family and a major power behind the throne of Joanna, Queen of Naples.

In the Preface (§1), Boccaccio informs us it was Petrarch's *Lives of Famous Men* (*De viris illustribus*) that prompted him to undertake his own work, for it was through Petrarch's work that he came to appreciate the need for a similar compilation dealing with famous women. Boccaccio further explains (§6) that his purpose in writing the *Famous Women* is to record for posterity the stories of women who were renowned for any sort of great deed. Inevitably, this means including both good and bad women, but the distaste aroused by recounting the wicked deeds of some protagonists will be offset, he claims, by the exhortations to virtue that have been included (§7). Boccaccio hopes that this mixture of the pleasant and the profitable will make its way into his reader's mind and function as a spur to virtue and a curb on vice.

Detailed studies of the more than one hundred manuscripts in which the text is preserved have distinguished at least nine stages in the composition of the *Famous Women*.[3] So large a number of codices shows, incidentally, that it was among the most popular works in the last age of the manuscript book; the relative obscurity in which the work now lies is a post-Renaissance phenomenon. But more to the point, the evidence these same manuscripts preserve of numerous authorial additions, deletions, rearrangements, and other textual changes demonstrates that his work on *Famous Women* was of persistent interest to Boccaccio in the last two decades of his life.

Indeed, by a fortunate chance we possess a manuscript witness, in Boccaccio's own hand, to the final (eighth and ninth) revisions, namely, Florence, Biblioteca Medicea Laurenziana 90

sup. 98¹ (Gaddi 593).⁴ This witness was the basis of Vittorio Zaccaria's authoritative edition of 1967,⁵ and it serves as well as the basis of the present edition and translation.

The various revisions to and expansions of the text made by Boccaccio help clarify its dating as well as the motives which prompted him to compile the work. Briefly, the nine stages in which the text was composed are as follows:⁶

Stages 1–3: (summer of 1361) Boccaccio composes a preface and 102 chapters in three successive groups comprising Eve-Enguldrada (74 chapters), Opis–Constance (21 chapters), and Sabina Poppaea–Thisbe (7 chapters).

Stage 4: (June 1362) Boccaccio is invited to Naples by Niccolò Acciaiuoli, Grand Seneschal of Queen Joanna. Lest (as scholars suppose) he arrive empty-handed, he draws together the completed portions of the work, penning a dedication to Andrea, Niccolò's sister. At this point he still considers the *Famous Women* an unfinished work (§7 "To you, therefore, I send, and to your name I dedicate, what I have *thus far* written about famous women" [emphasis added]).

Stage 5: he then writes the present chapters XXXI and LXXX and adds moralizing sections to chapters XXVI, XXVII, LI, and LXXVII.

Stage 6: still later he adopts a chronological arrangement of the text, eliminates three doublets (*Arachne, Manto, Niobe*), inserts three new chapters (LXXXVI, CV, CVI), adds a conclusion, and makes other alterations and additions to the existing text.

Stage 7: thereafter he continues to make small adjustments to the text.

Stage 8: towards the end of his life Boccaccio copies, in a neat, legible script, what is now MS Laur. 90 sup. 98¹ (Gaddi 593);⁷ the text contained therein exhibits still further modifications of earlier redactions.

Stage 9: the marginal notes and corrections to the autograph, Laur. 90 sup. 98[1] (Gaddi 593), are presumably afterthoughts and represent the final stage in Boccaccio's labors on the *Famous Women.*

The opening sentence of the dedication furnishes a clue as to the precise date when Boccaccio embarked upon his task. He tells the dedicatee that he has written a "slim volume" in praise of women "a short time ago during a carefree period." This period has been taken by students of Boccaccio to refer to the summer of 1361 when he ceded his house *oltr'Arno,* in the district of S. Spirito, to his half-brother Iacopo and withdrew to Certaldo.[8] There, during the late summer of that same year, he wrote to Pino de' Rossi that his removal to Certaldo had brought him tranquillity and freedom from the encumbrances of life in Florence.[9] Various references in the same letter to women whose biographies figure in the *Famous Women* provide additional evidence that Boccaccio was in the midst of writing the work.[10]

At least three more stages of Boccaccio's activity can be distinguished, thanks to the dedication to Andrea Acciaiuoli. Boccaccio did not leave for Naples until November 1362. Hence the sections in the *Famous Women* intended as compliments to his southern hosts — the dedicatory letter and chapters cv (Camiola, a Tuscan woman who had lived in Sicily) and cvi (Joanna, Queen of Naples) — suggest that the fourth, fifth, and sixth stages of revision took place in the five months following the arrival in June of Niccolò Acciaiuoli's invitation.

The text of the dedication is curious because to modern ears it seems to betray a certain tactlessness on Boccaccio's part. He begins with the observation that his "slim volume" (*libellum*) was intended to give pleasure to his friends; as it concerned women, it should be dedicated to "some distinguished lady." The first name to occur to him was that of Joanna, Queen of Naples.

But Boccaccio was afraid that his book was not worthy of so illustrious a personage; hence, after considering many other alternatives, he at length settled upon Andrea. While such frankness
seems clumsy to the modern reader, there is doubtless an intended compliment in Boccaccio's ranking of Andrea as second
only to the Queen; this was a compliment that Andrea, as a
member of Joanna's court, would have been obliged to accept
gracefully. As she would have known, courtly etiquette required
Boccaccio to explain why, upon arriving at a foreign court, he
should present his work to a feudal inferior rather than to the
Queen herself.

Even so, in view of the contents of the *Famous Women*, the dedication to Andrea may appear less than fully appropriate to modern eyes. Boccaccio expresses the hope (Dedication, §6) that his
book will bring Andrea as much fame as did her marriages to the
late Carlo d'Arto, Count of Monteodorisio, and her present husband Bartolomeo II of Capua, Count of Altavilla. Yet the *Famous
Women* contains numerous exhortations to women to preserve
their "illustrious widowhood" and many harsh condemnations of
women who remarry. It is hard at first glance to imagine that
Andrea would not have read this as a criticism of her own conduct.

But this was surely not Boccaccio's intention. The greater part
of the *Famous Women*, it will be remembered, was already written
before the arrival of Niccolò Acciaiuoli's invitation and the likeli-
hood is that Boccaccio was compelled by circumstances to present
his hosts with the one original work he had available at the moment, whether or not it was completely suitable to his purposes.
Nonetheless, we might have expected Boccaccio, in the manner of
other authors, to compose a dedicatory letter more in keeping with
the condition of its recipient. The fact that he did not may indicate a certain haste or maladroitness on his part. Or perhaps he

did not expect that Andrea Acciaiuoli would actually spend much time reading the *Famous Women*.

If she did, she might have sensed the changing attitudes of the time towards women and the position they should hold in the home and in society. For, though still influenced by medieval conceptions of women, Boccaccio provides in the *Famous Women* a striking foretaste of ideas that would later find clearer expression in the Renaissance — ideas such as the view that it was appropriate for gifted women (at least) to seek and acquire fame for their contributions to art, literature, and the active life of public affairs. Such themes would become common (if not quite commonplaces) in Quattrocento humanist writings.

The influence of Petrarchan humanism is already evident in the contents of the *Famous Women*. The series of lives starts with Eve (I), who is followed by the Assyrian queen Semiramis (II) and six pagan goddesses (III–VIII). There follows a series of thirty-four Greek and Roman mythological figures of heroic or semi-divine status (IX–XLII), closing with Nicaula (XLIII), a Biblical figure. Then there begins another long series (XLIV–CVI), in approximate chronological order, of what may be termed "historical" figures — historical in the sense that Boccaccio finds most of his information in sources usually classified as historical. This second series also includes Athaliah (LI) and Mariamme (LXXXVII), two women who have Biblical associations as well. Only the last six lives treat women who lived in post-classical times (a circumstance which has suggested to some scholars that Boccaccio's original plan may have called for an even one hundred biographies restricted to classical women). The work ends with a formal conclusion wherein Boccaccio tries to anticipate and answer his critics' objections to his choice of the women to be included, and to defend passages that some readers might consider inappropriate. This apologetic passage and similar ones scattered throughout the work recall the

elaborate justifications for the portrayal of vice typical of the *Decameron*.

The contents of *Famous Women* and his own explicit statements (Preface, §§9–10) make it plain that Boccaccio's principle of selection favored the pagan women of Greco-Roman antiquity. Nearly all Christian women were deliberately excluded on the grounds that they had been sufficiently celebrated already in hagiographical literature. Boccaccio states further that the life stories of Christian women are from a thematic point of view at odds with those of pagan women: the former sought eternal glory by means of an endurance that was often contrary to human nature; the latter achieved earthly fame with the help of gifts and instincts they had received from Nature, or through a desire for fleeting glory. Nevertheless (and here Boccaccio parts ways with the ancient Church Fathers and shows himself a humanist) their achievements are worthy of record and deserve to be emulated, even by Christian women.

The biographies of the *Famous Women* mostly follow the same formal pattern, borrowed from Jerome and Petrarch. Normally the life begins with the name of the woman, her parentage, and her rank. Next the reason for her fame is stated in general terms. Then Boccaccio explains in detail how her fame was acquired, usually in the form of a narrative. He authenticates his accounts by frequent allusions to learned authorities, almost always unspecified. At the conclusion of the biography comes a moral lesson or a moral exhortation or a passage of philosophical reflection. Further moralizing precepts are sometimes scattered throughout the narrative.

What sources were available to Boccaccio and how he exploited them is a subject that has yet to be investigated thoroughly by scholars.[11] Boccaccio never assumes that his authorities have supplied fully reliable information, and he does not hesitate to report differing opinions. The only sources explicitly cited are St. Paul

(XLII.22), the Bible (XLIII.2–3), and Jerome (LXXXVI.2). But the biographies themselves by their wording or substance yield evidence that Boccaccio used classical authors such as Livy, Ovid, Pliny the Elder, Statius, Suetonius, Valerius Maximus, and Virgil. He also drew upon late antique writers like Justinus, Lactantius, and Orosius, together with the mysterious "Theodontius" (whom he cites by name in the *Genealogiae deorum*). For the medieval biographies (CI–CVI) he relied on the chronicles of authors roughly contemporary with himself. Boccaccio's own library included many of these texts,[12] and his friend Petrarch would have made others accessible.

It is clear, however, that Boccaccio often retold the stories with far greater elaboration than can be found in his sources. Valerius Maximus, whose concise account sometimes furnishes the kernel of a story, is a good case in point: Boccaccio's account of the Minyan wives (XXXI), Hippo (LIII), Megullia Dotata (LIV), Claudia (LXII), Tertia Aemilia (LXXIV), and Sempronia (LXXVI) are all considerably longer and more finely wrought. Are these additional details the product of his own imagination or did he have recourse to another source as yet unidentified? Such problems still await scholarly solutions.

The still unresolved questions concerning the sources of *Famous Women* complicate the issue of Boccaccio's own view of women in this work. At first glance, his attitude does not appear especially positive: Boccaccio does not hesitate to pronounce women the inferior sex both in mind and in body (Dedication, §5; Preface, §4; XCIII.6). They are by nature obstinate and unbending (LXXVI.6), stingy (LXIX.6), timid (XCVI.4), suspicious (LXXIV.4), lascivious (XCV.2), avaricious (CV.32), less gifted than men (XXVI.9), and desirous of leading idle, useless lives in the confines of the household (LXXXVI.3; XCVII.10). Such praise as they do

merit they do not earn *qua* female; the highest accolade Boccaccio can bestow upon a woman is to describe her as "man-like" or as a woman capable of deeds beyond the powers of most men (e.g., II.13; LVII.10, 21; LXII.4; LXVI.2; LXIX.3; LXXVI.4; LXXXVI.4). This pattern is already established in the Dedication. Boccaccio's remarks (§5) on Andrea Acciaiuoli's gentle and upright character, elegance of speech, and intellectual powers culminate in the observation that she has been endowed with all these qualities to a degree surpassing the usual feminine estate, thus making her worthy to bear the name Andrea, which in Greek (says Boccaccio, in a typical false etymology) has the meaning of "man".

It should be remembered, however, that this condescending manner of praising with faint damns is characteristic of the cultural legacy inherited by Boccaccio from antiquity and the Middle Ages.[13] If such attitudes are Boccaccio's they are also attitudes common to the men of his time and education. In Boccaccio's defense it may be said that in certain respects he succeeds in escaping the prejudices of his sex and his sources. In general he is much more expansive than his sources in praising women's intellectual powers or their literary accomplishments or their moral virtues or their artistic creations. His sources will report that a given woman was known for such things, but will usually not go beyond a bare mention of the fact. Boccaccio's unqualified and apparently sincere admiration for the literary achievements of women like Isis (VI.4), Nicostrata (XXVII.1), Nicaula (XLIII.2), and Proba (XCVII.4); for the paintings of Tamaris (LVI.2); for the courage of Triaria (XCVI.4) and the endurance of Epicharis (XCIII.7) strikes a new note in the history of Latin literature.

Of course the rhetorical practice of praise and blame is fundamental to humanist literature, and it is from this point of view that we can best understand Boccaccio's broader reasons for compiling panegyrical accounts of female virtue and ability. The work

in fact displays several features that are typical of early Renaissance humanistic literature. It was a conviction of humanists from the time of Petrarch onwards that contemporary education did too little to provide the moral and intellectual formation needed by social and political elites in Italian cities. The humanist movement sought to provide that missing formation. It believed that a close study of classical literature and history would give the future leaders of Italian society (both male and female) the eloquence, prudence, and ethical models necessary for them to exercise power virtuously in the world. The literary pleasure afforded by the great classical writers would sweeten the pill of moral instruction contained in all sound literature. Classical history contained a treasury of wise and noble behavior upon which the future leader could model himself; hence the importance (evident in *Famous Women*) of separating historical truth from myth. Good literature (*bonae litterae, litterae humaniores*) taught that true nobility came not (or not only) from lineage, but (also) from noble conduct—that is, from virtue. Christianity was our best guide to ultimate salvation, but in the present life the noble Greeks and Romans provided the most fruitful examples of how to act in war and peace. Boccaccio clearly shares the admiration for old Roman virtue (later to become characteristic of the so-called civic humanists of the early Quattrocento): for Roman severity, dignity, eloquence, patriotism, self-sacrifice, and martial valor. These were the very qualities the humanists longed to bring to life again in the Italian society of their own day. Boccaccio's *Famous Women* underlines better than any other text of the period that the revival of Roman virtue and civilization we refer to as the Renaissance was intended to embrace women as well as men.

Boccaccio, who often expresses his desire in the *Famous Women* to rescue his subject from oblivion or to preserve her deeds for future

generations, would surely have been gratified by posterity's interest in his book. We have already noted that the work survives in more than a hundred manuscripts, an unusually high number, even in the last age of the hand-produced book. Another indication of the popularity of the work is the various vernacular renderings that appeared almost immediately after the Latin version began to circulate. Donato degli Albanzani, a friend of both Boccaccio and Petrarch, translated the work into Italian sometime in the last decades of the fourteenth century. Shortly thereafter fra Antonio di S. Lupidio made another *volgare* translation. A French version, at one time ascribed to Laurent de Premierfait, was produced at the beginning of the fifteenth century. Heinrich Steinhöwel translated into German an early redaction of the *Famous Women* when it still lacked chapters LXXXVI, CV, and CVI. Around 1440 there appeared a Middle English verse translation of twenty-one chapters, along with the Preface and Conclusion. In 1494 and 1528 a Spanish translation was published at Zaragoza and Seville. There are three more translations from the sixteenth century: Henry Parker's English rendering, dedicated to Henry VIII, of forty-six lives from the *Famous Women*, and the Italian versions of Giuseppe Betussi and Luca Antonio Ridolfi.

The work, clearly, remained popular for some time after the invention of printing. The first edition of the Latin text came from the press of Johan Zainer at Ulm in 1473. Two more incunabula followed, one ca. 1474–75 (? Strassburg?) and the other in 1487 (Louvain). The edition published by Mathias Apiarius at Bern in 1539 seems to be the only complete sixteenth-century printed text in Latin of the *Famous Women*. Then more than 400 years passed before Zaccaria's edition, based on the autograph manuscript, first appeared in 1967.

No list, however, of Latin and vernacular editions can by itself do justice to the literary and cultural influence exerted by *Famous*

Women on authors of England, France, Germany, Spain, and even Poland. In *The Canterbury Tales,* for example, Chaucer inserted a translation of the entire chapter on Zenobia (c) as one of the stories that make up *The Monk's Tale.* Christine de Pizan's *Livre de la cité des dames* (1405) used Boccaccio's work as its point of departure. Jean Lemaire, a Belgian rhetorician and a precursor of the Pléiade, drew on Boccaccio's work for his own *Couronne margaritique* (a panegyric of Marguerite of Austria). Edmund Spenser knew and used several works of Boccaccio, including the *Famous Women.* The *Famous Women* also inspired many imitators in the fifteenth and sixteenth centuries, among whom are Iacopo Filippo Foresti (*De plurimis claris selectisque mulieribus*), Giovanni Sabbadino degli Arienti (*Gynevera de le clare donne*), Alvaro de Luna (*De las virtuosas y claras mujeres*), Alonso of Cartagena (*De las mujeres ilustres*), and Thomas Elyot's *Defence of Good Women.*

Boccaccio's compilation is thus the fountainhead of the European tradition of female biography and for that reason alone deserves an honored place in the history of Western literature. Even though the book only rarely displays the wit that renders the *Decameron* an enduring classic,[14] even though its heavy-handed moralizing is as foreign to modern taste as it is possible to be, Boccaccio's stories, nevertheless, are usually well-told, memorable, and filled with piquant details. They are a valuable record of Italian humanist thought in its formative stages. And they provide the modern reader with a fascinating glimpse of medieval attitudes to women at a moment in history when such attitudes were beginning to give way to more modern views of the female sex and its potentialities.

While the present work was in preparation, the world of Latin philology lost two of its brightest ornaments, Giuseppe Billanovich and Jozef IJsewijn. As this is the first volume in a series designed to bring Renaissance Latin literature to the attention of a

broader public, it seems appropriate to dedicate this edition and translation to the memory of these two extraordinary scholars, *hortatores exemplaque laudum*, who did so much to establish Neo-Latin literature as a field of study in its own right.

V. B.

April 2000
Pontifical Institute of
Mediaeval Studies,
Toronto

NOTES

1. For an authoritative survey of Boccaccio's life and works see Vittore Branca, *Boccaccio: The Man and His Works*, tr. R. Monges (New York, 1976).

2. While the chapter numbering is consecutive from I through CVI, chapters XI–XII and XIX–XX are traditionally combined as they constitute joint biographies of Marpesia and Lampedon, Orithya and Antiope, respectively.

3. For listings of codices with the text of the *Famous Women*, see the Bibliography, under "Branca, V."

4. The relatively recent discovery of this autograph was made by P. G. Ricci ("Studi sulle opere latine e volgari del Boccaccio," *Rinascimento* 10 [1959] 3–12).

5. V. Branca, ed., *Tutte le opere di Giovanni Boccaccio*, vol. X: V. Zaccaria, ed. and trans., *De mulieribus claris* ([Milan,] 1967; 2nd edition, 1970). Henceforth all references to Zaccaria's text and translation will be to the 1970 edition.

6. Nine stages of redaction were established by V. Zaccaria, "Le fasi redazionali del 'De mulieribus claris'," *Studi sul Boccaccio* 1 (1963) 253–332. For earlier studies on the scope and number of the redactions of the *Famous Women*, see A. Hortis, *Studj sulle opere latine del Boccaccio* (Trieste, 1879); G. Traversari, "Appunti sulle redazioni del 'De claris mulieribus',"

in *Miscellanea di studi in onore di G. Mazzoni*, vol. 1 (Florence, 1907), pp. 225 ff.; G. Pasquali, *Storia della tradizione e critica del testo*, 3rd edition (Florence, 1988), pp. 443–48; and Ricci, "Studi sulle opere," pp. 12–21 (seven redactions). In the reprinted version of his article (see the Bibliography) Ricci still maintains that there are seven redactions, and points out (p. 130 n. 1) some difficulties with Zaccaria's hypothesis of nine redactions.

7. A. C. de la Mare, *The Handwriting of Italian Humanists*, vol. 1, fasc. 1 (London, 1973), p. 27, no. 8: "Copied very late in Boccaccio's life, probably *c.* 1373."

8. Ricci, "Studi sulle opere," pp. 25–26. The text of the act of donation, dated 2 July 1361, is printed in F. Corazzini, *Le lettere edite e inedite di messer Giovanni Boccaccio* (Florence, 1877), pp. CII–CV.

9. Boccaccio's letter (Corazzini, *ibid.*, pp. 67–97) was intended to bring comfort to Pino de' Rossi, who had been exiled in 1360. Ricci, *ibid.*, pp. 21–32 demonstrates that the date of this letter is late summer of 1361 (and not 1363, as previously believed).

10. See Corazzini, *ibid.*, pp. 85–86 for allusions to Helen, Cleopatra, Cassandra, Olympias, Hypsicratea, Sulpitia (wife of Lentulus Truscellio [= Cruscellio]), the wives of the Minyans, Portia, and Julia (daughter of Julius Caesar).

11. The fullest treatment of the sources currently available is that found in Zaccaria's edition. In the Notes below are listed, for each biography, the principal sources that have so far been identified. This list draws freely on the notes in Zaccaria's edition and G. A. Guarino's translation (see the Bibliography), though all references have been verified and corrected where necessary.

12. A. Mazza, "L'inventario della *parva libraria* di Santo Spirito e la biblioteca del Boccaccio," *Italia medioevale e umanistica* 9 (1966) 1–74, with a list of known surviving manuscripts written or owned by Boccaccio.

13. Some of the sources we can identify with certainty laud a woman for her courage (traditionally a male virtue) by comparing her to a man. For example, Valerius Maximus, *Factorum et dictorum memorabilium libri IX* V.4.6 (Claudia, a Vestal Virgin): "These were great works of manly pi-

ety, but I doubt whether any were more brave and spirited than the deed of Claudia the Vestal Virgin"; Justinus, *Epitoma Historiarum philippicarum Pompei Trogi* II.12.24 (Artemisia): "indeed, just as you would find in Xerxes a womanish fear, so in Artemisia there was virile audacity."

14. The biographies of Flora (LXIV) and Paulina (XCI) are the most "Boccaccian" of the lives.

FAMOUS WOMEN

꙰

Iohannes Boccaccius de Certaldo
mulieri clarissime Andree de Acciarolis de Florentia
Alteville comitisse

1 Pridie, mulierum egregia, paululum ab inerti vulgo semotus et a
ceteris fere solutus[1] curis, in eximiam muliebris sexus laudem ac
amicorum solatium, potius quam in magnum rei publice commo-
2 dum, libellum scripsi. Verum, dum mecum animo versarem cuinam illum primum transmicterem, ne penes me marceret ocio et
ut, alieno fultus favore, securior iret in publicum, adverteremque
satis non principi viro, sed potius, cum de mulieribus loqueretur,
alicui insigni femine destinandum fore, exquirenti digniorem, ante
alias venit in mentem ytalicum iubar illud prefulgidum ac singula-
ris, non tantum feminarum, sed regum gloria, Iohanna, serenis-
sima Ierusalem et Sicilie regina.

3 Cuius pensatis, tam inclite prosapie et avorum fulgoribus,
quam novis a se forti pectore quesitis laudibus, in desiderium mic-
tendi illum humilem devotumque ante solium sue celsitudinis in-
4 cidi. Tandem, quia adeo ingens regius fulgor est et opusculi tenuis
et fere semisopita favillula, timens ne a potiori lumine minor omnino fugaretur in tenebras, sensim retraxi consilium; et, nova inda-
gine multis aliis perquisitis, ad extremum ab illustri regina in te
5 votum deflexi meum; nec inmerito. Nam, dum mites ac celebres
mores tuos, dum honestatem eximiam, summum matronarum decus, dumque verborum elegantiam mente revolverem, et cum his

Dedication

꣠꣢꣠

Giovanni Boccaccio of Certaldo
to the Illustrious Lady Andrea Acciaiuoli of Florence,
Countess of Altavilla

A short time ago, gracious lady, at a moment when I was able   1
to isolate myself from the idle mob and was nearly carefree, I
wrote—more for my friends' pleasure than for the benefit of the
broader public—a slim volume in praise of women. I deliberated   2
as to whom I should first send this work so that it would not languish idly in my possession; supported by another's good will, I
thought, the book would have a better chance of reaching the public. Since women are the subject of the book, I saw that it ought to
be dedicated, not to a prince, but to some distinguished lady. As I
searched for a worthy recipient, the first woman who came to
mind was that radiant splendor of Italy, that unique glory not only
of women but of rulers: Joanna, Most Serene Queen of Sicily and
Jerusalem.[a]

I considered the brilliance of her celebrated family and fore-   3
bears as well as the more recent praises her own brave spirit had
recently won, and I was strongly tempted to place this humble and
pious work before Her Majesty's throne. In the end, however, as   4
her royal luster is so dazzling and the flickering flame of my little
book so small and weak, I gradually changed my mind, fearing
that the greater would altogether eclipse the lesser light. Renewing
my inquiries, at length I bent my desires upon you rather than
upon the illustrious queen, and justly so. For as I reflected on your   5
character, both gentle and renowned; your outstanding probity,
women's greatest ornament; and your elegance of speech; and as I
noted your generosity of soul and your powers of intellect far sur-

3

animi tui generositatem et ingenii vires, quibus longe femineas excedis, adverterem videremque quod sexui <in>firmiori² natura detraxerit, id tuo pectori Deus sua liberalitate miris virtutibus superinfuserit atque suppleverit, et eo, quo insignita es nomine, designari voluerit — cum *andres* Greci quod latine dicimus *homines* nuncupent — te equiparandam probissimis quibuscunque, etiam vetustissimis, arbitratus sum.

6   Et ideo, cum tempestate nostra multis atque splendidis facinoribus agentibus clarissimum vetustatis specimen sis, tanquam benemerito tuo fulgori huius libelli tituli munus adiecisse velim, existimans non minus apud posteros tuo nomini addidisse decoris quam fecerit, olim Montisodorisii et nunc Alteville comitatus, quibus te fortuna fecit illustrem.

7   Ad te igitur micto et tuo nomini dedico quod hactenus a me de mulieribus claris scriptum est; precorque, inclita mulier, per sanctum pudicitie nomen, quo inter mortales plurimum emines, grato animo munusculum scolastici hominis suscipias; et, si michi aliquid creditura es, aliquando legas suadeo; suis quippe suffragiis tuis blandietur ociis, dum feminea virtute et historiarum lepiditate

8 letaberis. Nec incassum, arbitror, agitabitur lectio si, facinorum preteritarum mulierum emula, egregium animum tuum concitabis in melius.

9   Et esto nonnunquam lasciva comperias immixta sacris — quod ut facerem recitandorum coegit oportunitas — ne omiseris vel horrescas; quin imo perseverans, uti viridarium intrans, eburneas manus, semotis spinarum aculeis, extendis in florem, sic, obscenis sepositis, collige laudanda; et quotiens in gentili muliere quid dignum, christianam religionem professa³ legeris, quod in te fore non senseris, ruborem mentis excita et te ipsam redargue quod, Christi delinita crismate, honestate aut pudicitia vel virtute supereris ab extera; et, provocato in vires ingenio, quo plurimum vales,

4

passing the endowments of womankind; as I saw that what nature
has denied the weaker sex God has freely instilled in your breast
and complemented with marvelous virtues, to the point where he
willed you to be known by the name you bear (*andres* being in
Greek the equivalent of the Latin word for 'men') — considering all
this, I felt that you deserved comparison with the most excellent
women anywhere, even among the ancients.

Your many splendid deeds have made you a shining model of   6
ancient virtue in our time, and so I should like to increase your
well-deserved fame by dedicating this little book to you. The
book, I believe, will do as much to keep your name bright for posterity as (with Fortune's help) the county of Monteodorisio did
formerly and as the county of Altavilla does now.[b]

To you, therefore, I send, and to your name I dedicate, what I   7
have thus far[c] written about famous women. Illustrious lady, I beg
you in the holy name of modesty, for which you are preeminent
among mortals, accept with favor this small gift from a scholar. If
you will take some advice from me, I urge you to read it occasionally: its counsels will sweeten your leisure, and you will find delight in the virtues of your sex and in the charm of the stories.
Nor will the perusal have been vain, I believe, if it spurs your no-   8
ble spirit to emulation of the deeds of women in the past.

You will find, at times, that an appropriate recital of the facts   9
has compelled me to mix the impure with the pure. Do not skip
over these parts and do not shy away from them, but persevere in
your reading. As on entering a garden you extend your ivory
hands towards the flowers, leaving aside the thorns, so in this case
relegate to one side offensive matters and gather what is praiseworthy. Whenever you, who profess the Christian religion, read
that a pagan woman has some worthy quality which you feel you
lack, blush and reproach yourself that, although marked with the
baptism of Christ, you have let yourself be surpassed by a pagan in
probity or chastity or resolution. Summon up the powers of your

non solum ne supereris patiare, sed ut superes quascunque egregia virtute coneris; ut, uti corpore leta iuventute ac florida venustate conspicua es, sic pre ceteris, non tantum coevis tuis, sed priscis etiam, animi integritate prestantior fias: memor non pigmentis — ut plereque facitis mulieres — decoranda formositas est, sed exornanda honestate sanctitate et primis operibus; ut, dum eidem qui tribuit gratam feceris, non solum hac in peritura mortalitate inter fulgidas una sis, sed ab eodem gratiarum Largitore, hominem exuens, in claritatem suscipiaris perpetuam.

10 Preterea si dignum duxeris, mulierum prestantissima, eidem
11 procedendi in medium audaciam prebeas. Ibit quidem, ut reor, tuo emissus auspicio, ab insultibus malignantium tutus; nomenque tuum, cum ceteris illustrium mulierum, per ora virum splendidum deferet, teque tuis cum meritis — cum minime possis ubique efferri presentia — presentibus cognitam faciet, et posteritati servabit eternam. Vale.

already strong character and do not allow yourself to be outdone,
but strive to outdo all women in noble virtues. Just as you are out-
wardly remarkable for your joyous youth and floral loveliness, so
you should surpass in spiritual excellence not only your contemporaries but even the women of antiquity. Remember that you
should not embellish your beauty with cosmetics, as do the majority of your sex, but increase its distinction through integrity, holiness, and the finest actions. In this fashion you will please Him
who granted you beauty; at the same time, you will stand out
among famous women in this earthly life and, after casting off
your mortal form, you will be received into eternal light by the
Giver of all blessings.

If you judge it worthy, most excellent lady, give this book the 10
boldness to appear in public. Under your auspices it will go forth, 11
I believe, safe from malicious criticism, and it will make your
name and the names of other illustrious women glorious on the
lips of humankind. As you cannot be physically present everywhere, my book will make you and your merits known to those
now alive and will preserve you forever for posterity.

Iohannis Boccaccii de Certaldo
De mulieribus claris
ad Andream de Acciarolis de Florentia Alteville comitissam
liber incipit feliciter

1 Scripsere iamdudum nonnulli veterum sub compendio de viris illustribus libros; et nostro evo, latiori tamen volumine et accura-
tiori stilo, vir insignis et poeta egregius Franciscus Petrarca, pre-
2 ceptor noster, scribit; et digne. Nam qui, ut ceteros anteirent claris
facinoribus, studium omne, substantias, sanguinem et animam,
exigente oportunitate, posuere, profecto ut eorum nomen in poste-
3 ros perpetua deducatur memoria meruere. Sane miratus sum plurimum adeo modicum apud huiusce viros potuisse mulieres, ut
nullam memorie gratiam in speciali aliqua descriptione consecute
sint, cum liquido ex amplioribus historiis constet quasdam tam
strenue quam fortiter egisse nonnulla.

4 Et si extollendi sunt homines dum, concesso sibi robore, magna
perfecerint, quanto amplius mulieres, quibus fere omnibus a natura rerum mollities insita et corpus debile ac tardum ingenium
datum est, si in virilem evaserint animum et ingenio celebri atque
virtute conspicua audeant atque perficiant etiam difficillima viris,
extollende sunt?

Et ideo, ne merito fraudentur suo, venit in animum ex his quas
memoria referet in glorie sue decus in unum deducere; eisque addere ex multis quasdam, quas aut audacia seu vires ingenii et in-

Preface

ༀ༈

Here Begins the Book on Famous Women
Written by Giovanni Boccaccio of Certaldo
and Dedicated to Andrea Acciaiuoli of Florence,
Countess of Altavilla

Long ago there were a few ancient authors who composed biographies of famous men in the form of compendia, and in our day that renowned man and great poet, my teacher Petrarch, is writing a similar work that will be even fuller and more carefully done.[a] This is fitting. For those who gave all their zeal, their fortunes, and (when the occasion required it) their blood and their lives in order to surpass other men in illustrious deeds have certainly earned the right to have their names remembered forever by posterity. What surprises me is how little attention women have attracted from writers of this genre, and the absence of any work devoted especially to their memory, even though lengthier histories show clearly that some women have performed acts requiring vigor and courage.

If we grant that men deserve praise whenever they perform great deeds with the strength bestowed upon them, how much more should women be extolled—almost all of whom are endowed by nature with soft, frail bodies and sluggish minds—when they take on a manly spirit, show remarkable intelligence and bravery, and dare to execute deeds that would be extremely difficult even for men?

Lest, therefore, such women be cheated of their just due, I had the idea of honoring their glory by assembling in a single volume the biographies of women whose memory is still green. To these I have added some lives from among the many women who are no-

dustria, aut nature munus, vel fortune gratia, seu iniuria, notabiles fecit; hisque paucas adnectere que, etsi non memoratu dignum aliquid fecere, causas tamen maximis facinoribus prebuere.

5 Nec volo legenti videatur incongruum si Penelopi, Lucretie Sulpitieve, pudicissimis matronis, immixtas Medeam, Floram Semproniamque compererint, vel conformes eisdem, quibus pregrande
6 sed pernitiosum forte fuit ingenium. Non enim est animus michi hoc claritatis nomen adeo strictim summere, ut semper in virtutem videatur exire; quin imo in ampliorem sensum—bona cum pace legentium—trahere et illas intelligere claras quas quocunque ex facinore orbi vulgato sermone notissimas novero; cum et inter Leonidas Scipiones Catonesque atque Fabritios, viros illustres, seditiosissimos Graccos, versipellem Hanibalem, proditorem Iugurtam, cruentos civilis sanguinis[1] Syllam Mariumque et eque divitem et avarum Crassum aliosque tales sepe legisse meminerim.

7 Verum, quoniam extulisse laudibus memoratu digna et depressisse increpationibus infanda nonnunquam, non solum erit hinc egisse generosos in gloriam et inde ignavos habenis ab infaustis paululum retraxisse, sed id restaurasse quod quarundam turpitudinibus venustatis opusculo demptum videtur, ratus sum quandoque historiis inserere nonnulla lepida blandimenta virtutis et in fugam atque detestationem scelerum aculeos addere; et sic fiet ut, inmixta hystoriarum delectationi, sacra mentes subintrabit utilitas.

8 Et ne more prisco apices tantum rerum tetigisse videar, ex quibus a fide dignis potuero cognovisse amplius in longiusculam hystoriam protraxisse non solum utile, sed oportunum arbitror; existimans harum facinora non minus mulieribus quam viris etiam

table for their boldness, intellectual powers, and perseverance, or for their natural endowments, or for fortune's favor or enmity. I have also included a few women who, although they performed no action worthy of remembrance, were nonetheless causal agents in the performance of mighty deeds.

Furthermore, I do not want readers to think it strange if they 5 find such chaste matrons as Penelope, Lucretia, and Sulpicia in company with Medea, Flora, and Sempronia or others like them, who had strong but, as it happened, destructive characters. It is 6 not in fact my intention to interpret the word 'famous' in such a strict sense that it will always appear to mean 'virtuous'. Instead, with the kind permission of my readers, I will adopt a wider meaning and consider as famous those women whom I know to have gained a reputation throughout the world for any deed whatsoever. Indeed, in the case of illustrious men I remember having read not only about the Leonidases, the Scipios, the Catos, and the Fabricii, but also about the turbulent Gracchi, sly Hannibal, and treacherous Jugurtha; about Sulla and Marius, stained with the blood of civil war; about Crassus, as avaricious as he was rich; and others of similar bent.

An account that praises deeds worthy of commemoration and 7 sometimes heaps reproaches upon crimes will not only drive the noble towards glory and to some degree restrain villains from their wicked acts; it will also restore to this little book the attractiveness lost as a result of the shameful exploits of certain of its heroines. Hence I have decided to insert at various places in these stories some pleasant exhortations to virtue and to add incentives for avoiding and detesting wickedness. Thus holy profit will mix with entertainment and so steal insensibly into my readers' minds.

To avoid the time-honored custom of dwelling only super- 8 ficially on events, I think it will be useful and appropriate to deal with the stories at somewhat greater length, learning where I can from trustworthy authors. It is my belief that the accomplish-

placitura; que cum, ut plurimum, hystoriarum ignare sint, sermone prolixiori indigent et letantur.

9   Attamen visum est, ne omiserim, excepta matre prima, his omnibus fere gentilibus nullas ex sacris mulieribus hebreis christianisque miscuisse; non enim satis bene conveniunt, nec equo incedere videntur gradu.

10   He quippe ob eternam et veram gloriam sese fere in adversam persepe humanitati tolerantiam coegere, sacrosancti Preceptoris tam iussa quam vestigia imitantes; ubi ille, seu quodam nature munere vel instinctu, seu potius huius momentanei fulgoris cupiditate percite, non absque tamen acri mentis robore, devenere; vel, fortune urgentis inpulsu, nonnunquam gravissima pertulere.

11   Preterea he, vera et indeficienti luce corusce, in meritam eternitatem non solum clarissime vivunt, sed earum virginitatem, castimoniam, sanctitatem, virtutem et, in superandis tam concupiscentiis carnis quam suppliciis tiramnorum invictam constantiam, ipsarum meritis exigentibus, singulis voluminibus a piis hominibus, sacris literis et veneranda maiestate conspicuis, descriptas esse cognoscimus; ubi illarum merita, nullo in hoc edito volumine speciali — uti iam dictum est — et a nemine demonstrata, describere, quasi aliquale reddituri premium, inchoamus.

Cui quidem pio operi ipse rerum omnium pater Deus assit; et, laboris assumpti fautor, quod scripsero in suam veram laudem scripsisse concedat.

ments of these ladies will please women no less than men. Moreover, since women are generally unacquainted with history, they
require and enjoy a more extended account.

Nevertheless, it seemed advisable, as I want to make plain, not 9
to mix these women, nearly all of them pagan, with Hebrew and
Christian women (except for Eve). The two groups do not harmo-
nize very well with each other, and they appear to proceed in
different ways.

Following the commands and example of their holy Teacher, 10
Hebrew and Christian women commonly steeled themselves for
the sake of true and everlasting glory to an endurance often at
odds with human nature. Pagan women, however, reached their
goal, admittedly with remarkable strength of character, either
through some natural gift or instinct or, as seems more likely,
through a keen desire for the fleeting glory of this world; sometimes they endured grievous troubles in the face of Fortune's as-
saults.

Besides, Christian women, resplendent in the true and unfail- 11
ing light, live gloriously in their deserved immortality; we know
too that their virginity, purity, holiness, and invincible firmness in
overcoming carnal desire and the punishments of tyrants have
been described in individual works, as their merits required, by pious men outstanding for their knowledge of sacred literature and
revered for their dignity. The merits of pagan women, on the
other hand, have not been published in any work designed especially for this purpose and have not been set forth by anyone, as I
have already pointed out. That is why I began to write this work:
it was a way of giving them some kind of reward.

May God, the Father of all things, assist me in this pious
endeavour; may He lavish his favor on what I shall write and grant
that I write it to his true glory.

De Eva parente prima

1 Scripturus igitur quibus fulgoribus mulieres claruerint insignes, a matre omnium sumpsisse exordium non apparebit indignum: ea quippe vetustissima parens, uti prima, sic magnificis fuit insignis

2 splendoribus. Nam, non in hac erumnosa miseriarum valle, in qua ad laborem ceteri mortales nascimur, producta est, nec eodem malleo aut incude etiam fabrefacta, seu eiulans nascendi crimen deflens, aut invalida, ceterorum ritu, venit in vitam; quin imo — quod nemini unquam alteri contigisse auditum est — cum iam ex limo terre rerum omnium Faber optimus Adam manu compegisset propria, et ex agro, cui postea Damascenus nomen inditum est, in orto delitiarum transtulisset eumque in soporem solvisset placidum, artificio sibi tantum cognito ex dormientis latere eduxit eandem, sui compotem et maturam viro et loci amenitate atque sui Factoris letabundam intuitu, immortalem et rerum dominam atque vigilantis iam viri sociam, et ab eodem Evam etiam nominatam.

3 Quid maius, quid splendidius potuit unquam contigisse nascenti? Preterea hanc arbitrari possumus corporea formositate mi-

4 rabilem. Quid enim Dei digito factum est quod cetera non excedat pulchritudine? Et quamvis formositas hec annositate peritura sit aut, medio in etatis flore, parvo egritudinis inpulsu, lapsura, tamen, quia inter precipuas dotes suas¹ mulieres numerant, et plurimum ex ea glorie, mortalium indiscreto iudicio, iam consecute sunt, non superflue inter claritates earum, tanquam fulgor precipuus, et apposita est et in sequentibus apponenda veniet.

5 Hec insuper, tam iure originis quam incolatus, paradisi civis facta et amicta splendore nobis incognito, dum una cum viro loci delitiis frueretur avide, invidus sue felicitatis hostis nepharia illi

Eve, Our First Mother

As I am going to write about the glories for which women have   1
become famous, it will not seem inappropriate to begin with the
mother of us all. She is the most ancient of mothers and, as the
first, she was singled out for special honors. She was not brought   2
forth in this wretched vale of misery in which the rest of us are
born to labor; she was not wrought with the same hammer or an-
vil; nor did she come into life like others, either weak or tearfully
bewailing original sin. Instead (and this never happened to anyone
else, so far as I know), after the most excellent Creator of all
things had formed Adam from earthly clay with his own hand and
had taken him from the field later called Damascene to the garden
of delights, he made Adam fall into peaceful slumber. With a skill
known only to himself, God brought forth a woman from Adam's
side as he lay sleeping. Adult, ripe for marriage, joyful at the
beauty of the place and at the sight of her Maker, she was also the
immortal mistress of nature and the companion of the man who,
now awake, named her Eve.

Could anything greater and more glorious ever happen to   3
someone at birth? We can imagine, besides, how marvelously
beautiful her body was, for whatever God creates with his own   4
hand will certainly surpass everything else in beauty. Beauty, to be
sure, perishes with old age, and even in the flower of youth it may
vanish from a slight attack of illness. Yet, since women count
beauty among their foremost endowments and have achieved, owing to the superficial judgment of mortals, much glory on that account, it will not seem excessive to place beauty here and in the
following pages as the most dazzling aspect of their fame.

Eve, furthermore, became a citizen of Paradise as much by right   5
of origin as of residence, and she was cloaked in a radiance unknown to us. While she and her husband were eagerly enjoying

suasione ingessit animo, si adversus unicam sibi legem a Deo im-
6 positam iret, in ampliorem gloriam iri posse. Cui dum levitate feminea, magis quam illi nobisque oportuerit, crederet seque stolide
ad altiora conscensuram arbitraretur, ante alia, blanda quadam
suggestione, virum flexibilem in sententiam suam traxit; et in legem agentes, arboris boni et mali poma dum gustassent, temerario
ausu seque genusque suum omne futurum ex quiete et eterni-
tate in labores anxios et miseram mortem et ex delectabili patria
inter vepres glebas et scopulos deduxere.

7 Nam, cum lux corusca, qua incedebant amicti, abiisset, a tur-
bato Creatore suo obiurgati, perizomatibus cincti, ex delitiarum
8 loco in agros Hebron[2] pulsi exulesque venere. Ibi egregia mulier,
his facinoribus clara, cum prima — ut a nonnullis creditum est —
vertente terram ligonibus viro, colo nere adinvenisset, sepius dolores partus experta est; et, quibus ob mortem filiorum atque nepotum angustiis angeretur animus, eque misere passa; et, ut algores
estusque sinam et incomoda cetera, fessa laboribus moritura devenit in senium.

: II :

De Semiramide regina Assyriorum

1 Semiramis insignis atque vetustissima Assyriorum regina fuit; a
quibus tamen parentibus genus duxerit, annositas abstulit, preter
quod fabulosum placet antiquis, aientibus eam filiam fuisse Neptuni, quem Saturni filium et maris deum erronea[1] credulitate

16

the garden's pleasures, the Enemy, envious of her happiness, impressed upon her with perverted eloquence the belief that she could attain greater glory if she disobeyed the one law that God had laid upon her. With a woman's fickleness, Eve believed him 6 more than was good for her or for us; foolishly, she thought that she was about to rise to greater heights. Her first step was to flatter her pliant husband into her way of thinking. Then they broke the law and tasted the apple of the Tree of Good and Evil. By this rash, foolhardy act they brought themselves and all their future descendants from peace and immortality to anxious labor and wretched death, and from a delightful country to thorns, clods, and rocks.

The gleaming light which clothed them disappeared. Rebuked 7 by their angry Creator and covered by a girdle of leaves, they were driven out of Eden and came as exiles to the fields of Hebron. There, while her husband tilled the soil with the hoe, this distin- 8 guished woman, famous for her above-mentioned deeds, discovered (so some believe) the art of spinning with the distaff. She experienced the pains of frequent childbirth and also suffered the grief which tortures the mind at the death of children and grandchildren. I shall pass over the cold and heat and her other sufferings. Finally she reached old age, tired out by her labors, waiting for death.

: II :

Semiramis, Queen of the Assyrians

Semiramis was a famous and very ancient queen of the Assyrians. 1 Time has obliterated any knowledge of her parents except for the legend of the ancients that she was the daughter of Neptune who, they falsely maintained, was the son of Saturn and god of the sea.

2 firmabant. Quod, etsi credi non oporteat, argumentum tamen est eam a nobilibus parentibus genitam.

Hec quidem Nino Assyriorum regi egregio nupsit et ex eo Ni-
3 niam filium peperit unicum. Sane Nino, omni Asya et postremo Bacthris subactis, sagitte ictu mortuo, cum adhuc hec iuvencula esset et filius puer, minime tutum existimans tam grandis et orientis imperii etati tam tenelle habenas commictere, adeo ingentis fuit animi ut, quas ferus homo armis subegerat nationes coercueratque viribus, arte et ingenio regendas[2] femina auderet assummere.

4 Nam astu quodam muliebri, excogitata fallacia pregrandi, mortui viri ante alia decepit exercitus. Erat, nec mirabile, Semiramis lineamentis oris persimilis filio: nude utrique gene, nec erat per etatem dissona a puerili feminea vox; et in statura corporis nil, vel
5 modicum, grandiuscula differebat a nato. Quibus iuvantibus, ne in processu quod fraudem detegere potuisset obesset, caput texit thyara, brachiis cruribusque velamentis absconditis; et quoniam insuetum eo usque esset Assyriis, egit, ne afferret novitas habitus admirationem accolis, ut ornatu simili omnis uteretur populus.[3]

6 Et sic Nini olim coniunx filium, et femina puerum simulans, mira cum diligentia maiestatem regiam adepta, eam militaremque disciplinam servavit et, mentita sexum, grandia multa et robustis-
7 simis viris egregia operata est. Et dum, nullo labori parcens aut periculo territa, inauditis facinoribus quorumcunque superasset invidiam, non est verita cuntis[4] aperire que foret quodve etiam fraude simulasset feminea, quasi vellet ostendere, non sexum, sed ani-
8 mum imperio oportunum. Quod quantum advertentibus ingessit admirationis, tantum mulieris maiestatem inclitam ampliavit.

We should not believe this story, but it is nonetheless an indica- 2
tion that Semiramis was born of noble parents.

She married Ninus, the eminent king of the Assyrians, and
bore him Ninyas, their only child. After his conquest of Asia in- 3
cluding, finally, the Bactrians, Ninus died of an arrow wound
while Semiramis was still quite young and their son a mere boy.
She thought it imprudent to entrust the reins of this new, large
empire to so young a child. Instead, Semiramis was possessed of
so courageous a spirit that she, a woman, dared undertake with
skill and intelligence the rule of those nations which her fierce
husband had subjugated and controlled with force of arms.

First she deceived her late husband's army by means of a colos- 4
sal trick plotted with feminine cunning. It is not surprising that
Semiramis' face looked very much like her son's; both were beard-
less; her woman's voice sounded no different at that time from her
young son's; and she was just a trifle taller, if at all. Taking advan- 5
tage of this resemblance, Semiramis always wore a turban and kept
her arms and legs covered so that nothing could reveal the deception and hinder her course of action. Previously it had never been
the custom of the Assyrians to dress like this, and so, to prevent
any wonder on her countrymen's part at the novelty of her garb,
she decreed that everyone should dress as she did.

Thus Semiramis, a woman once Ninus' wife, masqueraded as a 6
boy, his son. She energetically took up the royal power. Belying
her sex, she preserved both kingship and military discipline while
accomplishing many great deeds worthy of even the most powerful
men. Semiramis spared herself no labors, feared no dangers, and 7
with her incredible actions overcame all envy. Only then was she
unafraid to reveal to everyone who she really was and how with
womanly deceit she had pretended to be a man. It was almost as if
she wanted to show that spirit, not sex, was needed to govern.
Such an attitude enlarged the glorious majesty of this woman as 8
much as it gave rise to admiration in those who saw her.

Hec ut eius facinora paululum protensius deducamus in medium, sumptis post insigne figmentum virili animo armis, non solum quod vir suus quesiverat tutavit imperium, sed Ethyopiam, a se acri lacessitam bello atque superatam, iunxit eidem; et inde in Yndos vehementia arma convertit, ad quos nondum, preter virum, quisquam accesserat; Babiloniam insuper, vetustissimum Nembroth opus et ingentem ea etate in campis Senaar civitatem, restauravit murisque ex cocto latere[5] harena pice ac bitumine compactis, altitudine atque grossitie et circuitu longissimo admirandis, ambivit.

9   Et ut ex multitudine suorum gestorum unum memoratu dignissimum extollentes dicamus, certissimum asserunt, ea pacatis rebus et ocio quiescente ac die quadam feminea solertia cum pedissequis crines discriminante ac ritu patrio in tricas reducente, actum est, cum nondum preter medios deduxisset, ut illi nuntiaretur Babilo-

10   niam in dictionem defecisse privigni. Quod adeo egre tulit ut, proiecto pectine, confestim ab offitio muliebri irata consurgens, corriperet arma ac eductis copiis obsideret[6] urbem prevalidam; nec ante quod inordinatorum crinium superfuerat composuit, quam potentissimam civitatem longa obsidione affectam in deditionem

11   cogeret et suo sub dominio infestis revocaret armis. Cuius tam animosi facinoris diu exhibuit testimonium statua ingens ex ere conflata et in Babilonia erecta, feminam solutis ex altero latere crinibus, ex altero in tricam compositis, pretendens.

12   Multas preterea ex novo civitates condidit et ingentia facta peregit, que adeo vetustas absorbsit ut nil fere, preter quod dictum est, quod ad suam pertineat laudem, ad nos usque deductum est.

13   Ceterum hec omnia, nedum in femina, sed in quocunque viro strenuo, mirabilia atque laudabilia et perpetua memoria cele-

Let me now bring her achievements before the public at greater length. After perpetrating that marvelous subterfuge, Semiramis took up arms with manly spirit; and not only did she maintain the empire acquired by her husband, but she added to it Ethiopia, which she attacked and conquered in a hard-fought war. Then she turned her powerful forces against India, where no one had yet gone except her husband.[a] She also restored Babylon, the ancient and once great city built by Nimrod in the fields of Sennaar, and she surrounded it with brick walls cemented with sand, pitch, and tar. These walls were remarkable for their height, thickness, and length of circuit.

Of Semiramis' many deeds we shall single out the one most 9 worthy of remembrance, and the following story is reported as fact. One day, when all was peaceful and she was enjoying a leisurely rest, she was combing her hair with the dexterity of her sex. Surrounded by her maids, she was plaiting it into braids according to native custom. Her hair was not yet half finished when she was told that Babylon had defected to her stepson. So distressed was 10 Semiramis by this news that she threw aside her comb and instantly rose in anger from her womanly pursuits, took up arms, and led her troops to a siege of the powerful city. She did not finish arranging her hair until she had forced the surrender of that mighty place, weakened by a long blockade, and brought it back under her power by force of arms. A huge bronze statue of a 11 woman with her hair braided on one side and loose on the other stood in Babylon for a long time as witness to this brave deed.

Semiramis also built many new cities and performed great 12 deeds, but time has consigned them to oblivion. Consequently, almost nothing regarding her laudable actions has come down to us except what I have mentioned.

Her accomplishments would be extraordinary and praiseworthy 13 and deserving of perpetual memory for a vigorous male, to say nothing of a woman. But with one unspeakable act of seduction

branda, una obscena mulier fedavit illecebra. Nam cum, inter ceteras, quasi assidua libidinis prurigine, ureretur infelix, plurium miscuisse se concubitui creditum est; et inter mechos, bestiale quid
potius quam humanum, filius Ninias numeratur, unus prestantis-
sime forme iuvenis, qui, uti mutasset cum matre sexum, in thalamis marcebat ocio, ubi hec adversus hostes sudabat in armis.

14   O scelestum facinus! Ut quieta sinam, inter anxias regum curas,
inter cruenta certamina et, quod monstro simile est, inter lacrimas
et exilia, nulla temporis facta distinctione, hec evolat pestis et sensim incautas mentes occupans et in precipitium trahens, omne
15   decus turpi nota commaculat. Qua fedata Semiramis, dum putat
astutia abolere quod lascivia deturparat, legem illam insignem
condidisse aiunt, qua prestabatur subditis ut circa venerea agerent
quod liberet; timensque ne a domesticis feminis concubitu frauda-
retur filii—ut quidam volunt—prima usum femoralium excogitavit, eis omnes aulicas cinxit sub conclavi: quod, ut fertur, adhuc[7]
apud Egyptios observatur et Affros.

16   Alii tamen scribunt quod, cum in desiderium incidisset filii
eumque iam etate provectum in suos provocasset amplexus, ab eo-
17   dem, cum annis iam duobus et triginta regnasset, occisam. A quibus dissentiunt alii asserentes eam libidini miscuisse sevitiam soli-
tamque, quos ad explendum[8] sue uredinis votum advocasset, ut
occultaretur facinus, continuo post coitum iubere necari; verum,
cum aliquando concepisset, adulteria prodidisse partu; ad que ex-
cusanda, legem illam egregiam, cuius paulo ante mentio facta est,
proditam aiunt.

18   Tamen etsi visum sit pausillum contegisse ineptum crimen, filii
indignationem abstulisse minime potuit; quin, seu quod suum

Semiramis stained them all. Like others of her sex, this unhappy female was constantly burning with carnal desire, and it is believed that she gave herself to many men. Among her lovers — and this is something more beastly than human — was her own son Ninyas, a very handsome young man. As though he had changed sex with his mother, Ninyas languished idly in bed while she exerted herself in battle against her enemies.

What a heinous crime this was! The pestilence of lust, heedless of time or circumstances, flies about amidst the pressing concerns of kings, in bloody battles (not to mention in times of peace) and, monstrously, in sorrow and in exile. Imperceptibly it takes possession of unwary minds and drags them to the edge of the abyss, befouling every seemly thing with disgraceful infamy. Semiramis, tainted by this destructive force, thought cleverness could lessen the blot of lasciviousness. They say that she decreed the notorious law allowing her subjects to do as they pleased in matters of sexual conduct. According to some accounts, Semiramis was afraid that the women of her household would steal her son from her bed, and in this way she became the original inventor of the chastity belt. She forced all the ladies of her court to wear them locked. This is said to be the custom still in Egypt and Africa.

Others, however, write that Semiramis was stricken with desire for her son when he was already an adult; but that he killed her when she summoned him to her bed, and that this happened after she had reigned for thirty-two years. Yet another version claims that Semiramis mixed cruelty with lust: that she was accustomed to order, immediately after copulation, the death of the men she had called to satisfy her burning passion, and so was able to hide her crimes. But sometimes (they say) she became pregnant and her adultery was revealed through childbirth; and it was to excuse these actions that the famous law mentioned above was promulgated.

Nonetheless, even though it seems that Semiramis hid at least

tantum arbitrabatur cum aliis comunicatum incestum cerneret mi-
nusque equo animo ferret, seu quod in ruborem suum matris
luxuriam duceret aut forsan prolem in successionem imperii nasci-
turam expavesceret, reginam illecebrem, ira inpulsus, absumpsit.

:   III   :

De Opi Saturni coniuge

1   Opis seu Ops, vel Rhea, si priscis credimus, inter prospera et adversa plurima claritate emicuit. Nam Uranii, apud rudes adhuc
2   Grecos potentissimi hominis, et Veste coniugis filia fuit. Que,
Saturni regis soror pariter et coniunx, nullo, quod ad nos venerit,
facinore, se egregiam fecerat, ni muliebri astutia Iovem Neptunum
atque Plutonem filios a morte, cum Saturno a Tytone fratre pacta,
liberasset.

3   Qui cum inscitia, imo insania hominum evi illius, in claritatem
precipue deitatis evasissent homines, hec non solum regine decus
adepta est, quin imo errore mortalium dea insignis et deorum mater est habita eique templa, sacerdotes[1] et sacra, instituto publico,
constituta sunt; adeoque enorme malum convaluit ut, laborantibus
secundo bello punico Romanis, quasi pro salutari auxilio missis
consularibus viris, ab Attalo, Pergami rege, simulacrum eius expe-
titum precibus est ritusque sacrorum et e Pesimunte Asye oppido,
quasi quoddam deforme saxum, sumptum cum diligentia Romam
delatum atque summa cum reverentia susceptum et postremo, insigni locatum templo, tanquam sublime numen atque rei publice

24

to some extent her indecent crime, she was not able to avoid her son's wrath. In a fit of anger he killed the seductive queen either because he could not bear to see others share in that incest which he thought to be his alone, or because his mother's excesses brought him shame, or perhaps because he feared the birth of children who would succeed to the throne.

: III :

Opis, Wife of Saturn

Opis or Ops, or Rhea, if we believe the ancients, glittered with great fame in prosperous and adverse times. She was the daughter of Uranus, a very powerful man among the then uncivilized Greeks, and of his wife Vesta. Both sister and wife of the ruler Saturn, Opis did not distinguish herself for any deed which has come down to us, except that through feminine cunning she saved her children Jupiter, Neptune, and Pluto from a death planned by Saturn and her brother Titan.

Now Saturn and Titan were mortals who had been turned into divinities thanks to the ignorance, or rather madness, of the men of that time. So, too, did Opis acquire queenly status and, owing to human error, she was reputed to be an eminent goddess and the mother of the gods. Temples, priests, and sacrifices were accorded her by public decree. This shameful situation intensified to the point that, when the Romans were in danger during the Second Punic War, men of consular rank were sent in search of vital aid to Attalus, king of Pergamum. Fervently they asked for a likeness of Opis and the ritual procedure for her sacrifices. From the Asian city of Pessinus a certain oddly shaped stone was taken and carefully brought to Rome and there received with deep reverence.[a] Finally it was placed in a famous temple as a great deity and pro-

salutare, per multa secula cerimoniis plurimis apud Romanos et
Ytalos cultum est.

4   Mirabile profecto fortune ludibrium, seu potius cecitas hominum, an, velimus dicere, fraus et decipula demonum, quorum
opere actum est ut femina, longis agitata laboribus, demum anus
mortua et in cinerem versa et apud inferos alligata, et dea crederetur et in tam grande evum fere ab universo orbe divinis honorare-
tur obsequiis.

: IV :

De Iunone regnorum dea

1   Iuno, Saturni et Opis filia, poetarum carmine et errore gentilium
toto orbi pre ceteris mulieribus gentilitatis infectis labe celeber-
rima facta est, in tantum ut nequiverint taciti temporum dentes,
cum cuncta corrodant, adeo infame exesisse opus, quin ad etatem
usque nostram notissimum eius non evaserit nomen. Verum ex
hac potius fortunam egregiam recitare possumus, quam opus aliquod memorabile dictu[1] referre.

2   Fuit enim cum Iove illo cretensi, quem decepti veteres celi
finxere deum, eodem edita partu et ab infantia transmissa Samum
ibique ad pubertatem usque cum diligentia educata, Iovi demum
fratri nupta est; quod per multa secula eiusdem est statua in tem-
3   plo Sami testata. Nam existimantes Samii non modicum sibi po-
sterisque suis afferre glorie quod se penes alta atque desponsata
Iuno sit, quam celi reginam arbitrabantur et deam, ne memoria
hec dilueretur facile, templum ingens et pre ceteris orbis mirabile
construxere numinique dicavere suo et ex marmore pario, in ha-

tector of the state. For many ages the stone was venerated in numerous ceremonies by the Romans and the Italic peoples.

Certainly it was a marvelous jest on the part of Fortune, or   4
rather men's blindness, or better yet a deceitful snare of devils, that caused a woman troubled with long sufferings, who had finally died in old age, had turned to dust, and had been damned to hell, to be regarded as a goddess and honored for such a long time by almost the entire world with the respect accorded to deity.

: IV :

Juno, Goddess of Kingdoms

Thanks to the poets and pagan error, Juno, the daughter of Saturn   1
and Opis, has become the most famous of all the women in the world who were stained with the blot of paganism. So great is her fame that the silent teeth of time, which gnaw all things to pieces, have not been able to consume her notorious deeds and prevent her name, well known to all, from reaching even our age. Nonetheless, it is easier to speak of Juno's singular good fortune than to relate any great deed of hers that is worthy of comment.

She and that Jupiter of Crete (whom the ancients wrongly   2
imagined to be the god of heaven) were born twins. In her infancy Juno was sent to Samos and there was carefully brought up until she reached puberty and finally married her brother Jupiter. To this her statue in the temple at Samos for many centuries bore witness. Indeed, the people of Samos considered Juno a goddess   3
and queen of heaven and believed that her upbringing and marriage in their country brought glory to them and their descendants. To keep alive the memory of this connection, they built a huge temple consecrated to her divinity, more marvelous than any other in the world. They also ordered a statue of Juno, dressed as

bitu nubentis virginis, eiusdem ymaginem sculpi fecere temploque preposuere suo.

4   Hec tandem regi magno nupta, excrescente eius in dies imperio atque fama longe lateque nomen ipsius efferente, non modicum et
5   ipsa splendoris consecuta est. Sane, postquam poeticis fictionibus et insana antiquorum liberalitate celi regina facta est, que mortalis regina fuerat, Olympi regnis eam divitiisque prefecere necnon et illi coniugalia iura atque parientium auxilia commisere; et alia longe plura, ridenda potius quam credenda.

6   Ex quibus, sic humani generis hoste suadente, multa illi undique constructa sunt templa, altaria plurima, sacerdotes, ludi et sacra, more veteri instituta; et, ut de reliquis taceam, post Samos, celebri veneratione ab Argivis Achaye populis et a Cartaginensibus diu honorata est; et postremo a Veiis Romam delata in Capitolio et in cella Iovis optimi maximi, non aliter quam viro iuncta suo, locata, sub vocabulo Iunonis regine, a Romanis, rerum dominis, cerimoniis multis et diu culta est, etiam postquam in terris comparuit Deus homo.

: V :

De Cerere dea frugum et Syculorum regina

1   Ceres — ut nonnullis placet — vetustissima Syculorum regina fuit; tantoque ingenio valuit ut, cum agrorum excogitasset culturam, prima, apud suos, boves domuit et iugo assuefecit et, adinvento aratro atque vomere, eorum opere terram proscidit sulcisque semina tradidit; que cum in amplissimam segetem excrevissent, eam

a young girl for her wedding, to be carved out of Parian marble, and they placed it in front of her temple.

Juno herself gained no little glory through her marriage to the great king, whose power and fame were steadily increasing and spreading his name far and wide. Later the fictions of poets and the extravagant folly of the ancients made this woman, who had been a mortal queen, into the queen of heaven. They placed her in charge of the kingdom and wealth of Olympus and entrusted to her conjugal rights, the protection of women in childbirth, and many other things that arouse our amusement rather than our belief. 4 5

As a result, through the persuasion of the Enemy of humankind, numerous temples and altars were erected to Juno everywhere, and priests, games, and sacrifices were assigned to her according to ancient custom. For a long time she was honored with solemn reverence, after Samos, by the Argive peoples of Achaia and by the Carthaginians, not to mention others. At last Juno was brought to Rome from Veii and placed in the sanctuary of Jupiter Optimus Maximus on the Capitoline Hill, just as if she were joining her husband. The Romans, masters of the world, long honored her with many ceremonies under the name of Queen Juno, even after the time of Christ. 6

: V :

Ceres, Goddess of the Harvest and Queen of Sicily

Ceres, as some authorities report, was a very ancient queen of Sicily. Her intelligence was such that after discovering agriculture she was the first of her people to tame oxen and train them to the yoke. She invented the plow and the plowshare, broke up the earth with them, and sowed seed in the furrows. When the seeds ma- 1

spicis eruere, lapidibus terere, fermenta conficere et in cibum deducere homines, glandibus et pomis silvestribus assuetos, edocuit.

2 Quod ob meritum, cum mortalis esset femina, eam deam frugum arbitrati sunt et divinis honoribus extulere eamque Saturni et Cy-

3 beles credidere filiam. Huic preterea unicam ex Iove fratre fuisse filiam Proserpinam dicunt eamque maxima matris turbatione ab Orco Molossorum rege raptam et diu quesitam volunt, multis hinc fabulis occasionem prebentes.

4 Fuit preterea et Ceres altera apud Eleusim, attice regionis civitatem, eisdem meritis penes suos clara, cui Triptholemum obse-

5 quiosum fuisse volunt. Quas, eo quod vetustas deitate et honoribus eque extulit, sub uno tantum nomine ambarum ingenia retulisse satis visum est.

6 Harum edepol ingenium utrum laudem an execrer nescio. Quis enim damnet vagos silvestresque eductos in urbes e nemoribus homines? Quis, ritu ferarum viventes in meliorem evocatos frugem? Quis, glandes mutatas in segetem, quibus corpus lucidius, vegetiora membra et alimenta humano usui conformiora prestantur? Quis, musco vepribus arbustisque incompositis obsitum orbem, in cultum pulchritudinem et utilitatem publicam versum? Quis, rude seculum in civile? Quis, a desidia in contemplationem excitata ingenia? Quis, vires, torpentes in speleis, in urbicum seu rusticanum exercitium tractas, quibus tot ampliate urbes, tot de novo condite, tot aucta imperia, tot mores spectabiles inventi cultique sunt, fru-

7 mentarie artis adinventa notitia? Que, cum de se bona sit, et que

tured into an abundant harvest, she taught men who had been accustomed to living on acorns and wild fruit how to husk the grain,
grind it with stones, prepare yeast, and turn the flour into edible
fare. Although Ceres was only a mortal woman, this accomplish- 2
ment led people to regard her as the goddess of the harvest. They
exalted her with divine honors, believing her to be the daughter of
Saturn and Cybele. Proserpina, her only daughter, is said to have 3
been fathered by Ceres' brother Jupiter. It is alleged that, to her
mother's great distress, she was kidnapped by Orcus, king of the
Molossians, and became the object of a long search. This event
gave rise to many stories.

There was another Ceres in Eleusis, a town in the province of 4
Attica. This Ceres was famous among her people for the same
achievements and is said to have had Triptolemus in her service.
As the ancients elevated both women equally to divine honors, it 5
seemed appropriate for me to treat the genius of each under a single heading.

By heavens! I hardly know whether to praise or condemn their 6
ingenuity. Who will condemn the fact that wild, nomadic men
were led out of the woods and into cities? That men who were living like beasts were brought to a better form of sustenance? That
acorns were exchanged for grain, thanks to which the body becomes more refined, the limbs more vigorous, and nourishment
more suitable for human consumption is provided? Who will
complain that the world, filled with moss, thorns, and luxuriant
vegetation, was cultivated and made beautiful and useful for men?
That barbarous times were changed into a civilized age? That
man's mind was roused from idleness to rational thought? That,
after the discovery of the art of grain production, human energy,
listless from a life spent in caves, was directed towards urban or
rural life, with the resulting growth of many cities, the founding of
many new ones, the expansion of empires, the establishment and
practice of many admirable customs? If this and all the things just 7

dicta sunt omnia, reor, iudicio plurium, si quis faciat, dicetur insi-
pidus.

8   Demum versa vice, quis laudet multitudinem sparsam silvas in-
colentem, glandibus pomisque silvestribus ferino lacte herbisque
atque fluento assuetam, soluta curis habentem pectora, sola nature
lege contentam sobriam pudicam et doli nesciam, inimicam feris
9   tantum et avibus, in molliores atque incognitos evocatam cibos? E
quibus, nisi nos ipsos decipimus, secutum cernimus ut in abditis
adhuc latentibus vitiis exitumque timentibus aperiretur iter et procedendi prestaretur securitas.

10   Hinc arva, eo usque comunia, terminis et fossa distingui cepta
sunt, agricolationis[1] subiere cure et partiri inter mortales cepere labores; hinc meum et tuum venit in medium, nomina quidem ini-
mica pacis publice et private; hinc pauperies servitusque necnon et
litigia odia cruentaque bella et urens in circuitu evolavit invidia;
que egere ut vixdum curvate falces in messem, in acutos rectosque
in sanguinem gladios verterentur.

11   Hinc sulcata maria et occiduis eoa cognita et eois occidua; hinc
mollicies corporum, sagina ventris, ornatus vestium, accuratiores
mense, convivia splendida, torpor et otium advenere; et, que in
dies usque illos friguerat, Venus calefieri cepit, maximo orbis incommodo; et — quod deterius forsan est — si minus, eque labentibus annis, ut fit, celi seu bellorum ira, culta respondeant, subintrat
illico annone penuria et duriora priscis consurgunt ieiunia; seva fa-
mes, nunquam silvis cognita, gurgustiolos intrat inopum, non
12   absque divitum persepe periculo. Hinc turpis et effeta macies, in-

mentioned are good in themselves, I think (as most people would) that anyone who condemns agriculture will be called foolish.

On the other hand, who will praise the fact that delicate and   8 unfamiliar foods were introduced to scattered multitudes living in the forests and accustomed to acorns, wild fruit, the milk of animals, herbs and river water; who had no worries; who contented themselves with only the law of nature; who were sober, modest, and without deceit; who were hostile only to birds and beasts? If   9 we do not deceive ourselves, we shall see that the new practices opened the door to vices still latent — vices once afraid to come out into the open, but now given safe conduct.

Hence the fields, hitherto owned in common, began to be   10 marked off with ditches as boundaries. Hence came the cares of farming and the division of labor. Hence there emerged "mine" and "yours," words certainly inimical to public and private tranquillity. Hence arose poverty and servitude, as well as quarrels, hatred, cruel wars, and burning envy that spreads as swift as flight. These evils caused the sickles, only recently curved to harvest grain, to be turned into straight, sharp swords for purposes of bloodshed.

Hence came the navigation of the seas, and eastern and western   11 peoples became known to one another. Hence came that softening of the body, that fatness of the belly, ornament in dress, elaborate dinner tables, splendid banquets, laziness and leisure; hence, to the great detriment of the world, sexual desire, which had hitherto lain cold, burst into flame. There is perhaps still worse: if in the course of years the fields do not yield the expected harvest, as sometimes happens because of bad weather or war, immediately there is a shortage of food, and hunger is felt more harshly than was ever the case in primitive times; bitter starvation, which was never known in the forests, enters the huts of the poor and quite often menaces the wealthy. Hence arise repulsive, exhausted ema-   12

fernus pallor et titubanti incedens gradu debilitas morborumque et festinate mortis multiplices exoriuntur cause.

13   Quibus inspectis, una cum innumeris aliis, vix scio, imo scio, quia longe aurea illa, licet rudia et agrestia fuerint, his nostris ferreis comptisque seculis preponenda sint.

: VI :

De Minerva

1   Minerva, que et Pallas, virgo tanta claritate conspicua fuit ut non illi fuisse mortalem originem stolidi arbitrati sint homines. Aiunt quidem hanc Ogigii regis tempore apud lacum Tritonium, haud longe a sinu Syrtium minori, primo visam in terris et cognitam; et quoniam tractu temporis multa facientem vidissent ante non visa, non solum apud rudes Affros, verum apud Grecos, qui ea tempestate prudentia anteibant ceteros, absque matre ex Iovis cerebro genitam et celo[1] lapsam creditum est.

2   Cui ridiculo errori tanto plus fidei auctum est quanto occultior eius fuit origo. Hanc ante alia voluere perpetua floruisse virginitate; quod ut pleniori credatur fide, finxere Vulcanum, ignis deum, id est concupiscentie carnis fervorem, diu cum ea luctatum superatumque.

3   Huius insuper, incognitum omnino omnibus ante, lanificium inventum fuisse volunt; nam, ostenso quo ordine purgata superfluitatibus lana eaque dentibus mollita ferreis apponeretur colo atque demum digitis deduceretur in filum, textrine excogitavit offitium eoque docuit quo pacto internecterentur invicem fila et tractu

ciation, deadly pallor, weakness with shambling gait, and manifold causes of disease and untimely death.

After considering these and many other issues, I am tempted to believe—indeed I do believe—that those golden centuries, even if they were rude and uncivilized, are greatly to be preferred to our own iron age, refined though it is.[a]   13

: VI :

Minerva

Minerva, also known as Pallas, was a maiden of such celebrity that foolish people believed her to be of more than mortal origin. Our sources say that she was first seen and recognized on earth in Attica near Lake Tritonis, not far from the gulf of the Lesser Syrtis, at the time of King Ogyges. As time went by, it was observed that this woman did many things never before seen. Hence not only the barbarous Africans but also the Greeks, who at that time surpassed everyone else in good sense, believed that she had been born, not from a mother, but from Jupiter's head and had fallen from heaven.   1

The more hidden Minerva's origin, the more faith was put in this ridiculous error. Above all else, they claimed that she flowered in perpetual virginity. To render this more credible, the story was invented that Vulcan, the god of fire (that is, the ardor of carnal lust), had struggled with Minerva for a long time and had been defeated.   2

Minerva is further reported to have discovered woolworking, an art that previously had been entirely unknown. She showed how wool should be cleaned, softened with an iron comb, placed on the distaff, and spun with the fingers. Then Minerva invented weaving, demonstrating how the threads should be woven and joined   3

4   pectinis iungerentur et calce solidaretur intextum. In cuius opificii laudem pugna illa insignis eiusdem et Aragnis colophonie recitatur.

Usum insuper olei, eo usque mortalibus inauditum, hec invenit docuitque Acticos bachas mola terere trapetisque premere. Quod, quia multum utilitatis afferre visum sit, ei adversus Neptunum in nominandis a se Athenis attributa victoria creditur.

5   Volunt etiam huius fuisse opus, cum iam quadrigarum prima repperisset usum, ferrum in arma arte convertere, armis corpus tegere, aciem bellantium ordinare et leges omnes, quibus eatur in pugnam, edocere.

6   Dicunt preterea eam numeros invenisse et in ordinem deduxisse, quem in hodiernum usque servamus. Ceterum ex osse cruris alicuius avis, seu ex palustri potius calamo, eam tibias seu pastorales fistulas primam composuisse credidere easque in terras ex celo deiecisse, eo quod flantis redderent turgidum guctur et ora deformia.

7   Quid multa? Ob tot comperta, prodiga deitatum largintrix[2], antiquitas eidem sapientie numen attribuit. Quo intuitu tracti, Athenienses ab ea nuncupati; et eo quod civitas studiis apta videretur, per que quisque fit prudens et sapiens, eam in suam sumpsere tutelam eique arcem dicavere et, ingenti templo constructo suoque numini consecrato, in eodem illam effigiavere oculis torvam, eo quod raro noscatur in quem finem[3] sapientis tendat intentum; galeatam, volentes ob id sapientum tecta et armata significari consilia; indutam lorica, eo quod ad quoscunque fortune ictus semper armatus sit sapiens; longissima munitam hasta, ut comprehendatur sapientem in longinquo spicula figere; preterea

by the shuttle, and how the fabric should be strengthened by stamping on it. The famous contest that she had with Arachne of Colophon is cited in praise of the former's skill.[a]   4

In addition, Minerva found out how to use oil, which had not been known to men up to that time. She showed the Athenians how to crush olives with a grinding stone and how to press them in a mill. The discovery seemed very useful indeed, and it is for this reason she is thought to have defeated Neptune when Athens was deciding what to name itself.

It is claimed too that Minerva was the first to discover the use of the four-horse chariot, to make iron weapons, to use body armor, to draw up a battle-line, and to teach all the stratagems necessary for war.   5

Moreover, we are told that Minerva discovered numbers and arranged them in the order we still observe today. She is also believed to have been the first to make the flute or shepherd's bagpipes from the leg bone of some bird or, more plausibly, from swamp reeds; supposedly she threw them down from heaven because they swelled her throat and deformed her face as she was playing them.   6

In short, antiquity, that lavish dispenser of divinity, made Minerva the goddess of wisdom on account of these numerous inventions. It was for this reason that the Athenians named themselves after her. Since the city seemed to have a natural tendency for those studies which make one wise and prudent, the inhabitants took Minerva as their patron and dedicated their citadel to her. They built a great temple consecrated to this goddess, in which they represented Minerva as a statue with piercing eyes, because only rarely can the purpose of a wise man's intentions be discerned. She was helmeted to signify that the counsels of a wise man are hidden and well-defended; she was attired with a cuirass since the wise man is always armed against every blow of Fortune; she was fitted with an extremely long lance so that we might un-   7

cristallino egide, et in eo Gorgonis caput infixum, protectam, pretendentes ob hoc lucida sapienti omnia esse tegumenta, eosque serpentina semper astutia adeo premunitos, ut saxei eorum intuitu videantur ignari; eiusque in tutelam noctuam posuere, firmantes, prout in luce, sic et in tenebris videre prudentes.

8   Tandem huius mulieris fama atque numinis reverentia se adeo longe lateque diffudit tantumque favit illi veterum error, ut fere per universum eius in honorem templa construerentur et celebrarentur sacra; eoque usque conscenderet, ut in Capitolio penes Iovem optimum maximum cella dedicaretur eidem et inter potissimos Romanorum deos, cum Iunone regina et ipsa dea pariter haberetur.

9   Sunt tamen nonnulli gravissimi viri asserentes non unius Minerve, sed plurium que dicta sunt fuisse comperta. Quod ego libenter assentiam, ut clare mulieres ampliores sint numero.

: VII :

De Venere Cypriorum regina

1   Venerem cyprianam fuisse feminam quorundam arbitratur opinio; de parentibus autem a nonnullis ambigitur. Nam alii eam Cyri cuiusdam et Syrie volunt filiam; quidam vero Cyri et Dyonis cyprie mulieris. Nonnulli, reor ad extollendam eius[1] pulchritudinis

2   claritatem, Iovis et Dyonis predicte genitam asserunt. Sane, ex quocunque sit patre genita, eam inter claras mulieres potius ob illustrem eius pulchritudinem quam ob dedecorosum inventum describendam censui.

derstand that the wise man's arrow strikes far. This figure of Minerva was also protected by a crystal shield with the head of Medusa on it, thereby showing that all disguises are transparent to the wise man, and that wise men are always so armed with serpentine wisdom that ignorant people seem turned to stone at the sight of them. The owl was placed in her keeping to indicate that the man of sagacity sees in the darkness as well as in the light.

Eventually, with a great deal of help from the ancients' error, 8 the fame of this woman and reverence for her as a goddess spread so far and wide that temples were built and sacrifices held in her honor through almost the whole world. Devotion reached such a pitch that a sanctuary was erected to Minerva on the Capitoline Hill next to that of Jupiter Optimus Maximus; she was considered to be among the greatest Roman gods, a queen and a goddess herself, the equal of Juno.

Some authoritative sources, however, assert that the inventions 9 mentioned above do not belong to a single Minerva but to many. I shall gladly agree with them in order to increase the number of famous women.

: VII :

Venus, Queen of Cyprus

Some people think that Venus was a woman of Cyprus, but there 1 is disagreement as to her parents. One group claims that she was the daughter of a man called Cyrus and of Syria; others say that she was the daughter of Cyrus and Dione, a woman of Cyprus. Still others (to magnify the fame of her beauty, I believe) tell us that she was the daughter of Jupiter and the aforesaid Dione. No 2 matter who her father was, I certainly intend to place Venus among famous women on the basis of her outstanding beauty rather than because of some shameless fabrication.

3   Tanto igitur oris decore et totius corporis venustate emicuit, ut sepe intuentium falleretur credulitas. Nam quidam illam ipsum celi sydus, quod Venerem nuncupamus, dicebant; alii eam celes-
4 tem feminam in terras² ex Iovis gremio lapsam. Et breviter omnes, tetra obfuscati caligine, quam sciebant a mortali femina editam, immortalem asserebant deam eamque infausti amoris, quem Cupidinem vocitabant, genitricem totis nisibus affirmabant; nec illi intercipiendi stultorum intuentium mentes variis gesticulationibus deerant artes.

5   Quibus agentibus meritis eo usque itum est ut, nequeuntibus obsistere obscenitatibus mulieris, quas evestigio, non tamen omnes, scripturus sum, et Iovis filia et ex deabus una etiam vene-
6 randissima habita sit. Nec solum apud Paphos, vetustissimum Cypriorum oppidum, thure solo placata est — nam mortuam et incestuosam feminam eo delectari existimabant odore que vivens in prostibulorum volutabatur spurcitie — ; verum et apud nationes reliquas et Romanos, qui templum ei sub titulo Veneris genitricis³ et Verticordie aliisque insignibus olim struxere.

7   Sed quid multa? Hanc duobus nupsisse viris creditum est: cui primo, non satis certum. Nupsit ergo — ut placet aliquibus — ante Vulcano Lemniorum regi et Iovis cretensis filio; quo sublato, nu-
8 psit Adoni, filio Cynare atque Myrre, regi Cypriorum. Quod verisimilius michi videtur quam si primum virum Adonem dixerimus, eo quod, seu complexionis sue vitio, seu regionis infectione, in qua plurimum videtur posse lascivia, seu mentis corrupte malitia factum sit, Adone mortuo, in tam grandem luxurie pruritum lapsa est, ut omnem decoris sui claritatem crebris fornicationibus non

Indeed, Venus radiated such beauty in her face and her entire body that often those who saw her could hardly believe it. Some said that she was the very star we call Venus. Others believed that she was a celestial being who had fallen to earth from the lap of Jupiter. In short, since all these people were blinded by the blackest ignorance, they declared this woman to be an immortal goddess, although they knew that she had been born of a mortal woman. Moreover, they stoutly asserted that Venus was the mother of that unhappy love-god whom they called Cupid. Nor did she herself lack the skill to captivate with various pantomimic gestures the minds of the fools who looked at her. 3 4

The effect of these powers was such that men were unable to resist her lewd acts (only some of which I shall describe), and Venus was thought to be Jupiter's daughter and the goddess most worthy of adoration. She was honored with incense in Paphos, an ancient city of the Cypriots who thought that after death this sinful woman would love the scent of the filthy brothels she had wallowed in during her lifetime. She was honored as well by other peoples, including the Romans, who in olden times erected a temple to her under the names of Venus Genetrix, Venus Verticordia, and other titles. 5 6

But there is no need to belabor the point. Venus was believed to have had two husbands: it is not certain who was the first. Some think that she initially married Vulcan, king of Lemnos and son of Jupiter of Crete; when Vulcan died, she then married Adonis, king of Cyprus and son of Myrrha and Cinyras. This seems more plausible to me than saying that Adonis was her first husband. The reason is that, owing to her defects of character or the general influence of Cyprus (where lasciviousness seems to have been rampant) or through the corruption of a wicked mind, Venus so abandoned herself after Adonis' death to her wanton urges that in the eyes of those who had not been bewitched she seemed to tarnish all the splendor of her beauty with her incessant 7 8

obfuscatis oculis maculasse videretur, cum iam adiacentibus regionibus notum foret eam a Vulcano, viro primo, cum armigero compertam; ex quo creditum fabulam adulterii Martis et eiusdem sibi comperisse locum.

9   Postremo autem, ut ab impudica fronte paululum ruboris abstersisse videretur et lasciviendi sibi ampliorem concessisse licentiam, infanda turpitudine excogitata, prima — ut aiunt — meretricia publica adinvenit et fornices instituit et matronas inire compulit; quod satis execranda Cypriorum consuetudo in multa
10   protracta secula testata est. Servavere quidem diu mictere virgines suas ad litora, ut forensium uterentur concubitu et sic future castitatis sue libamenta persolvisse viderentur Veneri et suas in nuptias
11   quesisse dotes. Que quidem abominanda stultitia postea penetravit ad Ytalos usque, cum legatur hoc idem aliquando fecisse Locrenses.

: VIII :

De Yside regina atque dea Egyptiorum

1   Ysis, cui antea nomen Yo, clarissima non solum Egyptiorum regina, sed eorum postremo sanctissimum et venerabile numen fuit. Quibus tamen fuerit temporibus, aut ex quibus nata parentibus, apud illustres hystoriarum scriptores ambigitur.

2   Sunt autem qui dicant illam Ynaci primi regis Argivorum filiam et Phoronei sororem, quos constat Iacob, filii Ysaac, tempore imperasse; alii Promethei genitam asserunt, regnante apud Argos Phorbante, quod longe post primum tempus effluxit; nonnulli eam fuisse temporibus Cycropis, Athenarum regis, affirmant; et quidam insuper aiunt Lyncei regis Argivorum eam floruisse temporibus. Que quidem inter celebres viros varietates argumento non ca-

acts of fornication. In the neighboring regions it was already known that her first husband Vulcan had caught her with a soldier; and this gave rise to the myth of her adultery with Mars.

Finally, in order to lessen her shame and give herself greater 9 scope for wantonness, Venus devised something that was abominably foul. She was the first, so they say, to establish public prostitution by setting up brothels and forcing married women to enter them. Amply attesting to her invention was a detestable, centuries-old practice of the Cypriots. They were long accustomed to send 10 young girls to the beaches to lie with foreigners.[a] In this way the girls seem to have rendered to Venus the first fruits of their future chastity and to have earned dowries for their marriages. Later this 11 deplorable, stupid practice even reached Italy, since we read that at one time the Locrians did the same thing.

: VIII :

Isis, Queen and Goddess of Egypt

Isis, previously called Io, was an extremely famous queen of the 1 Egyptians who afterwards became a most holy and venerated goddess. Nevertheless, there is a discrepancy among distinguished historians as to when she lived or who her parents were.

Some sources say that Isis was the daughter of Inachus, the first 2 king of the Argives, and the sister of Phoroneus, both of whom ruled in the time of Jacob, son of Isaac. According to others, she was the daughter of Prometheus when Phorbas reigned at Argos, that is, at a much later time. Still others assert that she lived during the time of Cecrops, king of Athens; there are also some who place her *floruit* in the reign of Lynceus, king of the Argives. But this lack of consensus among illustrious men does not weaken the

rent, hanc inter feminas suo evo egregiam fuisse et memoratu dignissimam.

3 Verum—omissis scriptorum discordantiis—quod plurimi arbitrantur imitari mens est, eam scilicet Ynaci regis fuisse filiam; quam etsi poete veteres fingant ob venustatem forme placuisse Iovi et ab eo oppressam et, ad occultandum crimen, in vaccam transformatam petentique Iunoni concessam et Argum custodem a Mercurio cesum vacceque a Iunone oestrum subpositum et eam devectam cursu rapido in Egyptum ibidemque pristinam a se recuperatam formam et ex Yo Ysidem appellatam, ab hystorie veritate non discrepant; cum sint qui asserant a Iove adultero oppressam virginem eamque, ob perpetratum scelus metu patris inpulsam, cum quibusdam ex suis conscendisse navim, cui vacca esset insigne; et ingenio plurimo ac ingenti preditam animo, regnorum cupidine agitatam, secundo vento ad Egyptios transfretasse[1] et ibidem, apta desiderio regione comperta, constitisse.

4 Tandem, cum non habeatur quo pacto obtinuisset Egyptum, sat certum creditur ibi comperisse rudes inertesque populos et humanarum rerum omnium fere ignaros ac ritu potius brutorum viventes quam hominum; non absque labore et industria celebri illos docuit terras colere, cultis conmictere[2] semina et tandem collectas in tempore fruges in cibum deducere, preterea vagos et fere silvestres in unum se redigere et datis legibus civili more vivere; et, quod longe spectabilius in muliere est, coacto in vires ingenio, literarum ydiomati incolarum convenientium caracteribus adinventis aptioribus ad doctrinam, qua lege iungerentur ostendit.

5 Que—ut de reliquis taceam—adeo mirabilia insuetis hominibus visa sunt, ut arbitrarentur facile non ex Grecia venisse Ysidem, sed e celo lapsam et ob id spiranti adhuc divinos honores insti-

argument that Isis was preeminent among the women of her day and most worthy of remembrance.

Leaving aside the differences to be found in the sources, I intend to follow the view of the majority, namely, that she was the daughter of King Inachus. Ancient poets imagine that Jupiter was attracted to Isis because she was so beautiful, and that he seduced her. To hide this crime, she was transformed into a heifer and given to Juno at the latter's request. When Isis' guardian Argus was killed by Mercury, Juno planted a gadfly on the heifer, and she was driven at a rapid pace into Egypt, where she recovered her original form and her name was changed from Io to Isis. These events do not disagree with the historical version since there are those who claim that a virgin was seduced by Jupiter. Then, spurred on by fear of her father because of the sin she had committed, she and some of her friends boarded a ship on whose flag was depicted a cow. A person of great talent and courage who yearned for a kingdom, she sailed to Egypt with favorable winds. There she stayed, finding the region suitable to her wants. 3

Finally, although it is not known how she got control of Egypt, it is thought almost certain that she found an unskilled, lazy people, almost entirely ignorant of human affairs and living more like beasts than men. She worked hard and diligently to teach them how to till the soil, seed it, and finally, how to make food from grain after it had been harvested at the proper time. She also taught those nomadic and almost savage people to live together, and, having given them laws, she showed them how to live as civilized men. Next she did something that is even more admirable in a woman: marshalling her intellectual powers, she devised alphabetical characters suitable for teaching the language of the inhabitants and demonstrated how the letters should be placed together. 4

These feats (and others I could mention) seemed marvelous to people unaccustomed to them. So they found it easy to believe that Isis did not come from Greece but had fallen from heaven. 5

6　tuere omnes. Cuius quidem numen, fallente ignaros dyabolo, in tam grandem, ea mortua, atque famosam venerationem evasit, ut Rome, iam rerum domine, illi templum constitueretur pregrande, et egyptiaco ritu quotannis solemne sacrum institueretur; nec dubium quin ad occiduas usque barbaras nationes hic penetraret error.

7　Porro huius tam clare femine vir fuit Apis, quem vetustas erronea Iovis et Nyobis, Phoronei filie, filium arbitrata est; quem aiunt Egyaleo fratri, Acaye regno concesso, cum Argis triginta quinque regnasset annis, secessisse in Egyptum et una cum Yside imperasse, eque deum habitum, et Osyrim seu Serapim nuncupatum; esto sint qui dicant Ysidi Thelegonum quendam fuisse virum et ex ea suscepisse Epaphum; qui Egyptiis postea prefuit et Iovis ex ea filius extimatus est.

: IX :

De Europa Cretensium regina

1　Europam arbitrantur quidam filiam fuisse Phenicis; verum longe plures eam Agenoris, Phenicum regis, genitam dicunt; et tam mirabili formositate valuisse, ut amore invise cretensis caperetur Iuppiter. Ad cuius rapinam cum moliretur insidias potens homo, actum volunt lenocinio verborum cuiusdam, ut ex montibus in litus Phenicum lasciviens virgo armenta patris sequeretur et, exinde rapta confestim atque navi, cuius albus taurus erat insigne, inposita, deferretur in Cretam.

For this reason they accorded her every divine honor while she was
still alive. But the devil deceives the ignorant, and after Isis' death 6
her divinity became so renowned and revered that at Rome, already mistress of the world, a huge temple was accorded her, and
every year solemn sacrifices were held in the Egyptian manner.
Nor is there any doubt that this false belief spread even to the barbarous nations of the West.

The husband of this very famous woman was Apis, whom the 7
ancients were sufficiently deluded to regard as the son of Jupiter
and Niobe, the daughter of Phoroneus. They say that, after giving
the kingdom of Achaia to his brother Aegialeus, Apis ruled for
thirty-five years at Argos and then withdrew to Egypt where he
reigned together with Isis. He too was thought to be a god and
was called Osiris or Serapis. Others, however, claim that Isis' husband was a certain Telegonus, and that she bore him a son,
Epaphus, who afterwards governed Egypt and was thought to be
her son by Jupiter.

: IX :

Europa, Queen of Crete

Some people believe that Europa was the daughter of Phoenix, 1
but many more state that she was the daughter of Agenor, king of
Phoenicia. It is said that the power of her marvelous beauty was
such that Jupiter of Crete fell in love with her sight unseen. This 2
powerful man laid a trap to kidnap her, and the sources report
that it was effected through someone's flattering words. The result
was that the playful maiden followed her father's flocks from the
mountains down to the Phoenician shore; there she was immediately seized, put on a ship with a white bull as its standard, and
taken to Crete.

3   Vagari licentia nimia virginibus et aures faciles[1] cuiuscunque verbis prebere, minime laudandum reor, cum contigisse sepe legerim his agentibus honestati nonnunquam notas turpes imprimi, quas etiam perpetue demum castitatis decus abstersisse non potuit.

4   Ex his fabulam, qua legitur Mercurium inpulisse ad litus armenta Phenicum et Iovem in taurum versum natantemque in Cretam Europam virginem asportasse, causam sumpsisse liquido patet.

5   Verum in tempore rapine huius prisci discrepant: nam qui antiquiorem ponunt, regnante Argis Danao factam volunt; alii, regnante Acrisio; et qui postremi sunt, Pandione rege Atheniensibus imperante: quod magis Minois, filii Europe, temporibus convenire videtur. Hanc aliqui a Iove oppressam simpliciter volunt, et inde Astero Cretensium nupsisse regi, et ex eo Minoem, Radamantum et Sarpedonem filios peperisse, quos plurimi Iovis dicunt fuisse filios, asserentibus nonnullis Asterum Iovemque idem.

6   Que disceptatio cum spectet ad alios, claram tanti dei connubio plures Europam volunt, affirmantes insuper aliqui seu quia nobilitatis fuerit egregie — nam Phenices, multis agentibus meritis, suo evo pre ceteris stematibus claruere maiorum —, seu divini coniugis veneratione, seu filiorum regum gratia, vel ipsiusmet Europe virtute precipua, ab eius nomine Europam partem orbis tertiam in perpetuum nuncupatam.

7   Quam profecto ego insignem virtutibus mulierem, non solum ex concesso orbi nomine <arbitror>[2], sed ex <s>pectabili[3] ex ere statua a Pictagora, illustri philosopho, Tarenti Europe dicata nomini.

This is why I consider it highly inadvisable to give maidens too 3
much freedom to stroll about and listen too readily to the words
of just anyone. I have often read that girls who do this have seen
their reputations so stained that afterwards they could not be
washed clean, even by the glory of perpetual chastity.

The events I have related are clearly the source of the story we 4
read, that Mercury drove the flocks of the Phoenicians to the
shore, and that Jupiter, transformed into a bull, swam to Crete
with the maiden Europa.

But the ancients do not agree as to the time of this abduction. 5
Those who date it the earliest say it happened when Danaus was
king of Argos. Others say it occurred during the reign of Acrisius.
Authorities who place it more recently declare that it transpired
during the reign of Pandion, king of Athens, and this seems to fit
better with the dates of Europa's son Minos. Some sources simply
report that, after Jupiter raped her, Europa married Asterius, king
of Crete, to whom she bore three sons: Minos, Rhadamanthus,
and Sarpedon. The majority say that they were the sons of Jupiter,
and some identify Asterius with Jupiter.

Other sources could be cited, but most of them agree that 6
Europa became famous through her marriage to a great divinity.
In addition, some claim that the third part of the world has always
been called 'Europe' after her, either because she was of exceptional nobility (for numerous achievements made the Phoenicians
more famous in their own time than other peoples of ancient lineage) or through reverence for her divine husband, or through respect for her kingly sons, or because of the extraordinary virtue of
Europa herself.

I concede that Europa was a woman distinguished for her vir- 7
tues, not only because of the name she has given to the world, but
also because of the remarkable bronze statue dedicated to her in
Taranto by the illustrious philosopher Pythagoras.

: X :

De Lybia regina Lybie

1 Lybia—ut vetustissimi volunt autores—Epaphi Egyptiorum regis fuit filia ex Cassiopia coniuge; eaque nupsit Neptuno, id est extero atque potenti viro, cuius proprium nomen ad nos usque non venit; et ex eo peperit Busyridem, immanem postea superioris Egypti tiramnum.

2 Huius magnifica opera ab annis creduntur consumpta, sed ea fuisse permaxima satis argumenti prestat, eam tante apud suos fuisse autoritatis ut eius Affrice pars, cui imperavit, Lybia omnis de suo nomine appellata sit.

: XI–XII :

De Marpesia et Lampedone reginis Amazonum

1 Marpesia—seu Marthesia—et Lampedo sorores fuere, Amazonum invicem regine et ob illustrem bellorum gloriam sese Martis vocavere filias. Quarum, quoniam peregrina sit, hystoria paulo altius assummenda est.

2 E Scithia igitur, ea tempestate silvestri et fere inaccessa exteris regione et sub Arthoo se in Occeanum usque ab euxino sinu protendente, Sylisios et Scolopicus—ut aiunt—regii iuvenes factione maiorum pulsi, cum parte populorum iuxta Thermodohontem, Cappadocie amnem, devenere et, Cyriis occupatis arvis, raptu vi-
3 vere et incolas latrociniis infestare cepere. A quibus tractu temporis per insidias fere omnes trucidati sunt homines. Quod cum egre

: X :

Libya, Queen of Libya

Libya, according to the ancient authors, was the daughter of King 1
Epaphus of Egypt and his wife Cassiopeia. She married Neptune,
that is, a powerful foreigner whose real name has not come down
to us; she bore him Busiris, who later became a brutal tyrant of
Upper Egypt.

Her magnificent accomplishments are believed to have been 2
consumed by time, but she had so much authority among her people that the part of Africa which she ruled has been named Libya
after her, and this fact is sufficient proof that her deeds were extraordinary.

: XI–XII :

Marpesia and Lampedo, Queens of the Amazons

Marpesia (or Martesia) and Lampedo were sisters who served 1
jointly as queens of the Amazons and called themselves daughters
of Mars because of their glorious fame in war. Since the sisters'
story is foreign to our experience, we must begin in a somewhat
earlier period.

Our sources relate that an aristocratic faction sent into exile 2
Sylisios[a] and Scolopicus, two young men of royal blood from
Scythia, which at that time was a wild land almost inaccessible to
outsiders and extending from the Black Sea in a northerly direction towards Ocean. Accompanied by the popular faction, they
reached the Thermodon River in Cappadocia, seized the fields of
the Cyrian people,[b] and began to live by pillaging and robbing
the inhabitants. Eventually almost all the indigenous males were 3
slaughtered by the treachery of the newcomers. Their wives, now

ferrent viduate coniuges et in ardorem vindicte devenissent fervide, cum paucis qui supervixerant viris in arma prorupere et, primo impetu facto, hostes a suis amovere finibus; inde ultro circumstantibus intulere bellum.

4   Demum arbitrantes servitutem potius quam coniugium si exteris adhererent hominibus, et feminas solas posse sufficere bellis et armis, ne mitiores viderentur habuisse deos ceteris, he, quibus viros a cede finitimorum fortuna servasset, comuni consilio irruentes in eos, omnes interemere; inde in hostes furore converso, quasi virorum neces ulture, illos adeo contrivere ut ab eis facile pacem impetrarent.

5   Qua suscepta, ad successionem consequendam, vicissim finitimis adherebant et, cum concepissent, evestigio revertebantur in sedes. Tandem qui nascebantur mares occidebantur illico, virgines ad militiam cum diligentia servabantur, tenellis igne, seu medicamine alio, sublato incremento mammille[1] dextere, ne sagittandi exercitium impediretur adultis; sinixtra linquebatur intacta ut ex illa nutrimenta porrigerent nascituris; ex quo Amazonum vocabulum sortite sunt.

6   Nec eis in alendis virginibus fuit ea cura que nostris; nam colo calatisve aliisque muliebribus abiectis offitiis, venationibus discursionibus domationibus equorum laboribus armorum assiduis sagittationibus et huiusmodi exercitiis, maturiores puellulas durabant in aptitudinem et virile robur. Quibus artibus non solum

7   Cyrios tenuere campos, a suis olim maioribus occupatos, quin imo Europe ingenti parte bellorum iure quesita, plurimum Asye occupavere formidabilesque devenere omnibus.

8   Sane, ne viribus deesset regimen, ante alias Marpesiam et Lam-

widows, found the situation insupportable. Stirred by a burning desire for vengeance, they fell to arms together with the few remaining men, and in the first assault they drove the enemy from their country. Then, acting on their own, they extended the war against their neighbors.

Eventually these women concluded that, if they entered into relationships with foreign males, they would be slaves rather than wives; they also felt able to wage war by themselves. Hence, by common accord, they attacked and killed all the husbands who had survived so as to remove the appearance that a kinder fate had been reserved for those women whose spouses Fortune had saved from the Scythians' massacre. Then their fury was directed against the enemy. As if to avenge their dead husbands, the women so decimated the foe that the latter quickly sued for peace. 4

Afterwards, in order to assure the royal succession, they took turns sleeping with men of the neighboring regions and returned home as soon as they became pregnant. Male offspring were killed immediately after birth, and females were carefully brought up for military service. The right breast of very young girls was withered by means of fire or medicine, so that it would not grow and hinder them in the use of the bow during adult life. The left breast, however, was left unharmed, so that they would be able to suckle their future children. This practice gave rise to the name 'Amazon'.ᶜ 5

Their concerns, however, were different from our own vis-à-vis the upbringing of girls. The distaff, workbaskets, and other womanly tasks were set aside; through hunting, running, horse-taming, martial exercises, continuous practice in archery, and similar pursuits, the Amazons hardened the young girls and prepared them to acquire a man's strength. With such skills these women held not only the Cyrian fields once occupied by their ancestors, but they also acquired by right of conquest a large part of Europe, seized much of Asia, and became an object of terror to all. 6 7

After their husbands had been killed, the Amazons appointed 8

pedonem sibi post cesos viros instituere reginas, sub quarum au-
spitiis—ut premonstratum est—suum plurimum imperium au-
9 sere. He quidem, cum militari disciplina insignes essent, partitis
intra se provinciis, ut puta, cum una in regni tutelam subsisteret,
reliqua, parte copiarum sumpta, ad subiciendos finitimos earum
imperio incedebat; et sic vicissim, maximis partis[2] predis, auserunt
aliquandiu rem publicam.

10 Verum cum Lampedo ad ultimum in hostes duxisset exercitum,
repentino barbarorum circumadiacentium incursu, Marpesia nimium sui fidens, relictis aliquibus filiabus, cum parte copiarum
11 cesa est. Quid autem ex Lampedone secutum sit, legisse non
memini.

: XIII :

De Tisbe babilonia virgine

1 Tisbes, babilonia virgo, infelicis amoris exitu magis quam opere
alio inter mortales celebris facta est. Huius etsi non a maioribus
nostris qui parentes fuerint habuerimus, intra tamen Babiloniam
habuisse cum Pyramo, etatis sue puero, contiguas domos satis cre-
2 ditum est. Quorum cum esset iure convicinii quasi convictus assi-
duus et inde eis adhuc pueris puerilis affectio, egit iniqua sors ut,
crescentibus annis, cum ambo formosissimi essent, puerilis amor
in maximum augeretur incendium illudque inter se, nutibus saltem, aperirent aliquando, iam in puberem propinquantes etatem.

3 Sane, cum iam grandiuscula fieret Tisbes, a parentibus in futuros hymeneos domi detineri cepta est. Quod cum egerrime ferrent
ambo quererentque solliciti qua via possent saltem aliquando col-

Marpesia and Lampedo as queens to rule their forces. Under such leadership (as we have already said), the Amazons greatly increased their dominion. These two queens, both noted for their 9 military skill, divided the duties of office among themselves so that while one remained to guard the homeland, the other went forth with part of the army to subjugate their neighbors to the Amazonian empire. Thus by turns they enlarged for some time their state and procured great booty.

Finally, however, while Lampedo was away leading an army 10 against the enemy, the overly confident Marpesia was killed with part of her troops during a sudden invasion by the neighboring barbarians. She was survived by some daughters. But I do not re- 11 member reading what happened to Lampedo.

: XIII :

Thisbe, a Babylonian Maiden

Thisbe, a Babylonian maiden, became known to people more for 1 the outcome of her tragic love than for any other action. Although we have not learned from our ancient sources who her parents were, it is nevertheless believed that she had a house in Babylon next door to that of Pyramus, a young man her own age. Proxim- 2 ity gave them the right to continual intimacy, and hence, while they were still young, there arose a childish affection between them. Thanks to an unkind fate, their childhood love eventually grew into a powerful passion since both were extremely handsome. As they grew into puberty, they would sometimes reveal their mutual love to each other in subtle ways.

When Thisbe was nearly grown, her parents began to keep her 3 at home with a view towards her future marriage. The two young people could not endure this separation and tried anxiously to dis-

loqui, nulli adhuc visam comunis parietis invenere in seposito ri-
mulam; ad quam dum clam convenissent sepius et, consuetudine
paululum colloquendo, pariete etiam obice, quo minus erube-
scebant, ampliassent exprimendi affectiones suas licentiam, sepe
suspiria lacrimas fervores desideria et passiones omnes aperie-
bant vias, nonnunquam etiam orare invicem pacem animorum amplexus et oscula, pietatem fidem dilectionemque perpetuam.

4 Tandem, excrescente incendio, de fuga inivere consilium, sta-
tuentes ut nocte sequenti, quam primum quis posset suos fallere,
domos exiret; et seinvicem, si quis primus evaderet, in nemus civi-
tati proximum abiens, penes fontem Nini regis bustui proximum
tardiorem operiretur. Ardentior forte Tisbes prima suos fefellit et
amicta pallio, intempesta nocte, sola patriam domum exivit et,
luna monstrante viam, in nemus intrepida abiit; et dum secus fontem expectaret et ad quemcunque rei motum sollicita caput extol-
leret, leenam venientem advertens, relicto inadvertenter pallio, aufugit in bustum. Leena autem pasta, siti posita, comperto pallio,
aliquandiu ad illud cruento ore de more exfricato atque exterso,
unguibus laceratum liquit et abiit.

5 Interim tardior Pyramus, eque relicta domo, devenit in silvam;
dumque per silentia noctis intentus comperisset laceratum cruen-
tumque pallium Tisbis, ratus eam a belua devoratam, plangore
plurimo locum complevit, se miserum incusans quoniam dilectissime virgini seve mortis causam ipse dedisset; et aspernans de cetero vitam, exerto, quem gesserat, gladio, moribundus secus fontem pectori impegit suo.

6 Nec mora; Tisbes potatam leenam abiisse rata[1], ne decepisse vi-

cover a way to speak to each other at least occasionally; in a hidden part of the common wall between their houses they found a crack that had hitherto gone completely unnoticed. Pyramus and Thisbe secretly went to this opening many times and for a little while conversed in their accustomed manner. Then, less shy because of the wall that separated them, they grew bolder in expressing their affection and gave free rein to their sighs, tears, burning desires, and passions. At times they begged each other for consolation, embraces and kisses, for devotion, trust, and eternal love.

Finally, as their ardor grew, the lovers devised a plan of flight. 4 They decided that, on the following night, as soon as they could elude their families, they would leave their houses, go to a grove near the city, and there, near a spring close to King Ninus' tomb, whoever escaped first would wait for the other. Thisbe, being perhaps the more ardent, was the first to slip away from her parents. Wrapped in a cloak, she left her father's home alone in the dead of night and, with the moon lighting her way, went fearlessly into the grove. As Thisbe waited near the spring, raising her head apprehensively at the slightest motion, she saw a lioness approach; at this she fled towards the tomb, inadvertently leaving her cloak behind. The lioness, who had already eaten, now drank. Finding the cloak, she wiped her bloodstained mouth on it, as such animals commonly do. Then, after tearing the cloak with her claws, the creature dropped it and went away.

In the meantime Pyramus had also left his house and arrived finally at the grove. Searching intently in the silence of the night, he found Thisbe's torn and bloody cloak. Under the assumption that she had been devoured by some wild beast, he filled the place with loud wailing and accused his own wretched self of being the cause of his beloved's cruel death. Then, despising his own continued existence, Pyramus drew forth the sword he was wearing, plunged it into his breast, and lay dying near the spring.

Shortly afterwards, Thisbe, on the supposition that the lioness 6

deretur amantem aut diu expectatione suspensum teneret, pede-

7 tentim ad fontem regredi cepit. Cui iam propinqua, palpitantem adhuc Pyramum sentiens, pavefacta fere iterum abiit; tandem lune lumine percepit quoniam iacens suus esset Pyramus; et, dum eius in amplexus festina iret, eum sanguini per vulnus effuso incuban-

8 tem atque iam omnem effundentem animam comperit. Que cum aspectu obstupuisset primo mesta tandem ingenti cum fletu fru-stra prestare subsidia et animam retinere osculis et amplexu ali-quandiu conata est.

9 Verum cum nec verbum aurire posset sensissetque nil pendi tam ferventi pridie desiderio optata basia, et amantem in mortem festinare videret; rata, quoniam eam non comperisset, occisum, in acerbum fatum cum dilecto a se puero, amore pariter et dolore suadentibus, ire disposuit; et arrepto capulotenus ex vulnere gla-dio, cum gemitu ploratuque maximo nomen invocavit Pyrami ora-vitque ut Tisbem suam saltem morientem aspiceret et exeuntem expectaret animam, ut invicem in quascunque sedes incederent.

10 Mirum dictu! Sensit morientis deficiens intellectus amate virgi-nis nomen, nec extremum negare postulatum passus, oculos in

11 morte gravatos aperuit et invocantem aspexit. Que confestim pe-ctori adolescentis cultroque superincubuit et effuso sanguine se-cuta est animam iam defuncti. Et sic, quos amplexui placido invida fortuna iungi minime passa est, infelicem amborum sanguinem misceri prohibuisse non potuit.

12 Quis non compatietur iuvenibus? Quis tam infelici exitui lacri-mulam saltem unam non concedet? Saxeus erit. Amarunt pueri: non enim ob hoc infortunium meruere cruentum. Florentis etatis

had drunk and left, returned cautiously to the spring lest she should appear to have deceived her lover or to have kept him waiting long in suspense. When she came near the spring, she heard 7 Pyramus' twitchings; frightened, she almost left. At last she saw in the moonlight that it was her own Pyramus lying there. Thisbe hurried to embrace him and found him lying in the blood that had oozed from his wound and already breathing his last. She first ex- 8 perienced shock, then grief. With flooding tears she tried in vain to help him; with her kisses and embraces she sought long to keep his soul from flight.

But Thisbe was not able to get a word from Pyramus, and she 9 realized that he did not feel the kisses which a short time before he had so ardently desired. She saw that her lover was hastening to his death. Thisbe thought he had killed himself because he had not found her, and so, under the prompting in equal parts of love and sorrow, she determined to share with her beloved the same unhappy fate. She seized the sword embedded up to the hilt in his wound. Then, amidst great groaning and sobbing, she called out the name of Pyramus and begged him to look upon his Thisbe at least in death and to wait for her soul as it departed her body, so that they could go together to whatever might be their resting-place.

Wonderful to relate, the dying Pyramus still heard the name of 10 his beloved. Unable to deny her last wish, he opened his eyes, already heavy with death, and looked upon the woman who was calling him. Straightway Thisbe fell upon the young man's breast 11 and then upon his sword, poured out her blood, and followed the soul of her now dead lover. Thus envious Fortune could not prevent the mingling of the unhappy blood of those whom she had prevented from joining in a gentle embrace.

Who will not pity the two young people? Who does not shed 12 at least a single tear for their tragic end? Such a person must be made of stone. They had loved each other from the time they were

amor crimen est, nec horrendum solutis crimen; in coniugium ire poterat. Peccavit sors[2] pessima et forsan miseri peccavere parentes.

13 Sensim quippe frenandi sunt iuvenum impetus, ne, dum repentino obice illis obsistere volumus, desperantes in precipitium inpella-

14 mus. Immoderati vigoris est cupidinis passio et adolescentium fere pestis et comune flagitium, in quibus edepol patienti animo toleranda[3] est, quoniam sic rerum volente natura fit, ut scilicet dum etate valemus, ultro inclinemur in prolem, ne humanum genus in defectum corruat, si coitus differantur in senium.

: XIV :

De Ypermestra Argivorum regina et sacerdote Iunonis

1 Ypermestra, genere et dignitate clara, Danai, Argivorum regis, filia et Lyncei coniunx fuit. Colligitur autem ex hystoriis antiquorum duos quondam in Egypto fuisse fratres, Beli prisci filios, spectabili preminentes imperio, quorum Danaus unus, alter autem Egystus

2 nuncupatus est. Nec prolis ambobus fuit equa fortuna, esto numerus esset equus: nam Danao quinquaginta fuere filie filiique totidem Egysto.

3 Sane, cum habuisset oraculo Danaus quoniam manu nepotis ex fratre occideretur, et clam angeretur timore plurimo, cum ex tam ingenti multitudine nesciret cuius suspectas deberet habere manus, contigit ut, iam pubescentibus utriusque filiis, peteret Egystus ut

4 Danai filie omnes filiis suis iungerentur coniugio. Quod Danaus, sevo excogitato facinore, ultro concessit; desponsatisque filiabus

children: yet not for this did they deserve a bloody death. To love while in the flower of youth is a fault, but it is not a frightful crime for unmarried persons since they can proceed to matrimony. The worst sin was Fortune's, and perhaps their wretched parents were guilty as well. Certainly the impulses of the young should be   13 curbed, but this should be done gradually lest we drive them to ruin in their despair by setting up sudden obstacles in their path. Passionate desire is ungovernable; it is the plague and the disgrace   14 of youth, yet we should tolerate it with patience. Nature intends us, while young and fit, to feel spontaneously the procreative urge; the human race would die out if intercourse were delayed until old age.

: XIV :

Hypermnestra, Queen of the Argives and Priestess of Juno

Hypermnestra, famous for her lineage and merit, was the daugh-   1 ter of Danaus, king of the Argives, and the wife of Lynceus. Ac-cording to ancient sources there were once two brothers in Egypt, children of the ancient Belus, who were well known for their re-markable empire. One of them was called Danaus and the other Aegisthus. Although Fortune allotted them the same number of   2 offspring, she did not distribute them equally since Danaus had fifty girls and Aegisthus as many boys.

Danaus had learned from an oracle that he would die at the   3 hand of one of his brother's sons. Secretly he was gripped by great fear, but he did not know whom he should suspect since he had so many nephews. When the children of each brother were nearing adolescence, Aegisthus requested all the daughters of Danaus in marriage for his sons. Danaus, who was planning a terrible crime,   4 gladly gave his consent. After his daughters had been betrothed to

nepotibus, cum nuptiale sacrum pararetur, eas omnes summopere premonuit ut, si salutem suam vellent, unaqueque virum suum nocte prima, dum vino epulisque madentem somnoque illigatum gravi cognosceret, ferro perimeret.

5   Quod omnes cultris clam cubiculis suis illatis, marcentes externa crapula iuvenes iussu interfecere parentis; ast Ypermestra

6 sola abstinuit. Apposuerat quippe virgo iam animum suum in Lynum seu Lynceum virum suum; ut moris est puellarum, evestigio, viso sponso, illum diligere et ob id ei compassa, ingenti cum laude sua a nephasta cede abstinuit suasitque iuveni fugam; qua tutatus

7 est. Verum cum ceteris mane ob patratum scelus trux pater applausisset, Ypermestra sola obiurgata et carcere clausa, pium aliquandiu flevit opus.

8   Heu miseri mortales, quam cupido animo, quam ferventi peritura concupiscimus et occasum intueri aspernantes, quam execrandis viis, si prestetur, celsa conscendimus! <Quibus sceleribus conscensa servamus>,[1] quasi obscenis operibus arbitremur volubi-

9 lem firmari posse fortunam! Et, quod ridiculum est, quibus criminibus, quam scelestis facinoribus, volatilem fragilemque vite huius dieculam, non dicam longare, sed perpetuare conamur, cum in mortem ire ceteros cursu volucri videamus!

10   Quibus detestandis consiliis, quibus infandis operibus Dei irritamus iudicium! Ut alios sinam, testis infandus sit Danaus. Qui dum plurimo nepotum sanguine suos iam tremulos annos ampliare nititur, robusta se ac splendida nepotum nudavit acie et perenni labefactavit infamia. Arbitratus est homo nequam paucos frigidosque annos senectutis sue floridis adolescentie nepotum

11 suorum preponendos fore. Quod forsan, tanquam utiliores, existi-

his nephews and preparations for the marriage ceremony were un-
derway, Danaus warned each of his children, if she valued her life,
to stab her husband on her wedding night as the latter lay in heavy
slumber, dulled by food and wine.

In accord with their father's command, the daughters secretly 5
brought knives into their chambers and killed their husbands, who
had been rendered torpid by the previous day's drunkenness. Only
Hypermnestra held back. In fact, she had already fallen in love 6
with her husband, whose name was Linus or Lynceus. As girls often do, she loved at first sight and so took pity on him. To her
great credit, Hypermnestra refrained from this shameful murder
and advised the young man to flee; by this means he was saved. In 7
the morning, the cruel father lavished praise on his other daughters for the crime they had committed. Hypermnestra alone was
blamed and put in prison where for some time she tearfully lamented her kind action.

Alas, wretched mortals! how eagerly and passionately we desire 8
things that must perish! Heedless of falling, we scale the heights
by whatever accursed ways present themselves. With what crimes
do we cling to the positions we have reached, as if we thought
fickle fortune could be steadied with foul deeds! Laughable indeed 9
are the crimes, the detestable villainies we commit in order to
lengthen—nay, to perpetuate—the short span of our frail and
fleeting life, even while we see others rushing towards death.

With what abominable counsels and wicked deeds do we pro- 10
voke God's wrath! There is no need to mention anyone else: let
wicked Danaus stand a witness to this. Attempting to prolong his
trembling years with the bloodbath of his nephews, he deprived
himself of a vigorous and distinguished line of grandchildren and
incurred perpetual infamy. This vile man thought that the few
cold years of his old age should take precedence over the flowering
youth of his nephews. Another person might have thought those 11
years of old age more usefully spent in preserving an honorable

masset alius, dummodo servasset honeste; verum per vulnera iuvenum filiorum quesisse suum prolongasse senium, immane facinus iure videri potest.

12   Et, quod plurimum ignominie superaddit, non satellitum manus, sed filias armavit in scelus, ut non tantum nepotes auferret, sed ut scelere filias funestas haberet, quas habere pietate potuisset honestas; et dum vitam servare hoc crimine cupit, non advertit quantum audacie, quantum fraudis, quantum detestande enormitatis, futuris pernitiosis mulieribus infausti relicturus esset exempli.

13   Fidem coniugii calcari fecit perfidia. Ubi sacras inferri faces thalamis pius iussisse pater debuerat, nephastus gladios imperavit; ubi in coniugalem dilectionem natas hortari consuevimus, is in odium animavit et cedem; et, quod in omnes homo ausus non fuisset, in singulos natas immisit; quod die non attentasset, nocte perfici voluit; quod non presumpsisset in castris, thalamis mandavit impleri; non advertens quia, quot annos viridi iuventuti nepotum auferebat per scelus et fraudem, tot sibi fedata ignominiosi sui facinoris secula reservabat; et qui quinquaginta iure poterat habere generos hostis male merito letalis servatus est unus.

14   Cuius tandem manus, Dei iusto volente iudicio, truculentus senex evasisse non potuit quin ille nocuus effunderetur sanguis, quem tam multo nepotum sanguine redemisset. Qui tandem, seu pulsus, seu profugus, seu vocatus, transfretavit in Greciam et

15 Argivorum regnum ingenio et viribus occupatum tenuit. Quo sunt qui velint predictum facinus a Danao perpetratum; sed quocunque

mode of life. But seeking to lengthen his old age through the death of his young sons-in-law may rightly be regarded as inhuman.

What makes Danaus' shame all the greater is that to commit this crime he put weapons into the hands, not of accomplices, but of his own daughters. Not only did he cause the death of his nephews: he polluted his daughters with murder when they might have been honored for piety. Wanting to save his own life by means of this foul deed, Danaus did not notice what an unfortunate example of audacity, deceit, and detestable excess he would bequeath to evil women in the future.

His mistrust made him trample on the trust that belongs to marriage. Where a righteous father would have called for sacred torches to be carried into the bridal chambers, this wretch commanded swords; where we should have enjoined conjugal devotion upon our daughters, this man incited them to hatred and murder. What he as a man did not dare do to all his nephews together, he sent his daughters to do to each one singly; what he would not have attempted in daylight, he ordered done at night; what he would not have ventured on the battlefield, he ordered done in the bridal bed. Nor did he take into account that the number of years he took away from his nephews' youth through cruelty and deceit would be equalled by the number of centuries his hateful deed would be remembered. In the end Danaus, who by right could have had fifty sons, got the one he deserved: an enemy would prove his undoing.

At last, by this son's hand and by the just judgment of God, the bloodthirsty old man could not escape the spilling of his own wicked blood, the very blood he had purchased with so much of his nephews'. In due course Danaus went overseas to Greece — either driven away, exiled, or invited. There through shrewdness and strength he seized and held the kingdom of the Argives. Some sources report that Danaus' above-mentioned crime was committed there. But wherever it occurred, he was killed by Linus, who

factum sit, a Lyno truculentie memore occisus occubuit et pro eo
Lynus ipse regnavit Argivis eductaque e carcere Ypermestra, eaque
16 meliori omine sibi iuncta coniugio, regni participem fecit. Que
non solum regina refulsit, sed, Iunonis argive sacerdos effecta, can-
dore splendoris duplicis ornata comparuit; et, cum sorores in turpem abiissent infamiam, ipsa ob commendabilem pietatem nomen
suum laude dignum ad nos usque dimisit insigne.

: XV :

De Nyobe regina Thebanorum

1 Nyobes fere vulgo inter egregias notissima mulier, cum vetustissimi atque famosissimi Frigiorum regis Tantali nata fuisset et Pelo-
pis soror, nupsit Anphioni, Tebarum regi ea tempestate clarissimo[1], tam quia Iovis proles quam quia precipua valeret facundia; et
ex eo, perseverante regni gloria, septem peperit filios et filias toti-
2 dem. Sane quod sapienti profuisse debuerat, superbienti fuit exitium; nam tam splendore conspicue prolis quam maiorum suorum
fulgore elata, etiam in numina obloqui ausa est.

Erant equidem iussu Manthonis, Thyresie vatis filie, solliciti
dierum una Thebani circa sacrum Latone, matris Apollinis et
Dyane, veteri superstitione venerandis numinibus; cum quasi agitata Furiis, circumsepta natorum acie et regiis insignita notis, pro-
siluit in medium Nyobes, clamitans quenam illa esset Thebano-

remembered his father-in-law's cruelty and succeeded him as ruler of the Argives. Hypermnestra was freed from prison and, under better auspices, was joined to him in marriage and shared in his reign. Renowned as queen, she was also made a priestess of the   16
Argive Juno and thus appeared embellished with the sheen of a double glory. While her sisters fell into shameful infamy, Hypermnestra handed down even to our own time a name that is distinguished and worthy of esteem because of her own righteous conduct.

: XV :

Niobe, Queen of Thebes

Practically the most famous of noble women was Niobe, sister of   1
Pelops and daughter of Tantalus, the latter an ancient and famous king of Phrygia. Niobe married Amphion of Thebes, the most famous king of the time, who was renowned both as Jupiter's son and as a person of exceptional eloquence. During the course of Amphion's glorious reign, she gave birth to seven sons and seven daughters. It is certain that this achievement, which to a wise   2
woman ought to have been a source of good, was to her, in her pride, a source of destruction. For Niobe, carried away by the luster attached to her numerous children and the glory of her ancestors, dared to speak even against the gods.

One day the Thebans, at the command of Manto, daughter of the soothsayer Tiresias, were zealously sacrificing to Latona, mother of Apollo and Diana (all divinities revered at Thebes in the old superstitious era). Into their midst burst Niobe as if spurred on by the Furies. Dressed in her royal robes and surrounded by a crowd of her children, she cried out: "What mad-

rum dementia Latone sacra disponere et exteram feminam, Cey Tytanis genitam, duos tantum adulterio conceptos enixam filios, sibi, eorum regine, preponere, rege Tantalo nate, et que quattuordecim, eis videntibus, illis ex coniuge peperisset genitos; sibique, tanquam digniori, cerimonias illas deberi.

3   Tandem parvo temporis tractu factum est ut, ea vidente, letali peste nati omnes, pulchra iuventute florentes, infra breve spatium assummerentur usque ad unum; et Anphion, quod ex patre quattuordecim filiorum repente orbus effectus esset, dolore inpellente, manu propria gladio transfoderetur, existimantibus Thebanis hec ira superum, ulciscentium numinis iniuriam, contigisse.

4   Nyobes autem, tot funeribus superstes, vidua mestaque in tam grandem atque obstinatam taciturnitatem devenit, ut potius im-
5   mobile saxum videretur quam femina. Quam ob causam a poetis postmodum fictum est eam apud Sypilum, ubi sepulti fuerant filii, in lapideam statuam fuisse conversam.

6   Durum est et odiosum plurimum superbos, non dicam tolerare, sed spectare homines; mulieres autem fastidiosum et importabile; cum illos ferventis animi, ut plurimum, natura produxerit; has vero mitis ingenii et remisse virtutis, lautitiis potius quam impe-
7   riis aptas, produxit. Quam ob rem mirabile minus si in elatas dei proclivior ira sit et iudicium sevius, quotiens eas sue debilitatis contingat excedere terminos, ut insipiens Nyobes fecit, fortune lusa fallacia, et ignara quoniam ample prolis parentem fore, non virtutis parientis, sed nature opus esse, in se celi benignitatem flectentis.

8   Satis igitur illi, imo debitum, erat Deo ex concessis egisse gra-

ness prompts you Thebans to make sacrifices to Latona and give precedence to this foreign woman, daughter of Coeus (who was the son of Titan) and mother of only two children conceived in adultery, over me, your queen and the daughter of King Tantalus, who has borne the fourteen legitimate children whom you now see? It is I who am the more worthy; these sacrifices should be offered to me!"

Soon after it transpired that all her children, even down to the 3 last one, died of a fatal illness within a short time of each other while they were in the fair flower of youth; and Niobe was witness to it all. Amphion, once the father of fourteen children, suddenly found himself childless. Overcome by grief he impaled himself on a sword. The Thebans thought that these disasters had been brought on by the anger of the gods who were avenging Niobe's insult to Latona.

Now a widow and the lone survivor after so many losses, the 4 mournful Niobe fell into such deep and obstinate silence that she seemed a motionless rock rather than a woman. Hence the poetic 5 fiction that she had been changed into a stone statue near Sipylus, the burial place of her children.

It is a hard and especially hateful thing to look upon proud 6 men, to say nothing of enduring them. But it is perfectly unbearable to observe proud women. For the most part, Nature has made men high-spirited, while she has given a meek and submissive character to women, who are more suited to luxury than to power. For this reason, it should not be surprising if God's wrath 7 is swifter and his sentence more harsh against proud women whenever it happens that, like foolish Niobe, they go beyond the boundaries of their weakness. She was deluded by deceitful fortune and did not know that to have many children is not a work of virtue on the part of the mother who gives them birth, but a work of Nature who bends Heaven's goodness to that end.

Hence Niobe should have been satisfied to give thanks to 8

tias, quam sibi divinos qualescunque honores quesisse, tanquam sui fuisset operis tam numerosam prolem atque conspicuam pepe-

9 risse. Que, dum superbe potius quam prudenter operata est, egit ut infortunium viva fleret et post multa secula suum nomen posteritati foret exosum.

: XVI :

De Ysiphile regina Lemni

1 Ysiphiles insignis fuit femina, tam pietate in patrem quam infelici exilio et Archemori alumni morte atque subsidio natorum, oportuno in tempore repertorum.

2 Fuit etenim hec Thoantis, Lemniadum regis, filia, eo evo regnantis quo rabies illa subivit mulierum insule mentes, subtra-

3 hendi omnino indomita colla virorum iugo. Nam parvipenso senis regis imperio[1], adhibita secum Ysiphile, unanimes in eum devenere consilium ut sequenti nocte gladiis seviretur in quoscunque mas-

4 culos; nec defuit opus proposito. Sane, sevientibus reliquis, consilium mitius menti Ysiphilis occurrit; nam rata fedari paterno sanguine inhumanum fore, genitori detecto reliquarum facinore eoque in navim demisso ut Chium effugeret publicam iram; evestigio, ingenti constructo rogo, se patri postremum exhibere finxit officium.

5 Quod cum crederetur a cunctis, patrio imposita throno, loco regis, impiis mulieribus regina suffecta est.

6 Sanctissima quippe filiorum pietas in parentes est; quid enim decentius, quid iustius, quid laudabilius quam his humanitate

God—indeed it was her duty so to do—for granting her children, rather than seeking divine honors for herself as if the birth of such numerous and marvelous children had been her own accomplishment. By acting proudly rather than wisely, Niobe was the cause 9 of the sad misfortune she suffered while she lived, and she made sure that centuries later her name is still detested by posterity.

: XVI :

Hypsipyle, Queen of Lemnos

Hypsipyle was a woman famous for her devotion to her father 1 as well as for her unfortunate exile, the death of her ward Archemorus,[a] and the help she received from her children, whom she rediscovered at an opportune moment.

She was the daughter of Thoas, king of Lemnos, during whose 2 reign the women of that island were seized by a mad desire to escape their husbands' tyranny. Scorning the old king's rule and win- 3 ning over Hypsipyle to their side, they unanimously decided to put to the sword on the following night all the males. And their deeds matched their words. But while the rest of the women were 4 venting their rage, a more merciful idea occurred to Hypsipyle. She thought that it would be inhuman to sully herself with her father's blood, and so she told him of the others' crime and helped him to escape the general wrath by putting him on a ship bound for Chios. Thereupon she built a great pyre and pretended that she was performing the final rites for her father. Everyone believed 5 this. Hypsipyle was placed on her father's throne and, in place of their king, these wicked women now substituted a queen.

Most sacred indeed is the love of children for their parents. 6 What is more seemly, more just, more praiseworthy than to reward generously and honorably those from whose labor we re-

atque honore vices reddere, quorum labore invalidi alimenta sumpsimus, solertia tutati sumus et amore incessabili in provectiorem etatem deducti et instructi moribus et doctrina necnon honoribus atque facultatibus aucti, et ingenio valemus et moribus? Nil
7 equidem! Que cum ab Ysiphile inpensa sint cum cura parenti, non immerito illustribus addita mulieribus est.

Ea igitur regnante, seu vi ventorum inpulsus, seu ex proposito devectus, cum Argonautis in Colcos[2] tendentibus, Iason, frustra prohibentibus feminis, occupato litore, a regina hospicio atque
8 lecto susceptus est. Ex quo abeunte, cum geminos in tempore peperisset filios eosque Lemniadum lege cogeretur emictere, ut placet
9 aliquibus, in Chium ad avum nutriendos iussit efferri. Ex quo cognito quod, servato patre, decepisset reliquas, in eam concursum est; et vix, conscensa navi, a furore servata publico, dum patrem natosque quereret, a pyrratis capta et in servitutem deducta est; variisque exanclatis laboribus, Lygurgo nemeo regi dono data, curam Opheltis parvuli et unici Ligurgi filii suscepit.

10 Cui dum vacaret obsequio, transeunti atque propter estum siti periclitanti, Adrasti Argivorum regis exercitui in Thebas eunti, rogata, Langiam ostendit, relicto in pratis inter flores alumno.
11 Verum dum percontanti Adrasto preteritos exponeret casus, ab Eunoe et Thoante, adultis filiis et sub rege militantibus, cognita atque in spem fortune melioris erepta, ludentem inter herbas alumnum cum verbere caude serpentis comperisset occisum, fere plangoribus totum turbavit exercitum, a quo natisque furenti ob

ceived nourishment when we were helpless, who watched over us
with solicitude, brought us to maturity with constant love, taught
us manners and gave us knowledge, enriched us with honors and
skills, and made us strong in morals and in intellect? Surely nothing! Hypsipyle scrupulously repaid this debt to her father and thus   7
deserves to be placed among distinguished women.

It was during her reign that Jason, despite the women's opposition, landed on their shore. He was on his way to Colchis
with the Argonauts and came to Lemnos either because of a storm
or through his own design. The queen received him into her
house and into her bed. After his departure she bore him in due   8
course twin sons. Forced by the laws of Lemnos to send them
away, Hypsipyle ordered (so some sources report) that they be
taken to Chios to be brought up by their grandfather. Thus it be-   9
came known that in saving her father she had deceived the other
women, and her subjects rose up against her. Hypsipyle barely
saved herself from the general fury by boarding a ship. During the
journey in search of her father and her children she was captured
by pirates and enslaved. After enduring many hardships she was
given as a gift to Lycurgus, king of Nemea, and entrusted with the
care of the king's only son, a small boy named Opheltes.

While Hypsipyle was watching over him, Adrastus, king of   10
Argos, passed through the country with his army on the march
against Thebes. They were dying of thirst because of the heat. At
their request Hypsipyle showed them the spring of Langia, leaving
Opheltes in a meadow among the flowers. As she recounted her   11
misfortunes in answer to Adrastus' query, she was recognized by
her sons Euneus and Thoas, now grown, who were serving in the
king's army. Hypsipyle had just begun to hope for better fortune
when she discovered that Opheltes, who was playing in the grass,
had died from a serpent's bite. Her lamentations threw almost the
whole army into distress, and her children and the rest of the
soldiers took her away from Lycurgus, who had gone mad with

dolorem Lygurgo subtracta, incognito michi eventui mortique servata est.

: XVII :

De Medea regina Colcorum

1 Medea, sevissimum veteris perfidie documentum, Oete, clarissimi regis Colcorum, et Perse coniugis filia fuit: formosa satis et ma-
2 lefitiorum longe doctissima. Nam, a quocunque magistro instructa sit, adeo herbarum vires familiares habuit, ut nemo melius; novitque plene cantato carmine turbare celum, ventos ex antris[1] ciere, tempestates movere, flumina sistere, venena conficere, elaboratos ignes ad quodcunque incendium componere et huiusmodi perfi-
3 cere omnia. Nec illi—quod longe peius—ab artibus fuit dissonus animus; nam, deficientibus eis, ferro uti arbitrabatur levissimum.

4 Hec Iasonem thessalum, eo seculo conspicuum virtute iuvenem, a Pelia patruo, sue probitati insidiante, sub pretextu gloriosissime expeditionis missum in Colcos ad aureum surripiendum vellus, eiusdem capta prestantia, dilexit ardenter egitque, ad eius promerendam gratiam, ut, orta inter incolas seditione, patri suscitaretur bellum et consequendi votum Iasoni spatium prestaretur.

5 Quis hoc etiam sensatus arbitr<ar>etur[2] homo quod ex uno oculorum intuitu opulentissimi regis exterminium sequeretur? Eo igitur patrato scelere, cum dilecti iuvenis meruisset amplexus, cum eodem secum patriam substantiam omnem trahens, clam fugam arripuit; nec tam grandi facinore contenta, in peius trucem divertit animum.

6 Arbitrata quidem Oetam secuturum profugos, ad eum sisten-

grief. Thus Hypsipyle was preserved for a fate and a death unknown to me.

: XVII :   ·

Medea, Queen of Colchis

Medea, the cruelest example of ancient treachery, was the daugh-   1
ter of Aeetes, an eminent king of Colchis, and his wife Perse.
Medea was quite beautiful and by far the cleverest of witches.
Whoever her teacher may have been, no one had a more intimate   2
knowledge than she of the properties of herbs. She knew perfectly
well how, by singing enchantments, to stir up the heavens, summon the winds from their cave, raise storms, dam rivers, brew poi-
sons, make incendiary devices, and do all other things of this sort.
Far worse, her character was in keeping with her arts, for, if those   3
failed, Medea thought nothing of resorting to the sword.

She was attracted to the handsome Jason of Thessaly and fell   4
passionately in love with him. Famous at that time for his prowess, he had been sent to Colchis by his uncle Pelias under the pretext of a glorious expedition to steal the Golden Fleece; in reality
the uncle was plotting his nephew's downfall. To win Jason's love,
Medea used the occasion of a popular uprising to instigate a war
against her own father and gave Jason the opportunity to succeed
in his purpose.

What person of sense could imagine that a simple glance would   5
result in the destruction of a powerful king? Medea committed the
crime and so earned the embraces of her young lover. She fled
with him in secret, taking with her all her father's wealth. But she
was not satisfied with even this terrible action and turned her
cruel powers to hatching still worse schemes.

Medea had foreseen that Aeetes would follow the fugitives. He   6

dum in Thomitania Phasidis insula, per quam secuturo transitus futurus erat, Absyrtium seu Egyaleum puerum fratrem suum quem in hoc secum fuge comitem traxerat, obtruncari et eius membra passim per arva dispergi iussit, ut, dum spersa miserabilis colligeret genitor et eis lacrimas tumulumque daret, fugientibus

7 etiam fuge spatium commodaret. Nec eam fefellit opinio: sic enim factum est.

8   Tandem cum post errores plurimos in Thessaliam cum Iasone devenisset suo Esonemque socerum, tam ex reditu nati quam ex parta victoria predaque et illustri coniugio tanta replesset letitia, ut revocatus in floridam videretur etatem, Iasoni paratura regnum, arte sua zizaniam inter natas et Peliam sevit easque misere armavit in patrem.

9   Ceterum, labentibus annis, exosa Iasoni facta et ab eodem loco eius Creusa, filia Creontis, Corinthiorum regis, assumpta, inpatiens fremensque cum multa in Iasonem excogitasset, eo prorupit ut ingenio suo Creusam Creontisque regiam omnem assummeret igne volatili; et, spectante Iasone, quos ex eo susceperat filios trucidaret et effugeret in Athenas, ubi, Egeo nupta regi, cum Medum, a se denominatum, iam filium suscepisset ex eo, et frustra Theseum redeuntem veneno temptasset occidere, tertio fugam arripuit et, cum Iasonis in gratiam redisset, una cum eo³ omni Thesalia ab Agialeo, Pelie filio, pulsi repatriavit in Colcos senemque atque

10 exulem patrem regno restituit. Quid tandem egerit quove sub celo seu mortis genere diem clauserit, nec legisse memini nec audisse.

11   Sed, ne omiserim, non omnis oculis prestanda licentia est. Eis enim spectantibus, splendores cognoscimus, invidiam introducimus, concupiscentias attrahimus omnes; eis agentibus, excitatur

would have to come by way of Tomis, an island in the river Phasis. So, to hinder her father's pursuit, she took along her brother Absyrtus, or Aegialeus, who was just a boy, and had him dismembered there. Then Medea ordered parts of his body to be scattered through the fields on the supposition that, when her wretched father stopped to collect the body of his son whom he would mourn and bury, it would give Jason and herself time to flee. She was not deceived in her expectation, for this is exactly what happened. 7

After much wandering, Medea finally arrived in Thessaly with her Jason, where she made her father-in-law Aeson so happy for his son's return, as well as for his son's victory, his booty, and his noble marriage, that Aeson seemed to regain his youth. Wanting Jason to acquire the kingdom, Medea used her arts to sow discord between Aeson's brother Pelias and Pelias' daughters and, deplorably, armed them against their father. 8

As time passed, however, Jason came to hate Medea; Creusa, daughter of King Creon of Corinth, took Medea's place in his affections. Medea was unable to tolerate this and in her fury devised many plots against Jason. Finally her violent anger could be contained no longer. Using her craft, Medea destroyed Creon's palace in a raging fire that killed Creusa, and before Jason's very eyes she butchered the two sons she herself had borne him. Then Medea fled to Athens, where she married King Aegeus and bore him a son whose name, Medus, was derived from her own. After a vain attempt to poison Theseus, who was returning to the city, Medea fled for the third time. Restored to Jason's good graces, she was turned out of Thessaly with him by Aegialeus, son of Pelias. She returned to Colchis and restored to the throne her exiled, aged father. I do not remember having read or heard what Medea did later, or where or how she died. 10

I should not omit this observation: we must not give too much freedom to our eyes. Their wandering gaze dazzles us, makes us envious, and excites us to concupiscence. And it is by means of the 11

avaritia, laudatur formositas, damnatur squalor et paupertas indigne; et cum indocti sint iudices et superficiebus rerum tantum-
modo credant, sacris ignominiosa, ficta veris et anxia letis persepe
preficiunt; et dum abicienda commendant et brevi blandientia
12 tractu, inficiunt nonnunquam animos turpissima labe. Hi nescii a
formositate, etiam inhonesta, a lascivis gesticulationibus, a petulantia iuvenili mordacibus uncis capiuntur trahuntur rapiuntur te-
nenturque; et, cum pectoris ianua sint, per eos menti nuntios mic-
tit libido, per eos cupido inflat suspiria et cecos incendit ignes, per
eos emictit cor gemitus et affectus suos ostendit illecebres.

13 Quos, si quis recte saperet, aut clauderet, aut in celum erigeret,
aut in terram demergeret. Nullum illis inter utrumque tutum iter
est; quod si omnino peragendum sit, acri sunt cohibendi, ne lasci-
14 viant, freno. Apposuit illis natura fores, non ut in somnum claude-
rentur solum, sed ut obsisterent noxiis. Eos quippe si potens clausisset Medea, aut aliorsum flexisset dum erexit avida in Iasonem,
stetisset diutius potentia patris, vita fratris et sue virginitatis decus
infractum: que omnia horum impudicitia periere.

: XVIII :

De Aragne colophonia muliere

1 Aragnes, asyatica atque plebeia femina, Ydmonii, colophonii lana-
rum tinctoris, fuit filia. Que, quanquam origine minus clara fuerit,
2 nonnullis tamen meritis extollenda est. Asserunt quidem veteres

eyes that avarice is aroused; beauty praised; squalor and poverty unworthily condemned. Since, however, the eyes are unlearned judges and trust only the outward appearance of things, they often prefer the shameful to the sacred, the false to the true, and troubles to blessings. When the eyes praise things that should be condemned and whose pleasure is fleeting, they sometimes stain the soul in a shameful way. The eyes are unwittingly captivated, attracted, seized, and held fast in the sharp hooks of beauty (especially dishonorable beauty), of lascivious gestures, of youthful wantonness. The eyes are the gateway of the spirit: through them lust sends messages to the mind; through them love sighs and lights hidden fires; through them the heart sends out its groans and reveals its seductive intentions. 12

A person who was wise would either keep his eyes closed or raise them heavenward or fix them upon the ground. Between heaven and earth there is no safe direction for the eyes to turn. If one must use them, they should be severely restrained lest they fall into sin. Nature has provided eyelids not only for the eyes to be closed in sleep but also for resisting evil. Certainly, if powerful Medea had closed her eyes or turned them elsewhere when she first raised them longingly to Jason, her father's reign would have been of greater duration as would have been her brother's life, and her virginal honor would have remained unbroken. All these things were lost because of the shamelessness of her eyes. 13 14

: XVIII :

Arachne of Colophon

Arachne, an Asian woman of the common people, was the daughter of the wooldyer Idmon of Colophon. Although her lineage was undistinguished, she deserves nonetheless to be praised for several meritorious deeds. Some ancient writers maintain that she discov- 1 2

lini usum eius fuisse inventum eamque primam retia excogitasse, aucupatoria seu piscatoria fuerint, incertum. Et cum eius filius, cui Closter nomen fuit, fusos lanificio aptos reperisset, arbitrantur quidam hanc texture artis principatum suo evo[1] tenuisse, tanque circa hanc grandis ingenii, ut digitis filisque et spatula et aliis tali offitio oportunis id egisse quod pictor peregisset pinniculo: non equidem in muliere spernendum offitium.

3   Sane dum non solum Ypheis, quo habitans textrinam habebat, sed ubique se fama celebrem audiret, adeo elata est ut ausa sit adversus Palladem, huius artis repertricem, certamen inire; et cum se[2] superari equo animo ferre non posset, induto laqueo vitam finivit.

Ex quo locus fingentibus datus est; nam cum nomine et exercitio aranea vermis cum Aragne conveniat et filo pendeat, ut ipsa pependit laqueo, Aragnem miseratione deorum in araneam versam dixere et assidua cura pristino vacare servitio.

4   Alii vero dicunt quod, esto laqueum induerit moritura, non tamen mortuam, adiutorio interveniente suorum; sed, artificio posito, dolore vacasse.

5   Nunc autem si quis est, obsecro, qui se credat in aliquo anteire ceteros, dicat—dicat, si libet, Aragnes ipsa—an celum vertere et in se dignitates omnes trahere potuisse arbitretur, aut potius ipsum Deum, rerum satorem[3] omnium, precibus et meritis sic in se benignum fecisse potuerit ut, adaperto munificentie sue sinu, in illam gratias effundere cunctas coegerit, omissis ceteris. Sed quid

6   quero? Sic hec arbitrata videtur: stultissimum hercle. Vertit eterna

ered the use of linen and that she was the first to think of making nets (whether for catching birds or fish we do not know). Her son, who was named Closter, discovered the spindle for spinning wool. Consequently, according to some accounts, Arachne was the most skillful weaver of her time and so adept at it that she did with her fingers, thread, shuttle, and other tools of weaving what a painter does with his brush. A woman skilled in such tasks is by no means to be despised.

In fact, Arachne heard her praises sung not only in Hypaepa 3 where she lived and had her workshop, but everywhere else. She became so proud that she dared to enter a contest with Pallas Athena, who had discovered the art of weaving. Arachne, however, was unable to endure defeat with resignation and she hanged herself.

This circumstance gave the talemakers their chance. The spider[1] is connected in name and occupation with Arachne and hangs from a thread as she did from a rope; hence it is said that Arachne, through the mercy of the gods, was turned into a spider and plies her former art with unceasing diligence.

Other sources, however, report that although Arachne placed 4 the rope around her neck in an attempt to kill herself, she did not succeed because her servants intervened; but that once she put aside her work, she was liberated from her anguish.

And now, if there are any who think that they surpass others in 5 something, I beg them to tell me — or let Arachne herself speak if she will — whether she thought it possible to alter the heavens and usurp every honor for herself, or with her prayers and good actions render God, the Creator of all things, so well disposed towards her that she could force him to open the treasure of his munificence and bestow upon her all his favor to the exclusion of everyone else? But why do I ask this? Because Arachne seems to have thought so: and a really foolish idea it is. Nature turns the 6

lege natura celum et apta rebus variis ingenia cunctis prebet. Hec prout ocio atque desidia torpentia fiunt, sic studiis et exercitio luculenta et maximarum rerum capacia; et, eadem inpellente natura, in rerum omnes[4] notitiam desiderio vehimur, esto non eadem solertia vel fortuna.

7 Et, si sic est, quid obstat quin multi possint eadem in re pares effici? Et ob id quenquam se solum existimare, inter tam innumerabilem mortalium multitudinem, cursu prevalere ceteris ad gloriam, stolide mentis est. Optarem quippe ut Aragnes unica in hoc nobis esset ridiculum, cum sint innumeri tanta laqueati dementia qui, dum se in precipitium stolide presumptionis efferunt, Aragnem minus ridendam faciunt.

8

: XIX–XX :

De Orythia et Anthiope reginis Amazonum

1 Orythia Marpesie fuit filia et una cum Anthiopa, quam quidam sororem existimant suam, post Marpesiam Amazonum regina fuit et ante alia virginitate perpetua insignis et commendanda plurimum; tantum cum consorte regni Anthiope bellis valuit, ut multis Amazonum imperium honoribus ampliarit; et adeo militaris discipline suas laudes extulit, ut arbitraretur Euristeus, Micenarum rex, durum posse bello eius obtineri baltheum; et ob id aiunt debitori Herculi, tanquam maximum, iniunctum ut illud afferret eidem.

2 Eximia quippe mulieri gloria est sibi ob splendidam armorum

heavens by eternal law and produces talents appropriate for every kind of task. As these talents grow sluggish through idleness and laziness, so do they become brilliant and masterly through effort and practice. Stimulated by that same Nature, we are all carried forward by a desire for the knowledge of things, although not all with the same degree of skill or success.

If this is so, what is there to prevent many of us from becoming equally skillful in the same occupation? Consequently only a blockhead thinks that one person alone among the innumerable multitude of humankind can surpass the rest on the path to glory. I wish, indeed, that Arachne had been the only one to make herself ludicrous in this way, but the number of those in the noose of her madness is endless; as they throw themselves off the cliff of foolish presumption, they make Arachne less an object of ridicule. 7 8

: XIX–XX :

Orithya and Antiope, Queens of the Amazons

Orithya was the daughter of Marpesia and succeeded her as queen of the Amazons in company with Antiope, who is believed by some authorities to have been Orithya's sister. Orithya was primarily famous, and especially deserving of commendation, for her perpetual virginity. With the aid of her co-queen Antiope, she waged war so successfully that she enlarged and brought much honor to the Amazon empire. Orithya also elicited such great praise for her military prowess that Eurystheus, king of Mycenae, thought it would be difficult to capture her royal girdle in war. Hence the task of bringing it to Eurystheus is said to have been imposed on his debtor Hercules as the latter's greatest labor. 1

That Hercules, who overcame everything, was sent against 2

virtutem obiectum Herculem cuncta superantem. Qui cum expeditionem intrasset et novem longis navibus Amazonum occupasset litus, absente Orythia, in tumultuantes Amazones ob paucitatem et incuriam de se facile victoriam prebuere; capteque Menalippe et Ypolite, sorores Anthiope; dato regine baltheo, Menalippe restituta est.

3   Verum cum asportasse Ypolitem Theseum, expeditionis socium, audisset Orythia, in Greciam omnem, convocatis auxiliis, bellum movere ausa est; sed ob dissensionem ab auxiliis derelicta, ab Atheniensibus superata in regnum rediit, nec quid egerit ulterius invenisse recordor.

: XXI :

De Erytrea seu Eriphila sibilla

1   Erythrea seu Eriphile mulier ex sybillis una et insignis plurimum fuit. Quas quidem sybillas decem fuisse numero quidam putant easque propriis distinguunt nominibus; et quoniam plurimum va-
2   ticinio valuere omnes, sic illas cognominant. Nam *syos* eolico sermone, *deus* latine sonat; *biles* autem *mentem* dici dixere; et ideo *sybille*, quasi *mente divine* seu *mente deum gerentes*.

3   Ex quibus venerabilibus omnibus hanc fuisse celeberrimam referunt et eius apud Babilonios, aliquandiu ante troianum bellum, fuisse originem, esto nonnulli eam Romuli, Romanorum regis,
4   tempore vaticinatam putent. Huius—ut quidam dicunt—nomen

Orithya because of her great valor in arms is an uncommon source of glory for this Amazon queen. He started on his way and with nine warships occupied the shores of the Amazons while Orithya was away. The Amazons were thrown into confusion, and their reduced number and carelessness provided Hercules with an easy victory. He seized Menalippe and Hippolyte, Antiope's sisters, but returned Menalippe after he was given the queen's girdle.

When Orithya heard that Theseus, a member of the expedition, had carried off Hippolyte, she summoned reinforcements and dared to wage war against the whole of Greece. But dissension arose, her allies abandoned her, and Orithya was defeated by the Athenians and returned to her kingdom. I do not remember having found any evidence of what she did afterwards. 3

: XXI :

Erythraea or Herophile, a Sibyl

Erythraea, or Herophile, was one of the Sibyls and an especially famous woman. Some authorities believe that there were ten Sibyls, and they distinguish each one with a proper name. But the general term 'Sybil' applies to all of them because they were highly skilled in prophecy. In the Aeolian dialect, *sios* corresponds to the Latin word for 'god' (*deus*) and *byles* means 'mind' (*mens*); and so the 'sibyls' (*sibylle*) signify, as it were, 'women of divine mind' or 'women who bear God in their minds'. 1

2

Our sources report that the most renowned of all these venerable women was Erythraea, who was born in Babylonia some time before the Trojan War. Some think, however, that she exercised the art of prophecy when Romulus was king of the Romans. According to one opinion, her real name was Herophile, but she was 3

4

fuit Eriphyla, sed Erythrea ideo nominata, quia apud Erythream
insulam diu morata sit et ibidem plurima eius carmina sint com-
5 perta. Fuit igitur huius tanta vis ingenii aut orationis atque devotionis meritum in conspectu Dei, ut vigili studio, non absque divino munere, meruerit—si verum sit ab ea dictum quod legitur—
futura tanta claritate describere, ut evangelium potius quam vaticinium videatur.

6 Hec quidem percontantibus Grecis tam perlucide suos labores
et Ylionis excidium descripsit carmine, ut nil post factum quam
7 ante nosceretur clarius. Sic et Romanorum imperium casusque varios paucis verisque complexa est longe ante eius initium, ut nostro
seculo breve potius epythoma scripsisse videatur quam predixisse
futurum; et, quod longe maius meo iudicio est, archanum divine
mentis, nonnisi per figuras veterum et implicita prophetarum, imo
Sancti Spiritus per prophetas verba, predictum, aperuit: incar-
nandi Verbi misterium, iam nati vitam et opera, proditionem,
capturam, illusiones et inhonestam mortem resurrectionisque
triunphum et ascensionem et ad extremum iudicium reditum; ut
hystoriam dictasse, non venturos predixisse actus appareat.

8 Quibus meritis et dilectissimam Deo fuisse arbitror et pre cete-
9 ris gentilium mulieribus venerandam. Sunt qui asserant insuper
eam virginitate perpetua floruisse, quod ego facile credam: non
enim in contagioso pectore tanta futurorum lux effulsisse potuis-
10 set. Quo tempore, seu qua in parte decesserit, abolitum est.

called Erythraea because she lived for a long time on the island of Erythraea where many of her verses were found. The power of her 5 intellect was so great, or her prayers and devotion made her so deserving in God's eyes, that—if what we read about her sayings is true—through attentive study and divine generosity she earned the skill of prophesying the future. This she did with such clarity that she seemed to be less a prophet than an evangelist.

In response to an inquiry by the Greeks, Erythraea described in 6 verse their efforts and the destruction of Troy so lucidly that the events were as well known before the fact as after. Likewise, she 7 summarized briefly and accurately the varied fortunes of the Roman Empire long before its beginning: indeed, her words seem more like a historical epitome written in our time than a prediction of the future. But another accomplishment seems to me still greater. Erythraea unveiled the secret of divine thought which had been foreshadowed among the ancients only in symbols and in obscure utterances of prophets, or rather by the Holy Spirit speaking through the prophets: the mystery of the Word incarnate; the life and work of the Son; his betrayal, capture, mockery, and shameful death; the triumph of his Resurrection, the Ascension, and his return at the Last Judgment. All these events she seems not to have prophesied as future events but described as historical fact.

These worthy deeds show, I believe, that God loved Erythraea 8 very much and that she deserves greater reverence than other pagan women. Some accounts further claim that she preserved her 9 virginity. I can easily believe this, for I do not think that so clear a vision of the future could have shone forth in an unclean breast. When and where she died has been forgotten. 10

: XXII :

De Medusa filia Phorci

1 Medusa Phorci ditissimi regis heres fuit et filia eique opulentissi-
mum regnum extitit in athlantiaco mari, quod Hesperidas fuisse
insulas nonnulli credidere.

2 Hec, si vetustati fidem prestare possumus, tam admirande fuit
pulchritudinis, ut non solum excederet ceteras, sed, quasi quoddam preter naturam mirabile, quamplurimos ad se videndam exci-
3 ret homines. Fuit quidem illi capillitium aureum et numerosum,
faciei decus precipuum et digna proceritate corpus elatum; sed inter cetera tam grandis ac placidus oculorum illi fuit vigor ut, quos
4 benigne respiceret, fere immobiles et sui nescios redderet. Preterea
nonnulli eam agricolationis fuisse peritissimam asserunt eamque
inde Gorgonis consecutam cognomen: cuius opera mira cum sagacitate non solum patrias servavit divitias, sed in immensum ausit,
adeo ut qui novere crederent eam occiduos quoscunque reges an-
5 teire thesauris. Et sic tam pulchritudine eximia quam etiam opulentia et sagacitate in amplissimam famam apud remotas etiam nationes evasit.

6 Verum inter alios celebri rumore ad Argivos delata est, quos inter Perseus iuventutis achyve florentissimus, audito talium relatu,
in desiderium incidit et videndi spetiosissimam feminam et occu-
pandi thesauros; et sic, navi conscensa, cui Pegasus equus erat insigne, in occasum celeritate mirabili devectus est; ibique prudentia
usus et armis reginam occupavit et aurum, et opima honustus
preda remeavit ad suos.

7 Ex his locum sibi poetica adinvenit fictio qua legimus Medusam
gorgonem assuetam saxeos facere quos inspiceret eiusque crines

: XXII :

Medusa, Daughter of Phorcus

Medusa was the daughter and heir of Phorcus, a very wealthy king 1
whose opulent realm was located in the Atlantic Ocean. Some believe this kingdom is to be identified with the Islands of the
Hesperides.

If we can believe the ancients, Medusa was so astonishingly 2
beautiful that she not only surpassed every other woman but, like
something wondrous and supernatural, commanded the gaze of
many men. Her hair was golden and abundant, her face was 3
exceptionally attractive, and her figure was nobly tall and slender.
Her eyes in particular had a power in them so lofty and tranquil
that people she gazed upon favorably were rendered almost immo-
bile and forgetful of themselves. Some sources also assert that her 4
knowledge of agriculture explains why she acquired the name Gorgon. Thanks to this expertise, Medusa was able not only to preserve her father's wealth with extraordinary shrewdness but im-
measurably to increase it—so much so that informed persons
believed her to be the richest of all Western rulers. Hence she ac- 5
quired great fame even among far-off nations for her remarkable
beauty as well as for her riches and sagacity.

Reports of her fame reached, among other peoples, the Argives. 6
When Perseus, the most eminent young man in Achaia, had
heard these reports, there was kindled in him the desire to see this
beautiful woman and take possession of her treasure. He arrived
in the West with amazing speed aboard a ship whose standard
depicted the horse Pegasus. There Perseus deployed his forces
carefully, captured the queen and her gold, and returned home
laden with rich spoils.

These events inspired the following poetic fictions: that the 7
Gorgon Medusa commonly turned to stone those whom she

versos in angues ira Minerve, eo quod templum eius Neptuni concubitu vitiasset peperissetque Pegasum; et Perseum, equo insidentem alato, eius in regnum evolasse et Pallantei egydis usu superasse.

8   Infelix auri possessio est; quod, si lateat, possessori nullius est comodi; si fulgeat, mille concupiscentium nascuntur insidie; et si stent violentorum manus, non cessant possidentis anxie cure; fugatur enim quies animi, subtrahitur somnus, timor ingeritur, fides minuitur, augetur suspicio et omnis breviter vite usus impeditur misero; si vero casu quocunque pereat, anxietatibus excarnificatur, pauper factus, avarus, laudat liberalis, ridet invidus, consolatur inops et omne vulgus dolentis canit in fabulam.

: XXIII :

De Yole Etholorum regis filia

1   Yolem Euriti, regis Etholie, filiam, speciosissimam inter ceteras regionis illius virginem, sunt qui asserant amatam ab Hercule orbis domitore. Cuius nuptias cum illi Euritus spopondisset, aiunt poscenti, suasione filii, postea denegasse. Quam ob rem iratus Hercules acre bellum movit eidem eumque interemit, provincia capta, et dilectissimam sibi Yolem surripuit.

2   Que quidem, magis paterne cedis affecta quam sponsi dilectione, vindicte avida, mirabili atque constanti astutia, quem gereret animum ficto amore contexit; et blanditiis atque artificiosa quadam petulantia in tam ferventem sui dilectionem Herculem

looked upon; that an angry Minerva changed Medusa's hair into snakes because Medusa had defiled her temple by sleeping there with Neptune; that the offspring of this union was Pegasus; that Perseus, mounted on this winged horse, flew to Medusa's kingdom and conquered it using the shield of Pallas.

The possession of gold brings unhappiness. If the gold is kept 8 hidden, it is of no use to the owner; if displayed, it gives rise to a thousand plots on the part of those who covet it. Even if violent persons do not lay their hands on it, the worries and cares of the owner do not cease. His peace of mind is gone, he loses sleep, falls prey to fear, loses his sense of trust, becomes suspicious — in short, the wretched fellow has a hard time enjoying life. If by some mischance he loses his wealth, the miser, now a pauper, is tormented by anxiety while the gentleman calls him fortunate, the envious man laughs, the poor man offers consolation, and the vulgar all turn the tale of his grief into song.

: XXIII :

Iole, Daughter of the King of the Aetolians

Iole, daughter of King Eurytus of Aetolia, is reputed to have been 1 the most beautiful girl in her country and the sweetheart of Hercules, master of the world. It is said that Eurytus promised him Iole in marriage but later refused Hercules' suit at his son's insistence. Enraged at this turn of events, Hercules waged a bitter war against Eurytus, killed him, conquered his kingdom, and carried off his beloved Iole.

Iole, however, was moved more by love for her slain father than 2 for her husband and was eager for vengeance. With resolute cunning she hid her real attitude under a false show of affection. Her caresses and a certain artful wantonness made Hercules so besot-

3 traxit, ut satis adverteret nil eum negaturum quod posceret. At inde, quasi horreret tam hispidum habitu amantem, acri viro ante alia ponere clavam, qua monstra domuerat, imperavit; ponere leonis nemei spolium, sue fortitudinis insigne; ponere populeum sertum, pharetras sagittasque fecit.

4 Que cum non satis animo sufficerent suo, audacius in hostem inhermem precogitatis telis insiluit; et primo digitos anulis ornari precepit, caput asperum unguentis cypricis deliniri et hyrsutos pectine discriminari crines ac hyspidam ungi nardo barbam et puellaribus corollis et meonia etiam insigniri mitra; inde purpureos amictus mollesque vestes precepit indueret, existimans iuvencula, fraudibus erenata, longe plus decoris tam robustum hominem effeminasse lasciviis quam gladio vel aconithis occidisse.

5 Porro cum nec his satis sue indignationi satisfactum arbitraretur, in id egit mollitiei deditum, ut etiam inter mulierculas, femineo ritu sedens, fabellas laborum suorum narraret et, pensis a se susceptis, lanam colo neret digitosque, quos ad extinguendos in cunis, adhuc infans, angues duraverat, in valida iam, imo provecta etate, ad extenuanda fila molliret; equidem humane imbecillitatis et muliebrium astutiarum non minimum, intueri volentibus, argumentum est.

6 Hac igitur animadversione artificiosa iuvenis, cum perpetua in Herculem ignominie nota, patris mortem, non armis, sed dolis
7 et lascivia ulta est; et se eterno dignam nomine fecit. Nam quotquot ex quibuscunque monstris Euristeo triunphos victoriosus egit Alcides, ex tot victrix ipsius Yoles gloriosius triunphavit.

8 Consuevit pestifera hec passio delitiosas subire puellulas et lascivos ociososque persepe occupare iuvenes, cum gravitatis Cupido sit spretor et mollitiei cultor eximius; et ob id intrasse predurum

ted with her that she felt he would not refuse her anything. Feign- 3
ing disgust at her lover's rough dress, Iole first ordered this tough
fellow to put aside the club he had used to tame the monsters,
then the skin of the Nemean lion (the emblem of his strength).
She also made him remove the poplar wreath and his quiver and
arrows.

But all this was not enough for her purpose. Preparing her 4
weapons well in advance, Iole moved still more daringly against
her defenseless enemy. She began by instructing Hercules to adorn
his fingers with rings, anoint his rough scalp with Cyprian un-
guents, comb his shaggy hair, smear his prickly beard with nard,
and adorn himself with girlish garlands and a Maeonian headdress; next she had him wear purple cloaks and dainty garments.
The sweet young thing was naturally given to trickery, and so
thought there was more glory in weakening a strong man by seduction than in killing him by poison or the sword.

But even all this Iole deemed insufficient to satisfy her anger. 5
Finally she forced Hercules—by this time totally effeminate—to
sit in the midst of her servant girls and tell the story of his labors. Taking the distaff, he would spin wool, and though now an
adult—indeed a man of advanced years—he softened to stretch
threads the very fingers he had hardened to kill serpents while still
a baby. Indeed, for those who are willing to consider the facts, this
is no small proof of human weakness and feminine cunning.

To Hercules' eternal shame, the young woman cleverly avenged 6
by such punishment her father's death: she resorted not to arms
but to trickery and seduction, and so made herself worthy of eternal notoriety. In fact, his conqueror Iole triumphed as much and 7
in a more glorious fashion than did Hercules in his victorious
struggle, at Eurystheus' behest, with the monsters.

This destructive lust is wont to take hold of voluptuous young 8
girls, and quite frequently debauched and idle young men, because
Cupid scorns serious character and is a great worshipper of wan-

Herculis pectus, longe magis monstrum est, quam que sepe do-
9 muerat ipse fuerint. Quod non modicum salutis sue sollicitis de-
bet iniecisse timoris et torporis etiam excussisse, cum pateat quam
10 validus, quam potens hostis immineat. Vigilandum igitur est et robore plurimo nobis armanda sunt corda; non enim invitis incum-
bet. Obstandum ergo principiis, frenandi sunt oculi ne videant va-
nitates, obturande sunt more aspidis aures, laboribus assiduis est
premenda lascivia.

11 Blandus quippe incautis sese offert et placidus intuitu primo;
et si recipiatur spe leta, primo delectat ingressu, suadet ornatus
corporum, mores compositos, facetias urbicas choreas cantus et
12 carmina, ludos et commessationes atque similia. Postquam vero
approbatione stolida totum occupaverit hominem et, libertate subacta, mentibus catenis iniectis et vinculis, differentibus preter
spem votis, suspiria excitat, premit in artes ingenia, nullum discrimen faciens inter virtutes et vitia, dummodo consequatur optatum, in numero ponens hostium quecunque obstantia.

13 Hinc exurentibus flammis infelicium pectora, itur rediturque et
ambitu indefesso res amata perquiritur; et ex iterato sepius visu
semper nova contrahuntur incendia; et cum non sit prudentie
locus, itur in lacrimas, dictantur preces mellitis delinite blanditiis, instruuntur lene, promictuntur munera, donatur, proicitur, et
nonnunquam falluntur custodes et septa vigiliis capiuntur corda
14 et in concupitos quandoque devenitur amplexus. Tunc pudoris
hostis et scelerum suasor, rubore et honestate fugatis, parato volu-

tonness. Hence for such a feeling to have entered Hercules' rock-
hard breast is far more monstrous than were the monsters Hercules himself often mastered. It is clear that a strong and powerful   9
enemy threatens us, and those concerned for their own well-being
should be very much afraid and rouse themselves out of their
indifference. We must be vigilant and defend our hearts with great   10
constancy; lust will not come to those who do not welcome it. Resistance is necessary in the initial stages: the eyes must be curbed
to avoid vanities, the ears should be clasped shut. Passion has to
be restrained with continual effort.

To the unwary, love presents itself at first sight as gentle and ca-   11
ressing. If love is received joyously and happily, it gives pleasure at
its first appearance and encourages us in attractive dress, refined
behavior, sophisticated witticisms, dancing, song, verse, games,
conviviality, and other things of this kind. But after love has com-   12
pletely subdued a man through his own foolish consent, taken
away his freedom, chained and bound his mind; when desires have
been deferred beyond hope; then love awakens sighs and im-
plants cunning stratagems in our thoughts; it does not discrimi-
nate between vices and virtues so long as it achieves its goal — all
the while numbering among its enemies any obstacles it may encounter.

While the flames burn in the breast of the unhappy lovers,   13
there is much coming and going, and the beloved is the object of a
tireless search, with repeated encounters setting off new flames of
love. As prudence is out of place, recourse is had to tears, and entreaties sweetened with flattery are made; the services of panderers
are secured; gifts are promised, presented, refused. Sometimes
guards are tricked and hearts that have been well protected are
captured; sometimes the longed-for embraces are won. Then the   14
enemy of modesty and the counselor of wrongdoing casts shame
and honor aside, makes ready the pigsty, and incites the grunt-

tabro porcis, gannientes effundit in illecebres coitus; tunc sobrietate reiecta, Cerere et Bacho fervens advocatur Venus noctesque tote spurcido consumuntur in luxu.

15 Nec ob id furor semper extinguitur iste, quin imo persepe in ampliorem insaniam augetur. Ex quo fit ut in obedientiam illam detestabilem Alcides corruat, obliviscantur honores, effundantur substantie, armentur odia et vite sepissime subeantur pericula. Nec carent ista doloribus, interveniunt rixe et paces tenues, rur-

16 sum suspitiones et zelus, animarum consumptor et corporum. Ast si minus devenitur in votum, tum amor rationis inops, additis virge calcaribus, exaggerat curas, desideria cumulat, dolores fere intollerabiles infert, nullo nisi lacrimis et querelis et morte nonnunquam curandos remedio; adhibentur anicule, consuluntur Caldei, herbarum atque carminum et malefitiorum experiuntur vires, blanditie vertuntur in minas, paratur violentia, damnatur frustrata dilectio; nec deest quin aliquando tantum furoris ingerat malorum artifex iste ut miseros in laqueos impingat et gladios.

17 O quam dulcis, quam suavis hic amor! Quem cum horrere ac fugere debeamus, in deum extollimus, illum colimus, illum supplices oramus et sacrum ex suspiriis lacrimisque conficimus, stupra adulteria incestusque offerimus et obscenitatum nostrarum coronas immictimus!

: XXIV :

De Deyanira Herculis coniuge

1 Deyanira Oenei Etholorum regis — ut quidam asserunt — fuit filia et Meleagri soror: tanta insignis formositate virgo, ut ob eius nuptias consequendas certamen inter Acheloum et Herculem orire-

ing lovers to the allurements of copulation. Rejecting sobriety, inflamed by food and drink, they summon Venus and spend whole nights in disgusting wantonness.

Nor is that fury always extinguished as a result; indeed, it often 15 grows into a still greater madness. This explains why Hercules fell into an appalling state of subjection. For the same reason men forget their honor, squander their wealth, rekindle their hatreds, and very often endanger their lives. And such pleasures are not free of suffering. There are quarrels, fragile truces, then once again suspicions and jealousy which devour bodies and souls. If the lovers do 16 not attain their desires, then addlepated Love adds his spurs to the whip and thereby aggravates their worry, heightens desire, and inflicts almost unbearable pain for which the only remedies are tears, laments, and sometimes death. The lovers turn to fortunetellers, consult astrologers, try the powers of herbs and enchantments and witchcraft. From flattery they turn to threats; they plot acts of violence and curse their disappointed love. Occasionally this perpetrator of evil instills so much fury that he drives the poor wretches to the rope and the sword.

How sweet, how delicious is this Love! Although we should 17 flee from him in horror, we elevate him to the status of a god, honor him, pray to him as suppliants, and sacrifice to him with our tears and sighs. We offer him rape, adultery, and incest, and on him we place the crown of our lewdness.

: XXIV :

Deianira, Wife of Hercules

Some authorities tell us that Deianira was the daughter of 1 Oeneus, king of Aetolia, and the sister of Meleager. She was a maiden of such striking beauty that a contest arose between Her-

2 tur. Que cum victori cessisset Herculi, a Nesso centauro adamata
est; et cum illam Hercules e Calidonia transferret in patriam, ab
Ebeno Calidonie fluvio, imbrium pridianarum turgido, moratus,
obvium habuit amantem Nessum, se, quia eques esset, ad trans-
portandam Deyaniram ultro Herculi obsequiosum prebentem.

3 Cui cum concessisset Hercules, nataturus post coniugem ipse,
quasi voto potitus, cum transvadasset fluvium, cum dilecta fugam

4 arripuit. Quem cum non posset Hercules pedibus consequi, sagitta lerneo infecta tabo, fugientem actigit. Quod sentiens Nessus
seque mortuum arbitratus, vestem sanguine suo infectam confestim Deyanire tradidit, asserens, sic cruentam si induat, posse
Herculem ab omni extero in suum amorem retrahere. Quam
Deyanira credula, loco pregrandis muneris, summens, clam aliquandiu servatam, Herculi Omphalem, seu Yolem, amanti, per
Lycam servulum caute transmisit.

5 Ipse autem cum sudore cruorem, veneno infectum, resolvisset
porisque bibisset, versus in rabiem se igni comburendum ultro

6 concessit. Et sic Deyanira, tanto viduata viro, dum retrahere speraret, perdidit et Nessi cedem etiam expiavit.

: XXV :

De Yocasta Thebarum regina

1 Yocasta Thebarum regina fuit, magis infortunio suo clara quam
meritis aut regno. Hec quidem, cum a primis Thebarum condito-
ribus originem duceret splendidam, virgo nupsit Layo, Thebarum

cules and Achelous as to who would marry her. Hercules won   2
Deianira, and then the centaur Nessus fell in love with her. As
Hercules was bringing Deianira from Calydon to his own country,
he encountered a delay at the Evenus River, swollen by the previous day's rain. There he met her admirer Nessus. Since he was
on horseback, Nessus volunteered to help Hercules by taking
Deianira to the other side.

Hercules agreed, intending to swim after his wife. Nessus, his   3
prayers having, as it were, been answered, ran away with his beloved after crossing the river. Hercules could not catch him on   4
foot, so he shot the fugitive with an arrow dipped in the venom of
the Hydra. When he felt the wound, Nessus knew that he would
die and at once gave Deianira the cloak colored with his blood,
telling her that if she put it on Hercules, bloody as it was, she
would win him back from any other love. Deianira was all too
willing to believe this story; she accepted the cloak as she would a
great gift and kept it hidden for some time. When Hercules fell in
love with Omphale (also called Iole), she took care to send the
cloak to him by his servant Lichas.

Once the poisoned blood on the cloak mixed with his own   5
sweat and was absorbed through his pores, Hercules went mad,
and of his own will he threw himself into the fire. Thus was   6
Deianira widowed of her mighty husband: hoping to recapture his
love, she destroyed him and also avenged Nessus' death.

: XXV :

Jocasta, Queen of Thebes

Jocasta, queen of Thebes, was more famous for her misfortunes   1
than for her merits or her reign. She traced her splendid ancestry
back to the first founders of Thebes and thus, when she was a

regi, ex quo cum concepisset filium, ob adversum Layo responsum, ex oraculo sumptum, natum iussa feris obiciendum egra tradidit.

2   Quem cum evestigio devoratum existimasset, apud Corinthiorum regem pro filio educatum, atque iam etate provectum, occiso
ab eodem apud Phocenses Layo, vidua incognitum sumpsit in
coniugem et ex eo Ethyoclem et Polinicem filios et totidem feminas, Ysmenam scilicet et Anthigonam, peperit filias.

3   Et cum iam tam regno quam prole videretur felix, deorum responso, quem legitimum arbitrabatur virum, eum esse filium novit. Quod etsi ipsa ferret egerrime, egrius tamen ille, adeo ut ob
ruborem patrati sceleris eternam cuperet noctem, oculos abiecit et
regnum.

4   Quod discordes assummentes filii, in bellum, fractis federibus,
venere; etsi grandi Yocaste tristitia sepe adversum in certamen de-
scenderent, maxima[1] eos decertantes duello mutuis vulneribus oc-
5 cisos accepit. Cuius doloris inpatiens misera mater et avia, esto
Creontem fratrem iam regem cerneret et orbum filium virumque
captivum et Ysmenam Anthigonamque filias labanti fortune impli-
citas, reluctantem fessamque molis[2] animam ferro, iam anus, expu-
lit et anxietates cum vita finivit.

6   Sunt tamen qui velint eam tam diu noxios errores suos ferre
non potuisse, quin imo cum vidisset Edypum oculos eicientem, illico in se sevisse.

young girl, she married Laius, king of the Thebans, by whom she became pregnant. At his son's birth Laius received an unfavorable response from an oracle and bade Jocasta, her heart heavy, to expose the infant to wild animals.

She had assumed that the baby was immediately devoured, but   2 he was brought up by the king of Corinth as his own son. When the boy reached manhood, he killed Laius in Phocis. Afterwards the widowed Jocasta, not recognizing her own offspring, took him as her husband. She bore him two sons, Eteocles and Polynices, and two daughters, Ismene and Antigone.

Jocasta seemed happy in both her reign and her children. Then   3 she learned from an oracle that the man she regarded as her lawful spouse was actually her son. Although to her this was a terrible blow, it was still more so to her husband. Shamed by the sin he had committed and longing for eternal night, he gouged out his eyes and abandoned his kingdom.

The realm was taken over by his quarreling sons who broke   4 their agreement and started a war.[a] It was a great source of distress to Jocasta that they often joined battle on opposite sides, but her greatest sorrow came when she learned that her sons had fought a duel and died of mutually inflicted wounds. The pain of this   5 loss was unbearable to the wretched woman, who was both their mother and grandmother. Seeing her brother Creon now king, her husband-son blind and imprisoned, and her daughters Ismene and Antigone caught in the web of an uncertain destiny, the now elderly Jocasta banished her struggling and exhausted soul with the sword; she put an end to her sufferings and her life at the same moment.

Some authorities, however, say that Jocasta could not have long   6 endured her guilty mistakes and maintain instead that she immediately killed herself when she saw Oedipus gouge out his eyes.

: XXVI :

De Almathea seu Deyphebe[1] sybilla

1   Almathea virgo, quam quidam Deyphebem Glauci filiam vocant, ex Cumis Calchidiensium, Campanie veteri oppido, originem duxisse creditur; et, cum ex sybillis extiterit una, troiane desolationis tempore floruisse atque in tam longum devenisse evum, ut ad Prisci Tarquinii, Romanorum regis, usque tempus devenerit, arbitrantur aliqui.

2   Fuit huic, antiquorum testimonio, tanti virginitas ut tot seculorum spatio nulla viri contagione fedari passa sit. Et quanquam poetarum litere testentur hanc a Phebo dilectam et eius munere et longevos annos et divinitatem obtinuisse, ego quidem reor virginitatis merito illam ab illo vero Sole, qui illuminat omnem hominem venientem in hunc mundum, vaticinii suscepisse lumen, quo multa predixit scripsitque futuris.

3   Huic insuper in baiano litore secus Averni lacum dicunt insigne fuisse oraculum, quod quidem et ego vidi audivique quod servet ab ea cognomen usque in hodiernum; quod etsi corrosum sit vetustate plurima et incuria semirutum etiam sit, in ruinis maiestatem servat veterem et admirationem prestat, adhuc intuenti, magnitudinis sue.

4   Sunt preterea qui dicant hanc Enee profugo ducatum ad inferos prestitisse, quod ego non credo; sed de hoc alias.

5   Qui autem illam plura vidisse secula volunt, asserunt eam venisse Romam et Tarquinio Prisco novem attulisse libros, ex quibus, cum negaretur a Tarquinio precium postulatum, tres, eo vidente, combussit; et cum die sequenti ex sex reliquis illud idem

: XXVI :

Almathea or Deiphebe, a Sibyl

The maiden Almathea, whom some sources call Deiphebe, daugh-   1
ter of Glaucus, is believed to have been born in Cumae, an ancient
city of the Chalcidians in Campania. Since she was one of the
Sibyls, some authorities conclude that she flourished at the time of
Troy's destruction and lived to such an advanced age that she was
still alive in the reign of Tarquinius Priscus, king of Rome.

As some of the ancients testify, Almathea held virginity in such   2
high regard that for many hundreds of years she did not allow herself to be defiled by any contact with a man. Poets say that she received from Phoebus, who loved her, the gifts of longevity and
prophecy. I believe, however, that it was Almathea's virginity that
earned her the light of prophecy from that true Sun which enlightens every man who comes into this world.[a] Thanks to this
gift, she predicted and described many future events.

It is said that on the Baian shore near Lake Avernus she had a   3
famous sanctuary. Indeed, I have seen it, and I have heard that it
is still called after her down to the present day. This sanctuary, although in a state of decay because of its great age and its semi-de-
struction by negligence, retains an ancient majesty even in its ruin-
ous condition and a grandeur that still provokes wonder in those
who see it.

There are some who claim that, when Aeneas was a fugitive,   4
Almathea was his guide in the underworld, but I do not believe
this and I will discuss it elsewhere.[b]

The authorities who attribute a long life to Almathea declare   5
that she came to Rome and brought Tarquinius Priscus nine
books, of which she burned three in his presence when he refused
to give her the requested price. The next day Almathea demanded
for the remaining six books the price she had previously asked for

pretium, quod ante ex novem petiverat, postulasset asseruissetque,
ni daretur, tres evestigio exusturam, et die sequenti reliquos, a Tar-
6 quinio petitum suscepit. Quos cum servasset, a posteris compertum est eos Romanorum fata omnia continere. Quam ob causam
maxima cum diligentia post hec Romani servavere et iuxta oportunitatum exigentiam de futuris consulturi ad eosdem, quasi ad oraculum, recurrebant.

7 Michi quidem durum est credere hanc eandem extitisse cum
Deyphebe; eam tamen apud Syculos clausisse diem legimus et ibidem diu eius tumulum ab incolis demonstratum est.

8 Studiis igitur et divina gratia illustres efficimur; que nemini se
dignum facienti denegata sunt. Quod si spectaremus, desidia torpentes, sentiremus plane quod, tempore perdito, ab utero, etiam
annosi morientes, deferamur ad tumulum.

9 Demum si ingenio et divinitate pervigiles valent femine, quid
hominibus miseris arbitrandum est, quibus ad omnia aptitudo
promptior? Si pellatur ignavia, in ipsam quippe evaderent deita-
10 tem. Fleant igitur et tabescant quibus tam grande donum inertia
sublatum est; et se, inter homines animatos, fateantur lapides!

11 Quod fiet dum suum crimen confitebuntur elingues.

: XXVII :

De Nycostrata seu Carmenta Yonii regis filia

1 Nycostrata, cui postea Carmenta apud Ytalos nomen, fuit Yonii
regis Arcadum filia; secundum quosdam Pallanti arcado nupsit,
secundum alios nurus fuit eiusdem. Nec regni solum fulgore fuit

nine; she stated that, if he did not give it to her, she would immediately burn three more, and the last three on the following day.
Tarquinius then paid her the price she had originally asked. He 6
preserved these books, and posterity found that they contained the
entire destiny of Rome. For this reason the Romans guarded them
with great care from that time on, and, when the need arose for
counsel regarding the future, they had recourse to them as if to an
oracle.

It is difficult for me to believe that Almathea and Deiphebe were 7
the same person, for I have read that the latter died in Sicily, where
for a long time her grave was pointed out by the inhabitants.

We become famous through our own zeal and divine grace, and 8
these are not denied anyone who makes himself worthy of it. If we
consider this fact, we would realize that the slothful, even if they
live to an advanced age, are but filling the interval from womb to
tomb with wasted time.

Finally, if women are able to achieve so much through their 9
keenness of intellect and the gift of prophecy, what ought
wretched men to think who have greater aptitude for everything?
If they were to reject idleness, surely they could attain that same
divine quality? Let those weep and waste away who through indo- 10
lence lose so great a gift; let them confess that they are stones
among living men! And this shall come to pass so long as their 11
mute nature acknowledges their fault.

: XXVII :

Nicostrata or Carmenta, Daughter of King Ionius

Nicostrata, later called Carmenta by the Italians, was the daughter 1
of Ionius, king of Arcadia. According to some sources she married
Pallas, an Arcadian, but others say that she was his daughter-in-

insignis, quin imo grecarum literarum doctissima adeo versatilis fuit ingenii, ut ad vaticinium usque vigilanti penetraret studio et

2 vates[1] efficeretur notissima. Que cum querentibus et a se ipsa nonnunquam expromeret futura carmine, a Latinis, quasi primo Nycostrate aboleto nomine, Carmenta nuncupata est.

3 Hec autem mater fuit Evandri, Arcadum regis, quem fabule veterum, seu quia eloquens atque facundus homo, seu quia astutus

4 fuerit, ex Mercurio volunt fuisse conceptum. Qui—ut quidam dicunt—cum casu eum, qui verus erat pater, occidisset, seu—ut aliis placet—seditione civium suorum alia ex causa orta, e regno pulsus avito, suadente Carmenta matre, et magna vaticinio promictente, si has peteret quas ostenderet sedes, facta peregrinationis socia, conscensis navibus, cum parte populorum secundo vento ad hostia Tiberis ex Peloponeso deveniens, eadem matre duce, in Palatino monte, quem a Pallante patre, seu a Pallante filio, nominavit, ubi postea Roma ingens condita est, cum suis et matre consedit construxitque oppidum Pallanteum.

5 Sane Carmenta, cum indigenas fere silvestres comperisset homines, esto iamdudum, Saturni profugi munere, segetes didicissent serere, eosque nullo literarum usui, seu modico et hoc greco, assuetos, a longe divina mente prospiciens quanta loco regionique celebritas servaretur in posterum, indignum rata ut adminiculo exterarum literarum futuris seculis sua monstrarentur magnalia, in eum studium ivit totis ingenii viribus, ut proprias et omnino a ceteris nationibus diversas literas exhiberet populis; cui ceptui nec

6 defuit Deus. Sua enim gratia factum est ut, novis ab ea adinventis caracteribus secundum ytalicum ydioma, earum coniunctiones

law. It was not only for the splendor of her reign that she was famous: she also knew Greek very well, and her intellect was so versatile that with constant study she even learned the art of foretelling the future and became a famous seer. The Latins changed her 2 name from Nicostrata to Carmenta because at times, upon request or spontaneously, she disclosed the future in verse (*carmen*).

She was the mother of Evander, king of Arcadia, who, in view 3 of his eloquence or cleverness, was held by ancient legend to be the son of Mercury. Some authorities report that Evander was ex- 4 iled from the kingdom of his forebears because he had accidentally killed his true father, or, as others would have it, because of discord which had arisen for some other reason among his countrymen. On the advice of his mother Carmenta, who prophesied great things if he would go to a country that she would show him, Evander boarded a ship with his mother and some of his people. He left the Peloponnesus and reached the mouth of the Tiber with the help of a favorable wind. His mother guided him to the Palatine Hill, which he named after his father or son, both of whom were called Pallas. On this site, where mighty Rome was later founded, Evander settled with Carmenta and his followers and built the town of Pallanteum.

Carmenta found that the native inhabitants were still very 5 primitive. Although they had learned long ago how to plant seeds (thanks to Saturn who had come there as a fugitive), these people knew little or nothing of writing and what letters they did know were Greek. With divine farsightedness she perceived the fame lying in store for that place and region, and so she thought it unworthy that their great deeds should be told to future generations in a foreign tongue. Carmenta then used the full force of her genius to give them their own alphabet, completely different from that of other nations. Nor did God withhold his help from this enterprise. Through his grace she devised new characters suitable for 6 the Italic language and taught their various combinations, satisfied

edoceret, contenta sexdecim tantum excudisse figuras, et uti diu ante Cadmus, Thebarum conditor, adinvenerat Grecis. Quas nos in hodiernum usque latinas dicimus eiusque tenemus munere, dato aliquas, et oportune, quidam sapientes addiderint, nulla ex veteribus amota.

7 Cuius mulieris vaticinium, etsi plurimum mirati sint Latii, hoc tamen inventum adeo mirabile visum est, ut profecto crediderint rudes, non hominem sed potius deam esse Carmentam; quam ob rem cum viventem divinis celebrassent honoribus, mortue sub infima Capitolini montis parte, ubi vitam duxerat, sacellum suo condidere nomini et ad eius perpetuam memoriam a suo nomine 8 loca adiacentia Carmentalia vocavere. Quod quidem nec Roma iam grandis abolesse passa est; quin imo ianuam civitatis, quam ibi, exigente necessitate, cives construxerunt, Carmentalem per multa secula de Carmente nomine vocavere.

9 Multis olim dotibus Ytalia pre ceteris orbis regionibus florida fuit et fere celesti luce corusca; nec tantum suo sub celo tam splen-
10 didus quesitus est fulgor. Nam ab Asya opulentia venit et supellectilis regia; sanguinis claritas, etsi multum[2] addiderint Greci, a Troianis habita primo. Arismetricam et geometricam artes dedere Egyptii; phylosophia et eloquentia ac mechanicum fere opus omne
11 ab eisdem Grecis sumptum est. Agriculturam, paucis adhuc cognitam, Saturnus intulit exul; deorum infaustus cultus ab Etruscis et Numa Pompilio habitus; leges publicas Athene primo, inde senatusconsultus et Cesares prebuere; sacerdotium summum religionemque sinceram a Ierosolimis attulit Simon Petrus; disciplinam autem militarem veteres excogitavere Romani, qua et armorum atque corporum robore et in rem publicam caritate integra orbis totius sibi quesivere imperium.

to have produced only sixteen letters (just like Cadmus, founder of Thebes, who long before had done the same for the Greeks). The Latin alphabet we use down to the present day consists of the original letters inherited from her as well as some others added by certain wise men for the sake of convenience.

The Latins had marvelled at Carmenta's prophecies, but this 7 invention seemed so wonderful that these simple folk believed her to be a goddess and not a human being. Consequently they accorded her divine honors during her lifetime; when she died, they dedicated a shrine to her name on the lowest part of the Capitoline Hill where she had lived. To perpetuate her memory the nearby area was called *Carmentalis* after her. Even after Rome 8 achieved greatness, Carmenta's shrine was not allowed to perish; in fact, a gate which urgent necessity caused the citizens to build there was for many centuries called the *Porta Carmentalis*, a name derived from her own.

With its many blessings Italy was the most flourishing of any 9 region in the world and glittered with almost divine light. But such great splendor was not gained only under her own skies. From Asia came opulence and royal furnishings. Noble blood 10 originated with the Trojans, although the Greeks made a substantial contribution. The Egyptians contributed the arts of arithmetic and geometry. From the Greeks, too, came philosophy, eloquence, and almost all the mechanical arts. Saturn while in exile instituted 11 agriculture, which at that time was known only to a few. The unfortunate worship of the gods came from the Etruscans and from Numa Pompilius. Public laws first emanated from Athens and were then enacted by the senators and the emperors. Simon Peter brought from Jerusalem the papacy and true religion. Military training, however, was discovered by the ancient Romans who used this as well as their strength of spirit and body and their devotion to the republic to acquire for themselves dominion over the whole world.

12   Literarum caracteres satis ex dictis patet quoniam maioribus
nostris Carmenta concesserit, cum iam ex arcada devenisset yta-
13 lica. Sic et gramatice facultatis prima dedisse semina creditum,
que in ampliorem segetem successu temporum prisci traxere; quibus adeo fuit propitius Deus ut, hebraicis grecisque literis parte
maxima glorie dempta, omnis quasi Europa amplo terrarum tractu
nostris utatur.

Quibus delinita, facultatum omnium infinita splendent volu-
mina, hominum gesta Deique magnalia perpetua servantur memoria ut, que vidisse nequivimus ipsi, eis opitulantibus, cognoscamus.
His vota nostra transmictimus et aliena cum fide suscipimus, his
amicitias in longinquo iungimus et mutuis responsionibus conser-
14 vamus. He Deum — prout fieri potest — nobis describunt; he celum terrasque et maria et animantia cuncta designant; nec est
quod queras possibile quod ab his vigilans non possis percipere;
harum breviter opere quicquid amplitudine mentis complecti
15 atque teneri non potest, fidissime commendatur custodie. Que tamen, etsi aliis ex his nonnulla contingant, nil tamen nostris commendabile aufertur.

Ceterum ex tam egregiis dotibus quedam perdidimus, quedam
dedimus et nonnulla adhuc fere nomine potius quam effectu tene-
16 mus. Verum, quomodocunque de ceteris nostro crimine a fortuna
actum sit, nec germana rapacitas, nec gallicus furor, nec astutia an-
glica, nec hispana ferocitas, nec alicuius alterius nationis inculta
barbaries vel insultus, hanc tam grandem, tam spectabilem, tam
oportunam latino nomini gloriam surripuisse potuit unquam, ut
sui scilicet iuris prima literarum possent aut auderent dicere ele-

From what has been said, it is clear that the letters of the alpha-   12
bet were given to our ancestors by Carmenta after she had ceased
to be an Arcadian and had become an Italian. She is also believed   13
to have planted the first seeds of grammar, and these were harvested by the ancients over the course of time. God so favored
Carmenta's achievements that the Hebrew and Greek languages
have lost the greatest part of their glory while a vast area covering
almost all of Europe uses our alphabet.

An infinite number of books on all subjects has rendered the
Latin alphabet illustrious: in its letters is preserved a perpetual remembrance of divine and human accomplishments so that with
the help of Latin characters we know things which we cannot see.
In Latin characters we send our requests and receive with trust
those made by other people. Through these characters we enter
into friendship with people far away and preserve it by reciprocal
correspondence. Latin characters describe God for us insofar as   14
that can be done. They show forth the sky, the earth, the seas, and
all living things; there is nothing open to investigation that one
cannot understand by careful study of its letters. In short, Latin
characters enable us to entrust to faithful guardianship whatever   15
the mind cannot embrace and retain. Nor does the fact that a
number of the same advantages may be true of other alphabets detract in the least from the merits of our own.

Some of these noble gifts of Roman civilization we have lost,
some we have given away, and some we still preserve, in name at
least if not in practice. But regardless of the effects of fortune and   16
our neglect on these other gifts, neither the rapacity of the Ger-
mans, nor the fury of the Gauls, nor the wiles of the English, nor
the ferocity of the Spaniards, nor the rough barbarity and insolence of any other nation has been able to take away from the
Latin name this great, marvelous, and serviceable glory. These
other nations could never say, or have never dared to say, that the
invention of the alphabet was rightfully theirs, much less the in-

menta et longe minus suum compertum fuisse gramaticam³; quas,
uti comperimus ipsi, sic etiam dedimus ultro, nostro tamen sem-
17 per insignita vocabulo. Unde fit ut, quanto longius feruntur, tanto
magis latini nominis amplientur laudes et honores, clariusque vetustissimi decoris nobilitatis et ingenii testimonium deferunt et in-
corruptum nostre perspicacitatis servant, etiam indignante barbarie, argumentum.

Cuius tam eximii fulgoris, etsi Deo datori gratias agere debeamus, multum tamen laudis caritatis et fidei Carmente debemus.
Quam ob rem ne a quoquam, tanquam ingrati, iure redargui possimus, ut illud pro viribus in eternam memoriam efferamus piissi-
mum est.

: XXVIII :

De Pocri Cephali coniuge

1 Pocris Pandionis Athenarum regis nata et Cephalo, Eoli regis filio,
nupta, uti avaritia sua pudicis matronis exosa est, sic et viris ac-
cepta, quoniam per eam ceterarum mulierum vitium adaper-
tum sit.

2 Nam cum leto pioque amore vir et uxor iuvenes gauderent, eorum infortunio factum est ut desiderio Cephali caperetur Aura,
seu potius Aurora quedam, ut placet aliquibus, spectande pulchritudinis mulier, quem cupidine Pocris sue detentum aliquandiu
3 frustra in suam sententiam precibus trahere conata est. Ex quo inquit indignans: 'Penitebit te, Cephale, adeo fervide dilexisse Po-
crim: comperies, faxo, si sit qui temptet, eam aurum amori prepo-
suisse tuo.'

Quod audiens iuvenis, experiri avidus, peregrinationem longin-
quam fingens abiit flexoque in patriam gradu, per intermedium

vention of grammar. We discovered these things, and we gave them freely to others, though always marked with our Latin name. Hence it happens that the more remote their origin, the greater 17 are the praise and the honor of the Latin name; they make clearer the evidence for our ancient honor, nobility, and intellect, and preserve an incorruptible proof of our genius, however the barbarians may rage.

Although we should thank God who gave us this singular glory, nevertheless we owe Carmenta, too, great praise and gratitude. And so it is proper and just that we exert ourselves as much as possible to render her name eternal so that no one can accuse us, with good reason, of being ungrateful.

: XXVIII :

Pocris, Wife of Cephalus

Pocris was the offspring of Pandion, king of Athens,[2] and the wife 1 of Cephalus, who was King Aeolus' son. Her greed gained her in equal measure the hate of honest women and the approval of men, because through her example the faults of her sex were revealed.

The young couple loved each other with happy and devoted 2 affection. To their misfortune, it happened that an exceptionally beautiful woman called Aura (or Aurora in some sources) fell in love with Cephalus. For a while she tried to win him over with her entreaties, but in vain, for he remained bound by his love for Pocris. Angered by this, Aura said, "You will regret having loved 3 Pocris so ardently. You will see, I assure you, that if anyone shall tempt her, she will value gold more than your love."

When he heard this, young Cephalus was eager to find out if it was true. He left home under the pretext of making a long journey. Doubling back, he tested his wife's fidelity with the help of a

4   muneribus constantiam temptavit uxoris. Que, quantumcunque
grandia sponderentur, impetu primo movisse nequivere; eo tandem perseverante et iocalia augente, ad ultimum hesitantem flexit
animum, illique nox optatique amplexus, si detur sponsum aurum,
promissi sunt.

5   Tum Cephalus, merore consternatus, aperuit quoniam dolo fri-
volum Pocris amorem intercepisset; que, rubore conspersa et con-
scientia inpulsa facinoris, confestim in silvas abiit et se solitudini
dedit. Iuvenis autem amoris inpatiens, ultro venia data, precibus
aspernantem revocavit in gratiam.

Sed quid refert? Nulle sunt indulgentie vires adversus con-
6   scientie morsus. Agebatur Pocris in varios animi motus; et zelo
percita, ne forte id in se blanditiis Aurore vir ageret quod ipsa in
illum auro mercata fuerat, clam per scopulos et abrupta montium
7   iuga valliumque secreta venatorem consequi cepit. Quod peragens
contigit, dum inter vallium herbida calamosque palustres latitans
moveretur Pocris, credita a viro belua, sagitta confossa periit.

8   Ignoro[1] quid dix<e>rim[2] potius: an nil esse potentius auro in
terris, aut stolidius querere quod comperisse non velis. Quorum
dum utrunque insipiens mulier approbat, sibi indelebilem no-
9   tam et mortem invenit quam minime inquirebat. Sed, ut auri in-
moderatum[3] desiderium sinam, quo stolidi fere trahimur omnes,
queso, tam obstinato zelo correpti dicant quid inde sibi emolumenti sentiant, quid decoris, quid laudis aut glorie consequantur.

10   Meo quippe iudicio hec ridicula mentis est egritudo a pusillanimi-
tate patientis originem ducens, cum non alibi viderimus quam hos

go-between who promised gifts. Although large presents were   4
offered, these did not sway Pocris during the first assault. The in-
termediary persevered and added jewels; finally her determination,
which was already vacillating, crumbled. Pocris promised him the
night of love and the embraces he desired if he would give her the
gold he had pledged.

Then Cephalus, overwhelmed with grief, revealed how his   5
stratagem had exposed the shallowness of her love. Pocris was covered with shame. Driven by remorse for her misdeed, she immediately fled into the woods to live in solitude. The young man, however, still loved her passionately, and he forgave her of his own free
will. His pleading overcame her reluctance, and they were recon-
ciled.

But what good did it do? The power of pardon is helpless
against the pangs of conscience. Pocris' feelings changed con-   6
stantly. Torn by jealousy, she thought that, for the sake of Aurora's
caresses, her husband was doing to her what she had done to him
for the sake of money. Secretly Pocris began to follow Cephalus as
he hunted through the rocks and rough summits of the mountains
and hidden valleys. While spying on him among the swamp reeds   7
in a grassy valley, she happened to make a movement; her husband, believing that she was a wild animal, killed her with an arrow.

I do not know whether to say that nothing on earth is more   8
powerful than gold or that nothing is more foolish than to seek
something one does not wish to find. This silly woman proved the
truth of both maxims and acquired for herself perpetual infamy
and a death she had not sought. Leaving aside the unbridled love   9
of gold to which we are almost all foolishly attracted, I shall ask
those who fall prey to such blind jealousy to tell me what advantage, what honor, what praise or what glory they get from it. In   10
my opinion, jealousy is a ridiculous sickness of the mind caused by
the pusillanimity of the people who suffer from it; we see it only in

penes, qui se adeo deiecte virtutis existimant ut facile sibi quoscunque preponendos fore concedant.

: XXIX :

De Argia Polinicis coniuge et Adrasti regis filia

1 Argia greca mulier, ab antiquis Argivorum regibus generosam ducens originem, Adrasti regis filia fuit et spectabili pulchritudine sua, uti de se contemporaneis letum spectaculum prebuit, sic et posteris integerrimum atque preclarum coniugalis amoris testimonium perenne reliquit; ob quod in nostros usque dies nomen eius fulgidum precipua coruscatione devenit.

2 Hec igitur, nupta Polinici filio Edipi, Thebarum regis, et exuli, cum iam ex illo Thessandrum peperisset filium, advertens eum ob fratris fraudem mordacibus agitari curis, facta anxietatum particeps, patrem iam senem non solum exoravit lacrimis precibusque, verum et armavit in Ethioclem, preter pactionum leges cum fratre thebanum regnum occupantem tyramnice; et ne fatale responsum detrimentum susciperet, Euridici, Anphiorai vatis coniugi, preter naturam femineam liberalis effecta, pretiosum illud monile, matronis olim thebanis infaustum, ultro contulit; ex quo latitans patefactus Anphyoraus, in Thebas itum est, sed infelici omine.

3 Nam post plurimam certaminum stragem, ceteris interfectis ducibus et Adrasto auxiliis nudato atque semifugato, cum inter cetera sordidi vulgi cesique cadavera Polinicis corpus insepultum iacere anxia coniunx audisset, extemplo regio abiecto splendore et mollicie thalami atque debilitate feminei sexus seposita, paucis

those who deem themselves of such little worth that they stand ready to admit that anyone else takes precedence over themselves.

: XXIX :

Argia, Wife of Polynices and Daughter of King Adrastus

Argia, a Greek woman, was a noble descendant of Argos' ancient 1 rulers and the daughter of King Adrastus. She was remarkably beautiful, and her contemporaries rejoiced in the mere sight of her; in addition, she left to posterity a flawless, splendid, and eternal record of conjugal love. For this reason her name has shone even down to our own time with special brilliance.

Argia married Polynices, son of King Oedipus of Thebes, and 2 gave birth to a son named Thessander while her husband was in exile. Noticing that Polynices was tormented by bitter cares because of his brother's deceit, she made these concerns her own. Argia persuaded her aged father, with tears and prayers, to take up arms against Eteocles, whose tyrannical rule of the kingdom of Thebes violated the agreement made with his brother.[a] Moreover, to avoid the harm resulting from an unfavorable answer by the oracle, she turned generous beyond the nature of women and spontaneously presented Eurydice, wife of the seer Amphiaraus, with the precious necklace that had earlier proved unlucky for Theban women. This led to the discovery of Amphiaraus, who had been in hiding; subsequently an attack was launched against Thebes, but not with a happy omen.[b]

Heavy losses in battle, including the deaths of the other com- 3 manders, had left Adrastus helpless and half-routed. Argia, the anxious wife, heard that Polynices' body was lying unburied in the midst of the ignoble dead. Casting aside royal splendor, the comfort of her chamber, and womanly weakness, she immediately set

4 comitantibus, arripuit iter in castra. Nec eam terruere insiden-
tium itinera manus impie, non fere, non aves occisorum hominum
sequentes corpora, non circumvolantes, ut arbitrantur stolidi, cesorum manes, nec — quod terribilius videbatur — Creontis im-
perantis edictum, quo cavebatur pena capitalis suplicii, ne quis
cuiquam occisorum funebre prestaret officium; quin ardenti me-
stoque animo, nocte media, certaminis aream intrans, cesorum
atque tetro odore redolentia corpora nunc hec nunc illa devolveret,
ut parve facis auxilio ora tabentia dilectissimi viri cognosceret; nec
ante destitit quam quod querebat invenerit.

5 O mirum! Semesa iam facies armorum rubigine et squalore op-
pleta pulvereo et marcido iam cruore respersa, nulli iam edepol co-
gnoscenda, amantissime coniugi occultari non potuit; nec infecti
vultus sordes uxoris amovere potuerunt oscula, non voces, non
lacrimas, non ignes Creontis imperium; nam cum sepe vitalem
spiritum per oris oscula exquisisset lavissetque lacrimis fetidos ar-
tus et sepe vocibus in suos amplexus revocasset exanimem, flammis iam flagrantibus, ne quid pii offitii omissum linqueret, tradidit
consumptumque urna condidit nec, igne patefacto pio facinore, severi regis subire gladium et catenas expavit.

6 Flevere persepe plurime virorum egritudines carceres paupera-
tem et infortunia multa, stante tamen spe mitioris fortune et
7 amoto severioris pavore. Quod etsi laudabile videatur[1], extremum
tamen dilectionis inditium dici non potest, ut Argie dici obsequia
potuere. Hec hostiles petiit agros, dum flere posset in patria; feti-
dum tractavit cadaver, quod iniunxisse poterat aliis; flammis regium inpendit honorem, dum clam infodisse, qualitate temporis

out with a few companions for the battlefield. The bandits who 4
lay in wait for travelers did not frighten her, nor the wild beasts,
nor the birds seeking carrion, nor the spirits of the dead which (as
foolish report has it) fly about. Nor was Argia afraid of something
seemingly more terrible still: Creon's order forbidding, under pain
of capital punishment, the performance of funeral rites for any of
the slain. Instead, with eager, grim determination she went at midnight to the battlefield, where she turned over this or that reeking
body to see if she could recognize, with the help of a small torch,
the rotting face of her beloved husband. This search continued
until Argia found the one she sought.

It was a miracle! No one else except the loving wife could have 5
recognized that face half-consumed by the rusty armor, covered in
dust and filth, and sprinkled with putrid blood. His filthy and rotting face could not inhibit her kisses, nor could Creon's edict stop
her tears, her laments, and her immolation of the corpse. Argia
tried repeatedly to revive Polynices by kissing his face, and she
washed with tears his fetid limbs; over and over again she summoned the senseless corpse to her embraces. Then, that no part of
her pious duty should be left undone, she consigned his body to
the flames; when it was consumed, she placed the ashes in an urn.
The fire drew attention to her pious crime, but Argia feared neither prison nor the harsh king's sword.

While hope of a kindlier fortune remains and when fear of a 6
crueler one is removed, many women weep over the illnesses,
imprisonment, poverty, and numerous misfortunes of their husbands. This may seem praiseworthy, but one cannot claim that it 7
is an overwhelming proof of love, as can be said of Argia's last rites
for her husband. She went into the enemy's territory when she
could have wept at home; she touched the fetid corpse, something
which she could have ordered others to do; she paid it royal honors with fire when, in view of the circumstances, a secret burial
would have been sufficient; she lamented in womanly fashion

inspecta, satis erat; ululatus emisit femineos, ubi poterat pertransire tacita; nec quid speraret habebat ex occiso exule, cum quid timeret adesset ab hoste.

8   Sic verus amor, sic fides integra, sic coniugii sanctitas et illibata castitas suasisse potuere. Quo merito laudanda, colenda et splendido extollenda preconio venit Argia.

: XXX :

De Manthone Thyresie filia

1   Mantho, Thyresie, maximi Thebanorum vatis, filia, tempore Edipi
2   regis filiorumque fuit insignis. Hec quidem sub patre magistro tam pronpti atque capacis fuit ingenii, ut pyromantiam, vetustissimum Caldeorum, seu—ut volunt alii—Nembroth inventum, adeo egregie disceret, ut evo suo nemo melius flammarum motus colores et murmura, quibus, nescio quo dyabolico opere, futuro-
3   rum dicunt demonstrationes inesse, cognosceret. Preterea fibras pecudum et taurorum iecinora[1] et quorumcunque animalium exta perspicaci cognovit intuitu; traxitque sepissime—ut creditum est—suis artibus spiritus immundos et inferorum manes coegit in voces et responsa dare querentibus.

4   Sane cum iam bello cecidissent argivi reges qui Thebas obsederant[2], occupassetque Creon civitatis imperium, hec—ut placet aliquibus—regem novum fugiens, secessit in Asyam ibique Clarii Apollinis fanum, postea celeberrimum divinatione, instituit et Mopsum, inclitum sui seculi vatem, esto ex quo conceptum non prodat antiquitas, peperit.

5   Alii vero aliter sentiunt dicuntque eam cum complicibus qui-

when she could have passed by in silence. She had nothing to hope for from a husband who had died in exile, but she had much to fear from a very present enemy.

Such were the deeds taught her by true love, total devotion, the 8 sanctity of marriage, and an unshaken chastity. For these merits Argia became a woman whose praise, honor, and glory should be announced with shining trumpets.

: XXX :

Manto, Daughter of Tiresias

Manto, daughter of Tiresias, the greatest soothsayer of Thebes, 1 was renowned in the time of King Oedipus and his sons. Her fa- 2 ther's pupil, she had such a quick and capable mind that she became expert in the ancient art of pyromancy discovered by the Chaldeans or, as some authorities would have it, by Nimrod. In her age no one understood better the movements of flames, their colors and murmurings, wherein are said to be contained, as through some diabolical agency, indications of the future. More- 3 over, Manto also knew well how to interpret the entrails of sheep, the livers of oxen, and the vital organs of any other animal. Often, so people believed, she summoned up by means of her arts unclean spirits, and she compelled the shades of the dead to speak and to answer those who questioned them.

When the Argive kings besieging Thebes fell in battle and 4 Creon had taken control of the city, Manto (according to some sources) fled the new king and went to Asia. There she built the temple of Apollo Clarius, later famed for its oracle, and she gave birth to Mopsus, a distinguished soothsayer in his time, although the ancients do not tell us the name of his father.

A different version recounts that Manto wandered for a long 5

busdam suis, post thebanum bellum, errasse diu et tandem in Ytaliam devenisse ibique Tyberino iuncta cuidam, concepisse ex eo et
peperisse filium, quem Cithconum dixere, a quibusdam Byanorem
etiam vocitatum; et inde cum prole in Cisalpinam Galliam transie-
cisse, ubi cum palustria loca, Benaco contermina lacui, comperisset
sua natura munita, seu ut suis cantationibus posset vacare liberius,
seu vite residuum securius ducere, media in palude, in superemi-
nente aquis solo, posuisse sedem et ibidem post tempus mortuam
6 atque sepultam. Circa cuius tumulum aiunt Cithconum civitatem
suis constituisse eamque de matris nomine Manthuam vocitasse.

7   Quidam vero arbitrati sunt eam in mortem usque constanti
proposito virginitatem servasse: floridum quippe atque sanctissimum opus et laudabile plurimum, ni illud nephastis suis labefa-
ctasset artibus Deoque vero, cui dicanda est, virginitatem servasset.

: XXXI :

De coniugibus Meniarum

1 Meniarum uxorum numerus ac nomina, seu coevorum scribentium desidia, seu annositatis vitio, nobis subtracta sunt; equidem
indigne, cum non vulgari facinore meruerint in precipuam efferri
2 gloriam. Sed postquam invidenti fortune sic visum est, qua poteri-
mus arte, ornabimus innominatas digno preconio easque pro viribus in memoriam posteritatis educere, tanquam meritas bene, co-
nabimur.

3   Menie igitur fuere ex Iasonis atque Argonautarum sociis non
minime nobilitatis splendidissimi iuvenes; qui cum, peracta expe-
ditione colchida, redissent in Greciam, veteri relicto solo, apud La-

time after the Theban war with some of her companions and finally reached Italy. Here she married a certain Tiberinus, conceived, and gave birth to a son called Citheonus by some and Bianor by others. Manto then went with her child to Cisalpine Gaul. Finding naturally fortified swampy areas near Lake Garda, she settled on some higher ground in the middle of the marsh, either to be able to practice her spells with greater freedom or so as to spend the rest of her life in safer surroundings. There she eventually died and was buried. Citheonus is said to have built a city 6 for his followers near her grave and to have named it Mantua after his mother.

Other authorities, however, believe that Manto resolutely preserved her virginity until her death. This would have been a splendid, holy, and praiseworthy thing to do, had she not stained such an action with her wicked arts and had she preserved her virginity for the true God, to whom it should have been consecrated.

: XXXI :

The Wives of the Minyans

Negligence on the part of coeval writers or the lapse of time has 1 denied us the names and number of the wives of the Minyans — and unjustly so since they deserved particular glory for a remarkable exploit. But since jealous fortune has willed it thus, I shall 2 adorn with worthy praise as best I can these nameless women and try with all my strength to immortalize them, for they have well earned it.

To begin with the Minyans: they were fine young men of no little 3 nobility and figured among the companions of Jason and the Argonauts. When the expedition to Colchis was over, the Minyans returned to Greece, abandoned their ancient territory, and

4 cedemonios sibi delegere sedes. Quibus non solum a Lacedemoniis amicabiliter concessa civitas est, verum inter patres et reipublice presidentes assumpti sunt. Cuius tam splendide munificentie successores minus memores, libertatem publicam ignominiose servituti velle subigere ausi sunt.

5 Erant enim ea tempestate opulenti iuvenes, nec solum suo fulgore lucidi[1], verum et generosorum Lacedemonum affinitatibus septigemina fulgebant luce. Nam inter alia erant eis[2] spetiosissime coniuges a nobilissimis civibus ducentes originem, non edepol pars ultima mundani decoris; cui et clientele addebantur ingentes, ex quibus non gratiam publice patrie felicitati sensere, sed suis ascribentes meritis, eo se fatuitati permisere evehi, ut ceteris se preferendos fore existimarent; ex quo in cupidinem corruere imperii; et hinc ad occupandam rem publicam temere conatus exposuere

6 suos. Quam ob causam, detecto crimine, capti carcerique traditi et capitali supplicio, tanquam hostes, damnati sunt autoritate publica.

7 Et dum nocte sequenti, Lacedemonum veteri more, deberet illis a carnificibus mors inferri, meste flentesque coniuges pro liberatione damnatorum inauditum inivere consilium; nec cogitato dis-

8 tulere operam dare. Squalidis igitur vestimentis velatoque ore, opplete lacrimis, cum iam in noctem occumberet dies, quoniam nobiles essent femine, intrandi carcerem perituros visure viros, fa-

9 cile a custodibus obtinuere licentiam. Ad quos cum advenissent, non tempus consumpsere lacrimis et ploratu, sed repente explicato consilio, cum viris mutatis vestibus velatisque illis femineo ritu faciebus, flentes, deiectis in terram oculis fingentesque mestitiam,

chose Lacedaemon as their new residence. Not only did the Spartans graciously accord them citizenship: the Minyans were also included among the senators and governing class of the republic. Their descendants, however, did not remember that splendid courtesy and recklessly aimed to subject public liberty to shameful slavery. 4

At that time the Minyans were wealthy young men, notable not only for their own distinction, but many times more brilliant through their connections with noble Spartans. Among other advantages, they had beautiful wives who came from the noblest families of the city, and certainly this is not the least of worldly honors. They also had a large entourage. But the Minyans, instead of feeling grateful to their common fatherland for these blessings, attributed them to their own merits. As a result, they allowed themselves to be carried away to such a height of foolishness that they thought themselves superior to others. This attitude precipitated them into a lust for power; and thus they laid their rash plot to take over the state. When their criminal design was discovered, the Minyans were seized, imprisoned, and by public decree sentenced to death as enemies of the state. 5 6

On the following night the executioners, according to ancient Spartan custom, were to put them to death. The Minyan wives, in the midst of their grief and tears, hit upon a novel plan to liberate the condemned men and at once put it into action. When darkness was approaching, they dressed in unkempt fashion, with their tearful faces veiled; as noblewomen they easily received permission from the guards to enter the prison for a visit with their husbands who were soon to die. Once they arrived, the women did not waste time weeping and lamenting but immediately explained the plan to their husbands. They changed clothes with them, and their husbands veiled their faces as women do, wept, lowered their eyes to the ground, and feigned sorrow. With the help of darkness and the respect accorded to noblewomen, the doomed men 7 8 9

noctis etiam suffragantibus tenebris, et reverentia nobilibus feminis debita, deceptis custodibus, morituros emisere, ipsis damnatorum loco remanentibus; nec ante fraus comperta est quam, venien-
tibus suppliciorum ministris, ut damnatos in mortem educerent,
pro viris femine comperte sint.

10   Grandis profecto mulierum fides et egregius amor; sed sinamus
fraudis in custodes ludibrium, salutem damnatis exhibitam, quid
patribus visum sit et quid inde secutum; sacri coniugalis amoris vires et audaciam mulierum paululum contemplemur.

11   Instituto nature, veteri et indissolubili nexu firmato, nonnulli
volunt dissidentium coniugum nullum fore pernitiosius odium; sic
et convenientium amorem excedere ceteros. Nam rationis igne
succensus non urit ad insaniam, sed in complacentiam calefacit et
tanta caritate corda copulat, ut eque semper cuncta nolint ve-
lintque; et tam placide assuetus unitati, ad continuationem sui nil
omictit, nil agit tepide vel remisse; et si hostis fortuna sit, ultro labores et pericula subit et vigilantissimus in salutem meditatur
consilia, remedia comperit et excudit fallacias, si exigat indigentia.

12   Hic suavissimus, etiam placido convictu firmatus, coniugum
Meniarum tanto fervore inpulit animos, ut, quas nequissent ante
vidisse, periclitantibus viris, ingenii pressis viribus, decipulas in-
venirent, instrumenta pararent, rerum ordinem, tempus ratio-
nemque agendorum ut oculatos severosque custodes deciperent;
et, sublata sensualitatis nebula, advertentes quoniam nil honestum
pro salute amici omictendum sit, ex intimis cordis latebris excitata
pietate, ut viros periculo eximerent, temerario ausu in id irent ut,
quos publica damnaverat autoritas, pudicus coniugalis amor absol-

slipped past the guards, their places taken by their wives. The deception was not discovered until the executioners' assistants came to escort the condemned prisoners to their death and found the women instead of their husbands.

Great indeed was the devotion of these women and noble their love. But let us put aside the trick played on the guards, the saving of the lives of the condemned, the feelings of the senators, and the aftermath of the wives' action: instead let us consider briefly the power of sacred, wedded love and the daring of the women. 10

Some say that, since marriage is an ancient and indissoluble bond of nature, there is no more deadly hatred than that of discontented wives, just as there is no greater love than that of women who live in harmony with their husbands. For this fire of love, when ignited by reason, does not inflame to madness but warms to mutual accord; it joins hearts in such affection that husbands and wives share the same desires in equal measure. Accustomed to such peaceful union, love does whatever is necessary for its own preservation; it does nothing lax or lukewarm. If Fortune is unfriendly, love gladly endures toil and dangers and, ever watchful, makes plans for its safety, discovers remedies, and invents deceptions if need be. 11

It was this kind of sweet love, strengthened as well by peaceful intimacy, that moved with such fervor the spirits of the Minyan wives. When their husbands were in danger, they gathered their wits and found stratagems which normally they could not have discovered. They prepared the tools, the timetable, and the tactics for deceiving the stern and wary guards. Abandoning the clouds of sensuality, they realized that no honorable thing should be left undone for the safety of a friend. Evoking a sense of duty from the secret recesses of their hearts, they embarked on a reckless act of daring to save their husbands from peril. As a result, the chaste love of these wives exonerated and freed men whom public authority had condemned and confined to prison; that same love de- 12

veret, quos carceri manciparat, emicteret, quos iam tenere dirum videbatur et capitale supplicium, e carnificum manu subtractos securitati viteque donaret; et, quod permaximum visum est, lusa legum potestate, decreto publico ac patrum autoritate et totius civitatis voto frustrato, ut quod optabant impleretur non expavere loco damnatorum sub deceptorum custodum imperio sese claudere.

13   Non edepol tam sinceram fidem, amorem tam integrum admirari sufficio et ob id ratum habeo, si remisse amassent, si tenui fuissent astricte vinculo, cum illis per ocium domi torpere fas esset, hec tam grandia non fecissent.

Attamen, ut multa paucis claudam, has asserere audeo veros certosque fuisse viros, Meniasque iuvenes, quas simulabant, feminas extitisse.

:   XXXII   :

De Penthessilea regina Amazonum

1   Penthesilea virgo Amazonum regina fuit, et successit Orythie et Anthyopi reginis: quibus tamen procreata parentibus, non legi. Hanc aiunt, oris incliti spreto decore et superata mollicie feminei corporis, arma induere maiorum suarum aggressam; et auream cesariem tegere galea ac latus munire faretra; et militari, non muliebri, ritu currus et equos ascendere; seque pre ceteris preteritis regi-
2   nis mirabilem exhibere, viribus et disciplina, ausa est. Cui nec ingenium validum defuisse constat, cum legatur securis usum, in seculum usque suum incognitum, eius[1] fuisse compertum.

3   Hec — ut placet aliquibus —, audita troiani Hectoris virtute, invisum ardenter amavit, et cupidine, in successionem regni, inclite

livered from the executioners' hands and returned to life and safety those bound by capital punishment. The most extraordinary thing is that these women, who had eluded the power of the law and thwarted the public decree, the authority of the Senate, and the will of the whole city in order to attain their goal, were not afraid to imprison themselves in place of the condemned men under the eyes of the very guards whom they had tricked.

Truly, I cannot admire enough such utter devotion and selfless love. I feel certain that if these women had loved less fervently, if they had been bound to their husbands by feebler ties, if they had remained idly at home as was their right, they would not have accomplished such great deeds. 13

To sum up: I do not hesitate to affirm that these wives were tried and true men, while the Minyan youths they impersonated were women.

: XXXII :

Penthesilea, Queen of the Amazons

The virgin Penthesilea succeeded Antiope and Orithya as queen of the Amazons, but I have read nothing about her parents. It is said that Penthesilea scorned her great beauty and overcame the softness of her woman's body; that she began to wear the armor of her ancestors, to cover her golden tresses with a helmet, to wear a quiver at her side, and to mount chariots and horses not like a woman but like a soldier. In matters of strength and skill she dared to show herself superior to all previous queens. And clearly Penthesilea did not lack intelligence since we read that she invented the ax, which had been unknown up to her time. 2

Some sources report that when Penthesilea heard of the prowess of Trojan Hector, she fell passionately in love with him sight 3

prolis ex eo suscipiendi, in tam grandem oportunitatem cum maxima suarum copia eius in auxilium adversus Graios facile provocata descendit.

4 Nec eam clara grecorum principum perterruit fama, quin Hectori armis et virtute cupiens quam formositate placere, sepissime certamina frequentium armatorum intraret; et nonnunquam hasta prosternere, quandoque obsistentes gladio aperire et persepe arcu versas in fugam turmas pellere et tot tanque grandia viriliter agere, ut ipsum spectantem aliquando Hectorem[2] in admirationem sui
5 deduceret. Tandem dum in confertissimos hostes virago hec die preliaretur una, seque ultra solitum tanto amasio dignam ostenderet, multis ex suis iam cesis, letali suscepto vulnere, miseranda medios inter Grecos a se stratos occubuit.

6 Alii vero volunt eam, Hectore iam mortuo, applicuisse Troiam et ibidem — ut scribitur — acri in pugna cesam.

7 Essent qui possent mirari mulieres, quantumcunque armatas, in viros unquam incurrere ausas, ni admirationem subtraheret quoniam usus in naturam vertatur alteram, quo hec et huiusmodi longe magis in armis homines facte sunt, quam sint quos sexu masculos natura fecit, et ociositas et voluptas vertit in feminas seu lepores galeatos.

unseen. She wanted as her successor an illustrious child fathered by Hector, and with this end in view she fell readily upon the chance to help him against the Greeks, bringing with her a great body of troops.

Penthesilea wished to please Hector with her skill in combat 4 rather than by her beauty. Hence the distinguished reputation of the Greek princes did not deter her from frequent participation in battles where the fighting was thick. At times she struck down the enemy with her lance and broke the enemy line with her sword; often she routed entire squadrons with her bow. In fact, Penthesilea accomplished in manly fashion so many and such illustrious deeds that she gained the admiration of Hector himself who would sometimes watch her. One day this valiant woman was 5 fighting against concentrated enemy forces and, more than usual, proving herself worthy of so great a lover. But after many of her followers had been killed, she at length received a mortal blow and fell, poor wretch, among the Greeks whom she herself had slain.

Other accounts relate that Penthesilea arrived in Troy only after 6 Hector's death and was killed there in a hard-fought battle.

Some may marvel at the fact that there are women, however 7 well armed, who dare to fight against men. But admiration will cease if we remember that practical experience can change natural dispositions. Through practice, Penthesilea and women like her became much more manly in arms than those born male who have been changed into women — or helmeted hares — by idleness and love of pleasure.

: XXXIII :

De Polysena Priami regis filia

1 Polysena virgo Priami, regis Troianorum, ex Hecuba fuit filia, tam
floride pulchritudinis adolescentula[1], ut severo pectori Achillis Pe-
liadis flammas immictere potuerit cupidinis eumque, matris He-
cube fraude, in suam necem nocte solum in templum usque Apol-
2 linis Tymbrei deducere. Ob quam minus debito lapsis troianis
viribus et Ylione deiecto, a Neoptholemo in piaculum manium patris et ad eius tumulum deducta est; ibique — si maiorum literis
fides ulla prestari potest — videns acrem iuvenem expedisse gladium, flentibus ceteris circumstantibus, innocens adeo constanti
pectore et intrepido vultu iugulum prebuit, ut non minus admira-
tio fortitudinis eius quam pietas pereuntis moveret animos.

3 Magnum quippe et memoratu dignum nequivisse tenella etas,
sexus femineus, mollicies regia, mutata fortuna, grandem pressisse
virginis animum et potissime sub victoris et hostis gladio, sub quo
nonnunquam egregiorum virorum nutant et persepe deficiunt ani-
4 mosa pectora. Crediderim facile hoc generose nature opus, ut ostenderet hac mortis parvipensione quam feminam produxisset, ni
tam cito hostis surripuisset fortuna.

⠆ XXXIII ⠆

Polyxena, Daughter of King Priam

The maiden Polyxena, daughter of Hecuba and King Priam of 1
Troy, was a young woman of such radiant beauty that she inflamed
with love the stern breast of Achilles, son of Peleus. A trick devised by her mother Hecuba enabled her to lead Achilles to a violent death by bringing him alone at night into the temple of
Thymbraean Apollo. Hence, after the undeserved collapse of the 2
Trojan forces and the fall of Troy, Neoptolemus brought Polyxena
to his father's grave to be sacrificed in appeasement of his spirit.
There, if we are to believe the writings of the ancients, the girl
watched the embittered youth draw his sword and, while the onlookers wept, she offered him her throat, innocent as she was,
with such a steadfast heart and fearless expression that everyone
was moved equally by admiration for her strength and by regret
for her death.

It was certainly a great thing and worthy of remembrance that 3
her tender age, female sex, royal delicacy, and altered fortune could
not overcome the sublime spirit of this girl, especially under the
sword of a victorious enemy, in the face of which the brave resolve
of noble men will waver and often fail. I can easily believe that 4
Polyxena's action was the creation of noble Nature who wished to
show by the maiden's scorn of death what kind of woman she
might have grown into had a hostile fortune not snatched her
away so quickly.

: XXXIV :

De Hecuba regina Troianorum

1 Hecuba Troianorum preclarissima regina fuit, eque perituri splendoris fulgor eximius[1] et miseriarum certissimum documentum.

2 Hec secundum quosdam Dymantis Aonis filia extitit. Alii vero Cipsei regis Tracie volunt, quod quidem et ipse arbitror, cum sic opinetur a pluribus. Nupsit hec virgo Priamo Troianorum regi illustri, et ex eo mixtim utriusque sexus concepit peperitque filios decem et novem, inter quos iubar illud eximium Frigie probitatis Hector; cuius tantus fuit militie fulgor, ut non se tantum eterna fama splendidum faceret, quin imo et parentes patriamque perenni nobilitaret gloria.

3 Verum non tantum felicis regni decore ac multiplicis prolis serenitate fulgida facta est, quin, urgente adversa fortuna, orbi toto longe deveniret cognita.

4 Hectorem nempe dilectissimum sibi et Troilum adolescentem et iam maiora viribus audentem, manu Achillis cesos et ea cede re-
5 gni solidam basem fere eversam mestissime flevit. Sic et a Pyrro Paridem trucidatum, inde auribus naribusque truncatum Deyphebum atque fede exanimatum, Ylyonem igne cremari danao, Polytem patris in gremio confodi, Priamum ipsum senem secus domesticas aras exenterari, Cassandram filiam, Andromacam nurum seque captivam ab hostibus trahi, Polysenam ante Achillis tumulum obtruncari, Astianactem nepotem ex latebris surreptum saxo
6 illidi miseranda conspexit. Et postremo tracio in litore tumulatum

: XXXIV :

Hecuba, Queen of the Trojans

Hecuba, the most famous queen of the Trojans, provides a notable   1
illustration of fleeting glory as well as a sure example of human
misery. In some accounts she was the daughter of Dymas, son of
Aon. Other sources, however, assert that Hecuba's father was   2
Cisseus, king of Thrace, and this I myself believe since the majority of sources so concurs. A young girl when she married Priam,
the illustrious king of the Trojans, she bore him nineteen children,
both male and female. Among these was Hector, that singular
glory of Phrygian virtue. His brilliance in war was such that he
gained everlasting renown for himself and ennobled his parents
and his country with eternal fame.

Yet Hecuba did not become famous only for the splendor of a   3
happy reign and satisfaction in her many children. Quite the contrary: it was the blows of adverse fortune that made her known
throughout the whole world.

With great sadness Hecuba mourned the death of two of her   4
sons at the hands of Achilles: Hector, whom she loved dearly,
and Troilus, a boy whose daring was greater than his strength.
She wept as well over the near destruction of the kingdom's foundations brought on by that slaughter. So, too, the wretched   5
woman witnessed Pyrrhus' butchering of Paris; the foul death of
Deiphobus after his ears and nose were cut off; the burning of
Troy by the Greeks; Polites cut down in his father's lap; aged
Priam himself disemboweled before the altars of his own
house; herself, her daughter Cassandra, and her daughter-in-law
Andromache taken captive by the enemy. She saw Polyxena killed
before the grave of Achilles and her grandson Astyanax snatched
from his hiding place and dashed against a rock. At last, find-   6
ing his tomb on the Thracian shore, she wept over her son

adolescentulum Polydorum, Polymestoris fraude occisum, comperit atque flevit.

7 Quibus tot tanque immanibus oppressam[2] doloribus in rabiem
versam volunt aliqui traciosque per agros ritu ululasse canum; et
sic mortuam et in tumulo hellespontiaci litoris, cui nomen a se
8 Cynosema[3], sepultam. Nonnulli dicunt in servitutem ab hostibus
cum reliquis tractam et, ne miseriarum illi particula deesset ulla,
vidisse ultimo Cassandram, occiso iam Agamenone, Clitemestre
iugulari iussu.

: XXXV :

De Cassandra Priami Troianorum regis filia

1 Cassandra Priami fuit, Troianorum regis, filia. Huic quidem—ut
vetustas asserit—vaticinii mens fuit, seu quesita studiis, seu Dei
dono, seu potius dyabolica fraude, non satis certum est.

2 Hoc tamen affirmatur a multis, eam longe ante rapinam Helene, audaciam Paridis et adventum Tyndaridis et longam civitatis
obsidionem et postremam Priami atque Ylionis desolationem persepe et clara cecinisse voce; et ob hoc, cum nulla dictis suis prestaretur fides, a patre et fratribus verberibus castigatam volunt; ac
etiam fabulam inde confictam, eam scilicet ab Apolline dilectam et
in eius concubitum requisitam; quem se prestaturam promisisse[1]
dicunt, si ab eodem ante eidem futurorum notitia prestaretur.

3 Quod cum suscepisset negassetque promissum, nec Apollo posset
auferre concessum, aiunt illum muneri adiecisse neminem quod
diceret crediturum; et sic factum est ut quod diceret tanquam
fatue dictum crederetur a cunctis.

4 Hec aut[2] nobili cuidam Corebo desponsata iuveni, prius

Polydorus, who died in adolescence thanks to the faithlessness of Polymestor.[a]

Some authorities report that these sorrows, so numerous and so brutal, caused Hecuba to go mad and to howl like a dog through the Thracian fields. Thus, they say, she died and was buried on the shore of the Hellespont in a mound named 'Cynossema' after her.[b] Others claim that the enemy took Hecuba into slavery along with the remaining survivors, and that her misery was complete when she saw Cassandra's throat cut at Clytemnestra's order after the murder of Agamemnon.

: XXXV :

Cassandra, Daughter of King Priam of Troy

Cassandra was the daughter of Priam, king of Troy. The ancient writers tell us that she possessed the art of prophecy, but we do not know if she acquired this by study or through God's bounty or, as is more likely, because of some trick of the devil.

Nevertheless, many sources affirm that, long before the abduction of Helen, Cassandra had clearly and often predicted the bold deed of Paris, the arrival of Helen, the long siege of Troy, and the final destruction of Priam and his city. But her prophecies, they say, did not gain credence, and Cassandra was subsequently beaten by her father and brothers. This gave rise to the story that she was loved by Apollo who sought to sleep with her. Cassandra is said to have agreed on the condition that he would first give her the art of knowing the future. But once she had received the gift, she reneged on her promise. Apollo, unable to take back what he had bestowed, added to the gift the proviso that no one would believe what Cassandra said. And so it happened that, whenever she spoke, everyone regarded her words as silly.

Cassandra, who had been betrothed to a young nobleman

illum in bello perdidit quam ab eo susciperetur in thalamum; et
demum, pereuntibus rebus, captiva Agamenoni cessit in sortem. A
quo cum Micenas traheretur, eidem cecinit sibi a Clitemestra pre-
5 paratas insidias atque mortem. Cuius verbis cum fides daretur
nulla, post mille maris pericula, Micenas cum Agamenone devenit, ubi, eo Clitemestre fraude ceso, et ipsa eiusdem Clitemestre
iussu iugulata est.

: XXXVI :

De Clitemestra Micenarum regina

1 Clitemestra Tyndari, regis Oebalie, filia fuit ex Leda et Castoris
atque Pollucis et Helene soror, virgoque nupsit Agamenoni, Micenarum regi.

2   Que etsi genere satis et coniugio clara esset, nephario tamen
ausu clarior facta est. Nam imperante Agamenone viro Grecorum
copiis apud Troiam, cum ex eo iam plures filios peperisset, ociosi
atque desidis iuvenis Egysti, olim Thiestis ex Pelopia filii, qui ob
sacerdotium abstinebat ab armis, in concupiscentiam incidit; et —
ut placet aliquibus — Nauplii senis, Palamedis olim patris, suasionibus, eius in amplexus et concubitum venit.

3   Ex quo scelere secutum est ut, seu timore ob patratum facinus
redeuntis Agamenonis, seu amasii suasione et regni cupidine, seu
indignationis concepte ob Cassandram, que ab Agamenone dedu-
cebatur Micenas, animosa mulier armato animo et fraudibus te-

named Coroebus, lost him in the war before he could take her to the marriage bed. Finally, after the fall of Troy, she was captured and fell by lot to Agamemnon. During their journey to Mycenae she foretold the snares and the death that Clytemnestra was preparing for him. Her words, however, were not believed. After a long and dangerous voyage they arrived at Mycenae; there Agamemnon was killed through Clytemnestra's treachery, and Cassandra had her throat cut at the latter's order. 5

: XXXVI :

Clytemnestra, Queen of Mycenae

Clytemnestra was the daughter of Tyndareus, king of Sparta, by Leda; she was also the sister of Castor, Pollux, and Helen; while still a young girl, she married Agamemnon, king of Mycenae. 1

Already well known because of her ancestry and her marriage, Clytemnestra's wicked daring made her still more famous. When her husband Agamemnon was commanding the Greek forces at Troy, despite the fact that she had already given the king a number of children, Clytemnestra fell in love with Aegisthus, who was the son of the deceased Thyestes and Pelopia. An idle and worthless young man, he had not taken up arms because he was a priest. Some sources report that Clytemnestra slept with Aegisthus at the encouragement of the aged Nauplius, whose son Palamedes had been killed. 2

Such wickedness encouraged this bold woman to arm her spirit with treachery and to rise with reckless audacity against her husband, either through fear of the sin she had committed (since Agamemnon was returning); or through the instigation of her lover and a desire for power; or through indignation (since Agamemnon was bringing Cassandra to Mycenae). When Agamemnon came 3

merario ausu surrexit in virum eumque victorem Ylii redeuntem et maris tempestatibus fessum, ficta oris letitia, suscepit in regiam; et — ut quibusdam placet — cenantem et vino iam forte madentem percuti iussit ab adultero ex insidiis prodeunte.

4   Alii autem dicunt, cum recubaret, vestimentis victoria quesitis implicitus, quasi grecanicis festum clarius esset futurum, placide adultera coniunx illi suasit ut patrias indueret vestes et quas ipsa in hoc ante confecerat; easque exitu capiti<s>[1] carentes audax porrexit eidem; et cum iam brachia manicis iniecisset vir quereretque circumvolutus unde posset emictere caput, semiligatus adultero percussori, ab eadem suadente, concessus est et sic, eo neminem vidente, percussus est. Quo facto regnum occupavit omne et cum adultero Egysto per septennium imperavit.

5   Sane cum excrevisset interim Horestes, Agamenonis ex ea filius, quem clam servaverant a furore matris amici, animumque in necem patris ulciscendam sumpsisset, tempore sumpto eam cum adultero interemit.

6   Quid incusem magis nescio: scelus an audaciam? Primum, pregrande malum non meruerat vir inclitus; secundum, quanto minus decebat perfidam mulierem, tanto abominabile magis. Habeo tamen quid laudem, Horestis scilicet virtutem, que diu substinere passa non est a pietate inceste matris retrahi quin in inmeriti patris necem animosus ultor irrueret et in male meritam matrem filius ageret quod minus meritus genitor ab adultero sacerdote, incesta imperante femina, passus fuerat; et eorum, quorum imperio et opere paternus sanguis effusus fuerat, ut in autores verteretur scelus, effuso sanguine piaretur.

back victorious from Troy and exhausted by the storms that he
had encountered at sea, Clytemnestra received him in the royal
palace with a feigned expression of joy. According to some accounts, she ordered the adulterous Aegisthus, who emerged from
hiding, to kill Agamemnon when the latter was dining and perhaps already drunk with wine.

Others, however, say that while he was reclining in triumphal 4
dress at the table, his faithless wife, as if to make the feast an even
greater occasion for the Greeks, coaxed him to put on the clothes
of his own country, which she herself had earlier prepared for this
purpose. Brazenly Clytemnestra handed him garments lacking an
opening at the neck. When Agamemnon had put his arms in the
sleeves and, all tangled up, was trying to find a way to put his head
through, she handed him half-bound to her lover whom she had
recruited as an assassin. Thus Agamemnon was killed without
seeing his murderer. Then Clytemnestra took over the kingdom
and reigned for seven years with the adulterous Aegisthus.

During this time, however, Agamemnon's son Orestes, whom 5
friends had secretly saved from his mother's fury, grew up. He
made up his mind to avenge his father's death and, at an opportune moment, killed Clytemnestra along with her lover.

I do not know which I condemn more, the crime or the impu- 6
dence of the crime. The first was a great evil which that noble man
did not deserve; the second was the more abominable as it was unbecoming to that perfidious woman. I do, however, have to praise
Orestes' virtue. Although he endured the situation for a long time,
he was not deterred by any feeling of respect for his lewd mother
from bravely avenging his father's undeserved death. The son inflicted on his guilty mother what his innocent father had suffered
at the hands of an adulterous priest acting under orders from an
indecent woman. Thus his father's blood was expiated by the
blood of those through whose command and whose agency it had
been shed, so that the crime turned against the perpetrators.

: XXXVII :

De Helena Menelai regis coniuge

1 Helena tam ob suam lasciviam—ut multis visum est—quam ob diuturnum bellum ex ea consecutum toto orbi notissima femina, filia fuit Tyndari, Oebalie regis, et Lede, formosissime mulieris, et
2 Menelai Lacedemonum regis coniunx. Huius—ut omnes aiunt veteres greci latinique post eos—tam celebris pulchritudo fuit ut
3 preponatur facile ceteris. Fatigavit enim—ut reliquos sinam—divini ingenii virum Homerum, antequam illam posset secundum precepta[1] satis convenienter describere carmine.

Preterea pictores et sculptores multiplices egregii omnes eundem sumpsere laborem ut tam eximii decoris saltem effigiem, si
4 possent, posteritati relinquerent. Quos inter, summa conductus a Crotoniensibus pecunia Zeusis heracleotes, illius seculi famosissimus pictor et prepositus ceteris, ad illam pinniculo formandam, ingenium omne artisque vires exposuit; et cum, preter Homeri carmen et magnam undique famam, nullum aliud haberet exemplum, ut per hec duo de facie et cetero persone statu potuerat mente concipere, excogitavit se ex aliis plurium pulcherrimis formis divinam illam Helene effigiem posse percipere et aliis poscentibus designatam ostendere; et ostensis postulanti a Crotoniatibus, primo formosissimis pueris et inde sororibus, ex formosioribus quinque precipuo decore spectabiles selegit; et collecta secum ex pulchritudine omnium forma una, totis ex ingenio celebri emunctis viribus, vix creditum est satis plene quod optabat arte potuisse percipere.

5 Nec ego miror: quis enim picture vel statue pinniculo aut celo potuerit inscribere leticiam[2] oculorum, totius oris placidam affabilitatem, celestem risum motusque faciei varios et decoros secun-

: XXXVII :

Helen, Wife of King Menelaus

The view is widely held that Helen was notorious throughout   1
the entire world as much for her lustfulness as for the long war
which resulted from it. She was the wife of Menelaus, king of
Lacedaemon, and her parents were Tyndareus, king of Oebalia,
and Leda, a woman of great loveliness. Every ancient source, first   2
Greek and then Latin, reports that Helen's beauty was so extraordinary as easily to surpass that of other women. To mention only   3
one instance, even Homer, a man of divine talents, exhausted the
resources of his art without describing her fittingly in verse.

Moreover, many distinguished painters and sculptors embarked
on the same task of leaving to posterity, if they could, at least a
likeness of Helen's marvelous beauty. Among them was Zeuxis of   4
Heraclea, the most famous and respected painter of the time, who
was hired at great expense by the people of Croton. He put all his
skill and the powers of his art into the attempt to depict her with
his brush. The only models he had were Homer's poetry and
Helen's own universal fame. Since these had given him an idea
of her face and the rest of her person, Zeuxis thought that he
would be able to represent Helen's divine appearance on the basis
of the beauty of many others, and so to exhibit a sketch of his
painting to the people who had commissioned it. At his request,
the Crotoniatae showed him their most beautiful boys and girls;
from them Zeuxis chose five who were especially notable. Calling
on all his creative powers, he produced an image of their collective
beauty. But it is hardly to be believed that he realized fully his artistic objective.

This does not surprise me. The happiness in Helen's eyes, the   5
pleasant serenity of her entire face, her heavenly laugh, and the
charming changes of expression reflecting what she heard and

dum verborum et actuum qualitates? Cum solius hoc nature officium sit.

6   Fecit ergo quod potuit; et quod pinxerat, tanquam celeste simulacri decus, posteritati reliquit. Hinc acutiores finxere fabulam eamque ob sydereum oculorum fulgorem, ob invisam mortalibus lucem, ob insignem faciei candorem aureamque come volatilis copiam, hinc inde per humeros petulantibus recidentem cincinnulis, et lepidam sonoramque vocis suavitatem necnon et gestus quosdam, tam cinnamei roseique oris quam splendide frontis et eburnei gucturis ac ex invisis delitiis pectoris assurgentis, nonnisi ex aspirantis concipiendis aspectu, Iovis in cignum versi descripsere filiam, ut, preter quam a matre suscepisse poterat formositatem, intelligeretur ex infuso numine quod pinniculis coloribusque ingenio suo imprimere nequibant artifices.

7   Ab hac tam spectanda pulcritudine in Laconas Theseus ab Athenis evocatus ante alios, virginem et etate tenellam, in palestra patrio ludentem more, audax rapuit; et etsi preter oscula pauca eidem auferre nequiverit, aliqualem tamen labefactate virginitatis iniecit notam. Que fratribus ab Eletra Thesei matre, seu—ut volunt alii—a Protheo rege egyptio, absente Theseo, repetentibus restituta; et tandem matura viro Menelao, Lacedemonum regi, coniugio iuncta est, cui Hermionam filiam peperit unicam.

8

9   Post hec, fluentibus annis, cum redisset Ylionem Paris, qui ob somnium pregnantis matris in Yda fuerat expositus, et in lucta Hectorem fratrem superasset non cognitus, mortem, crepundiis ostensis et a matre cognitis, evitasset, memor sponsionis spetiosis-

saw — who could represent these with a painter's brush or a sculptor's chisel? That is the prerogative of Nature alone.

Zeuxis, therefore, did what he could, and what he left to posterity was but a simulacrum of her celestial grace. Hence the more ingenious authors invented the myth that Helen was the daughter of Jupiter transformed into a swan. Their accounts described the starry splendor of her eyes whose light had never before been seen by humankind; the marvelous whiteness of her complexion; her mass of golden hair falling and swirling on her shoulders in saucy curls; the charming and resonant sweetness of her voice; certain movements of her scented and rosy mouth; her dazzling forehead and ivory throat rising above the hidden delights of her breast that were imaginable only from the rhythm of her breathing. In this way they wished it to be understood that Helen possessed beauty from some divine source, besides that inherited from her mother, which the artists, despite their talents, could not express with brush and paint.

Theseus was the first to be attracted by Helen's spectacular beauty. Proceeding to Sparta from Athens, he boldly abducted the girl, still of tender years, while she was exercising, as was the local custom, in the palestra. Although he had in fact been able to take from her nothing except a few kisses, he nevertheless left some doubt regarding the matter of her virginity. Electra, Theseus' mother, gave Helen back to her brothers when they came looking for her, or, as other sources claim, Helen was returned during Theseus' absence by Proteus, king of Egypt. Finally, when she came of age, she was married to Menelaus, king of Sparta, to whom she bore one child, a daughter named Hermione.

With the passing of years, Paris, who had been abandoned on Mount Ida because of a dream his mother had when she was pregnant,[a] returned to Troy. Still unrecognized when he overcame his brother Hector in wrestling, he escaped death after displaying certain baby toys which his mother recognized. Remembering Venus'

sime coniugis sibi a Venere, ob latam a se apud Ydam sententiam, seu — ut alii volunt — postulaturus Hesyonam, fabrefactis ex Yda navibus, regio comitatu sotiatus, transfretavit in Greciam et a Menelao fuit susceptus hospitio.

10 Ibi cum vidisset Helenam celesti decore conspicuam atque regio in cultu lascivientem seque intueri cupientem, captus illico et ex moribus spe sumpta, captatis temporibus, scintillantibus fervore oculis, furtim impudico pectori ignem sue dilectionis ingessit. Ceptisque fortuna favit: nam, exigente oportunitate, eo relicto, 11 Cretam Menelaus perrexerat. Quam ob rem placet aliquibus, eis equis flammis urentibus, ex composito factum esse ut Paris ignem, per quietem visum ab Hecuba, portaret in patriam et vaticinia adimpleret; maxima cum parte thesaurorum Menelai, noctu, ex laconico litore, seu — ut aliis placet — ex Citharea, ibidem vicina insula, dum <erat>[3] in templo quodam, patrio ritu, ob sacrum conficiendum, Helenam vigilantem raperet parateque classi imponeret; et cum ea post multa pericula deveniret in Troiam: ubi cum precipuo honore a Priamo suscepta est, eo extimante potius notam iniurie abstersisse ob detentam a Thelamone Hesionam, quam postremam regni sui desolationem suscepisse in patria.

12 Hac huius illecebra mulieris universa Grecia commota est; et cum gray principes omnes Paridis potius iniuriam ponderarent quam Helene lasciviam, ea frustra repetita sepius, in Troie excidium coniurarunt unanimes; collectisque viribus, cum mille vel amplius navibus, armatorum honustis, litus inter Sygeum et Retheum, promontoria Frigie, occupavere et Ylionem obsederunt,

promise of a very beautiful wife which she had made to him as a reward for his judgment delivered on Mount Ida,[b] or (as some sources claim) intending to ask for the return of Hesione,[c] Paris built a flotilla near Mount Ida and sailed in the company of a noble retinue to Greece where he enjoyed Menelaus' hospitality.

Once in Sparta, Paris fell in love with Helen as soon as he saw 10 her resplendent in celestial beauty, wanton in royal elegance, and yearning for admiration. Her behavior offered reason for hope, and so, his eyes sparkling with passion, Paris took advantage of every opportunity to instill secretly in her unchaste breast a desire for his love. Fortune favored his efforts: Menelaus had gone to Crete on business and had left Paris in the house. Hence some 11 sources relate that, since Paris and Helen were both in love, mutual agreement was behind Paris' bringing to his country the 'fire' seen by his mother Hecuba in a dream and his fulfillment of the prophecy. During the night he seized Helen and carried her off, along with the bulk of Menelaus' treasure, from the Laconian shore. (Or, as some accounts prefer, he took her from the nearby island of Cythera while she was in a temple keeping vigil in order to perform a sacrifice according to the local custom). He brought her on board the waiting ship and after many dangers they reached Troy. There Helen was received with special honor by Priam, who thought that by so doing he had purged the shame of Telamon's refusal to surrender Hesione. The king did not understand that instead he had welcomed to Troy the cause of the final devastation of his kingdom.

Helen's charm threw the whole of Greece into turmoil. The 12 Greek princes all placed more weight on Paris' wrongdoing than on Helen's wantonness; in vain they called repeatedly for her return. Then they banded together for the destruction of Troy. Pooling their forces, the princes landed on the shore between the Phrygian promontories of Sigeum and Rhoeteum with a thousand or more ships loaded with armed men. They laid siege to Troy

13 frustra obsistentibus Frigiis. Helena quidem quanti foret sua formositas ex muris obsesse civitatis vidisse potuit, cernens litus omne completum hostibus et igne ferroque circumdesolari omnia, populos inire certamina ac per mutua vulnera in mortem iri et tam troiano quam greco sanguine cuncta fedari.

14 Que quidem tam pertinaci proposito repetita est atque detenta, ut, dum non redderetur, per decennium cede multorum nobilium cruenta perseveraret obsidio. Qua stante, Hectore iam mortuo et Achille, atque a Pyrro, acerrimo iuvene, trucidato Paride, quasi parvum sibi visum sit peccasse semel, Helena secundas inivit nuptias nupsitque Deyphebo iuniori.

15 Tandem cum proditione tentaretur quod armis obtineri non posse videbatur, hec, que obsidioni causam dederat, ut opus daret excidio et ad viri primi gratiam promerendam, in eandem volens sciensque devenit; et cum dolo simulassent Greci discessum, Troianis preteritis fessis laboribus et nova letitia festisque epulis victis somnoque sepultis, Helena choream simulans accensa face in tempore ex arce revocavit intentos. Qui redeuntes, cum tacite semisopitam urbem reseratis ianuis intrassent, ea incensa et Deyphebo fede ceso, Helenam post vigesimum a raptu annum Menelao restituere coniugi.

16 Alii vero asserunt Helenam non sponte sua a Paride raptam et ob id a viro meruisse suscipi. Qui cum ea Greciam repetens, a tempestate et adverso vento agitatus plurimum, in Egyptum cursum vertere coactus, a Polibo rege susceptus est. Post hec[4] sedatis procellis in Lacedemonam[5] cum reacquisita coniuge fere post octa-

amid futile Phrygian opposition. From the walls of the besieged 13
city, Helen could recognize the worth of her beauty: she saw the
shore completely filled with the enemy and everything around destroyed by fire and sword, people fighting and dying of mutually
inflicted wounds, and the earth everywhere stained with Trojan as
well as Greek blood.

With such stubborn resolve was Helen sought by the Greeks 14
and held captive by the Trojans that the siege lasted ten years and
resulted in the horrific slaughter of many noble men. During the
siege, after the deaths of Hector and Achilles and the brutal murder of Paris by the cruel youth Pyrrhus, Helen entered into wed-
lock again and married Deiphobus, a younger man—as if she
thought she had not sinned enough the first time.

Finally, an attempt was made to achieve by means of treason 15
what did not seem possible to obtain with force. Helen, who had
been the cause of the siege, entered willingly and knowingly into
the plot so that she could aid in the destruction of the city and return to the good graces of her first husband. After the Greeks had
feigned their retreat, the Trojans were exhausted both by their past
efforts and by their present joy. When they were sleeping soundly
after their celebratory banquets, Helen pretended to dance; at the
proper moment she lit a torch, thereby sending a signal from
the citadel to the waiting Greeks. They returned and silently entered through the open gates a city now half asleep. Troy was
burned, Deiphobus cruelly slain, and Helen restored to her husband Menelaus more than twenty years after her abduction.

Other sources, however, claim that Helen was carried off by 16
Paris against her will and thus deserved to be taken back by her
husband. Fierce storms and adverse winds hindered their return to
Greece. Menelaus was forced to turn his course towards Egypt
and there he was kindly received by King Polybus. Later, when the
storms abated, he returned with the wife he had regained to

17 vum annum a desolato Ylione susceptus est. Ipsa autem quam diu
post hec vixerit, aut quid egerit, seu quo sub celo mortua sit, nusquam legisse recordor.

: XXXVIII :

De Circe Solis filia

1 Circes, cantationibus suis in hodiernum usque famosissima mulier, ut poetarum testantur carmina, filia fuit Solis et Perse
nynphe, Occeani filie, sororque Oethe Colcorum regis: Solis, ut
arbitror, ideo filia dicta, quia singulari floruerit pulchritudine, seu
quia circa notitiam herbarum fuerit eruditissima, vel potius quia
prudentissima in agendis: que omnia solem, variis habitis respecti-
bus, dare nascentibus mathematici arbitrantur.

2 Quo autem pacto, relictis Colcis, Italiam petierit, minime legisse memini. Eam Etheum Volscorum montem, quem de suo nomine dicimus in hodiernum usque Circeum, incoluisse omnes testantur historie; et cum nil preter poeticum legatur ex hac tam
celebri muliere, recitatis succincte poeticis, quo prestabitur ingenio
mentem excutiemus credentium.

3 Volunt igitur ante alia quoscunque nautas, seu ex proposito, seu
tempestatis inpulsu, ad dicti montis, olim insule, litora applican-
tes, huius artibus cantatis carminibus, seu infectis veneno poculis,
in feras diversarum specierum fuisse conversos; et hos inter vagi
4 Ulixis fuisse sotios, eo, Mercurii mediante consilio, servato. Qui
cum evaginato gladio mortem minaretur venefice, socios reas-
sumpsisse in formam redactos pristinam et per annum contuber-

Sparta, where he was welcomed almost eight years after the destruction of Troy. But I do not remember reading how long Helen 17 lived afterwards, or what she did, or where she died.

: XXXVIII :

Circe, Daughter of the Sun

Poets say that Circe, a woman famous even in our own time for 1 her magical spells, was the daughter of the Sun and the nymph Perse, whose father was Oceanus. Circe was also the sister of Aeetes, king of Colchis. In my opinion, she was called the daughter of the Sun because of her extraordinary beauty or her great knowledge of herbs or, more probably, her shrewdness in conducting her affairs. Astrologers believe that these are all qualities which the sun gives to mortals at birth in proportion to their varying dispositions.

I do not recall reading how she arrived in Italy once she had left 2 Colchis. The histories, however, state unanimously that she lived on Aetheus, a mountain in the region of the Volscians, whose present name of Circeo is derived from her own. The works of the poets are our only sources for this celebrated woman; after touching briefly on their reports I shall explain, to the best of my ability, the meaning of what they believe.

First of all, they say that any sailors who landed on purpose or 3 were driven by storms onto the shore of the promontory, formerly an island, were changed into various kinds of animals through Circe's enchantments or poisonous potions. It is reported that the companions of Ulysses during his wanderings were among those who suffered such a fate, but he himself was saved thanks to Mercury's advice. When Ulysses drew his sword and threatened the 4

nio[1] usus eiusdem, ex ea Thelegonum suscepisse filium dicunt; et ab ea plenum consilii discessisse.

Quo sub cortice hos existimo latere sensus.

5   Sunt qui dicant hanc feminam haud longe a Caieta, Campanie oppido, potentissimam fuisse viribus et sermone, nec magni facientem, dummodo aliquid consequeretur optatum, a nota illesam servasse pudicitiam; et sic multos ex applicantibus litori suo blanditiis et ornatu sermonis non solum in suas illecebras traxisse, verum alios in rapinam et pyrraticam inpulisse, nonnullos, omni honestate postposita, ad exercenda negotia et mercimonia dolis incitasse, et plures ob sui singularem dilectionem in superbiam extulisse. Et sic hi, quibus infauste mulieris opera humana subtracta videbatur ratio, eos ab eadem in sui facinoris feras merito crederetur fuisse conversos.

6   Ex quibus satis comprehendere possumus, hominum mulierumque conspectis moribus, multas ubique Cyrces esse et longe
7   plures homines lascivia et crimine suo versos in beluas. Ulixes autem, Mercurii consilio predoctus, prudentem virum satis evidenter ostendit, quem adulantium nequeunt laqueare decipule, quin imo et documentis suis laqueatos persepe solvit a vinculo.

8   Reliquum satis patet ad hystoriam pertinere: qua constat Ulixem aliquandiu permansisse cum Circe. Fertur preterea hanc eandem feminam Pici, Saturni filii, Latinorum regis, fuisse coniugem eumque augurandi docuisse scientiam, et ob zelum, quia Pomonam nynpham adamaret, eum in avem sui transformasse nominis. Erat enim illi domesticus picus avis, ex cantu cuius et motibus

sorceress with death, she changed his companions back to their original form. He lived with Circe for a year, fathered her son Telegonus, and then, full of wisdom, left her.

I believe that the sense underlying this story is as follows.

In some versions, this woman, who lived not far from the Campanian city of Gaeta, was forceful and eloquent but not overly concerned with keeping her chastity untarnished so long as she got something she wanted. With her wiles and charming words not only did she entice many who reached her shore to join in her wantonness: some she pushed into robbery and piracy; others she induced with her tricks to cast all honor aside and take up commerce and trading; many she made arrogant because they loved her inordinately. We would thus be right in believing that the men changed into the kinds of wild beasts appropriate to their misdeeds were those who had lost their human reason through this unfortunate woman's influence.

If we consider human behavior, we see plainly enough from this instance that there are many Circes everywhere, and many more men whose lust and vice change them into beasts. Ulysses, however, equipped in advance with Mercury's counsel, obviously signifies the wise man who cannot be ensnared by fawning tricksters but rather through his example often frees from their bonds those who have been trapped.

Clearly the remaining details have to do with history, which tells us that Ulysses stayed for some time with Circe. It is also said that this same Circe was the wife of Picus, whose father was Saturn, king of the Latins, and that she taught her husband the art of foretelling the future. Jealous of Picus' love for the nymph Pomona, Circe is alleged to have changed him into the bird which bears his name. Actually, the man had a woodpecker (*picus*) at home from whose singing and motions he took auguries of the future; thus, because he regulated his life according to the actions of

summebat de futuris augurium; et, quia secundum actus pici vitam duceret, in picum versus dictus est.

9   Quando seu quo mortis genere aut ubi hec defuncta sit Circes, compertum non habeo.

: XXXIX :

De Camilla Volscorum regina

1 Camilla insignis et memoratu dignissima virgo fuit et Volscorum regina. Hec ex Methabo Volscorum rege antiquissimo et Casmilla coniuge genita, nascens matri mortis causa fuit; nam cum enixa parvulam moreretur, a Methabo patre, una tantum ex materno nomine dempta litera, Camillam filiam nuncupavit in sui solatium.

2 Huius quidem virginis a natali suo die severa fortuna fuit; nam paululum post matris funus, Methabus, Privernatum civium suorum repentina seditione regno pulsus, nil, fugam arripiens, preter parvulam hanc filiam suam, sibi pre ceteris rebus dilectam, aspor-

3 tasse in exilium potuit. In quod cum solus pedesque miser effugeret et in ulnis sociam deportaret Camillam, ad Amasenum fluvium, pridiano imbre tumentem, devenit; nec cum, onere infantule prepeditus, posset enare, in oportunum devenit consilium, porrigente Deo qui celebrem futuram virginem ignobili assummi

4 fato nolebat. Illam igitur suberis cortice involutam iaculo, quod forte ferebat, alligavit atque Dyane devovit, si servasset incolumem; et vibratum totis viribus brachio iaculum, cum filia, in ripam transiecit adversam, quam evestigio nando secutus est; et

this bird, he was reported to have been changed into a wood-pecker.

I have not discovered when, how, or where Circe died.   9

: XXXIX :

Camilla, Queen of the Volscians

Camilla, queen of the Volscians, was an illustrious maiden worthy   1
of memory. She was the daughter of Metabus, an ancient Volscian
king, and his wife Casmilla, who died in giving birth to her daughter. For this reason, and to console himself, Metabus named the
child Camilla after her mother (with only the letter *s* removed).

Fortune dealt harshly with this young woman from the day she   2
was born. Soon after her mother's death, Metabus was driven
from his kingdom by a sudden rebellion of the Privernates. He
could take nothing on his hurried flight into exile except this little
daughter, whom he loved above all else. As the wretched man   3
made his way on foot, accompanied only by Camilla whom he carried in his arms, he reached the Amasenus River. Hampered as he
was by his young burden, he could not swim across the waters,
swollen with the rain of the previous day. At just this moment
Metabus was inspired by God, who did not want the child, destined for fame, to suffer an ignoble fate. Accordingly, he wrapped   4
Camilla in the bark of a cork tree, tied her to the lance that he
happened to be carrying, and promised her to Diana if she would
save his daughter. With all his strength Metabus hurled the quiv-
ering lance bearing his child to the opposite bank and immediately
swam towards it. Through God's grace he found her uninjured.
Happy, then, even in his misery, he proceeded to a hiding place in

cum illam Dei munere comperisset illesam, in miseria letus, silva-
rum petiit latebras nec absque labore plurimo parvulam educavit
lacte ferino.

5   Que cum in validiorem evasisset etatem, tegere ferarum corpus
cepit exuviis et tela vibrare lacertis fundasque circumagere, arcus
tendere, gestare pharetras, cursu cervos capreasque silvestres insequi atque superare, labores femineos omnes despicere, virginitatem
pre ceteris inviolatam servare, iuvenum amores ludere et connubia
potentum procerum omnino respuere ac sese totam Dyane obse-
6   quio, cui pater devoverat, exhibere. Quibus exercitiis durata virgo,
in patrium revocata regnum, servavit robore inflexo propositum.

Tandem cum a Troia veniens Eneas Lavinam[1] sumpsisset in
coniugem, et ob id bellum inter eum Turnumque rutulum esset
exortum, congregantibus eis undique copias, Camilla, Turni parti-
bus favens, cum grandi Volscorum agmine venit auxiliatrix eidem;
et cum sepius armata irruisset in Teucros et die una acriter pugnans multos occidisset ex eis, et novissime Corebum quendam,
Cybelis sacerdotem, armorum eius avida, sequeretur, ab Arrunte
quodam ex hostibus, sagitta sub papilla letaliter percussa, maximo
Rutulorum damno moribunda collapsa est; et sic inter amata exer-
citia expiravit.

7   Hanc intueantur velim puellule hodierne; et dum sui iuris virginem adultam et pro libito nunc latos agros, nunc silvas et lustra ferarum accintam faretra discurrentem, labore assiduo lascivias illecebris appetitus prementem, delitias atque molliciem accuratas
offas et elaborata pocula fugientem et constantissimo animo coevorum iuvenum, non dicam amplexus, sed verba etiam respuentem
viderint, monite discant quid eas in domo patria, quid in templis,

the forest and there laboriously raised the little girl on the milk of wild animals.

When Camilla reached a more active age, she began to cover 5 her body with the skins of animals, hurl the spear, use a slingshot, stretch the bow, wear a quiver, chase and catch deer and wild goats, and disdain all womanly work. Especially concerned to preserve her virginity, she mocked her youthful lovers and rejected outright the offers of marriage from many princes. Instead she dedicated herself wholly to the service of Diana, to whom her father had promised her. Strengthened by her physical pursuits, 6 Camilla was summoned back to her father's kingdom but remained inflexible in her resolve.

Finally war broke out between Aeneas and Turnus, a Rutulian, after the former's arrival from Troy and subsequent marriage to Lavinia. Both sides gathered their forces. Camilla favored Turnus and went to his aid with a large army of Volscians. She made repeated attacks against the Trojans. One day, when she was fighting fiercely and had already killed many of the enemy, she pursued last of all a priest of Cybele called Corebus, whose armor she wanted. Then one of her foes, Arruns by name, wounded her mortally with an arrow beneath her breast. She fell to the ground, her death a great loss to the Rutulians. Thus Camilla lost her life in the midst of the pursuits she had loved.

I wish that the girls of our time would consider Camilla's exam- 7 ple. When they imagine this mature and self-possessed young woman wearing a quiver and running freely through the open fields, forests, and the lairs of animals, constantly curbing wanton desire with its enticements, refusing the pleasures and luxury of elaborate food and drink, and steadfastly rejecting not only the embraces but even the conversation of young men of her own age—when they have imagined this, let them learn from her example the proper demeanor in their parents' home, in churches, and in theaters where many onlookers and the most severe judges

quid in theatris, in quibus spectantium multitudo et severissimi morum censores conveniunt, deceat; minus quidem honestis negare aures, os taciturnitate frenare, oculos gravitate compescere, mores componere et gestus omnes suos honestatis mole comprimere, ocia, commesationes, lautitias nimias, choreas et iuvenum vitare consortia; sentiantque quoniam nec optare quod libet, nec quod licet agere sanctum sit aut castitati conforme; ut prudentiores facte et laudabili virginitate florentes in sacras nuptias mature, maioribus obtemperantes suis, deveniant.

: XL :

De Penelope Ulixis coniuge

1 Penelopes Ycari regis filia fuit et Ulixis strenuissimi viri coniunx: illibati decoris atque intemerate pudicitie matronis exemplum sanctissimum et eternum.

2 Huius quidem pudoris vires a fortuna acriter agitate, sed frustra, sunt, nam cum iuvencula virgo, et ob venustatem forme plurimum diligenda, a patre iuncta fuisset Ulixi peperissetque ex eo Thelemacum; et ecce in expeditionem troiani belli vocatus, imo vi fere tractus, Ulixes, ab eo cum Laerte patre iam sene et Anthyclia matre et parvo filio relicta est.

3 Sane, perseverante bello, nullam preter decennalem viduitatis iniuriam passa est. Attamen, Ylione deiecto, cum repetentes domum proceres aut in scopulos tempestate maris illisos, aut in peregrinum litus inpulsos aut undis absortos, seu paucos in patriam re-

of conduct assemble. Let them learn also not to listen to less than honorable persons, to keep silent, have a serious look in their eyes, be well-mannered, gesture modestly, and avoid idleness, feasting, excessive luxury, dancing, and consorting with young men. Young women should also realize that it is neither pious nor in keeping with a chaste life to desire everything that is pleasurable and to do everything that is allowed. When they become wiser and blossom in their precious virginity, let them enter into holy matrimony in due season and under the direction of their elders.

: XL :

Penelope, Wife of Ulysses

Penelope, daughter of King Icarius, was the wife of Ulysses, a man   1
of great activity: for married women she is the most sacred and lasting example of untarnished honor and undefiled purity.

The constancy of her virtue was sternly tested by fortune, but   2
in vain. When Penelope was a young girl, greatly admired for her beauty and still a virgin, her father married her to Ulysses; she gave him a son named Telemachus. Suddenly Ulysses was called, or rather, practically hauled off by force, to take part in the expedition against Troy. He left Penelope behind with his father Laertes, who was already an old man, his mother Anticlea, and their little son.

Throughout the war Penelope suffered no injury, except that   3
she was without a husband for ten years. When the Greek commanders were returning home after the destruction of Troy, word came that some of them had been dashed against the rocks by storms at sea or forced to land on foreign shores or swallowed up by the waves, and that few had returned to their own countries.

ceptos, fama monstraret, solius Ulixis erat incertum quo cursum
4 tenuissent naves. Quam ob rem cum expectatus diu non revertere-
tur in patriam, nec appareret ab ullo usquam visum, mortuus existimatus est; qua credulitate Anthyclia genitrix miseranda, ad le-
niendum dolorem, vitam terminavit laqueo.
5 Penelopes autem, etsi egre plurimum ferret viri absentiam,
6 longe tulit egrius sinistram mortis eius suspitionem. Sed post multas lacrimas et Ulixem frustra vocatum sepissime, inter senem
Laertem et Thelemacum puerum in castissimam et perpetuam viduitatem senescere firmato animo disposuit.
7 Verum cum et forma decens moresque probabiles et egregium
genus ad se diligendam atque concupiscendam quorundam nobilium ex Ythachia atque Cephalania et Etholia provocasset animos,
8 plurimum instigationibus eorum vexata est. Nam cum in dies spes
vite Ulixis aut reditus eiusdem continue[1] videretur minui, eo ventum est ut, abeunte rus ob fastidium procatorum Laerte, procatores ipsi Ulixis occuparent regiam et Penelopem precibus atque
suasionibus pro viribus, et sepissime, in suum provocarent coniu-
9 gium. Ast mulier, metuens ne forte sacri pectoris violaretur propositum, cum iam cerneret viam negationibus auferri, divino profecto
illustrata lumine, terminis et astutia infestos, saltem ad tempus,
fallendos esse arbitrata est; petiit instantibus sibi tam diu liceret
expectare virum donec telam, quam more regalium mulierum ce-
10 perat, perfecisse posset. Quod cum facile concessissent competito-
res egregii, ipsa femineo astu quicquid in die solerti studio texens
videbatur operi iungere, clam revocatis filis, subtrahebat in nocte.
11 Qua arte cum eos in regia Ulixis bona assiduis conviviis consu-
mentes aliquandiu lusisset, nec iam amplius videretur locum
fraudi posse prestari, Dei pietate factum est ut ex Pheycum regno

Only in Ulysses' case was it uncertain what course his ships had followed. Consequently, when his long-expected homecoming did 4 not take place and it appeared that no one had seen him, Ulysses was presumed dead. His wretched mother Anticlea believed this all too readily and hanged herself to put an end to her grief.

As for Penelope, while her husband's absence had been a cause 5 of great sorrow to her, she took the terrible surmise of his death even more to heart. After much weeping and many vain invoca- 6 tions to Ulysses, she firmly resolved to maintain, in the company of aged Laertes and her son Telemachus, a chaste and perpetual widowhood until she herself grew old.

But her beauty, good character, and noble birth prompted some 7 of the nobility from Ithaca, Cephalonia, and Aetolia to love and desire her, and Penelope was much harassed by their entreaties. Every day there seemed less reason to hope that Ulysses was alive 8 and would return. Finally it reached the point that Laertes retired to the country because of his aversion to Penelope's suitors, who took over Ulysses' own palace and, as best they could with pleas and flattery, repeatedly urged Penelope to marry one of them. She 9 saw no possibility of refusal and was afraid that the resolution she had taken within her chaste breast would be broken. It was surely by divine inspiration that she devised a clever way to deceive her enemies, at least temporarily, by setting a date for her decision. Penelope asked the persistent suitors that she be allowed to wait for her husband until she could finish weaving the cloth that she had begun in accord with queenly custom. This the noble rivals 10 readily conceded. Penelope, however, with feminine cunning se- cretly undid at night all that she had diligently woven during the day.

With this trick she fooled them for some time while they con- 11 sumed Ulysses' wealth in continual feasting at his palace. When it seemed impossible to deceive them any longer, divine mercy saw to

navigans, post vigesimum sui discessus annum, solus et incognitus
Ulixes Ythachiam veniret pastoresque suos scitaturus rerum suarum statum adiret; et cum ex astutia pauper incessisset habitu, a
Sybote iam sene porcario suo comiter susceptus, ab eodem refe-
rente fere omnem rerum suarum comprehendit seriem et Thelemacum a Menelao redeuntem vidit seque clam illi cognitum fecit
et consilium suum aperuit omne; factumque est ut a Sybote incognitus deduceretur in patriam.

12   Quo cum vidisset quo pacto rem suam traherent procatores
atque pudicam Penelopem eorum renuentem coniugium, irritatus,
cum Sybote subulco et Phylitia opilione suo atque Thelemaco
filio, clausis regie ianuis, in procatores convivantes insurgens, Euri-
macum, Polibi filium, et Anthinoum, Anphinonem atque Clisip-
pum samium, Agelaum aliosque, frustra veniam exorantes, una
cum Melantheo caprario suo, hostibus arma ministrante, atque
mulieribus domesticis, quas noverat cum procatoribus contubernium habuisse, occidit; suamque Penelopem ab insidiis procan-
13   tium liberavit. Que tandem, cum vix eum recognoscere potuisset,
summo perfusa gaudio, diu desideratum suscepit.

Vult tamen Lycophron quidam, novissimus poetarum ex Grecis, hanc suasionibus Nauplii senis, ob vindictam occisi Palamedis
filii sui, fere omnes Grecorum coniuges lenocinio in meretricium
deducentis, Penelopem cum aliquo ex procatoribus in amplexus et
14   concubitum venisse. Quod absit ut credam, celebrem castimonia
multorum autorum literis mulierem, unius in contrarium asseren-
tis, Penelopem preter castissimam extitisse. Cuius quidem virtus
tanto clarior atque commendabilior quanto rarior invenitur et,
maiori inpulsa certamine, perseveravit constantior inconcussa.

it that Ulysses, sailing from the kingdom of the Phaeacians, returned to Ithaca alone and unknown twenty years after his departure. To obtain information about the state of his affairs, he approached his shepherds. Since he had cleverly dressed himself as
a beggar, he was received in a friendly way by his swineherd
Sybotes,[a] now an old man. From him Ulysses learned almost everything that had happened. He saw Telemachus, who was returning from a visit to Menelaus, secretly made himself known to his
son, and told him of his plans. Sybotes then took Ulysses, still unrecognized, to the palace.

When he saw the suitors wasting his property and the chaste   12
Penelope rejecting their offers of marriage, Ulysses became enraged. Aided by the swineherd Sybotes, his shepherd Philitia,
and his son Telemachus, Ulysses rose up against the carousers.
The doors of the palace were closed, and he killed Polybus' son
Eurymachus, Antinous, Anphinon, Clisippus of Samos, Agelaus,
and others who pleaded in vain for mercy. Also killed were his
goatherd Melanthius, who was giving arms to the enemy, and
some women servants whom Ulysses knew to have been mistresses
of the suitors. Thus he freed Penelope from the plottings of her
would-be lovers. Though barely able to recognize him, she wel-   13
comed with great joy the husband she had longed for all that time.

But according to Lycophron, the last of the Greek poets,
Penelope committed adultery with one of the suitors at the persuasion of the aged Nauplius, who avenged the death of his son
Palamedes by enticing almost all the wives of the Greeks into
prostitution. Far be it from me to believe that Penelope, whom   14
many authors have celebrated for the purity of her morals, was
anything but completely chaste, just because one writer states the
opposite. Her virtue is the more renowned and praiseworthy in
that it is only rarely found; the more urgently she was assailed, the
more constantly and firmly did she persevere.

: XLI :

De Lavinia Laurentum regina

1 Lavinia Laurentum regina, genus a Saturno cretensi ducens, Latini regis et Amate coniugis eius filia fuit unica; et tandem Enee, strenuissimi Troianorum ducis, coniunx, magis belli Enee Turnique rutuli causa clara quam alio facinore suo.

2 Hec equidem ob insigne formositatis sue decus et patrium regnum, cui successura videbatur, a Turno Rutulorum rege ardentissimo iuvene in coniugium instantissime petebatur eique ex eo spem fecerat Amata mater, que, avia, desiderio nepotis favebat in-

3 pense. Sane Latinus augurandi peritus, cum ab oraculo suscepisset filiam extero duci tradendam coniugio, tardius ibat in votum; quin imo cum a Troia profugus advenisset Eneas, Latinus, tam ob generis claritatem quam ob oraculi monitus, eidem poscenti amicitiam

4 spopondit et filiam. Quam ob rem inter Eneam Turnumque bellum suscitatum est; et post multa certamina obtinentibus Troianis per vulnera et sanguinem mortesque[1] plurium nobilium, ab Enea in Lavinie nuptias itum est, mortua iam ob indignationem Amata laqueo.

5 Sunt tamen qui velint bellum post nuptias exortum, sed, qualitercunque gestum sit, constat Laviniam ex Enea clarissimo principe concepisse filium et, eo ante diem partus apud Numicum fluvium rebus humanis subtracto, cum Ascanium privignum regnantem timeret, secessisse in silvas et ibi postumum peperisse

6 atque — ut volunt aliqui — Iulium nominasse Silvium. Sane cum mitior credito esset in novercam Ascanius et sibi Albam civitatem

: XLI :

Lavinia, Queen of Laurentum

Lavinia, queen of Laurentum and a descendant of Saturn of Crete, 1
was the only child of King Latinus and his wife Amata and eventually became the wife of Aeneas, the valorous Trojan leader. She
was famous more for the war between Aeneas and Turnus the
Rutulian than for any deed of her own.

Thanks to her remarkable beauty and her father's kingdom, to 2
which she was the heir, Lavinia was eagerly sought as a wife by
Turnus, a passionate youth who was the king of the Rutulians.
Lavinia's mother Amata had given Turnus reason to hope; she was
also Turnus' grandmother and zealously furthered her grandson's
interests. But Latinus, who was a skilful soothsayer, learned from 3
an oracle that he was to give his daughter in marriage to a foreign
prince; hence he was reluctant to go along with his wife's wishes.
In fact, when Aeneas arrived in flight from Troy, Latinus was
moved by the oracle's command as well as by the Trojan's noble
ancestry to promise him his daughter and the alliance Aeneas was
seeking. This resulted in a war between Aeneas and Turnus. After 4
numerous battles in which many noble men were wounded and
slaughtered, the Trojans triumphed and Aeneas married Lavinia.
Her mother Amata had already hanged herself in a fit of rage.

Some authorities, however, claim that the war started after the 5
marriage. But whatever happened, it is agreed that Lavinia conceived a son by the illustrious prince Aeneas. Before she could give
birth, Aeneas left this mortal vale near the Numicus River. Lavinia
was afraid of her stepson Ascanius, who now ruled in his father's
place, and she retreated into the forest. There she bore Aeneas'
posthumous son whom (according to some sources) she named
Julius Silvius. Ascanius, however, was kinder to his stepmother 6
than she had expected; he voluntarily withdrew to Alba, a city

condidisset, ultro secedens Lavinie regnum patrium liquit, quod
Lavinia, veterem pectori generositatem gerens, honeste atque pudice vivens summa cum diligentia tenuit illudque tam diu servavit
donec Silvio pubescenti resignaret in nichilo diminutum.

7   Volunt tamen aliqui eam a silvis revocatam Melampodi cuidam
nupsisse et Silvium ab Ascanio fraterna benivolentia educatum.

: XLII :

De Didone seu Elissa Cartaginensium regina

1   Dido, cui prius Elyssa nomen, Cartaginis eque conditrix et regina
fuit. Huius quidem in veras laudes, paululum ampliatis fimbriis,
ire libet, si forte paucis literulis meis saltem pro parte notam, indigne obiectam decori sue viduitatis, abstergere queam.

2   Et ut altius in suam gloriam aliquantisper assummam, Phenices, ut satis vulgatum est, populi industria preclarissimi, ab extrema fere Egypti plaga in syrium venientes litus, plurimas et pre-
claras ibidem condidere urbes. Quibus inter alios rex fuit Agenor,
nostro, nedum suo, evo prefulgidus fama, a quo genus Didonis in-
3   clitum manasse creditum est. Cuius pater Belus Phenicum rex
cum, Cypro insula subacta, clausisset diem, eam virgunculam cum
Pygmaleone fratre grandiusculo Phenicum reliquit fidei. Qui Pyg-
maleonem constituentes genitoris in solium, Elyssam, puellulam et
forma eximiam, Acerbe seu Syceo vel Sycarbe—ut dicunt alii—
Herculis sacerdoti, qui primus erat post regem apud Tyrios honor,
coniugio iunxere.

4   Hi autem invicem sanctissime se amarunt. Erat pre ceteris mor-

which he had built for himself, and left Lavinia in possession of her father's kingdom. She carried the spirit of the ancient nobility in her breast and so lived honorably and virtuously, administering the realm with the utmost care until she turned it over intact to Silvius, now a young man.

Other versions, however, report that after Lavinia was recalled 7 from the forest, she married someone called Melampus, and that Silvius was raised with brotherly kindness by Ascanius.

: XLII :

Dido or Elissa, Queen of Carthage

Dido, formerly called Elissa, was both founder and queen of 1 Carthage. I should like, in genuine praise of this woman, to embroider somewhat upon my account, and I hope that my modest remarks may cleanse away (at least in part) the infamy undeservedly cast on the honor of her widowhood.

Regarding the question of Dido's glory, let us go back to antiq- 2 uity. As is well known, the Phoenicians were a people renowned for their industry who came from what is practically the remotest part of Egypt to the shores of Syria. There they built many famous cities. One of the Phoenician kings was Agenor, celebrated in our time, to say nothing of his own; Dido's glorious line is believed to trace its descent from him. Her father was Belus, king of 3 Phoenicia, who died on Cyprus after he had conquered the island. At his death he entrusted Elissa, still a young girl, and her brother Pygmalion, who was slightly older, to the care of the Phoenicians. They placed Pygmalion on his father's throne and gave the beautiful young Elissa in marriage to Acerbas or Sychaeus (or Sicarbas as he is sometimes called), a priest of Hercules. (Among the Tyrians priesthood was the next highest honor after that of king).

Extremely virtuous was the love that Dido and Acerbas had for 4

talibus cupidissimus et inexplebilis Pygmalion auri, sic et Acerba
ditissimus; esto, regis avaritia cognita, illud occultasset latebris.
Verum cum famam occultasse nequiverit, in aviditatem tractus,
Pygmalion, spe potiundi, per fraudem occidit incautum.

5   Quod cum cognovisset Elyssa, adeo inpatienter tulit ut vix abstineret a morte. Sane cum multum temporis consumpsisset in lacrimis et frustra sepius dilectissimum sibi vocasset Acerbam atque
in fratrem diras omnes execrationes expetisset, seu in somnis[1] mo-
nita — ut placet aliquibus — seu ex proprio mentis sue consilio, fugam capessere deliberavit, ne forsan et ipsa avaritia fratris traheretur in necem; et posita feminea mollicie et firmato in virile robur
animo, ex quo postea Didonis nomen meruit, Phenicum lingua
sonans quod virago latina, ante alia nonnullos ex principibus civi-
tatum, quibus variis ex causis Pygmalionem sciebat exosum, in
suam deduxit sententiam; et sumpta fratris classe, ad eam transfe-
rendam, seu in aliud, preparata, confestim navalibus compleri sotiis iussit et nocte, sumptis thesauris omnibus quos viri noverat et
quos fratri subtraxisse potuit, clam navibus imponi fecit et excogitata astutia, pluribus involucris harena repletis, sub figmento thesaurorum Sycei, videntibus omnibus, easdem honeravit; et cum
iam altum teneret pelagi, mirantibus ignaris, in mari proici involu-
cra iussit; et lacrimis se mortem, quam diu desideraverat, thesaurorum Acerbe summersione adinvenisse testata est, sed sotiis com-
pati, quos non dubitabat, si ad Pygmalionem irent, diris suppliciis
una secum ab avarissimo atque truci rege scarnificari; sane si se-

each other. Pygmalion, who was the greediest of men, had an insatiable desire for gold, and Acerbas was very rich. Although he was aware of the king's avarice and kept his own treasures hidden, Acerbas could not conceal the fact of his own wealth. Pygmalion, carried away by greed and hoping to get his hands on his brother-in-law's riches, treacherously killed the unsuspecting Acerbas.

When Elissa learned the news, she took it so much to heart 5 that she almost died. She wept for a long time, calling in vain, over and over again, to her beloved Acerbas; she also called down every frightful curse on her brother's head. Then, lest Pygmalion's greed bring about her own death, Elissa resolved to flee, either because she was warned to do so in a dream (according to some sources) or because it was her own idea. Womanly weakness was cast aside and her spirit hardened to manly strength; for this she later earned the name of 'Dido', the Phoenician equivalent of the Latin *virago*. She began by winning over to her side some princes in the city whom she knew to hate Pygmalion for various reasons. Next she seized her brother's ships, which had been readied for her own deportation or for some other purpose, and immediately had them manned by her own faithful sailors. During the night she secretly had placed on board all the riches she knew had belonged to her husband as well as whatever else she could take secretly from her brother. The third step in her shrewdly devised plan was to fill many bags with sand and, under the pretext that they were Sychaeus' treasure, to have them loaded on the ships in full view of everyone. Once they were out on the high seas—much to the surprise of those who who did not know of the trick—Dido ordered these bags to be thrown into the water. In tears she declared that, with the sinking of Acerbas' treasure, she would also find the death she had long sought. But she said that she felt pity for the sailors, who, if they returned to Pygmalion, would certainly be cut to pieces along with herself by the avaricious and cruel king. If,

cum fugam arripere vellent, non se illis et eorum oportunitatibus defuturam asseruit.

6 Quod miseri audientes naute, etsi egre natale solum patriosque penates linquerent, timore tamen seve mortis exterriti, in consensum exilii venere faciles; et, flexis proris, ea duce, in Cyprum ventum est, ubi virgines Veneri in litore libamenta, suorum more, solventes, ad solatium iuventutis et prolem procreandam rapuit; et Iovis antistitem cum omni familia premonitum, et magna huic fuge subsecutura vaticinantem, socium peregrinationis suscepit.

7 Et iam Creta post tergum et Sycilia a dextris relicta, litus flexit in affrum et, Massuliorum oram radens, sinum intravit, postea satis notum, quo tutam navibus stationem arbitrata, dare pausillum quietis fatigatis remigio statuit; ubi advenientibus vicinis desiderio visendi forenses et aliis comeatus et mercimonia portantibus, ut moris est, collocutiones et amicitie iniri cepte; et cum gratum appareret incolis eos ibidem mansuros esse et ab Uticensibus, olim a Tyro eque profectis, legatio suasisset sedes; confestim, esto audisset fratrem bella minantem, nullo territa metu, ne iniuriam inferre cuiquam videretur, et ne quis eam magnum aliquid suspicaretur facturam, non amplius quam quantum quis posset bovis occupare corio, ad sedem sibi constituendam, ab accolis telluris in litore mercata est.

8 O mulieris astutia! In frusta iussu suo concisum bovis corium fracturisque iunctis, longe amplius quam arbitrari potuerint venditores amplexa est et auspicio equini capitis bellicosam civitatem condidit, quam Cartaginem nuncupavit; et arcem a corio bovis Byrsam; et cum, quos fraude texerat, ostendisset thesauros, et in-

however, they wanted to join her in flight, she assured them that she would not fail to take care of them and their needs.

On hearing this, the wretched sailors, sorry as they were at 6 leaving their homes and the country of their birth, were also terrified at the prospect of a cruel death, and so readily consented to go into exile. They changed course and at Dido's command sailed to Cyprus. There, to comfort the young men and for purposes of procreation, Dido seized some girls who were on the shore making the customary sacrifice to Venus.[b] She also took as companion on her voyage a priest of Jupiter and all his family; he had been forewarned of her arrival and had prophesied that great things would come of this flight.

Leaving Crete behind and Sicily on her right, Dido headed for 7 Africa. She skirted the Massylian shore and finally entered the gulf that was later to become well known. Here, believing that she had found safe harbor for her ships, she decided to allow the weary oarsmen some rest. The people living nearby came to see the foreigners, and some brought provisions and merchandise. As usually happens, they began to converse and to form friendships. The natives seemed to want the newcomers to stay, and ambassadors from Utica, a city whose people had also emigrated from Tyre, urged them to settle in the region. Although Dido knew that her brother was threatening war, she was not afraid. For her new abode she immediately bought from the landowners on the coast only as much land as could be covered by the hide of an ox. This she did to avoid offending anyone and to allay any suspicion that she had great plans for the future.

What a clever woman she was! At Dido's order the hide of the 8 ox was cut into thin strips which, when joined together, encompassed much more land than the sellers had thought. Under the auspices of a horse's head that had been found, Dido built a warlike city; she called it Carthage and named the fortress Byrsa, after the oxhide. Displaying the treasure which she had hidden through

9 genti spe fuge animasset socios, surrexere illico menia, templa, forum et edificia publica et privata. Ipsa autem, datis populo legibus et norma vivendi, cum repente civitas evasisset egregia et ipsa inclita fama pulchritudinis invise et inaudite virtutis atque castimonie per omnem Affricam delata est.

10 Quam ob rem, cum in libidinem pronissimi homines Affri sint, factum est ut Musitanorum rex in concupiscentiam veniret eiusdem eamque quibusdam ex principibus civitatis sub belli atque desolationis surgentis civitatis denunciatione, ni daretur, in coniu-

11 gium postulavit. Qui cum novissent vidue regine sacrum atque inflexibile castitatis propositum et sibi timerent plurimum ne, petitoris frustrato desiderio, bello absorberentur, non ausi Didoni interoganti² quod poscebatur exponere verbis, reginam fallere et in optatum deducere sua sententia cogitarunt, eique dixere regem cupere eorum doctrina efferatam barbariem suam in mores humaniores redigere; et ob id, sub belli interminatione, preceptores ex eis poscere; verum eos ambigere quisnam ex eis tam grande vellet onus assummere ut, relicta patria, apud tam immanem regem moraturus iret.

12 Non sensit regina dolos, quin imo in eos versa: 'Egregii cives' inquit 'que segnities hec, que socordia? An ignoratis quia patri nascamur et patrie? nec eum rite civem dici posse qui pro salute publica mortem, si casus expostulet, nedum incomodum aliud renuat? Ite igitur alacres et parvo periculo vestro a patria ingens belli incendium removete.'

13 His regine redargutionibus visum est principibus obtinuisse quod vellent et vera regis detexere iussa. Quibus auditis, satis regine visum est se sua sententia petitum approbasse coniugium ingemuitque secum, non ausa suorum adversari dolo. Stante tamen

her stratagems, she inspired her fellow exiles with high hopes. Immediately there sprang up city walls, temples, a forum, and public and private buildings. She gave the people laws and a code of conduct. Soon Dido was known throughout Africa both for the rapid emergence of her splendid city and for her remarkable beauty and exceptional virtue and purity. 9

In consequence, the king of the Massitani lusted after Dido 10 (Africans being much inclined to sensuality) and besought the elders of Carthage that he might marry her, threatening war and the destruction of the growing city if she were not given to him. These 11 men knew of the widowed queen's sacred and inflexible resolve to maintain her chastity, and they were very much afraid that they would be destroyed by this war if the king's request were denied. When she questioned them, the elders did not dare to tell Dido plainly what the king wanted. Instead, they planned to deceive the queen and make her accede to their wishes through her own decision. And so the elders told her that the king wanted, with the help of their instruction, to bring his savage people to a more civilized way of life; hence he was asking them (under threat of war) for teachers; but they claimed not to know anyone who would be willing to undertake such a heavy task since it meant leaving one's own country to go and live with so barbarous a king.

The queen did not detect the trick. She turned to them and 12 said: "O noble citizens, what sloth, what negligence is this? Do you not know that we are born for father and for fatherland? Can that person rightly be called a true citizen who, when circumstances require it, refuses to sacrifice his interests, even his life, to preserve the public weal? Go forth gladly, then, and take a small risk to free your country from the enormous conflagration of war."

In light of these reproaches from the queen, it seemed to the el- 13 ders that they had obtained their objective. Then they revealed to her what the king really wanted. After she heard this, Dido realized that by her own pronouncement she had approved the re-

proposito, repente in consilium ivit quod sue pudicitie oportunum visum est dixitque se, si terminus adeundi virum detur, ituram.

14 Quo concesso atque adveniente Enea troiano nunquam viso, mori potius quam infringendam fore castimoniam rata, in sublimiori patrie parte, opinione civium manes placatura Sicei, rogum construxit ingentem et pulla tecta veste et cerimoniis servatis variis, ac hostiis cesis plurimis, illum conscendit, civibus frequenti 15 multitudine spectantibus quidnam factura esset. Que cum omnia pro votis egisset, cultro, quem sub vestibus gesserat, exerto ac castissimo apposito pectori vocatoque Syceo inquit: 'Prout vultis cives optimi, ad virum vado.' Et vix verbis tam paucis finitis, summa omnium intuentium mestitia, in cultrum sese precipitem dedit et auxiliis frustra admotis, cum perfodisset vitalia, pudicissimum effundens sanguinem, ivit in mortem.

16 O pudicitie inviolatum decus! O viduitatis infracte venerandum eternumque specimen, Dido! In te velim ingerant oculos vidue mulieres et potissime christiane tuum robur inspiciant; te, si possunt, castissimum effundentem sanguinem, tota mente considerent, et he potissime quibus fuit, ne ad secunda solum dicam, sed ad tertia et ulteriora etiam vota transvolasse levissimum! Quid inquient, queso, spectantes, Christi insignite caractere, exteram[3] mulierem gentilem, infidelem, cui omnino Christus incognitus, ad consequendam perituram laudem tam perseveranti animo, tam forti pectore in mortem usque pergere, non aliena sed sua illatam

quest for marriage, and she groaned inwardly but did not dare object to her people's subterfuge. Remaining firm, nonetheless, in her resolve, she suddenly adopted a plan that seemed compatible with her sense of virtue. Dido said that she would go if she were given a fixed date for going to her husband.

The reprieve was granted. Thus, even before the arrival of the 14 Trojan Aeneas (whom she never saw), Dido had already decided to die rather than violate her chastity. In the highest part of the city she built a great pyre; this the people believed she had constructed in order to appease the shade of Sychaeus. Dressed in a black robe, she performed the various rites, offered many sacrifices, and mounted the pyre in the presence of a great throng watching to see what she would do. When she had completed all 15 the ceremonies, Dido took out the knife that she had brought under her clothing. Placing it against her chaste breast and calling out to Sychaeus, she said: "In accordance with your wish, my people, I go to my husband." Hardly had she finished uttering these few words when, to the great sorrow of all the spectators, she threw herself headlong onto the knife. The vital organs were pierced and she died, shedding her pure blood as the onlookers rushed vainly to her aid.

What glory there is in inviolate chastity! O Dido, venerable and 16 eternal model of unsullied widowhood! I wish that women who have lost their husbands would turn their eyes upon you and that Christian women in particular would contemplate your strength. If they can, let them meditate upon how you shed your chaste blood—especially women for whom it is a trivial matter to drift into second, third, and even more marriages. These women, marked with the emblem of Christ—what will they say, I wonder, when they see before them a foreign woman, a pagan, an unbeliever, to whom Christ was completely unknown, go to her death for the sake of fleeting reputation? Rather than marry again,

manu, antequam in secundas nuptias iret? antequam venerandissimum observantie propositum violari permicteret?

Dicet arbitror aliqua, cum perspicacissime ad excusationes nostre sint femine: 'Sic faciendum fuit; destituta eram, in mortem parentes et fratres abierant, instabant blanditiis procatores, nequibam obsistere, carnea, non ferrea sum.'

17 O ridiculum! Dido quorum subsidio confidebat, cui exuli frater unicus erat hostis? Nonne et Didoni procatores fuere plurimi? Imo, et ipsa Dido eratne saxea aut lignea magis quam hodierne sint? Non equidem. Ergo mente saltem valens, cuius non arbitrabatur posse viribus evitare illecebras, moriens, ea via qua potuit evitavit.

Sed nobis, qui nos tam desertos dicimus, nonne Christus refugium est? Ipse quidem Redemptor pius in se sperantibus semper adest. An putas, qui pueros de camino ignis eripuit, qui Susannam de falso crimine liberavit, te de manibus adversantium non possit auferre, si velis? Flecte in terram oculos et aures obsera atque ad instar scopuli undas venientes expelle et immota ventos efflare sine: salvaberis.

18 Insurget forsan et altera dicens: 'Erant michi longe lateque protensus ager, domus splendida et[4] supellectilis regia et divitiarum ampla possessio; cupiebam effici mater, ne tam grandis substantia ad exteros deferretur.' O insanum desiderium! Nonne et Didoni absque filiis regnum erat? nonne[5] divitie regie? Erant equidem. Quid et ipsa mater effici recusavit? Quia sapientissime arbitrata est nil stolidius fore quam tibi destruere ut edifices alteri.

19 'Ergo castimoniam maculabo ut agris, ut splendide domui, ut supellectili pariam possessorem?' Sino, quod contigit sepissime, destructorem. Nonne, etsi tibi divitie ingentes, que profecto expendende, non abiciende sunt, et Christi pauperes multi sunt?

rather than break her holy resolve, she died by her own hand, steadfast in spirit, unshaken in her determination.

Our women show great acuity in excusing themselves, so I believe that someone will reply: "I *had* to marry again: I had been abandoned; my parents and my brothers were dead; suitors were urgent in their flattery; I couldn't resist; I'm made of flesh, not iron."

How ridiculous! Dido's only brother was an enemy to his exiled 17 sister — on whose help could *she* depend? Did Dido not have many suitors? Was Dido made of stone or wood any more than the women of our time? Certainly not! That is why she used her mental strength to escape in the only way she could — through death — the snares she lacked the physical strength to avoid.

But we who say that we are so abandoned, do we not have Christ as our refuge? Truly our holy Redeemer is always there for those who place their hopes in Him. Do you think that He who snatched the boys from the fiery furnace, who freed Susanna from false accusations, cannot rescue you from the hands of your enemies if you so desire? Lower your eyes to the ground, close your ears, and like a rock hurl back the oncoming waves; be still and let the winds blow. You will be saved.

Perhaps another woman will rise and say: "My domains 18 stretched far and wide, I had a beautiful house, royal furnishings, and great wealth. I wanted to be a mother so that this great fortune would not end up among strangers." What an insane desire! Did childless Dido not also have a kingdom? Did she not have a king's wealth? She certainly did! Why did she refuse to become a mother? Because she was of the wise opinion that nothing is more foolish than to ruin oneself so as to aggrandize another.

"Shall I then stain my virtue in order to give birth to an owner 19 for my fields, my splendid house, my furnishings?" (I pass over the fact that the heir very often proves to be a wastrel). Even if you have great wealth which should be spent and not thrown away, are

20 Quibus dum exhibes, tibi eterna palatia construis; quibus dum exhibes, castimoniam alio fulgore illustras. Preterea et amici sunt, quorum nulli aptiores heredes, cum tales habeas quales ipsa quesitos probaveris; filios autem, non quales volueris, sed quales natura concedet, habebis.

21 Veniet et tertia asserens quia sic illi fuerit agendum, cum parentes iusserint, consanguinei coegerint et affines suaserint; quasi ignoremus, ni sua concupiscentia suasisset, imo effrenata iussisset, predicta omnia frustrasset negatione unica. Potuit mori Dido ne viveret impudica; hec, ut pudica viveret, connubium negare non potuit.

22 Aderit, suo iudicio, astutior ceteris una que dicat: 'Iuvenis eram; fervet, ut nosti, iuventus; continere non poteram; doctoris gentium aientis: 'Melius est nubere quam uri' sum secuta consilium.' O quam bene dictum! Quasi ego aniculis imperem castitatem, vel non fuerit, dum firmavit animo castimoniam, iuvencula Dido! O scelestum facinus! Non a Paulo tam sancte consilium illud datur quin in defensionem facinoris persepe turpius alligetur. Exhaustas vires sensim cibis restaurare possumus: superfluas abstinentia minorare non possumus? Gentilis femina ob inanem gloriam fervori suo imperare potuit et leges imponere; christiana, ut consequatur eternam, imperare non potest! Hei michi! Dum fallere Deum talibus arbitramur, nos ipsos et honori caduco—ut eternum sinam—subtrahimus et in precipitium eterne damnationis inpellimus.

23 Erubescant igitur intuentes Didonis cadaver exanime; et dum causam mortis eius excogitant, vultus deiciant, dolentes quod a membro dyaboli christicole pudicitia superentur; nec putent, dum

not the poor of Christ numerous? In giving to them you build ev- 20
erlasting palaces for yourself; in giving to them you illumine your
virtue with new splendor. Besides, your friends make more suitable heirs than anyone else since they are as you have sought and
tested them. Children, however, are not as we would like them but
as nature permits.

A third woman will come and declare that she had to marry 21
again because her parents ordered her, her relatives forced her, and
her neighbors encouraged her. As if we did not know that with a
single denial she could have overcome everything had her own passion not spurred her on — nay, had not unbridled lust commanded
her. This woman could not refuse marriage to live honorably, but
Dido could die so as not to live dishonorably.

Still another will present herself who (in her own opinion) is 22
more clever than the rest, and she will say: "I was young. As you
know, youth is ardent; I could not remain continent. St. Paul says
that it is better to marry than to burn,ᶜ and I followed his advice."
How well spoken! As if I recommended chastity only to old
women, or as if Dido had not been a young woman when she determined to remain chaste! How wicked it is that Paul's holy
counsel should so often be dishonorably quoted in defense of a
shameful act! We can gradually restore our spent forces with food:
can we not diminish superfluous forces with abstinence? That pagan woman, for the sake of empty glory, was able to master her ardor and subject herself to principle; but a Christian woman cannot practice such control in order to acquire eternal glory! Alas! In
our belief that we can deceive God in this way, we forego transi-
tory glory, not to mention that which is eternal, and we plunge towards the brink of eternal damnation.

Let the women of today blush, then, as they contemplate 23
Dido's lifeless body. While they ponder the reason for her death,
let them bow their heads in sorrow that Christian women are surpassed in chastity by a woman who was a limb of Satan. Let them

lacrimas dederint et pullas assumpserint vestes, defuncto peregisse omnia. In finem usque servandus est amor, si adimplere velint vi-
24 duitatis officium. Nec existiment ad ulteriora vota transire; quod nonnulle persepe faciunt, potius ut sue prurigini, sub ficto coniugii nomine, satisfaciant, quam ut sacro obsequantur connubio, impudicitie labe carea<n>t[6]. Quid enim aliud est tot hominum amplexus exposcere, tot inire, quam, post Valeriam Messalinam, caveas et fornices intrare?

25 Sed de hoc alias. Fateor enim[7] laboris incepti nimium excessisse terminos; sed quis adeo sui compos est quin aliquando ultra propositum efferatur ab impetu? Ignoscant queso qui legerint et nos unde divertimus revertamur.

26 Didonem igitur exanguem cum lacrimis publicis et merore cives, non solum humanis, sed divinis etiam honoribus funus exercentes magnificum, extulere pro viribus; nec tantum publice matris et regine loco, sed deitatis inclite eisque faventis assidue, dum stetit Cartago, aris templisque excogitatis sacrificiis coluere.

: XLIII :

De Nicaula Ethyopum regina

1 Nicaulam extrema — ut percipi potest — Ethyopum produxit[1] barbaries; que quidem tanto memoratu dignior est quanto, inter incultiores exorta, moribus effulsit splendidior.

Constat enim — si fides datur antiquis — hanc, deficientibus Pharaonibus, seu eorum prolem seu alteram, Ethyopum atque

not think that by mourning and dressing in black they have executed all the duties owed to the dead. Love must be maintained to the end if they want to fulfill the obligations of widowhood. Nor 24 should they think of contracting another marriage; this some do under the false name of matrimony more to satisfy their passion than to observe its sacramental character and avoid the defilement caused by lust. In fact, how can seeking and having intercourse with so many men differ from frequenting the brothels after the example of Valeria Messalina?[d]

But I shall speak of this at another time, for I admit that I have 25 greatly exceeded the limits of the task I have undertaken. Who, however, is so self-controlled that he is not occasionally diverted from his purpose by the force of his arguments? I beg the reader's pardon and return to the point where I digressed.

And so Dido's countrymen, amid public mourning and grief, 26 honored her in death as best they could and staged a magnificent funeral at which she was accorded both human and divine honors. While Carthage stood, they venerated her with altars, temples, and special sacrifices, not only as their common mother and their ruler, but also as an illustrious goddess and their constant protector.

: XLIII :

Nicaula, Queen of Ethiopia

As far as I can determine, Nicaula was a product of remote and 1 barbaric Ethiopia. She is the more worthy of remembrance as her splendid moral principles had their origin among uncivilized folk.

The following facts are known (if we can believe the ancient sources): when the dynasty of the Pharaohs came to an end,

Egyptiorum et—ut nonnulli asserunt—Arabum clariss[...]
fuisse reginam et in Meroe, insula Nyli permaxima, habu[...]
giam ibique tam grandi divitiarum habundasse copia ut [...]
in hac fere mortales excessisse ceteros.

2 Quas inter divitiarum delitias, non ocio et molliciei f[...]
ditam legimus, quin imo, etsi preceptorem ignoremus[...]
rerum periturarum scientia preditam sensimus, ut m[...]
sit; quod etiam sacre testari videntur litere, quar[...]
monstratur.

3 Hanc, quam Sabam vocant, audita scientie Sal[...]
florentis, fama, que celebris totum iam complever[...]
fuisse miratam, cum consueverint stolidi seu ign[...]
lia, non mirari. Et, quod longe magis, non sol[...]
imo a Meroe, fere altero orbis ex angulo, insig[...]
Ethyopes Egyptiosque et Rubri Maris litora[...]
dines, tam splendido comitatu tanque magn[...]
permaximo famulatu venit illum auditura[...]
mon, regum omnium ditissimus, mulier[...]
tus sit.

4 Que summo cum honore ab eo sus[...]
suisset quedam, et eorum solutiones[...]
tro confessa est Salomonis sapientia[...]
norum ingeniorum capacitatem excede[...]

5 non studio quesitam fuisse. Inde dona exhibuit m[...]
que fuisse creduntur balsama sudantes arbuscule, quas p[...]

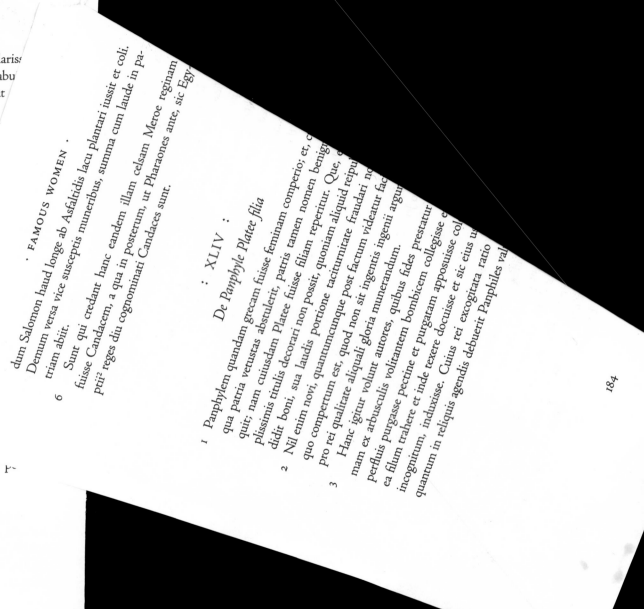

dum Salomon haud longe ab Asfaltidis lacu plantari iussit et coli.
Demum versa vice susceptis muneribus, summa cum laude in patriam abiit.

6 Sunt qui credant hanc eandem illam celsam Meroe reginam
fuisse Candacem, a qua in posterum, ut Pharaones ante, sic Egy[...]
ptii? reges diu cognominati Candaces sunt.

: XLIV :

De Panphyle Platee filia

1 Panphylem quandam grecam fuisse feminam comperio; et, c[...]
qua patria vetustas abstulerit, patris tamen nomen benig[...]
quit; nam cuiusdam Platee fuisse filiam reperitur. Que, [...]
plissimis titulis decorari non possit, quoniam aliquid repu[...]
didit boni, sua laudis portione taciturnitate fraudari n[...]

2 Nil enim novi, quantumcunque post factum videatur fac[...]
quo compertum est, quod non sit ingentis ingenii argu[...]
pro rei qualitate aliquali gloria munerandum.

3 Hanc igitur volunt autores, quibus fides prestatur[...]
mam ex arbusculis volitantem bombicem collegisse e[...]
perfluis purgasse pectine et purgatam appossuisse col[...]
ea filum trahere et inde texere docuisse et sic eius us[...]
incognitum, induxisse. Cuius rei excogitata ratio[...]
quantum in reliquis agendis debuerit Panphiles val[...]

CHAPTER XLIV

Asphaltites. In turn Nicaula received gifts from him and at last returned home with great praise.

Some authorities believe that this woman can be identified with   6
Candace, the great queen of Meroe, after whom the kings of
Egypt (formerly known as Pharaohs) were for a long time called
Candaces.

: XLIV :

Pamphile, Daughter of Platea

Pamphile, I find, was a Greek woman. Time has erased any   1
knowledge of her country,[a] but it has kindly left us her father's
name: we know that she was the daughter of a man called Platea.
Although Pamphile cannot be adorned with grand titles, she did
benefit the commonwealth and so must not be passed over in silence and thus cheated of her share of praise. No matter how easy   2
it may appear afterwards, no one has ever discovered something
new without its proving the power of the inventor's intellect and
without bringing glory in proportion to its quality.

Trustworthy sources report, therefore, that Pamphile was the   3
first to pick the cotton wool given off by plants, cleanse it of resid-
ual matter by means of a comb, and place it on the distaff. Then
she demonstrated how to make thread from the cotton and how to
weave, and so introduced for this material a use that had been unknown up to her own time. This invention of the art of weaving
will easily show how capable Pamphile must have been in other respects.

: XLV :

De Rhea Ylia vestali virgine

1 Rhea Ylia generosi sanguinis precipua claritate inter Ytalos emicuit olim; nam per Silvios, Albanorum reges, successive regnantes atque descendentes ab Enea, inclito Troianorum duce, traxit originem, Numitore ex dictis Albanorum rege prestante. Ea quippe adhuc existente virguncula, factum est ut Amulius, Numitoris frater iunior, inpulsus regni cupidine, iure gentium parvipenso, Numitorem vi regno privaret; in quem ne seviret, fraterna intercessit pietas: contentus ut ruri relegatus privato vacaret ocio.

2 In Lausum vero adolescentulum, Numitoris filium, ut regni amoveret emulum, animo truci desevit eoque ceso Yliam, Lausi sororem, adhuc puellulam servavit. Verum ut illi auferretur connubii spes omnis et prolis, vestalibus virginibus addidit eamque perpetuam virginitatem profiteri coegit.

3 Que cum in pleniorem devenisset etatem, stimulis acta venereis, quo pacto nescitur, eam tamen in amplexus devenisse viri turgidus patefecit uterus; nam pregnans effecta Romulum Remumque, romane urbis parentes uno et eodem partu enixa est.

4 Quod ob crimen, quantumcunque regia fuerit femina, instituto veteri regioque iussu expositi sunt filii et ipsa viva infossa est. Sane etsi eius corpus terra obrutum sit, natorum opus egregium in sublime culmen ipsius nomen evexit egitque ut id posteritati venerabile foret quod tyramnus lege sacra abolesse conatus est.

5 Hanc dum mente intueor videoque sacras vestes et sanctimonialium velamenta Veneris aliquandiu tegere furta, quin quorundam insaniam rideam continere nequeo. Sunt quidam qui, ut avari portiunculam dotis natis subtrahant, sub pretextu devotionis par-

: XLV :

Rhea Ilia, a Vestal Virgin

In former times Rhea Ilia shone among the people of Italy for the   1
exceptional brilliance of her noble lineage. Her ancestors were the
Silvii, hereditary kings of the Albans as well as descendants of
Aeneas, glorious leader of the Trojans. She was the daughter of
King Numitor of Alba, a member of the Silvii family.

While Ilia was still a girl, Numitor's younger brother Amulius,
spurred by desire for power and scorning the law of nations, over-
threw Numitor by force. Fraternal sentiment forbade him to treat
Numitor cruelly, and Amulius was satisfied to banish his brother
to a life of retirement in the country. However, to remove a poten-   2
tial rival for the throne, he acted violently and pitilessly against
Lausus, Numitor's youthful son. Amulius killed Lausus but
spared his young sister Ilia. By making her a Vestal and forcing her
to take a vow of perpetual virginity, he took away all her hopes of
having a husband and children.

When Ilia grew up, she came somehow under the powerful in-   3
fluence of concupiscence. Her swelling womb disclosed an intimate relationship with a man, and she gave birth to Romulus and
Remus, twins and founders of the city of Rome. As punishment   4
for this sin, ancient law and royal decree ordained that, despite her
royal parentage, she should be buried alive and her children exposed. Yet although her body may have been covered with earth,
her children's noble achievement raised her name to the highest
pinnacle of fame. They ensured the reverence of posterity for their
mother's memory which a tyrant had attempted to destroy on the
grounds of sacred law.

So, when I reflect upon the case of this woman and see the holy   5
vestments and veils of nuns hiding furtive love, I cannot help
laughing at the madness of some people. There are certain individ-

vulas filias aut quandoque puberes sed coactas monasticis claustris, nescio utrum dicam, claudunt aut perdunt: aientes se Deo[1] dicasse virginem que intenta precibus rem suam deducet in melius morientique piorum lucrabitur sedes.

6   O ridiculum stolidum! Ignorant ociosam feminam Veneri militare et summe publicis invidere meretriculis earumque cellas suis preponere claustris; et dum secularia coniugia spectant, vestes ornatusque varios, choreas et festos dies, se, nulla coniugii habita experientia, vere et ab ipso vite huius ingressu viduas deflent, fortunam suam, parentum animas, victas et claustra tota execrantur mente, nec alibi solature mesta precordia recurrunt quam in meditationem quo pacto in fugam carcerem erumpere possint aut saltem intromictere mechos, incestu[2] querentes agere furtim quod palam illis sublatum est fecisse coniugio.

7   He sunt, non dicam omnium, sed plurimarum, contemplationes in Deum precesque transcendentes[3] ethera, quibus aucti salvique fient qui illas intrusere carceri. Heu miseri parentes <et>[4] necessarii quicunque alii, dum alias <cogitant>[5] posse perpeti quod ipsi nequirent et fugiunt miseri! Persepe flentur stupra turpissima, infames partus, nepotes expositi aut infanda morte necati, exclusiones ignominiose fugeque; et postremo dehonestatas oportet alere quas honestas potuisset avarus coniugibus iungere.

8   Sentiant ergo dementes, si alienas vires suis metiri non volunt, quoniam non inscie, non parvule, non coacte, Deo dicande sint virgines, quin imo persancte ab infantia patria in domo nutrite,

uals who are greedy enough to take away from their daughters their pittance of a dowry. Under the pretext of religion, they confine—or should I say condemn?—these girls to nuns' cells, sometimes when they are still very young, sometimes when almost mature, but always under force. Then the claim is made that a virgin has been dedicated to God whose prayers will advance her father's affairs and gain Paradise for him when he dies.

How ridiculous and foolish! These people do not know that an 6 idle woman serves Venus and is consumed with envy of the public prostitutes, whose brothels she prefers to her own cloister. When nuns see the weddings of secular women, their dresses and various ornaments, dances and festivals, and realize that they themselves will have no experience of marriage, they feel sorry for themselves. As though widowed on the doorstep of life, they curse mightily their destiny, the souls of their parents, their own veils, and their cloisters. As consolation for the sadness in their hearts, their sole recourse is to plan how they can escape from their prison or at least bring their lovers inside, trying to take secretly the sexual pleasure whose open enjoyment in marriage has been denied them.

Such are the holy meditations typical of, I won't say all, but certainly the majority of nuns. Such are the prayers which rise up to heaven for the prosperity and salvation of those who have imprisoned these women. Wretched are those parents and near relations and anyone else at all who think that others can endure what they themselves flee from as intolerable! Often do they weep over dishonorable acts of adultery, shameful births, grandchildren abandoned or foully murdered, and the ignominious expulsion or flight of their daughters. In the end, it is necessary to provide for the disgraced women whom the greedy father could have given away in marriage while they were still pure.

Let these fools realize, then, if they do not want to measure the 8 strength of others by their own, that girls must not be consecrated to God while they are ignorant or too young or under coercion.

honestate et probandis moribus imbute; etate provecte et quid
agant integra mente noscentes, sponte sua, non coacte, iugum sub-
9 euntes virginitatis perpetue. Quas rarissimas inveniri arbitror; sed
longe melius est talium parvum esse numerum quam multitudine
illecebri Dei sanctuarium prophanare.

: XLVI :

De Gaia Cirilla Tarquinii Prisci regis coniuge

1 Gaia Cirilla, etsi eius originis nullam stare memoriam compere-
rim, romanam tamen aut etruscam fuisse mulierem reor, et veterum constat autoritate quoniam Tarquinii Prisci Romanorum regis fuerit gratissima coniunx.

2   Hec cum esset prestantissimi ingenii femina, quantumcunque
regia coniunx et in regia esset domo, ocio torpere passa non est,
quin imo cum se lanificio dedisset (quod credam eo tempore apud
Latinos honorabile) adeo erga illud egregiam opificem atque soler-
tem fecit ut in hodiernum usque nominis sui fama protensa sit;
3 nec evo suo publico caruit munere. Nam cum apud Romanos mi-
rabilis et amantissima femina haberetur, nondum eis marcentibus
deliciis asyaticis, instituto publico cautum est ut ab intrantibus
novis nuptis[1] primitus sponsorum suorum domos unaqueque ro-
garetur quo vocaretur nomine, rogataque se evestigio Gaiam vocari profiteretur, quasi ex hoc sumpture essent future frugalitatis
omen.

4   Quod quantumcunque apud insolentes modernorum animos

On the contrary, they should be well brought up from childhood in their father's home and taught honesty and virtuous behavior. Then, when they are grown and know full well what they are doing, let them submit voluntarily and without duress to the yoke of perpetual virginity. I believe there would be very few such women, 9 but it is far better for their number to be small than to profane the sanctuary of God with a crowd of frivolous, pleasure-seeking females.

꞉ XLVI ꞉

Gaia Cyrilla, Wife of King Tarquinius Priscus

Although I do not find any record of her origin, I think that Gaia 1 Cyrilla was a Roman or an Etruscan woman. Ancient testimony confirms that she was the beloved wife of Tarquinius Priscus, king of Rome.

A woman of extraordinary intellectual capabilities, Gaia did 2 not allow herself to idle away her time, despite the fact that she was the wife of a king and lived in a royal palace. She dedicated herself instead to the art of woolworking, which I believe was an honorable occupation at that time among the Latins. In this she was such an eminent and skillful artisan that her fame has endured down to our own age. Nor did she lack public recognition among her contemporaries. In fact, she was admired and greatly 3 loved by the Romans, who had not yet been corrupted by Asiatic luxury. Indeed, it was ordered by public decree that every new bride entering her husband's house for the first time should be asked her name; the immediate response was to be 'Gaia', as if these women were adopting an omen of future frugality.

However trifling this may seem to the proud modern spirit, I 4

videatur perminimum, non dubitem quin apud prudentiores, illius seculi simplicitate pensata, optime et plurimum laudande mulieris videatur inditium.

: XLVII :

De Sapho puella lesbia et poeta

1 Saphos lesbia ex Mitilena urbe puella fuit, nec amplius sue originis posteritati relictum est. Sane, si studium inspexerimus, quod annositas abstulit pro parte restitutum videbimus, eam scilicet ex honestis atque claris parentibus genitam; non enim illud unquam degener animus potuit desiderasse vel actigisse plebeius.

2 Hec etenim, etsi quibus temporibus claruerit ignoremus, adeo generose fuit mentis ut, etate florens et forma, non contenta solum literas iungere novisse, ampliori fervore animi et ingenii suasa vivacitate, conscenso studio vigili per abruta Parnasi vertice celso, se felici ausu, Musis non renuentibus, immiscuit; et laureo pervagato nemore in antrum usque Apollinis evasit et, Castalio proluta latice, Phebi sumpto plectro, sacris nynphis choream traentibus, sonore cithare fides tangere et expromere modulos puella non dubitavit; que quidem etiam studiosissimis viris difficilia plurimum visa sunt.

3 Quid multa? Eo studio devenit suo ut usque in hodiernum clarissimum suum carmen testimonio veterum lucens sit, et erecta illi fuerit statua enea et suo dicata nomini, et ipsa inter poetas celebres numerata; quo splendore profecto, non clariora sunt re-

do not doubt that wiser men, after taking into account the simplicity of that era, will consider it the mark of an excellent woman
who deserves the highest praise.

: XLVII :

Sappho, Girl of Lesbos and Poetess

Sappho was a girl from the city of Mytilene on the island of   1
Lesbos. No other fact has reached us about her origin. But if
we consider her *métier*, we will see restored to her part of what
time has destroyed: namely, that Sappho must have been born of
honorable and distinguished parents, for no ignoble soul could
have wanted to write poetry, nor could a vulgar one have actually
done it.

We do not know when Sappho lived. She was, however, of   2
such a noble disposition that, in the bloom of youth and beauty,
she was not satisfied solely to write in prose. Spurred on by a
wider spiritual and intellectual fervor, Sappho studied diligently
and ascended the steep slopes of Parnassus. On that lofty summit,
with happy daring she joined the welcoming Muses. Wandering
through the laurel grove, she arrived at the cave of Apollo, bathed
in the Castalian spring, and took up Phoebus' plectrum. As the sacred nymphs danced, this young girl did not hesitate to strike the
strings of the resonant cithara and bring forth melodies, something that seems extremely difficult even for the most skilled of
males.

In short, Sappho's art reached such heights that her poetry, re-   3
nowned in ancient testimony, is still famous in our own day. A
bronze statue was erected and dedicated to her, and she was included among the famous poets. Such glory neither the crowns of

gum dyademata, non pontificum infule, nec etiam triunphantium lauree.

4   Verum — si danda fides est — uti feliciter studuit, sic infelici amore capta est. Nam, seu facetia seu decore seu alia gratia, cuiusdam iuvenis dilectione, imo intolerabili occupata peste, cum ille desiderio suo non esset accomodus, ingemiscens in eius obstinatam duritiem, dicunt versus flebiles cecinisse; quos ego elegos fuisse putassem, cum tali sint elegi attributi materie, ni legissem ab ea, quasi preteritorum carminum formis spretis, novum adinventum genus, diversis a ceteris incedens pedibus, quod adhuc ex eius nomine saphycum appellatur.

5   Sed quid? Accusande videntur Pyerides que, tangente Anphyone liram[1], ogygia saxa movisse potuerunt et adolescentis cor, Sapho canente, mollisse noluerunt.

: XLVIII :

De Lucretia Collatini coniuge

1   Lucretia romane pudicitie dux egregia atque sanctissimum vetuste parsimonie decus, filia fuit Lucretii Spurii Tricipitini, clarissimi inter Romanos viri, et coniunx Tarquinii Collatini, olim Egerii fratris Tarquinii Prisci filii; incertum utrum oris formositate an honestate morum inter romanas matronas speciosior visa sit.

2   Que cum obsidente Tarquinio Superbo Ardeam civitatem, apud Collatii oppidum haud longe ab Urbe, in viri edes secessisset, actum est ut in castris, cum obsidio traheretur in longum, cenanti-

kings nor pontifical mitres nor even the conquerors' laurel can surpass.

But, if the story is true, Sappho was as unhappy in love as she   4
was happy in her poetic craft. Either because of his wit or good
looks or because of some other charm she became infatuated with
a young man (better still, fell prey to an intolerable pestilence).
He, however, did not reciprocate her passion. Lamenting his stubborn resistance, Sappho is said to have composed mournful verses.
I should have thought that these would be elegiac distichs, since
they are appropriate to such subjects, had I not read that Sappho
scorned the verse forms used by her predecessors and wrote a new
kind of verse in a completely different meter which is still called
'Sapphic' after her.

But to what effect? The Muses, it seems, should be blamed: 5
they were able to move the stones of Ogygia when Amphion
played the lyre, but they were unwilling to soften the young man's
heart when Sappho sang.

: XLVIII :

Lucretia, Wife of Collatinus

Lucretia, a leading example of Roman modesty and most divine   1
ornament of ancient frugality, was the daughter of Spurius
Lucretius Tricipitinus, a famous Roman. Her husband was
Tarquinius Collatinus, son of the late Egerius who had been the
brother of Tarquinius Priscus. Whether Lucretia appeared lovelier
among the Roman matrons because of the beauty of her countenance or because of her upright conduct is open to debate.

When Tarquinius Superbus was besieging the city of Ardea,   2
Lucretia retreated to her husband's house near Collatia, a town
not far from Rome. The siege lasted a long time. One evening the

bus regiis iuvenibus, inter quos et Collatinus erat, et forte nimio calentibus vino, caderet sermo de coniugum honestate. Et cum suam ceteris — ut moris est — unusquisque preferret, in consilium hoc[1] itum est ut, conscensis citatis equis visisque quibus noctu, eis bella gerentibus, ignare coniuges exercerentur offitiis, probabiliorem oculata fide perciperent.

3   Sane cum iuvenes regias Romam inter coequales ludentes invenissent, versis equis devenere Collatium; ubi cum mulieribus suis lanificio vacantem et nullo exornatam cultu invenere Lucretiam; quam ob rem iudicio omnium laudabilior visa est. Collatinus autem reliquos iuvenes benigne suscepit in domum, in qua, dum honorantur, Sextus, Superbi filius, impudicos oculos in honestatem atque formositatem caste mulieris iniecit; et nephasto succensus igne, per vim potiundam, si aliter non detur, eiusdem venustatem tacito secum consilio disponit.

4   Nec multis interpositis diebus, urgente insania, clam castris relictis, nocte venit Collatium. Ubi, eo quod viri consanguineus esset, a Lucretia comiter susceptus et honoratus, postquam domum omnem tacitam sensit et sic omnes sopitos arbitratus, exerto gladio, cubiculum intravit Lucretie, quis esset aperuit minatusque illi mortem si vocem emicteret aut sue non acquiesceret voluntati.

5   Quam cum reluctantem desiderio suo et mortis impavidam cerneret, ad damnandam recurrens astutiam, inquit se illam secus servum ex suis occisurum[2]; et cunctis eam a se ob adulterium cum adultero cesam dicere. Substitit his auditis tremebunda mulier et a tam obscena infamia terrefacta, timens, si eo occideretur pacto,

young men of royal blood, including Collatinus, were having supper together. Warmed perhaps by too much wine, they began to
argue about the honor of their spouses. Naturally each placed his
own wife ahead of the others. At last they decided to return
swiftly on horseback to see how the unsuspecting wives were occupying their time at night while their husbands were away at war;
they could then verify with their own eyes whose was the most
praiseworthy wife.

In Rome the young men found their wives enjoying the com- 3
panionship of other women of similar age. They turned their
horses around and went to Collatia, where they discovered
Lucretia, plainly dressed, spinning wool with her ladies. Thereupon everyone agreed that she seemed more deserving of praise
than the others. Collatinus then graciously welcomed the other
young men into his house. While they were being entertained
there, Sextus, the son of Superbus, cast immodest looks at the
beauty and virtue of the chaste Lucretia. Burning with illicit passion, he decided in his own mind to possess her through force if
he could not enjoy her charms in any other way.

Not many days had passed when, driven on by his mad love, 4
Sextus secretly left the camp and went at night to Collatia. He was
her husband's relative, so Lucretia received him courteously and
hospitably. Later, when Sextus observed that the house had fallen
silent, he assumed that everyone was asleep and entered Lucretia's
bedroom with his sword drawn. Making himself known to her, he
threatened her with death if she cried out or did not yield to his
will. When Sextus saw that Lucretia resisted his desire and was 5
not afraid to die, he resorted to a damnable trick: he said that he
would kill her, along with one of her male servants, and tell ev-
erybody that he had killed them because they had committed
adultery. Hearing this, the trembling woman could not move,
terrified as she was at the prospect of such an obscene slur. Fearing
that, if she died under these circumstances, there would be no one

purgatorem sue innocentie defuturum; et ob id aspernanti animo corpus permisit adultero.

6   Qui cum illecebri voluptati sue satisfecisset et abiisset iudicio suo victor, egra tam scelesti facinoris, Lucretia, elucescente die, Tricipitinum patrem et Brutum, Collatini affinem, amentem usque in diem illam existimatum, aliosque necessarios confestim accersiri

7   iussit, et virum. Quibus advenientibus, que a Sexto nocte intempesta in eam gesta sint, cum lacrimis et ordine retulit; et cum eam flentem misere solarentur affines, cultrum, quem sub veste texerat, educens inquit: 'Ego me, si peccato absolvo, supplicio non libero; nec ulla deinceps impudica Lucretie vivet exemplo.'

8   Hisque dictis illum in pectus impegit innocuum et vulneri incumbens, vidente viro ac patre, moribunda collapsa est; nec diu et animam cum sanguine fudit.

9   Infelix equidem pulcritudo eius et tanto clarius, nunquam satis laudata, pudicitia sua dignis preconiis extollenda est, quanto acrius ingesta vi ignominia expiata; cum ex eadem non solum reintegratum sit decus, quod feditate facinoris iuvenis labefactarat ineptus, sed consecuta sit romana libertas.

: XLIX :

De Thamiri Scitharum regina

1   Tamiris Scitharum regina fuit. Qui quidem Scythe, cum in sterili solo et sub gelida celi plaga Rypheis[1] Yperboreisque annexi montibus sint et inde sibi tantum fere cogniti, ex quibus Thamiris sit orta parentibus, seu cui iuncta connubio, incognitum est; et ideo

to clear her innocent name, Lucretia unwillingly gave her body to the adulterer.

Sextus satisfied his wicked desire and went away, as he thought, 6 victorious. At daybreak, Lucretia, much distressed by so wicked a crime, immediately sent for her father Tricipitinus, Collatinus' relative Brutus (hitherto considered mad), and other members of the family as well as her husband. Upon their arrival, she told them 7 tearfully, but coherently, what Sextus had done to her in the dead of night. While her relatives consoled her as she wept miserably, Lucretia took out a knife that she had hidden under her garment and said: "Although I absolve myself of the sin, I do not exempt myself from the punishment, and in future no woman will live dishonorably because of Lucretia's example."

No sooner had she said this than she drove the knife into her 8 innocent breast, bent forward over her wound, and fell dying before the very eyes of her husband and her father. Shortly thereafter Lucretia poured out her soul together with her blood.

Hers was an unfortunate beauty. Her purity, which can never 9 be sufficiently commended, should be extolled all the more highly as she expiated with such severity the ignominy thrust violently upon her. Her action not only restored the reputation that a dissolute young man had destroyed with his filthy crime, but led ultimately to freedom for Rome.[a]

: XLIX :

Tamyris, Queen of Scythia

Tamyris was queen of Scythia. We know nothing of her parents 1 or her husband: the Scythians inhabit a sterile region under cold skies near the Riphaean and the Hyperborean Mountains, and so they are known to few people apart from themselves. As for the

hac tantum, quantum ad insigne nobilitatis, nota conspicua est, quod feris et indomitis populis imperarit, Cyro iam Asye regna tenente.

2   Qui cum — forsan ut clarius nosceretur Thamiris — in cupidinem regni scythici deveniret, magis ad suam gloriam extollendam quam imperium augendum (audierat quippe pauperes et silvestres homines Scythas fore, sed a maximis regibus eo usque fuisse invictos); hac ergo tractus aviditate, in Thamirim reginam viduam egit exercitum.

3   Cuius cum prenovisset adventum Thamiris, esto toti Asye et fere orbi gestorum amplitudine formidabilis foret, non tamen, ut femina territa, latebras petiit, seu leges pacis caduceatore postulavit medio; quin imo congregatis copiis et belli dux facta, cum posset navato opere obsistere, eum cum omni exercitu Araxem transire passa est et suos intrare fines, arbitrata sagax femina longe melius expugnari Cyri rabiem infra terminos suos posse quam extra.

4   Et certior facta eum ad interiora penetrasse regni, adolescentulo filio unico tercia copiarum parte concessa, iussit ut Cyro obviam pugnaturus procederet. Cyrus vero, tam qualitate locorum et gentium moribus pensatis quam auditis, sentiens venientem cum exercitu iuvenem, fraude quam armis vincere statuit; castrisque vino, quod nondum noverant Scythe, epulisque et deliciis ceteris confertis relictis, fugam finxit.

5   Que vacua cum intrasset iuvenis, quasi victor hosteque fugato letus, cum Scythis non ad bellum, sed ad epulas invitatus, ample cibos et pocula incognita ingurgitare cepere. Ex quo, soluta disci-

distinction of nobility, she is famous for only one thing, namely, that she governed a fierce and invincible people during the period when Cyrus had already acquired his Asian kingdoms.

What transpired next may have occurred in order to make   2 Tamyris better known. Cyrus began to covet the Scythian realm, though more as an enhancement of his own glory than an expansion of his empire: he had heard that the Scythians were a poor and wild people, but one that so far had never been conquered by even the greatest kings. This greed eventually drove Cyrus to lead his army against the widowed queen.

Tamyris knew in advance of his arrival. Despite the fact that   3 Cyrus was feared throughout Asia and almost the whole world because of his great exploits, she did not, like some timid female, look for a place to hide, nor did she seek terms of peace through the mediation of an ambassador. Instead she gathered her forces and became their commander during the war. Tamyris could have put up an active resistance, but she allowed Cyrus and his entire army to cross the Araxes River and enter her country. This clever woman thought that she could defeat Cyrus' fury far better within, rather than outside, the borders of her own land.

When she had been informed that he had penetrated the interior of her kingdom, Tamyris entrusted a third of her army to her   4 only son, still a youth, and ordered him to go and fight Cyrus. Hearing that the young man was coming with his army, Cyrus weighed both the features of the terrain and the customs of those people against what he had been told; then he decided to win by deceit rather than by battle. Hence he feigned flight and left his camp full of wine (which was still unknown to the Scythians), fine food, and other luxuries.

Tamyris' youthful son entered the abandoned camp as if he   5 were a conqueror rejoicing in his rout of the enemy and as if he had been invited, along with the other Scythians, not to fight but to feast. They all began to gorge themselves on the unfamiliar food

plina militari, somnus affuit; quo sepulti, superveniens Cyrus, illum cum reliquis dedit in mortem; et quasi certus victorie ad ulteriora processit.

6   Tamiris autem cum audisset suorum cedem, etsi plurimum ob unici filii necem vidua moveretur, non tamen femineo more se dedit in lacrimas, quin imo, illis ira et vindicte cupiditate sedatis, cum residuo copiarum, ea arte qua captum filium audierat, etiamsi non omicterentur referta poculis castra, hostem, etsi astutissimus esset, capi posse existimavit; et locorum gnara, fugam simulans, avidum secutorem inter steriles geluque horridos montes, non longo viarum tractu, deduxit atque conclusit et inopem oportunitatum fere omnium, inter aspreta saltusque montium conversa, cum omni exercitu, fere delevit; nec ipse Cyrus evasit quin cruenta morte vidue satiaret iram.

7   Thamiris autem efferato animo iussit inter cadavera Cyri corpus exquiri; cui comperto auferri caput et in utrem, sanguine suorum plenum, immicti mandavit; et quasi superbo regi dignum exhibuisset tumulum, dixit: 'Satiare sanguine quem sitisti.'

Sed quid tandem? Nil preter hoc facinus Thamiris habemus, tanto clarius quanto Cyri maius fuerat imperium.

and drink. This loosened the soldiers' discipline, and they soon fell asleep. As they lay buried in slumber, Cyrus returned and put the young man and his army to the sword. Then, feeling almost certain of victory, he advanced farther into Scythian territory.

At the news of the slaughter of her troops, Tamyris, already a 6 widow, grieved deeply for the death of her only son. But she did not burst out weeping as women usually do. Anger and a lust for vengeance restrained her tears, and she reckoned that with her remaining forces she could deceive the enemy, despite his shrewdness, by using the same stratagem which had ensnared her son (even if she did not leave a camp full of wine). Knowing well the lay of the land, Tamyris pretended to flee. She led the enemy in eager pursuit along a short stretch of road into the bare, bitter-cold mountains where they could be entrapped. Then, in the midst of the rough mountain ravines, she turned on her foe. By now they were almost entirely without supplies, and she destroyed practically the whole army. Even Cyrus did not escape; and his bloody death satisfied the widow's wrath.

In a rage, Tamyris ordered a search for Cyrus' body among the 7 fallen. After it was found, she had the head cut off and placed in a leather bag filled with the blood of her troops. Then, as if she had given worthy burial to the proud king, she said: "Take your fill of the blood for which you have thirsted."

What else is there left to say? Nothing: we know nothing about Tamyris except this deed, as famous as Cyrus' empire was great.

: L :

De Leena meretrice

1 Leenam grecam arbitror fuisse feminam; quam, etsi minus fuerit
pudica, bona tamen honestarum matronarum atque reginarum illustrium pace, inter claras feminas descripsisse velim. Nam—ut in
superioribus dictum est—claras ob quodcunque facinus mulieres,
non pudicas tantum apponere pollicitus sum.

Insuper, adeo virtuti obnoxii sumus ut, non solum quam insigni
loco consitam cernimus, elevemus, sed et obrutam tegmine turpi
in lucem meritam conari debemus educere; est enim ubique pretiosa,[1] nec aliter fedatur, scelerum contagione, quam solaris radius
2 ceno inficiatur immixtus. Si ergo aliquando pectori, detestabili
offitio dedito, eam infixam viderimus, ita detestari debemus offitium, ut sue laudes non minuantur virtuti, cum tanto mirabilior
digniorque in tali sit, quanto ab eadem putabatur remotior.

3 Quam ob rem non semper meretricum aspernanda memoria
est, quin imo, dum ob aliquod virtutis meritum se fecerint memoratu dignas, latiori letiorique sunt preconio extollende, cum in eis
hoc agat comperta virtus, ut lascivientibus reginis ruborem incu-
tiat, cum earum lubricos luxus excuset reginarum ignavia; preterea, ut appareat non semper ingentes animos solum titulis illustribus connexos esse et virtutem neminem dedignari volentem se,
tam celebri mulierum cetui adnectenda est Leena, ut etiam in ea
parte in qua strenue egit, tanquam bene merita laudetur.

4 Leena igitur turpi meretricio dedita, detestabili obsequio fecit
ut eius origo ignoretur et patria. Hec tamen, regnante apud Macedonas[2] Aminta, cum Armonius et Ariston egregii iuvenes, seu ob
liberandam patriam turpi subiectam tyramnidi, seu ob aliam in-
pulsi causam, Hyparcum immanem tyramnum occidissent, inter

: L :

Leaena, a Prostitute

It is my opinion that Leaena was a Greek woman. Even though 1
she was hardly chaste, I would like, with the kind permission of
virtuous ladies and illustrious queens, to include her in the ranks
of famous women. As I have said earlier, I did not promise to
speak only of chaste women but of those who are famous, whatever might be the cause of their renown.[a]

Moreover, such is our devotion to virtue that we cannot glorify
only merits found in high places but are also bound to bring to
light merit that lies hidden under a shameful exterior. Virtue is
precious everywhere; it is not stained from contact with vice any
more than the rays of the sun are sullied when they touch mud. If 2
at times we see virtue implanted in the breast of someone given to
detestable practices, we must condemn those practices but in such
a manner that we do not lessen the praise of virtue. In such instances, virtue is more worthy of admiration since the person in
question was thought incapable of it.

Prostitutes, therefore, are not always to be remembered with 3
scorn. On the contrary, they should be praised the more widely
and joyously if they earn remembrance through some service to
virtue. Virtue found in these women shames wanton queens, while
queenly vice excuses the debaucheries of whores. Besides, Leaena
must be included in the class of famous women in order to show
that a noble spirit is not always connected to grand titles only, and
that virtue does not scorn anyone who desires it. She will then be
justly praised for the brave role she played.

Leaena's involvement in the disgusting and hateful trade of 4
prostitution has rendered anonymous her family and her country.
When Amyntas was king of Macedonia, the young nobles
Harmonius and Ariston were driven to kill the cruel tyrant

alios, a successore, tanquam gestorum conscia, eo quod eorum contubernio[3] uteretur, capta est; et cum ad prodendos coniurationis conscios diris cogeretur suppliciis, secum lubrica mulier, quantum esset sanctum atque venerabile nomen amicitie, pia volvens consideratione, ne illi, ut sibi parceret, in aliquo violentiam inferret, primo diu, ne diceret quod querebatur, mira constantia animo imperavit suo; tandem, convalescentibus cruciatibus et corporeis deficientibus viribus, timens, virilis femina, ne, debilitata virtute corporea, etiam enervaretur propositum, in robur maius excessit egitque ut eque cum viribus et dicendi potestas auferretur; et acri morsu linguam precidit suam et expuit; et sic actu unico, sed clarissimo, spem omnem a se noscendi quod exquirebatur tortoribus abstulit.

5   Quis dicet Leenam, nisi fortune crimine, fornices inhabitasse? Profecto non eam norat qui feminas dixit id tacere quod nesciunt.

Hei michi! Nonnunquam lasciviens opulentia domus et parentum indulgentia nimia virgines deduxit in lubricum; quarum petulca facilitas, ni austerulis coherceatur frenis et a matribus potissime observantia retrahatur vigili, aliquando, etiam non inpulsa, labitur; et si lapsus a desperatione decoris honestatis pristine calcetur, a nullis demum viribus revocatur.

6   Hac ego puto Leenam desidia corruisse, non nature malitia; et potissime dum virile eius robur circa cruciatus intueor. Quo equidem non minus, et muta prius et inde precisa eius lingua, splendoris consecuta est, quam florida persepe oratione apud suos valens meruerit forsitan Demosthenes.[4]

Hipparchus, either by a desire to free their country from servitude to shameful tyranny or for some other reason. Among those seized by the tyrant's successor was Leaena, who was suspected of complicity in the murder because of her intimacy with its perpetrators. During the cruel torture to which she was subjected in an effort to make her reveal the conspirators, this dissolute woman reflected with gratitude on the value of the holy and venerable name of friendship. At first she steeled herself for a long time with marvelous constancy and did not answer any questions lest she save herself by harming others. Finally, as the tortures increased and the strength ebbed from her body, this manly woman feared that her resolve would weaken along with her physical forces. Leaena then rose to an even greater resolve and acted so that her ability to speak was lost together with her strength. She bit down sharply on her tongue, severed it, and spat it out. Thus, by a single but most noble act, she deprived her tormentors of all hope of getting information from her.

Who will deny that fortune was to blame for Leaena's life in the brothels? Certainly, the person who said that women keep silence best when they are ignorant was not acquainted with Leaena.[b]

Alas! Sometimes insolent wealth at home and excessive parental indulgence have led girls to their ruin. If the feminine tendency towards wantonness is not strictly curbed and restrained by the unsleeping vigilance of their mothers, it will give way at some point, even without temptation. And if this fall is aggravated by despair for the loss of maidenly honor, the recovery of virtue is impossible.

I believe, particularly when I reflect on her manly strength in the face of torture, that Leaena went astray because of idleness and not because of an evil nature. In my view, this woman may have gained no less glory by holding, then biting off her tongue than Demosthenes earned from his compatriots by all the flowers of his eloquence.

: LI :

De Atalia regina Ierusalem

1 Atalie efferata mens notiorem illam fecit Syris Egyptiisque quam
oportunum fuerit davitico generi; esto domus eius, undique cruore
suorum ac multiplici cede feda, non minus nomini suo infauste
claritatis addiderit quam fulgoris dyademata regum.

Hec igitur Achab, regis Israelitarum, et Iezabelis regine, nequis-
sime mulieris, filia fuit et nupta Ioram, filio Iosaphat regis Ierusa-
2 lem. Et tandem Iosaphat atque Ozia filio natu maiore, in quem
morte patris devenerat regni successio, de medio sublatis, Ioram
vir eius preter opinionem rex Ierusalem coronatus est; qui et hanc
3 coniugem suam voluit esse reginam. Cui splendori, Achab genitore
defuncto, Ioram frater eius patri suffectus suo solio non modicum
lucis iniunxit. Temporis vero successu, multis ante infortuniis agitata, viro diem functo, Ocoziam filium suum vidit patris in throno
sedentem, ut undique mulier regiis coruscare<t>[1] honoribus.

4 Sane cum et Ocozias sagitta ictus ivisset in mortem, trux mulier, in desiderium regni accensa, cum memorabile excogitasset facinus et animi satis ad perpetrandum collegisset, pulsa feminea
pietate, non solum dare lacrimas exanimi filio omisit, quin imo in
ampliores fletus, si femineum illi cor fuisset, progressa, madente
adhuc nati terra cruore, in omnem davitice prolis posteritatem expedivit gladios; et tam diu in illam debachata est, donec ex mascu-
5 lis nullum omicteret quin per vulnera in necem compelleret. Solus
quidem immanitati sue Ioas, Ocozie regis parvulus filius, subtractus est, ea minime advertente. Nam Iosabe eiusdem filia et

: LI :

Athaliah, Queen of Jerusalem

Athaliah's savage nature made her better known to the Syrians and 1
the Egyptians than was expedient for the descendants of David,
even though her family, stained throughout by the murder of its
own members and multiple deaths, added as much notoriety to
her name as her royal diadem contributed to her glory.

To begin with, Athaliah was the daughter of Ahab, king of Israel, and of the wicked Queen Jezebel; she married Jehoram,
whose father Jehoshaphat was the king of Jerusalem. After the 2
deaths of Jehoshaphat and his elder son Ahaziah, on whom the
right of succession had fallen when his father died, Athaliah's husband Jehoram was unexpectedly crowned king of Jerusalem. He
wanted his wife to be queen. Athaliah's brother Jehoram, adding 3
further glory to his sister's splendor, replaced his father Ahab on
the throne when the latter died. Over the years Athaliah was troubled with many misfortunes, but after her husband's death she saw
her son Ahaziah on his father's throne. So this woman glittered
with honors on every side.

When Ahaziah died of an arrow wound, the cruel Athaliah 4
was inflamed with a desire to rule. She devised a memorable plan
and gathered her courage to put it into action. Casting aside every
tender feminine sentiment, Athaliah failed to mourn her dead son
and provided instead a reason for more tears — if she had had
a woman's heart. While the earth was still wet with her son's
blood, she drew her sword against all the descendants of the line
of David. Furiously she persecuted them until all the males had
been slaughtered. Only King Ahaziah's little son Joash, who was 5
spirited away without Athaliah's knowledge, escaped her ferocity.
In fact, it was Athaliah's daughter Jehosheba, sister of the late
Ahaziah, who secretly removed the boy and brought him to the

Ocozie olim soror, furtive subtractum parvulum in domum Ioadam pontificis viri sui, servandum nutriendumque tulerat.

6   Et sic per tot impie occisorum sanguinem mulier audax, tanquam in vacuam, suo opere, possessionem, regium conscendere solium ausa est et regalia disponere cuncta.

7   Quid Atreum, quid Dyonisium, quid Iugurtam mirabimur, homines acris ingenii, si, regni cupidine tractos, per vulnera quorundam suorum imperii conscendisse apicem audiamus, postquam, ut
eo perveniret, sobolem omnem regiam confodisse nec suis propriis
pepercisse mulierem cernimus?

8   Fulsit igitur dyademate regio Athalia, equidem magis purpureo
respersa cruore spectabilis, quam regia nota. Sane sicuti ultro in
innocuas davitice stirpis animas gladio truculenta sevierat, sic in
suos exasperatos alienos sensisse potuit. Ioram quidem Israel regem fratrem suum in agro Nabaoth iacentem et sanguinem per
mille vulnera canibus exhibentem vidisse cupiens potuisset facile;
sic et Iezabelem matrem regiis ornatam e turri celsa deiectam et
discurrentium calcatam pedibus atque adeo calcibus et rotarum
orbitis attritam, ut in cenum versa nullum infausti corporis rema-
neret vestigium; sic et septuaginta fratres suos una hora apud
Samariam victoris iussu percussos, et circa Iezraelam civitatem
eorum palis infixa capita, egregii facinoris argumenta prestantia;
sic et ceteros quoscunque cognatos ne unus evaderet quin eiusdem
percussoris ferro confoderetur.

9   Et postremo ne sanguinum scelesta mulier pertransiret impune,
se, cum septem regnasset annis, opera Ioadam pontificis elevato
Ioas nepote suo in regem, quem ipsa cum reliquis arbitrabatur occisum, e regia sede vi detrahi vidit et, clamante in eam populo, servorum atque lurconum manibus dedecorose² ad portam usque
mulorum frustra clamitantem atque minantem deduci ibique pro

house of her husband, the high priest Jehoiada, to be brought up in safety.

Hence, thanks to the blood of so many who had been slain 6 without pity, reckless Athaliah dared to seat herself upon the royal throne (a possession emptied, as it were, through her handiwork) and to govern the kingdom.

Why should it surprise us if we hear that Atreus, Dionysius, 7 and Jugurtha, men of violent character, were spurred on by a desire for power and gained control by murdering some of their own kinsmen? Have we not seen that, to reach the same goal, a woman killed an entire royal line and did not spare even her own family?

So Athaliah was resplendent in her regal headdress — but the 8 blood that bespattered her was surely more noticeable than her royal insignia. She had certainly cut down of her own free will and without mercy the innocent descendants of David; in the same way she might well have witnessed the cruelty of others against her own kin. If she had wanted, she could easily have seen her brother Jehoram, king of Israel, lying in the field of Naboth and pouring out his blood to the dogs through a thousand wounds. She could also have seen how her mother Jezebel, decked in royal garb, was thrown from a lofty tower, trampled by the feet of passers-by, and squashed by horses' hooves and wagon wheels to the point where she was turned into mud, with no traces left of her wretched body. Or she could have seen her seventy brothers killed by the victor's order in a single hour near Samaria and their heads, impaled on sharp poles, planted around the city of Jezreel as clear evidence of the shocking deed. Or she could have seen the murder of her other relatives, none of whom escaped the enemy's sword.

In the end Athaliah, who was guilty of so much bloodshed, 9 would not herself remain unpunished. After she had reigned for seven years, she saw herself forced violently from the royal throne and her grandchild Joash, whom she thought had been killed with the others, made king through the agency of the high priest

meritis trucidari, ut non alio tramite ad inferos pergeret nocua quam ire coegisset innocuos.

10 Sic agit divina iustitia, que, etsi differat, non obliviscitur; agitque supplicio severiori in quos diu expectatos mores mutari non videt. Quod dum cogitare negligimus, credere nolumus nec emendari curamus, et nos ipsos amplioribus flagitiis illigamus; dum minime arbitramur, absorti procella, dum non prodest, miseri commissa deflemus.

11 Dira quippe preter ius regni concupiscentia est et, ut plurimum, occupatio truculenta. In quam raro itur ex casu, per fraudem aut per violentiam conscendas necesse est; si per fraudem, dolis insidiis periuriis proditionibus similibusque agiteris meditatione conveniet; si violentia, iactationibus tumultu rumoribus sevitia rabieque vexeris incumbit; et per quam mavis iturus viam es, preparasse vires oportet. Que omnes scelestorum hominum habentur opere, quibus, nisi servus efficiaris, regni dominus esse non possis.

12 Quid tandem? Itur in thronum: obtures necesse est querelis aures, lacrimis sceleribus cedibusque avertas oculos, in saxum dures precordia, armetur crudelitas, pietas excludatur, negligatur ratio, colatur iniuria, potestas sacris legibus auferatur, prestetur libidini, accersatur malitia, simplicitas ludatur, rapacitas luxuria ingluvies commendentur, incliti regis prenuntie, divinis nec humanis parcatur, sacra atque prophana[3] misceantur, et, misericordia pressa, per

Jehoiada. Amid the hostile shouts of her people, Athaliah was dragged in disgrace by slaves and ruffians to the Mule Gate. Her cries and threats were useless. There she was killed in accordance with her deserts, and so this wicked woman went to the lower regions by the same road she had forced her innocent victims to travel.

Thus does divine justice operate. Even if it is slow to act, it does not forget and moves with harsher punishment against those who fail to mend their accustomed ways. As long as we ignore this truth, refuse to believe it, and take no steps to reform ourselves, we only involve ourselves in still greater sins. When we least expect it, we are swallowed up by the tempest, and in misery weep over our misdeeds when it is of no avail. 10

Truly, a craving for illegitimate rule is a terrible thing and, in the majority of cases, to acquire it demands cruelty. Rarely is mere chance responsible for the longed-for ascent; usually it is necessary to employ subterfuge or violence. If subterfuge is used, you will be assailed by thoughts of deception, traps, perjury, treachery, and similar things. If recourse is had to violence, you can expect to be plagued by upheavals, riots, calumny, cruelty, and rage. Whatever path to the throne you choose to travel, you must have your forces ready. All these means are considered actions proper to wicked men; unless you become the servant of such practices, you cannot become the ruler of a kingdom. 11

And what then? Say that the ascent to the throne has been achieved: you will have to close your ears to complaints, avert your eyes from tears, crimes, and murders, and harden your heart into stone; you must give arms to cruelty, banish compassion, cast aside reason, encourage wrongdoing, do away with the sacred force of law, dance attendance on lust, invoke wickedness, mock candor, praise pillage, dissipation, and gluttony—such are the harbingers of this glorious king. Neither divine nor human concerns may be spared; the sacred and the profane must be confused. Since mercy 12

summum nephas eatur in sanguinem, sternantur pii homines, impii sublimentur, stuprentur virgines, in abusum pueri trahantur ingenui, damnetur virtus et ignoscatur vitio; et ubique pulsa pace triunphos agat discordia. O spectabilis regis accessus!

13   Sed quid? In thronum per sanguinem et indigna facinora itum est: utinam, in quocunque modo quesitum, innocue viveretur! Illico, urgente suspicione, primores pelluntur exilio, in pauperiem rediguntur divites, relegantur amici veteres, fratres filii nepotes parentesque, tanquam emuli, carcerantur, occiduntur; nulla fides, nulla sanctitas, iustitia nulla servatur, anxie vigilatur, cum difficultate dormitur, nec cibus absque timore gustatur; pulsisque fidelibus, scelestis omnis vita commictitur.

14   O pulchra, o appetenda, o laudanda, quesita curis possessio! Erat equidem satius gurgustiolum intrasse pauperis, pace plenum, securitate validum et sollicitudine vacuum. Hec ardua, quanto cum cruore queruntur, tanto cum timore tenentur; et qui fidos suspicantes emisimus, dum infidis, procurante crimine, nos ipsos commictimus, fit persepe ut, eorum opere, quales habuimus introitus, tales aut detestabiliores exitus habeamus et una, nostro cum interitu, subtrahatur hora, quod per multos infaustos dies nequiter fuerat congestum.

15   Quod sero cognovisse potuit Athalia.

must be suppressed, wickedness must issue in bloodshed, with good men stricken to the ground, the wicked exalted, virgins raped, and innocent boys abused. It will be necessary to condemn virtue and excuse vice. With the expulsion of peace, discord will triumph everywhere. How marvelous is the accession of such a king!

And then? Once one has ascended the throne through bloodshed and shameful deeds, would that, no matter how it was acquired, one could live free of harm! Immediately, however, suspicion is at work. The leading men are exiled, the wealthy reduced to poverty, and old friends banished; because they are potential rivals, brothers, children, grandchildren, and relatives are imprisoned and killed. There is no sense of trust or piety or justice. One lies awake in anxiety, sleeps badly, and cannot eat without fear. Those who have been loyal are cast aside and one's life is in the hands of the wicked. 13

O how beautiful, desirable, and praiseworthy is this possession obtained with such care! Surely it would have been better to enter a poor man's small hut, filled with peace, strong in its safety, and free of worry. These lofty places acquired with loss of life are retained with an equal amount of fear. When we in our suspicion banish those on whom we can rely and, at the urging of calumny, entrust ourselves to disloyal persons, it often happens that through their doing our exit is similar to, or worse than, our entrance. Thus, in a single hour we lose in death what we have wickedly accumulated during our unfortunate lifetime. 14

Athaliah learned this, but too late. 15

: LII :

De Cloelia romana virgine

1 Cloelia insignis virgo romana, a quibus parentibus originem traxerit, aut posteris non reliquere priores, aut vetustate abolitum est; sed eam ex claris natam satis arbitrari potest, cum generositas testetur animi et quia pacis obses inter alios nobiles Romanorum, Porsenne Etruscorum regi, tempore belli Tarquinii Superbi, data sit.

2 Cuius ut laudandam audaciam verbis amplioribus explicem, advertendum est quoniam, pulso Tarquinio Superbo ob scelus enorme in Lucretiam patratum, nec succederent temptanti reditum fraudes, in bellum patens ventum est. In quod cum venisset Porsenna rex clusinus, precibus Tarquinii accitus et, probitate Oratii Coclitis pontem Sublicium defendentis, Etrusci amoverentur a transitu[1] et, Mutii Scevole audacia atque commento territus, venisset in concordiam Romanorum et ad servandam suscepisset obsides plures, factum est ut cum aliis virginibus pluribus micteretur Cloelia.

3 Cui cum forsan videretur minus de republica apud exterum regem tot detineri virgines, in audaciam virilem virgineum pectus armavit et, deceptis custodibus, equum, quem forte non ante conscenderat, pascentem secus Tiberim, nocte, cum multas eduxisset in ripam, conscendit, nec exterrita profunditate fluminis aut aquarum vertiginibus sospites in adversam partem omnes eduxit suisque restituit.

4 Quod a Porsenna mane compertum conquestus est; frequentique senatu iussum est ut transfugarum dux regi restitueretur poscenti, adiecto ut inviolata suis in tempore redderetur a rege.

: LII :

Cloelia, a Roman Maiden

Either the ancients did not preserve for posterity, or time has de- 1
stroyed, any knowledge of the parents of Cloelia, a distinguished
young Roman woman. But we can assume with some confidence
that she was born of an illustrious family: attesting to this is her
noble spirit and also the fact that during the war with Tarquinius
Superbus she was handed over, along with other leading Romans,
as a hostage of peace to Porsenna, king of the Etruscans.

In order to explain and praise more fully her daring, we must 2
remember that after Tarquinius Superbus was expelled (owing to
the terrible crime committed by his son Sextus against Lucretia[a]),
war broke out openly when Tarquinius' secret plots to return to
Rome did not succeed. At his request, Porsenna, king of Chiusi,
entered the fray. The Etruscans, however, were prevented from
crossing the Tiber by Horatius Cocles' brave defense of the Sub-
lician Bridge. Then Porsenna, terrified by the boldness and the
ruse of Mucius Scaevola, came to terms with the Romans. As a
guaranty of peace, he received a number of hostages, and Cloelia
was among the group of young women sent to him.

Perhaps she did not deem it honorable for the state that so 3
many young females were in the control of a foreign king. At any
rate, Cloelia armed her maiden's breast with a man's boldness. One
night she evaded the guards and led many of the women hostages
to the bank of the Tiber. There she mounted a horse grazing
nearby—perhaps her first time to ride such an animal. Unafraid
of the deep river and the swirling waters, Cloelia brought her companions safely to the other shore and returned them to their families.

The next morning Porsenna learned what had happened, and 4
he complained. At a crowded meeting of the Roman Senate an or-

5 Rex autem virginis miratus virtutem et delectatus audacia, non solum ad suos illi concessit reditum, sed potestatem fecit ut quos vellet ex obsidibus reliquis posset educere. Que ex omnibus solos sumpsit impuberes; quod et honestati virginee commendabile visum est et urbi fuit acceptissimum, eo quod eam potissime etatem liberasset que aptior videretur iniurie.

Quam ob causam a gratis civibus inusitati honoris genere decorata est eique concessa equestris statua fuit que, in summo vie Sacre apposita, diu permansit intacta.

: LIII :

De Hyppone greca muliere

1 Hyppo greca fuit mulier, ut ex codicibus veterum satis percipitur; quam vix credam unico tantum optimo valuisse opere, cum ad altiora conscendamus gradibus, eo quod nemo summus repente fiat. Sed postquam vetustatis malignitate et genus et patria ac cetera eius facinora sublata sunt, quod ad nos usque venit ne pereat, aut illi meritum subtrahatur decus, in medium deducere mens est.

2 Accepimus igitur Hypponem hanc casu a nautis hostibus captam. Que cum forte forma valeret sentiretque predonum in se pudicitiamque suam teneri consilium, tanti castitatis decus existimavit ut, cum nisi per mortem servari posse cerneret, non expectata violentia, in undas se dedit precipitem; a quibus sublata vita et pudicitia servata est.

der was given that the leader of the fugitives should be restored to
the king who was demanding her back, with the proviso that at
the proper time he was to return her unharmed to her people. But 5
Porsenna, amazed by the young woman's courage and pleased by
her daring, allowed her to return to her family and also gave her
permission to take along whatever remaining hostages she wished.
From the entire group Cloelia selected only the young boys. This
choice seemed to accord well with her maidenly virtue, and it
pleased the Romans greatly because she had freed those who were
of an age more susceptible to hurt.

Hence she received an extraordinary honor from her grateful
countrymen, namely, the decree of an equestrian statue. This
statue was placed at the highest point of the Sacred Way, where it
remained intact for a long time.

: LIII :

Hippo, a Greek Woman

It is clear from ancient books that Hippo was a Greek woman. I 1
can hardly believe that she distinguished herself by only a single illustrious exploit since no one suddenly achieves greatness; our rise
to lofty heights is gradual. As the malevolence of time has deprived us of any knowledge of her family, country, and other accomplishments, I thought that I would report what little has come
down to us, lest it perish or the honor due her be lost.

Well then, we are told that Hippo happened to be captured by 2
enemy sailors. A beautiful woman, she overheard the pirates making plans to rape her. But she reckoned her chastity at so high a
rate that, when she saw it could not be preserved except through
death, she forestalled her violation by throwing herself headlong
into the sea. Among the waves she lost her life but saved her honor.

3   Quis tam severum mulieris consilium non laudet? Paucis quidem annis, quibus forsan vita protendi poterat, castitatem redemit
et immatura morte sibi perenne decus quesivit. Quod virtutis opus
procellosum nequivit mare contegere nec desertum auferre litus
quin literarum perpetuis monimentis suo cum honore servaretur
in luce.

4   Corpus autem postquam ab undis aliquandiu ludibrii more vo-
lutatum est, ab eisdem in eritreum litus inpulsum, a litoranis nau-
fragi ritu sepultum est. Tandem cum ferret ab hostibus exorta
fama quenam foret et mortis causam, ab Eritreis summa cum
veneratione sepulcri locus in litore ingenti tumulo atque diu man-
suro, in servati decoris testimonium, exornatus est, ut nosca-
mus quoniam nullis adverse fortune tenebris lux possit obfuscari
virtutis.

: LIV :

De Megulia Dotata

1   Meguliam, quam Romani veteres cognominavere Dotatam, romanam fuisse feminam atque nobilem reor: rudi illo atque—ut ita
dixerim—sancto evo, quo nondum ex ulnis paupertatis, altricis
optime, Quirites in splendores asyaticos et magnorum regum ga-
zas, ea neglecta, proruperant, illustrem habitam. Que quidem hoc
2   Dotate consecuta cognomen est—ut arbitror—magis maiorum
suorum prodigalitate quam aliquo[1] sui operis merito. Nam, datis
in dotem viro quingentis milibus eris, adeo monstruosum illo seculo visum est, ut danti sit Dotate cognomen inditum et per multa
perseveratum tempora in tantum ut, si quid preter consuetum ci-

CHAPTER LIV

Who will not praise so austere a resolve on the part of this 3
woman? At the cost of the few years by which she might have pro-
longed her life, Hippo ransomed her chastity, exchanging a premature death for everlasting glory. The tempestuous sea could not
hide her virtuous deed, nor could the deserted shore prevent its
brilliant preservation, with the accompanying personal renown, in
the enduring records of literature.

For a while her body was tossed about by the waves like a toy. 4
Then it was hurled onto the shore of Erythrae and buried by the
inhabitants in a ceremony reserved for the shipwrecked. When
Hippo's enemies finally disclosed her identity and the reason for
her death, the Erythraeans reverently adorned the burial place on
the shore with a mighty tomb. This was destined to remain for a
long time as a memorial to the chastity she had preserved; it
teaches us that the light of virtue cannot be obscured by the shadows of adverse fortune.

: LIV :

Megullia Dotata

I believe that Megullia, also called Dotata ('Dowry girl') by the 1
ancient Romans, was a Roman noblewoman. She was regarded as
famous in that primitive and, if I may say so, holy age when her
countrymen had not yet repudiated the embrace of poverty, best
of nurses, to rush forth seeking eastern glory and kingly treasures.
I also think that Megullia acquired the name of Dotata more 2
through the lavishness of her ancestors than through any meritorious undertaking of her own. At that time it seemed so marvelous
a thing to give one's husband a dowry of 500,000 pennies that the
name of Dotata was bestowed on the female giver. This appella-
tion lasted for such a long time that, if anything extra was added

vium morem doti superadderetur cuiquam virgini, confestim et ipsa Dotata Megulia diceretur.

3   O bona simplicitas, o laudanda paupertas! Quod tu monstruo-sum, et merito, arbitrari faciebas, ridiculum videretur lascivie ho-dierne. In tantum enim mensuram undique rerum excessimus, ut vix cerdo, vix lignarius faber, vix mercennarius lixa vel villicus ob tam parvam stipem comperies qui domum velit uxorem inducere.

4   Nec mirum; etiam plebeie muliercule reginarum coronas, aureas fibulas et armillas et insignia reliqua ascripsere sibi: eis non dicam inverecunde, sed superbe utuntur.

Hei michi! Nescio utrum dixerim: 'Sic ampliati sunt animi dum nobis invicem nimium cedimus'; an potius (quod verissimum arbitror): 'Nostro crimine sic exculta vitia sunt, ambitiones et inexplebilia[2] mortalium vota.'

: LV :

De Veturia romana matrona

1   Veturia nobilis et romana mulier iam senex laudabili opere annos suos in viriditatem traxit perpetuam. Erat huic adolescens Gneus Martius, strenue virtutis filius, consilio et manu promptus; et cum, oppugnantibus Romanis, Coriolos, oppidum Volscorum, eius inclita probitate captum videretur, Coriolani cognomen ade-ptus est; et tam grandem nobilitatis favorem ut omnia verbis et opere auderet.

2   Quam ob rem, laborante Urbe annone penuria et opere patrum plurima ex Sycilia delata foret, severa oratione prohibuit ne plebi partiretur priusquam, quos paulo ante in Sacro monte secedens, honores propter reditum nobilitati abstulerat[1], dimisisset. In quem

to some girl's dowry, she too was henceforth called Megullia Dotata.

O beautiful simplicity! O praiseworthy poverty! The sum you 3 made people believe was extraordinary (and justly so) would seem laughable to our modern licentiousness. We have exceeded due measure in everything to such an extreme that you will hardly find an artisan, carpenter, street vendor, or peasant who would marry a woman for so small a dowry. But this is not surprising: even ordi- 4 nary women have claimed for themselves queenly crowns, gold brooches, bracelets, and other ornaments and wear them proudly, not to say shamelessly.

Alas, I doubt whether our minds are enlarged when we make overlarge gifts to each other, or whether (and this I think is more correct) we only cultivate, through this wicked practice of ours, the vices, ambitions, and insatiable desires of mankind.

: LV :

Veturia, a Roman Matron

A praiseworthy deed of Veturia, an aged Roman noblewoman, has 1 rendered her advanced years perennially fresh. She had a son named Gnaeus Marcius, a courageous young man who was quick in thought and action. He acquired the toponymic 'Coriolanus' when, during a Roman siege, the Volscian city of Corioli was taken as a result of his exceptional valor. Henceforth the youth en-joyed such great favor among the nobility that there was nothing he did not dare to do and say.

Once when Rome was suffering from famine, the Senate or- 2 dered a great quantity of grain to be brought from Sicily. Cori-olanus sternly opposed its distribution among the plebs until such time as the latter should restore to the nobility the privileges they,

infesta plebs, ut erat famelica, manus profecto iniecisset, ni illi a tribuno peroportune dies ad dicendam causam indicta fuisset.

3   Qui cum non paruisset indignans, exilio damnatus est; et in Volscos, paulo ante Romanorum hostes, secessit. A quibus benigne et honorifice susceptus, ubique enim virtus in pretio est, hos iste tam sua quam Accii Tullii volsci fraude in bellum adversus Romanos redegit et belli dux ab eisdem factus, ad fossas Cluillas, ad quartum a Roma lapidem, deduxit exercitum; eoque rem romanam redegit, ut a senatu qui pacem equis legibus impetrarent ad eum exulem micterentur.

4   Quos Martius atroci cum responso dimisit in patriam. Ob quod iterum missi, sed minime recepti sunt. Ivere tertio cum infulis velati pontifices et suis cum insignibus supplices, sed frustrati rediere; et ideo undique desperatio Romanorum intraverat animos, cum ad Veturiam Coriolani matrem et Volumniam[2] coniugem frequentes et querule venientes matrone obtinuere ut magno iam natu mulier in castra hostium precibus lacrimisque placatura filium, postquam armis ab hominibus non posse respublica tutari videretur, iret cum coniuge; neque ex eis ingens prosequentium caterva defuit.

5   Cuius adventum cum cognovisset Coriolanus, etsi animo turgidus esset, consternatus tamen matris adventu, e sella consurgens exivit tabernaculum et suscepturus illam obvius factus est.

Sane Veturia, hinc coniugem, inde liberos Coriolani tenens, non ante filium vidit quam, pietate patria posita, se succendit in iram; et ubi supplex exiverat urbem, in hostium castra veniens

the plebs, had usurped as the price of their return to Rome from the Sacred Mount, whither they had recently seceded. Starved as they were, the hostile plebs would certainly have attacked him if their tribune had not opportunely appointed a day for discussing the question.

Coriolanus, angered by this, did not appear and was condemned to exile. He fled to the Volscians, who only a little while before had been the enemies of Rome. There Coriolanus was kindly and honorably received, for bravery is universally valued. The stratagems which he and Attius Tullius devised brought Tullius' fellow Volscians into another war against the Romans. Coriolanus was elected commander and led the army to the Cluilian Trenches situated four miles from Rome. Here he reduced the Romans to the point that they dispatched ambassadors to the exiled enemy leader to sue for peace on fair terms.

Coriolanus sent them back home with a harsh answer. Once again ambassadors were sent, but this time they were not received. On the third attempt, priests adorned with their headbands and badges of office went to him as suppliants but returned empty-handed. Despair had already entered the souls of Romans everywhere when a crowd of plaintive women went to Coriolanus' mother Veturia and his wife Volumnia. They prevailed on the aged mother to go, along with the wife, to the enemy's camp and appease her son with tearful entreaties, since the men of the commonwealth seemed unable to defend it by force of arms. Veturia and Volumnia were escorted there by a large troop of women.

When Coriolanus learned of her arrival, he was dismayed at her coming, though his heart was thick with rage. He rose from his chair, left the tent, and went to receive his mother.

With Coriolanus' wife on one side and his children on the other, Veturia put aside her patriotic duty and burst into a fit of anger as soon as she saw her son. She had left Rome as a suppliant but, now that she was actually in the enemy's camp, she became a

3

4

5

obiurgatrix effecta est; et suscitatis in effeto pectore viribus inquit: 'Siste gradum, infeste iuvenis; scire velim, antequam in amplexus veniam tuos, an matrem an captivam hostem suscepturus adve-

6 nias; hostem puto. Me miseram! In hoc exoptata mortalibus evi longitudo deduxisse me debuit ut te damnatum exilio et inde reipublice hostem cernerem? Cognoscis queso quo armatus hostis consistas in solo? Cognoscis quam habeas in conspectu patriam? Cognoscis equidem, et si nescis, hec est in quo genitus, in quo natus, in quo labore meo educatus es.

7 'Quo igitur animo, qua mente, quo inpulsu hostilia potuisti inferre arma? Non intranti tibi parenti debitus honos, dulcis uxoris amor, filiorum pietas et native patrie reverentia obvii facti sunt? Non acre pectus moverunt, non iras, quantumcunque iuste susceptas, obruisse potuerunt? Non, dum primo illa spectares menia, in memoriam venit: "Ibi domus et penates patrii mei sunt, ibi coniunx et liberi, ibi infortunio suo et opere meo infelix mater est"?

8 'Venere patres, venere pontifices, nec saxeum pectus movisse potuere tuum ut id rogatus ageres quod sponte fecisse tua debueras. Satis, me miseram, adverto fecunditatem meam patrie michique fuisse adversam; ubi filium et civem peperisse arbitrabar, hostem et infestissimum atque inflexibilem peperisse me video.

9 'Satius quippe non concepisse fuerat: potuerat sterilitate mea Roma absque oppugnatione consistere et ego misella anus in libera mori patria. Sed ego nil iam pati michi miserius quam tibi turpius possum; nec ut sim miserrima diu futura sum; de his natis

scold. Strength awoke in her feeble breast, and she told Coriolanus: "Stop right there, you troublesome young man! Before I embrace you, I want to know whether you have come to receive me as your mother or as an enemy prisoner. The latter, I think. O 6 wretched woman that I am! Must my longevity—the very longevity for which mortals yearn—bring me to this, that I see you condemned to exile and become an adversary of the republic? I ask you: do you know on what soil you stand, armed as an enemy? Do you recognize the country you see before you? Indeed you do. But in case you do not, this is the land where you were conceived, where you were born, where you were raised through my efforts.

"What is going on in your spirit, your mind, your passions that 7 you have been able to bear arms against it like an enemy? The respect owed your mother, love for your sweet wife, compassion for your children, reverence for your fatherland—did not these feelings come to meet you as you entered your country? Did they not move your embittered heart? Could they not extinguish your wrath, however justified? As soon as you saw these walls, did you not remember: 'There is my home, there my household gods; there are my wife and children; there, to her misfortune, is my mother, made wretched through my deeds'?

"The senators came to you, and the priests too, but they were 8 not able to move your stony breast to do at their entreaty what you should have done of your own free will. Wretched woman that I am, I see well enough that my fertility has become a curse directed against my country and against me. I thought that I had given birth to a son and a citizen, but now I realize that I have produced a dangerous and implacable enemy.

"Better, truly, not to have conceived! By my sterility Rome 9 could have remained free from siege, and I, a poor old woman, could have died in a free country. But now I can never suffer anything worse for me and more shameful for you, nor shall I endure for long this life of wretchedness. As for these children of yours,

tuis videris, quos, si pergis, aut immatura mors aut longa servitus manet.'

10   Verba lacrime secute sunt; et inde coniugis preces atque natorum et amplexus mutui clamoresque flentium et orantium matronarum. Quibus verbis et gemitibus precibusque actum est ut, quod legatorum maiestas et sacerdotum reverentia nequiverant, matris veneratione ducis acerrimi frangeretur ira et propositum verteretur et, suis complexis atque dimissis, retro ab urbe castra hostium moverentur.

11   Ex quo secutum est, ne glorie mulieris ingratitudine detraheretur, ut ex senatu<s>[3] consulto eo in loco in quo Veturia filii iram molliverat, templum ad eius rei perpetuam memoriam et ara Fortune muliebri ex cocto construeretur lapide (quod quidem, etsi vetustissimum sit, in nullo fere diminutum[4], in nostrum usque perdurat evum) sanxitque ut, pretereuntibus mulieribus, quibus nullus vel minimus usque ad illam etatem a viris prestabatur honor, et assurgerent homines et via cederent; quod nostra in patria ritu veteri servatur huc usque; et quod eis liceret uti aurium vetusto orientalium mulierum insigni et purpurea veste aureisque fibulis et armillis. Nec desunt qui asserant eodem senatus consulto adiectum ut, quod ante non licebat, possent hereditates consequi quorumcunque.

12   Huius igitur meritum, virisne exosum esse magis debeat an mulieribus gratum, putant quidam pendere sententiam; quam ego certissimam reor. Nam, ornamentis agentibus, virorum exhauriuntur substantie et mulieres incedunt cultu insignite regio, depauperantur viri, maiorum hereditatibus demptis, ditantur femine consequentes, honorantur insignes, honorantur etiam non illustres; multa his incommoda et illis commoda inde secuta sunt.

you surely realize that, if you persevere, there awaits them either untimely death or lasting slavery."

Her words were followed by tears, then the pleas of wife and children, mutual embraces, and the cries of the weeping, suppliant matrons. With their words, groanings, and prayers they accomplished what the majesty of ambassadors and the reverence owed to priests had not been able to achieve: out of respect for his mother, the anger of this ferocious general vanished and his purpose was altered. When Coriolanus had embraced his family and sent them away, he withdrew his army from Rome. 10

Naturally, the Senate did not want this woman's glory to be diminished through ingratitude, so it decreed the construction of a temple in perpetual memory of her deed at the very place where Veturia had softened her son's wrath; there a brick altar was erected to Fortuna Muliebris. (This temple, although very old, has endured to our own day almost intact). Hitherto women had received little or no male respect: now the Senate decreed that, when they passed by, men should rise to their feet and give way; and this ancient practice is still observed in our country. In addition, women were permitted to wear earrings, the ancient ornament of Eastern women, and dresses of royal purple, gold brooches and bracelets. Some authorities claim that this same decree of the Senate enabled women to receive inheritances from anyone, a privilege which earlier had not been allowed. 11

Whether Veturia's reward ought to be more disliked by men or more welcomed by women is, in the opinion of certain people, a moot question. But I think that there is no room at all for doubt. Thanks to feminine ornaments, masculine wealth has been depleted while women parade about in royal finery; men become paupers through the loss of their ancestral inheritance while women become rich gaining it; deserving women are honored, but so are ignoble ones. All this has brought many disadvantages to men and many advantages to women. 12

13 Maledictis in Veturiam irem ob ex his consecutam superbiam feminis, ni suis precibus stetisset romana libertas. Sed liberalitatem illam senatus nimiam et perseveratum per tot secula damnosum morem laudare non possum. Minori fuissent contente munere; permaximum videbatur muliebri Fortune dicatum templum.

14 Sed quid? Muliebris est mundus, sic et homines muliebres. Quod autem adversum fuit hominibus, etas, que multa consumpsit utilia, consumpsisse non potuit nec minorasse mulieribus ius suum tenaci perseveratione servantibus.

15 Veturie igitur applaudant, eius colant nomen et meritum quotiens caris lapillis purpura et aureis ornantur fibulis et incedentibus a viris assurgitur ociosisque morientium substancie numerantur.

: LVI :

De Thamari Miconis[1] filia

1 Thamaris mulier evo suo pictrix egregia fuit; cuius virtu<ti>s[2] etsi forsan veternositas plurimum abstulerit, nomen tamen egregium nec artificium adhuc abstulisse potuit. Volunt igitur hanc nonagesima olympiade filiam fuisse Myconis pictoris; verum cuius, cum duos fuisse Mycones et ambo pictores et eodem tempore Athenis floruisse legamus, non distinguunt, nisi his paucis verbis eam filiam fuisse Myconis cui minoris cognomen additum ferunt.

2 Sane cuiuscunque fuerit, tam miro ingenio, despectis muliebribus officiis, paternam artem imitata est ut, regnante apud Mace-

CHAPTER LVI

If Rome's liberty had not been saved by her pleas, I would curse 13
Veturia for the haughtiness that women have assumed as a result
of her actions. I cannot praise, however, the excessive generosity of
the Senate and the harmful custom that has lasted for so many
centuries. Those women might have been satisfied with a lesser
gift; the temple consecrated to Fortuna Muliebris would have
seemed to them a great reward.

But what is there to say? This is a woman's world, and men 14
have become womanish. Although time has consumed many useful things, it has not been able to destroy what in this instance was
detrimental to men, nor to diminish women's tenacious and persistent hold on their own prerogatives.

Let women applaud Veturia, then, and honor her name and her 15
worthy deed whenever they adorn themselves with precious jewels,
with purple cloth, and with gold brooches; whenever men stand
up as they go by; and whenever they calmly calculate the wealth of
dying testators.

: LVI :

Tamaris, Daughter of Micon

Tamaris[a] was a female artist famous in her own day. Time may 1
have destroyed most of her efforts but not, at least up to now, her
distinguished reputation and her skill. Reportedly she was the
daughter of the painter Micon and lived during the ninetieth
Olympiad. We read, however, that two artists named Micon flourished in Athens at the same time, and our sources do not specify
which of the two was her father except to indicate briefly that she
was the daughter of Micon the Younger.

No matter what her parentage may have been, Tamaris scorned 2
womanly tasks and practiced her father's craft with remarkable

donas Archelao, singularem picture gloriam adepta sit, in tantum
ut Ephesi, apud quos honore precipuo Dyana colebatur, eiusdem
Dyane effigiem, in tabula quadam manu eius pictam, tanquam
3 celebrem servaverint diu. Que cum in longissimam etatem perse-
verasset, artificii huius testimonium tam grande prebuit, ut in
hodiernum usque memorabile videatur: equidem laudabile plurimum, si prospectemus fusos et calathos aliarum.

: LVII :

De Arthemisia regina Carie

1 Arthemisia Carie regina fuit ingentis animi femina et sanctissimi
amoris atque perrarissimi et integre viduitatis exemplum posteris
sempiternum. Hec, esto a quibus progressa parentibus nec ex qua
fuerit patria in dies nostros venerit, satis ad eius nobilitatis laudem
est novisse eam Mausoli, tum potentissimi regis Carie, fuisse coniugem. Quem adeo dilexit in vita ut superstes mortuum oblivisci
non posset.
2   Cuius rei stetere diu insignia monimenta[1]. Nam, si fides claris
scriptoribus prestanda est, cum primum vir amantissimus clausisset diem, exquisitis eius cadaver honoribus extulit; nec passa est,
post funebres ignes, collectos diligenter cineres aurea in urna ser-
vandos condi, existimans tam amati coniugis omne aliud vas incongruum esse preter id pectus in quo veteris amoris flamme longe
3 plus solito, eo defuncto, flagrabant. Quam ob rem ut ibi quod ter-
reum supererat consisteret, quo perpetua preterite vite memoria
consistebat, collectos, donec explerentur, immixtos paulatim pocu-

talent. When Archelaus was king of Macedonia, she gained such acclaim for her painting that the Ephesians, who had a particular veneration for Diana, long preserved as a celebrated image of this goddess a panel painting done by Tamaris. This work of art en- 3 dured for many years and provided such convincing proof of her ability that it seems worthy of remembrance even today—indeed, eminently so if we compare it with the usual spinning and weaving of other women.

: LVII :

Artemisia, Queen of Caria

Artemisia, queen of Caria, was a woman of great character; to 1 posterity she is a lasting example of chaste widowhood and of the purest and rarest kind of love. Knowledge of her parents or native country has not reached us, but it is sufficient to know in praise of her nobility that she was the wife of Mausolus, a powerful king of Caria. Artemisia loved him so much when he was alive that after his death she could never forget him so long as she lived.

There endured for a long time wonderful monuments to her 2 devotion. If we can believe well-known sources, as soon as her much-loved husband died, she adorned his corpse with choice marks of honor. After he had been cremated and his ashes care-fully gathered, Artemisia did not allow them to be placed for safekeeping in a golden urn. She thought there was no receptacle more suitable for so beloved a spouse than that breast wherein the flames of her old love burned—still more brightly now that Mausolus was gone. Hence, in order to give his earthly remains a 3 resting place where his life would be remembered, she dissolved all his collected ashes in a drink, which she then slowly consumed. Her remaining years were devoted to constant mourning. After a

lis exhauxit omnes, vita residua perpetuis dicata lacrimis. Et sic humore consumpto, se ad virum ituram credens, leta devenit in mortem; verum vidua ingentia peregit facinora.

4   Vetus fuit consuetudo viris egregiis insignia sepulcra erigi; quod ut amori conforme appareret, opus Arthimisia[2] mirabile nimis et sumptuosum, avaritia omni seposita, excogitavit; nec uno nec populari contenta artifice, Scopam Briaxem Thimotheum atque Leocarem, quos eo seculo totius orbis conspectiores predicabat Grecia, accersiri iussit fecitque iuxta eorum iudicium Mausolo magnificum designari mausoleum et paratis marmoribus construi, ut ob mirabile opus illud, si aliter non daretur, dilecti viri nomen efficeretur eternum.

5   Cuius quidem, eo quod tam arte quam inpensa omnia fere orbis edificia excesserit, et inter septem mundi miracula unum diu memoratum sit, singularem fecisse mentionem non erit absurdum; nam virebit artificum fama et mulieris inclite fiet magnificentia clarior.

6   Architecti igitur apud Alicarnasum, precipuam Carie civitatem, regine iussu quadrata in forma firmavere bustum; et que austrum et arthos prospectant facies, sexaginta trium pedum in longitudinem deduxere; breviores relique fuere; et illud in altitudinem centum quadraginta pedum extulere et ut omne cingeretur triginta

7   sex columnis marmoreis voluere. Ceterum eam partem que spectat Eoum Scopam sculpsisse dicunt; eam vero que in Boream vergitur Briaxem, cum eam que in occiduum versa est celandam sumpsisset Leocares; quarta Thimoteo relicta; qui in sculpendis statuis et hystoriis aliisque operi contingentibus, tanta solertia vires ingenii expressere, cupientes singuli anteire magisterio reliquos, ut vivos e marmore vultus eduxisse nonnunquam a prospectantibus credi-

lifetime spent in this manner, Artemisia died happy in the belief that she was going to her husband. Before this happened, however, she accomplished great things during her widowhood.

It was an ancient custom to erect impressive funerary monuments to prominent men. To produce something for Mausolus that would be equal to her love, Artemisia gave no thought to expense and planned a striking, extravagant memorial. Not satisfied with just one artist, nor with someone from her own people, she summoned Scopas, Bryaxis, Timotheus, and Leochares, whom Greece acclaimed in that age as the greatest artists in the world. Following their advice, she had a magnificent tomb designed for Mausolus and built of marble procured for the purpose. Thus, if for no other reason, the name of her dear husband would live forever thanks to this extraordinary structure.   4

The monument surpassed in beauty as well as cost practically every other building on the globe and was long remembered as one of the seven wonders of the world. So it will not be out of place for me to make special mention of the edifice. This will ensure that the fame of the artists remains ever fresh and that the remarkable liberality of this noble woman shines even more brightly.   5

Well then, the architects, at the queen's request, laid the foundations for a sepulcher of rectangular shape near Halicarnassus, the capital of Caria. The two sides facing north and south were sixty-three feet long, while the other two sides were shorter. The building rose to a height of one hundred and forty feet, and it was girt round on all sides with thirty-six marble columns. The part facing east is reported to have been sculpted by Scopas, that facing north by Bryaxis, and that facing west by Leochares; the fourth part was left to Timotheus. Each artist aimed to surpass the others in skill. In carving the statues, friezes, and other appropriate decorations, they expressed the power of their genius with such subtlety that spectators sometimes believed them to have brought   6   7

tum; ac nedum tunc, sed multa post secula visum sit pro gloria manus ibidem decertasse artificum.

8 Nec contigit Arthemisiam opus tam celebre perfectum vidisse, morte subtractam. Tamen ob regine obitum non reliquere opus artifices, quin imo arbitrantes illud futurum suorum ingeniorum posteritati documentum certissimum, in finem usque quod cepe-

9 rant deduxerunt. Sed et accessit et Yteron quintus artifex, qui altitudinem superioris pyramidis per viginti quatuor gradus equavit; et his superadditus sculptor sextus Pithis, cuius opus fuit quadriga marmorea fastigio totius edificii superaddita. Huic tam eximio operi perfecto, a Mausolo rege pro quo factum fuit, Mausoleum nomen impositum est, a quo tanquam a digniori, sequentium regum sepulcra mausolea denominata sunt.

10 Clarus ergo Arthemisie coniugii amor, clariores perseveratio viduitatis et lacrime, nec minus sepulcrum spectabile, seu sculptum velis, seu Arthemisie pectus in quo poti viri[3] cineres quievere. Ceterum non his tantum extollendis laudibus Arthemisie virtus inclusa permansit; nam et virili robore et audacia ac militari disciplina plurimum valuit femina et triunphis maiestatem sui nominis exornavit.

11 Hanc quidem, etsi forte sepius, saltem post viri mortem, positis ad tempus lacrimis, bis arma sumpsisse legimus; primo ut salutem patrie tutaretur, secundo ut socialem fidem requisita servaret.

12 Nam mortuo Mausolo, cum indignarentur haud longe ab Alicarnaso Rhodii mulierem regno Carie preesse, armata classe, quasi certa spe potiundi, frequentes ad occupandum illud venere.

13 Sane Alicarnasus civitas, mari iminens ycaro, in loco natura

forth living faces from the marble. It seemed, not only then but many centuries later, that the sculptors' hands had competed for glory.

Artemisia did not live to see the completion of her famous pro- 8 ject. But the artists did not abandon their work on account of the queen's death: in fact, they brought to a close what they had begun because they considered the monument to be the most certain proof for posterity of their own genius. A fifth artist was 9 summoned, namely, Pteron, who crowned the structure with an equally tall pyramid of twenty-four steps.[a] A sixth sculptor called Pythius was added to the group, and his contribution, a marble chariot with four horses, was placed atop the edifice. When this remarkable building was completed, it was named the 'Mausoleum' after King Mausolus, for whom it had been erected. From that time on, the tombs of kings have been called mausoleums after this one, the best example of the genre.

Thus the conjugal love of Artemisia gained renown, and even 10 more so her perseverance in widowhood and mourning. No less famous was the marvelous sepulcher, whether you prefer the carved version or Artemisia's own breast, wherein rested her husband's ashes which she had drunk. But Artemisia's virtue cannot be confined only to these praiseworthy accomplishments: a woman exceptionally capable of masculine vigor, daring, and military prowess, she adorned with triumphs the majesty of her name.

We read that, perhaps more often but at least twice after her 11 husband's death, she temporarily put aside her sorrow and took up arms — once to defend her country's security and on a second occasion to maintain faith with her allies at their request. When 12 Mausolus died, the people of nearby Rhodes were angered by the fact that a woman now ruled the kingdom of Caria. They came in great numbers with an armed fleet to besiege that state and, so it seemed, with every expectation of taking possession.

The city of Halicarnassus, which overlooks the Icarian Sea, is 13

munito sita est, geminos habens portus: quorum unus, qui minor dicitur, intra urbem arto introitu quasi absconditus sic iacet ut in illum, ex regia illi iminente, oportuna omnia parari atque deferri, nemine civium, nedum exterorum, vidente, possint qui regiam servant; alter, qui maior est, secus urbis menia, aperte mari continuus est.

14   In quem cum Arthemisia novisset hostes accessuros rhodios, suos iussit esse in armis et assumptis nauticis sociis et epypatis, quos oportunos ad peragendum iam conceptum animo facinus in regiam <celaverat>[4], imperavit civibus, dum signum ipsa daret, applauderent Rhodiis eosque e muris vocarent eisque spem deditionis facerent et, si possent, in forum usque contraherent.

15   Demum evestigio, quomodocunque factum sit, minime advertentibus hostibus, a minori portu in amplum mare erupit et, cum videret signo dato iam Rhodios, a civibus evocatos, relicta classe, tanquam victores cursim in forum tendere, infestis navibus et maximo nautarum conatu Rhodiorum occupata vacua classe et clamore sublato, in Rhodios undique cives suos iussit irruere; quam ob causam actum est, cum non esset fuge locus Rhodiis, ut ab Alicharnasiis cederentur omnes.

16   Hoc peracto Arthemisia, laureata Rhodiorum classe, proras direxit in Rhodum. Rhodii autem e speculis videntes laureas classi, suos obtinuisse credentes, patefacto portu portisque civitatis, non advertentes victricem hostem loco civium suscepere; et sic eorum repente ab Arthemisia civitas occupata est; iussique a victrice Rho-

17   diorum principes cedi. Ast hinc tropheum parte victorie signum in

naturally fortified and has two harbors. Of these, the one known as the lesser lies within the city; it has a narrow approach and is so hidden that from the royal palace above it one can prepare and bring into this harbor everything needed without being seen by those outside or even by the citizens protecting the palace itself. The other, larger harbor is located outside the walls of the city and is connected with the open sea.

When Artemisia learned that the Rhodian enemy would enter 14 this outer harbor, she ordered her people to arm themselves. She took with her some oarsmen and sailors whom she had hidden in the palace to help her in carrying out a stratagem of her own devising. Artemisia then ordered the citizens of Halicarnassus, until she signalled them otherwise, to cheer on the Rhodians, to call to them from the walls, to give them hope of a surrender, and, if possible, to lure them into the marketplace.

Finally, in some way or other and without the enemy's knowl- 15 edge, Artemisia suddenly sailed out of the smaller harbor into the open sea. After the signal agreed upon had been given, she saw that the Rhodians, summoned into the city by the people of Halicarnassus, had abandoned their ships and were running towards the forum like conquerors. Thereupon with her own vessels and with a mighty effort on the part of the sailors, she seized the abandoned Rhodian fleet. Then, with a loud cry, she ordered her countrymen to attack the enemy from all sides. The Rhodians had no way to escape and were all killed by the Halicarnassians.

Afterwards Artemisia sailed to Rhodes in the enemy's ships, 16 now crowned with laurel. From their lookout points, the Rhodians saw the laurel on the fleet and believed that their own soldiers had prevailed. They opened the port and the gates of the city, not realizing that they were welcoming a conquering foe instead of their compatriots. Thus the city was unexpectedly seized by Artemisia, and the Rhodian princes killed at her order. As a sign of the 17

foro Rhodiorum mandavit erigi; actumque est ut due enee statue levarentur in publico, quarum altera victricis Arthemisie represen-

18 tabat effigiem, reliqua victe rhodie civitatis. In qua stematibus positis, quod ab ea actum erat significantibus, vectigalem sibi, domum rediens, insulam liquit.

Preterea cum adversus Lacedemonas Xerxes, Persarum rex potentissimus, terras pedestribus exercitibus complesset, et litus omne occupasset classibus, omnem suo iudicio non capturus sed absorturus Greciam, requisita Arthemisia, cum armatis navibus venit in bellum; fractisque iam terrestribus Xerxis copiis, cum in conspectu Salamine in navale prelium Xerxis classis et Atheniensium sub Themistode[5] duce convenissent, spectante ex tuto Xerxe, Arthemisia inter primos principes suos exhortans atque acriter pugnans, quasi cum Xerxe sexum mutasset, visa est adeo ut, si tam audax robustusque Xerxi fuisset animus, non de facili classis eius proras vertisset in fugam.

19 Sunt tamen qui velint non Arthemisiam hanc fuisse, sed Arthemidoram, eque Alicharnasi reginam, asserentes, in testimonium sue credulitatis, navale bellum Xerxis apud Salaminam olympiade septuagesima quarta fuisse commissum, cum centesima constet mausoleum ab Arthemisia fuisse constructum.

20 Ego quidem his adhereo qui unam eandem fuisse Arthemisiam et Arthemidoram putant, cum que de Arthemisia certa narrantur plurimum fidei incertis de se exhibeant et auferant alienis.

21 Quicunque tamen legerit, quod maluerit id credat: seu una seu due fuerint, opus quippe fuit femineum unumquodque. Sed quid, Arthemisie acta spectantes, arbitrari possumus, nisi nature labo-

victory she had won, Artemisia had a memorial erected in the Rhodian forum. Two bronze statues were raised in the public square: one represented Artemisia victorious; the other, the conquered city of Rhodes, with marks of disgrace[b] signifying the defeat inflicted by Artemisia. She left the island after making it her tributary and returned home.

18

There was a second occasion when Artemisia went to war with an armed fleet. Xerxes, the powerful king of the Persians, asked for her help when he attacked the Spartans. He had covered the land with his infantry and the coast with his ships in the belief that he would not only seize but devour all of Greece. But Xerxes' land forces were already shattered when his ships encountered the Greek fleet commanded by Themistocles in a naval battle off Salamis. The king watched from a safe place while Artemisia, in the midst of her admirals, was seen urging on her men and fighting bitterly; it was almost as if she had changed sex with Xerxes. If the latter had possessed as daring and brave a spirit, his ships would not so easily have been turned to flight.

Some sources, however, report that this was not Artemisia but Artemidora, another queen of Halicarnassus. To prove their point, they adduce the fact that Xerxes' naval battle near Salamis took place during the seventy-fourth Olympiad, and it is known that Artemisia had the Mausoleum built during the one-hundredth Olympiad.

19

But I agree with those who believe that Artemisia and Artemidora were one and the same person. The trustworthy accounts we have of Artemisia lend considerable weight to the reports that are doubtful and take away our confidence in other hypotheses.

20

Whoever my readers are, let them believe what they prefer. Whether one or two women were involved, each undertaking was still that of a woman. As we admire the deeds of Artemisia, what

21

rantis errore factum ut corpori, cui Deus virilem et magnificam in-
fuderat animam, sexus femineus datus sit?

: LVIII :

De Virginea virgine Virginii filia

1 Virginea nomine et facto romana virgo pia est recolenda memoria:
fuit enim insignis decoris conspicui[1] et Auli Virginii, plebei hominis sed honesti, filia. Que esto optime esset indolis, non tantum
tamen sua constantia clara quantum scelere amantis infausti et severi nimium patris facinore, ac ex illo Romanorum libertate secuta, facta est.

2 Hec equidem, imperantibus iam anno secundo romane urbi decemviris, a genitore Lucilio Icilio tribunitio et acri iuveni desponsata est; eiusque forte distulerat nuptias expeditio a Romanis in
Algidum adversus Equos sumpta, eo quod in eadem Virginius mi-
3 litaret. Quibus sic se habentibus, infortunio Virginie factum est ut
Appio Claudio decemviro, qui ad urbem tutandam cum Spurio
Appio ex sociis militantibus solus remanserat, eius adeo formositas placeret ut ab eo amaretur perdite.

4 Cuius adhuc tenella virgo cum frustrasset blanditias, nec illis
nec donis ingentibus neque precibus aut minis flecteretur imbutum sanctitate pectus, tanto insano furore succensus est Appius
ut, cum in varia labantem volvisset animum, nec satis tutum vim
publice inferre arbitraretur, in fraudem ingenium verteret egitque
ex composito ut Marcus Claudius eiusdem libertus, homo audacie
prime, transeuntem aliquando virginem secus forum, quam primo
daretur occasio, tanquam suum mancipium fugitivum arriperet et

can we think except that the workings of nature erred in bestowing female sex on a body which God had endowed with a virile and lofty spirit?

: LVIII :

Virginia, Virgin and Daughter of Virginius

Virginia, a Roman, was a virgin in name and in fact, and she   1
should be remembered with reverence. Notable for her remarkable virtue, she was the daughter of Aulus Virginius, a plebeian but an honorable man. Although Virginia had an excellent character, she became famous not so much for her constancy as for the wickedness of her ill-starred lover, the extraordinary severity of her father, and the liberty of the Romans that resulted from it.

During the second year of the decemvirs' rule in Rome, Vir-   2
ginia's father betrothed her to Lucius Icilius, a fiery young man and a former tribune. Chance delayed the wedding, for Virginius took part in an expedition sent by the Romans to Mount Algidus against the Aequians. This was the situation when, to Virginia's   3
misfortune, the decemvir Appius Claudius was so taken with her beauty that he fell desperately in love with her. (While the others were away campaigning, he alone had remained, along with Spurius Appius, to defend Rome).

The young girl spurned his advances, and her pure heart was   4
not swayed by his flattery or extravagant gifts or entreaties or threats. Appius burned with such mad passion that, after hesitantly turning over various possibilities in his mind, he opted for cunning, regarding a public display of force as unsafe. His plan involved his freedman Marcus Claudius, a man unequalled in daring, who at the first opportunity was to seize Virginia as she passed near the forum, under the pretext that she was his runaway

in suam deduceret domum; et si quid forsan obstaret incepto, confestim se coram in causam traheret.

5   Quam cum paucos post dies ausu temerario transeuntem cepisset libertus et suam diceret, proclamante virgine atque pro viribus impuro homini obsistente, iuvantibus matronis, cum quibus una 6 incedebat, factus est repente hominum concursus. Inter quos et advenit Icilius; et multis hinc inde dictis, eo ventum est ut in pretorium coram amante iudice ducta, vix ab ardente Appio ut usque in diem futuram differretur iudicium obtentum est.

7   In qua, nil proficiente Claudii fraude, qua itum erat in castra ne venire Romam, si vocaretur, Virginius permicteretur a ducibus, evocatus affuit presto pater et cum filia et reliquis amicis et Icilio sordidatus venit in curiam, ubi econtrario Marco Claudio[2] mancipium petenti, non audito Virginio a libidinoso preside, Virginia 8 tanquam fugitiva serva adiudicata est. Quam cum capere voluisset Marcus et multa frustra[3] in Appium dixisset Virginius, ab eo tandem ira frendente obtentum est ut sibi saltem paululum et nutrici loqui fas esset, ut forte, erroris veteris comperta veritate, mancipium minori cum noxa sui concederet.

9   Cumque cum eis apud Cloatinas tabernas in conspectu tamen curie evasisset, sumpto lanii cultro, inquit: 'Qua possum via, dilecta filia, libertatem tuam vendico'; et omnem virgineo infixit pectori, maximo dolore spectantium. Ex quo infelix virgo concidens, cernentibus cunctis astantibus, sanguinem cum anima fudit; et sic libidinosi Appii per innocentis cedem spes turpissima exinanita est

slave, and take her to his house. If Virginia put up any opposition, Claudius was to bring her immediately before Appius for arraignment.

A few days later, the freedman seized Virginia with reckless 5 boldness as she passed by, and he claimed that she was his slave. The girl cried out and resisted the wicked man with all her might. The women with whom she was walking tried to help her, and a crowd of people quickly gathered. Icilius was among them. After 6 a lengthy exchange between the two sides, Virginia was finally brought to the pretorium to face the judge, her would-be lover. Only with great difficulty was the concession won from the ardent Appius that judgment would be delayed to a future day.

Then Claudius went to the camp and ordered that, if Virginius 7 were sent for, his officers should not allow him to come to Rome. This stratagem, however, did not work, for the father came immediately upon being summoned. Still wearing his dirty clothes, he entered the court with his daughter, Icilius, and other friends. There, in opposition, was Marcus Claudius who claimed the girl as his property. The lustful judge, without giving Virginius a hearing, decreed that Virginia was a fugitive slave. Marcus wanted to 8 take her away, and Virginius launched many fruitless verbal attacks against Appius. Finally the furious parent obtained permission for himself and her nurse to speak briefly with the girl, on the grounds that he might perhaps hand over the slave with less loss of dignity should the truth behind an old error be brought to light.

He left with the two women and went to a place, still in sight 9 of the court, near the shops around the temple of Venus Cloacina. Seizing a butcher knife, Virginius cried, "Dear daughter, I restore your liberty in the only way I can," and, to the shock of the onlookers, he plunged the knife into his daughter's breast. The unfortunate girl fell to the ground, bleeding profusely, and died in front of everyone. Thus did the innocent victim's death thwart the

et opere Virginii ac Icilii facta secunda plebis secessione, actum est ut decemviri coacti abdicarent imperium et romano populo quam occupaverant libertatem linquerent.

10 Nec multo post, Virginio plebis tribuno procurante, Appio Claudio dies dicta est. Qui cum causam dicturus accederet, in carcerem iussu Virginii tractus et cathenis implicitus, ut meritum effugeret dedecus, nocuus manes innocue piavit Virginie, laqueo

11 seu gladio vel veneno ibidem vitam eiecit. Temerarius autem cliens Marcus Claudius crimen, non qua debuit via, nam fuga tutatus, deflevit exilio, bonis tam patroni quam suis redactis in publicum.

12 Nil pernitiosius iniquo iudice. Hic quotiens sceleste mentis imperium sequitur, omnis iuris ordo pervertatur necesse est, legum potestas solvatur, virtutis enervetur opus, sceleri laxentur habene et breviter omne bonum publicum in ruinam⁴ trahatur.

Quod si non satis alias apparet, nepharium Appii ceptum et

13 que inde secuta sunt in lucem deducunt. Nam dum male libidini sue potens homo frenum poneret, ex libera servam, ex virgine adulteram, ex desponsata pelicem, per imbutum fraude libertum fere peregit suoque detestabili decreto factum est ut armaretur pater in filiam, verteretur pietas in sevitiam et, ne voto fraude quesito gauderet incestus homo, occideretur innocua, clamaretur in urbe, tumultuaretur in castris, separatio plebis a patribus oriretur et fere in discrimine res omnis poneretur romana.

lecherous Appius' vile hopes. The efforts of Virginius and Icilius resulted in the withdrawal of the plebeians for a second time, and the decemvirs were forced to resign and give back to the people the freedom they had seized.

Not long after, on the initiative of Virginius, who was now tri-   10 bune of the plebs, Appius Claudius was indicted. When Claudius went to answer the charges, he was dragged off to prison at Virginius' orders and bound with chains. In order to escape his deserved infamy, the guilty perpetrator expiated the death of the innocent Virginia by taking his own life with a rope or a sword or poison. But his reckless follower Marcus Claudius did not pay for   11 his crime as he should have; taking safety in flight, he bemoaned his wicked deed in exile, and both his property and that of his patron were confiscated by the state.

There is nothing more dangerous than a corrupt judge. When-   12 ever he follows the dictates of his wicked mind, every due procedure of justice is necessarily perverted, the power of the laws is broken, virtuous activity is weakened, curbs on crime are loosened: in short, the public welfare as a whole is dragged down to ruin.

If this is not sufficiently obvious from other events, then Appius' nefarious scheme and its consequences make it clear as day. This powerful man did not restrain his concupiscence; with the   13 help of his corrupt freedman, he almost succeeded in making a slave of a free woman, an adulteress of a virgin, and a whore of a woman who was engaged to be married. As a result of Appius' abominable decision, a father took up arms against his own daughter and parental love turned into cruelty. To prevent his lewd enjoyment of a pleasure gained through a trick, an innocent girl was killed, a city was thrown into an uproar, a military camp into rebellion, the plebeians seceded from the patricians, and practically the entire Roman state was endangered.

14   O preses inclitus et legum lator egregius! Quod in alios diro
supplicio punisse debuerat, ipse perpetrare veritus non est.

Hei michi! Quotiens hac periclitamur peste mortales, quotiens
in exitium immeriti trahimur et turpi premimur iugo, agimur spo-
15   liamur et occidimur, urgente nequitia! Quid hoc mali est? Non ve-
rentur prefecti, quod in temperamentum libidinum adinventum
est, id nullo Dei timore territi, in licentiam vertere scelerum; et
cum oporteat presidem oculos et animum eque pudicos habere,
eloquium mite, graves sanctosque mores et manus a muneribus
omnino immunes, non oculis tantum, sed insana mente lasciviunt,
nec legum sed lenonum sequuntur[5] iudicia; superbiunt nec mite-
scunt nisi meretricula imperet, aut iras leniat aurum; nec solum
dona suscipiunt, sed exposcunt mercantur et subtrahunt et in violentiam usque, si aliter nequit fieri quod cupiunt, furore succensi
prorumpunt.

16   Et sic optime legum interpretes[6] facte, hinc luxuria inde pecunia, incassum pro rostris ius poscitur, nisi ab his vel ab earum altera suffragia inpendantur.

: LIX :

De Yrene Cratini filia

1   Yrenes utrum fuerit greca mulier, aut qua floruerit etate, non satis
certum est; greca tamen creditur constatque eam Cratini cuiusdam
pictoris fuisse filiam atque discipulam. Quam tantum laudabilio-
rem existimo quantum arte et fama videtur superasse magistrum,
cum eius adhuc in pluribus nomen vigeat, existente patre nisi per

CHAPTER LIX

What an outstanding magistrate and noble administrator of the 14
law he was! Appius himself was not afraid to commit what it was
his duty to punish severely in others.

Alas! How often are we mortals endangered by a plague like
this! How often are we brought undeservedly to ruin and held in
dishonorable restraint, persecuted, robbed, and killed at the bidding of such wickedness! How evil is this act? The authorities, 15
with no fear of God, dare to turn into a license for crime an insti-
tution established to moderate the passions. An official should exercise an equal self-control over his eyes and his mind; he should
possess temperate speech, austere and upright conduct, and hands
immune from bribes. Instead, they embrace licentiousness not
only with their eyes but also with their frenzied minds; they follow the counsels of panderers rather than of the *Pandects*.[a] They
are proud and economical of mercy — unless a prostitute demands
it, or their wrath is softened by gold. Not only do they receive
gifts: they insist on them, traffic in them, and steal them. If they
cannot otherwise obtain what they covet, they burn with fury and
rush to use violence.

Thus dissipation and gold have been established as the best in- 16
terpreters of the laws: if we do not have the help of one or both of
them, we shall seek justice from the courts in vain.

: LIX :

Irene, Daughter of Cratinus

It is not really clear if Irene was a Greek woman and when she 1
flourished; she is, nevertheless, believed to have been a Greek. We
know that she was the daughter and pupil of a certain painter
named Cratinus. I regard Irene as all the more worthy of praise
since she surpassed her master in art and in fame. Her name is

eam fere innominato, excepto si is fuit de quo legitur qui frondes
atque radices herbarum omnium, ad earum prestandam notitiam,
in forma descripsit propria, esto hic Cratinax non Cratinus ab aliquibus nuncupetur.

2   Huius autem Yrene celebre[1] fuit ingenium et artificium memorabile; cuius quidem magisterii in longum argumenta fuere: puella
quedam que[2] apud Eleusinam civitatem diu tabula visa est; sic et
senex Calipso, preterea et gladiator Theodorus necnon et Abstite-
nes, suo tempore saltator egregius.

3   Que, ideo quod officium est a femina, ut plurimum, alienum
nec absque[3] vi maxima ingenii consecutum, quod in eis tardissi-
mum esse consuevit, dignum aliqua celebrari laude ratus sum.

: LX :

De Leuntio

1   Leuntium, si satis bene arbitror, greca fuit mulier et forsan
Alexandri magni, macedonici regis, evo conspicua. Cuius, si ma-
tronalem pudicitiam servasset, cum ingenii eius permaxime fuerint
vires, longe fulgidior nominis fuisset gloria.

2   Veterum enim testimonio tantum in studiis literarum valuit, ut
aut invidia percita, aut muliebri temeritate inpulsa, in Theophra-
stum, celeberrimum ea tempestate[1] phylosophum, scribere inve-
hendo ausa sit: quid, ego non vidi. Sane postquam per[2] tot secula
in etatem usque nostram fama devenit, non minimum fuisse nec
etiam parve facultatis inditium existimare possumus, esto invidi
animi sit certissimum argumentum.

still respected by many, while her father is hardly known except on her account, unless he was the man who is said to have given us full and accurate information about the leaves and roots of all plants. Some sources, however, give the latter's name as Cratinax, not Cratinus.

Irene was famous for her talent, and her skill deserves to be 2 remembered. Proofs of her masterly ability survived for a long time: a girl seen on a panel painting at Eleusis, the aged Calypso, Theodorus the gladiator, and Alcisthenes, a celebrated dancer in his day.

I thought that these achievements merited some praise because 3 the art of painting is mostly alien to the feminine mind and cannot be attained without that great intellectual concentration which women, as a rule, are very slow to acquire.

: LX :

Leontium

If I am right, Leontium was a Greek woman who achieved fame 1 perhaps in the time of Alexander the Great, king of Macedonia. If she had preserved her matronly honor, the glory attached to her name would have been much more radiant, for she had extraordinary intellectual powers.

According to the testimony of ancient authors, Leontium so 2 excelled in the study of literature that, prompted either by envy or feminine temerity, she dared to write an invective against Theophrastus, a famous philosopher of that period. I have not seen this work. But its fame has lasted throughout the centuries down to our own age; hence we cannot say that the work was a trifle or showed a lack of ability, although it is a clear sign of an envious disposition.

3   Et si adeo studiis tam splendidis valuit, non facile credam eam ex plebeia fece duxisse originem; raro quippe ex ea sorde ingenium su<b>lime[3] surgit; nam etsi quandoque e celo infundatur, caligine

4   extreme sortis claritas eius opprimitur. Sed quid progenitorum generosus sanguis, si morum indecentia sit, veri possunt fulgoris inpendere? Si amplissimis fidem prestemus viris, hec seposito pudore femineo meretrix, imo meretricula, fuit.

5   Heu facinus indignum! Inter lenones impurosque mechos et scorta atque fornices versata, potuit magistram rerum phylosophiam inhonestis in cellulis et ignominiosis deturpare notis atque impudicis calcare vestigiis et cloacis immergere fetidis, si phylosophie splendor obfuscari potest impudici pectoris labe. Dolendum equidem est ingenium tam celebre, sacro superumque munere datum, adeo spurcido[4] exercitio subigi potuisse.

6   Edepol nescio utrum illam fortiorem dixerim, in tam scelestum locum phylosophiam trahendo, an phylosophiam ipsam remissiorem, doctum pectus subigi lasciviis permictendo.

: LXI :

De Olympiade regina Macedonie

1   Olympias Macedonum regina titulorum multiplicium fuit illustris. Primo quidem, si possunt stemata aliquid claritatis afferre mortalibus, ex Eacidarum sanguine, qui tunc pre ceteris totius Grecie seu orbis terrarum habebatur splendidior, Neoptholemi, regis Molossorum, filia traxit originem; et cum illi ab infantia Mistilis nomen

Since she was so brilliant in such a distinguished field of study, 3
I will not easily believe that Leontium was of humble plebeian origin. It is rare indeed for sublime genius to spring from those dregs,
for even if genius is sometimes implanted there by heaven, its radiance is darkened by the shadows of lowly estate. Yet what true 4
splendor can the noble blood of ancestors impart where there
is unbecoming conduct? If we may believe trustworthy sources,
Leontium disregarded feminine decency and was a courtesan, or
rather, a little trollop.

What disgraceful behavior! Living in the brothels among 5
pimps, vile adulterers, and whores, she was able to stain Philosophy, the teacher of truth, with ignominy in those disgraceful
chambers, trample it with wanton feet, and plunge it into filthy
sewers—if indeed the splendor of Philosophy can be dimmed by
the infamous action of an unchaste heart. We must certainly be-
wail the fact that so brilliant a talent, bestowed as a sacred gift
from heaven, could be subjected to so filthy a way of life.

Quite honestly, I do not know whether to say that Leontium 6
was the stronger of the two in that she dragged Philosophy down
to so wicked a place, or that Philosophy was the weaker because she allowed an enlightened heart to be dominated by licentiousness.

: LXI :

Olympias, Queen of Macedonia

Olympias, queen of Macedonia, had many titles to fame. First, if 1
lineage can confer any distinction upon mortal beings, she was the
daughter of Neoptolemus, king of the Molossians, and thus descended from the Aeacidae, who were regarded as the most illustrious family in Greece or, rather, in the entire world. Her name at
birth was Mistilis; it was only when she married Philip, who at the

esset, nupta Phylippo, serenissimo ea tempestate Macedonum regi, Olympias — ut placet aliquibus — primo vocata est.

2   Preterea et Alexandrum Epyri regem fratrem habuit et Macedonie, Phylippo mortuo, filium Alexandrum; cuius tam ingentia fuere facinora, ut qui superaret illum gloria, inani tamen, nec audi-

3 retur natus, nec nasceretur in posterum. Quod Olympiadi non modicum fulgoris adiunxit, si matribus fulgor est prestantes peperisse filios. Sed non omnino iubar hoc evasisse potuit quin notis aliquando iniectis fuscaretur, esto ex illis Olympias evasisset notior.

    Nam adulterii illecebra, eius etate florente, Olympias labefactata est, qua nil fere dedecorosius regine contigisse potuit; et, quod

4 turpius fuit, suspicatum est Alexandrum adulterio genitum. Que quidem suspicio adeo commovit Phylippum ut, non solum aliquando palam diceret, ex se scilicet non genitum Alexandrum, verum et Olympiadem ignominia notaret repudii et Cleopatram,

5 Alexandri epyrote filiam, in uxorem duceret. Quod quantum Olympias egre tulerit, dissimulare non potuit. Nam que usque in diem illam, hac excepta labe, regiis tantum fulgoribus clara erat, enormitatibus variis sese fecit insignem.

    Creditum quidem est a se agitatum atque inpulsum Pausaniam iuvenem, ex splendido Horestis sanguine natum, in Phylippi viri

6 sui necem, conscio etiam Alexandro. Nam Pausanie, ob occisum Phylippum, in cruce pendentis, caput, opere Olympie, mane sequenti a die qua cruci affixus fuerat, aurea insignitum corona compertum est; et, paucis interpositis diebus, Olympiade iubente, eius cadaver depositum super reliquiis regi\<s\>[1] Phylippi honorifice ma-

7 cedonico ritu exustum est et funebri cum pompa sepultum. Gladium preterea, quo Phylippum Pausanias occiderat, regina sub nomine Mistilis[2] in templo Apollinis iussit apponi et Cleopatram sibi

time was the Most Serene King of Macedonia, that (as is sometimes reported) she began to be called Olympias.

In addition, Olympias' brother was Alexander, king of Epirus, 2
and at Philip's death her son Alexander became king of Macedonia. The latter's deeds were so awesome that the man who would
surpass him in glory (empty though it is) has never been born, so
far as we know, nor is he likely ever to be born. Accordingly, a 3
great deal of luster accrued to Olympias, if it is glorious for mothers to give birth to outstanding sons. But her radiance could not
wholly escape occultation by some darker hues, though Olympias
emerged from these occasional episodes with still greater fame.

For example, in her youth she fell prey to the snare of adultery—and hardly anything more shameful could have happened to
a queen. Still worse, however, was the suspicion that Alexander
had been born of her adulterous union. Philip was so troubled by 4
this notion that, not only did he say openly at times that Alexander was not his son, but he also disgraced Olympias by repudiat-
ing her and marrying Cleopatra, daughter of Alexander of Epirus.
Olympias could not conceal how bitter a blow this was to her. Un- 5
til that day, she had been famous only (excepting her infamous act
of adultery) for regal splendor; henceforth she distinguished herself by various monstrous actions.

It was believed, for instance, that Olympias incited Pausanias, a
young man descended from the eminent line of Orestes, to kill her
husband Philip, and that Alexander was in on the plot. While 6
Pausanias was hanging on the cross the day after he had been
crucified for the murder of Philip, he was found to have on his
head a golden crown put there by Olympias. A few days later, at
Olympias' orders, his body was placed over the remains of King
Philip and cremated with honors according to the Macedonian
rite, then buried in a solemn funeral. The queen ordered the 7
sword Pausanias had used to kill Philip to be hung in the temple
of Apollo under the name of Mistilis. She also had Cleopatra's

superinductam, post illisam saxo filiam, in tantum exasperavit verbis et ignominia ut miseram ad laqueum induendum compelleret.

8 Aucto tandem maximis victoriis filio Alexandro, eoque apud Babiloniam veneno assumpto, et Alexandro fratre apud Lucanos ceso, ac Arideo Macedonie rege et Euridice coniuge, eam Macedoniam ab Epyro venientem intrare prohibentibus, favore veterum Macedonum datis in mortem, Macedonum regnum sola obtinuit vidua et regina; verum cum passim in cruorem tam nobilium quam plebeiorum Macedonum quasi belua bacharetur, a Cassandro in Epydua civitate obsessa est adeoque coacta ut una cum oppidanis, rerum omnium inopia, deveniret in famem; qua cogente actum est ut, conditionibus appositis, se in fidem Cassandri commicteret.

9 Qui fraude exornatis occisorum amicis, post deditionem in mortem postulata est. Ad quam occidendam cum Cassander ubi detinebatur scelerum ministros intromisisset, ea iam advertente se manu venientium morituram, duabus innixa ancillis imperterrita surrexit et vestimentis crinibusque composita, ne quid cadens videretur inhonestum, nec orare passa est nec audita voces aut ululatus femineos emictere, quin imo percussoribus obvia facta paratum in vulnera corpus obtulit ultro, quasi pauci penderet quod robustissimi etiam homines consuevere, ut plurimum, expavescere: actu illo confessa se vere extitisse imperatoris tam egregii genitricem.

daughter dashed to pieces on a rock. Then with her slanderous words Olympias so infuriated Cleopatra, the illegitimate wife who had supplanted her, that she drove the poor woman to hang herself.

At length Olympias' son Alexander, grown famous for his brilliant victories, died of poison in Babylonia, and her brother Alexander was killed in Lucania. Olympias was on her way to Macedonia from Epirus when Arrhidaeus, king of Macedonia, and his wife Eurydice forbade her to enter; they were murdered by some elderly Macedonian accomplices. Thus Olympias, a widowed queen, became the sole ruler of Macedonia. But she raged like a wild beast and everywhere slaughtered Macedonian nobles as well as commoners. She was besieged by Cassander in the city of Pydna and eventually reduced, along with the inhabitants, to starvation and penury. This forced Olympias to come to terms with the enemy and to entrust herself to Cassander's protection. 8

After she had surrendered, the friends of those whom she had killed were suborned to demand Olympias' execution. Cassander sent assassins to kill her in the prison where she was being kept. Realizing that she was to die at the hands of the approaching men, Olympias arose undaunted and, supported by two maidservants, combed her hair and arranged her clothes so that there would be nothing undignified about her fall. She did not permit herself any entreaty, nor was she heard to utter any cries or womanly laments. Instead, she walked towards her executioners and voluntarily offered her body to their blows, as if she scorned what even the bravest of men are wont to fear. With that act Olympias proclaimed herself truly to be the mother of so illustrious a commander as Alexander. 9

: LXII :

De Claudia vestali virgine

1 Claudiam vestalem virginem, digne ex Romanorum generoso sanguine procreatam crediderim, dum intueor insignem pietatem eius
in patrem. Pompa quippe spectabili pre se ex senatus consulto
triunphum pater agebat, frequenti Romanorum spectante plebe,
cum se tribunorum plebis unus, ob privatam simultatem in eum
non aliter quam in male meritum prorumpens, dedit in medium;
et insolenti, more tribunitio, audacia violentas manus in triun-
phantem iniciens, eum de curru evolvere conatus est.

2 Quod cum inter spectantes Claudia virgo conspiceret, illico urgente pietate commota, tristis et oblita sexus honestatisque victa-
rum, quibus obtecta erat, pati non potuit, quin imo, repente me-
dias inter catervas impetuosa prorumpens, et sibi audaci nisu
cedere turbam cogens, inter tribuni arrogantiam et patris gloriam
se indefesso robore immiscuit et, quibuscunque ausis factum sit,
amoto tribuno, liberum in Capitolium patri concessit ascensum.

3 O dulcis amor! O infracta pietas! Quid credemus vires imbecilli
corpori prestitisse virginis, quid religionis oblivionem iniecisse,
preter eum cernere iniuria opprimi quem meminerat infantie sue
educatorem et piis delenitorem blanditiis, votorum in suam salutem exhibitorem, noxiorum amotorem omnium et provectioris
etatis instructorem?

4 Sed, ut de hoc satis dictum sit, queso: quis ob[1] hoc tumultuantibus hominibus sanctimonialem immixtam virginem de inhone-
state redarguet? Quis temerariam dicet? Quis tanquam in tribuni-
tiam potestatem ausam iure damnabit, cum adeo pulchrum atque

: LXII :

Claudia, a Vestal Virgin

Considering the remarkable devotion she had for her father, I am inclined to believe that Claudia, a Vestal virgin, was a worthy descendant of noble Roman stock. By decree of the Senate, her father was celebrating a triumph with great pomp before a large crowd of Romans. Suddenly, moved by private enmity, a tribune of the plebs stepped forward and lunged towards him as if against one who deserved ill. With the arrogant boldness characteristic of the tribunes, this man laid violent hands on the victor and tried to pull him down from the chariot.   1

The virgin Claudia, who was among the spectators, saw what had happened and was distressed and saddened because of the love she bore her father. Unable to endure the situation, she forgot her sex and the dignity of the headbands she was wearing. At once she rushed impetuously into the midst of the crowd. Her bold dash compelled the bystanders to give way, and Claudia forced herself between the arrogant tribune and her father who was in the midst of his triumph. In her daring she somehow managed to push the tribune aside and assure her father free ascent to the Capitol.   2

What sweet love! What firm devotion! What shall we believe gave strength to the maiden's weak body? What shall we believe made her forget to act as a Vestal, if not the sight of a shameful attack on her father — the father she remembered nurturing her as a child, consoling her with his affectionate caresses, granting those desires which were for her own good, keeping her safe from all harm, and guiding her as she grew to womanhood?   3

But enough of this, please. Who will use her action as a pretext to accuse a cloistered virgin of indecency because she mingled with riotous men? Who will say that she was rash? Who can in justice condemn her for defying the tribune's power in order to defend   4

memorabile pietatis opus in tutandum patrium decus egerit, ut
etiam robustissimus iuvenis acriori animo fecisse nequiverit?

5   Equidem non immerito dubitem quis spectabiliorem triunphum: an pater in Capitolium traxerit, an nata in edem reportave-
rit Veste.

: LXIII :

De Virginea Lucii Volupnii coniuge

1 Verginea[1] apud Romanos equidem clara matrona fuit, altera tamen a superiori, esto eque Auli cuiusdam, sed patritii viri, fuerit
genita. Hec enim, preter nobilitatis insignia, suo evo castimonie
meritis ceteris fuit preferenda Romanis. Cuius actum unicum sed
laudandissimum retulisse, ad eius omnem vitam cognoscendam,
eique ad claritatem meritam inpendendam, sat erit.

2 Ut satis igitur constat, fuit olim in urbe Roma in foro boario ad
rotundam Herculis edem sacellum celebre patritie Pudicitie du-
3 dum a nobilibus mulieribus persancte dicatum. In quo, Q. Fabio,
quinto, et P. Decio Mure, quarto, consulibus, cum senatus iussu,
uti et in ceteris templis, supplicationes ad expianda prodigia fie-
rent, et ibidem patritie tantum femine sacra ritu veteri castissime
peragerent, contigit ut Virginea cum ceteris peracta sacrum accederet; a quo cum, matronis patritiis imperantibus, superbe se-
mota esset, eo quod Lucio Volumnio, plebeio homini, anno tamen
preterito consuli, nupta foret, brevis apud sacram edem feminea
altercatio orta est; que tandem muliebri indignatione in maius ani-

her father by an act of devotion so beautiful and memorable as to be impossible for even a young man of great strength and passion?

Certainly I question, and not without reason, which of the two 5 celebrated the more glorious triumph: the father ascending the Capitol or the daughter returning to the temple of Vesta.

: LXIII :

Virginia, Wife of Lucius Volumnius

Virginia was a famous Roman matron, but she is different from 1 the Virginia mentioned above.[a] Although the father of this Virginia was also named Aulus, he was a patrician. Her purity in addition to her nobility entitled her to a preeminent position among the Roman women of her time. It will be sufficient to relate a single but highly laudable deed of hers in order to know her entire life and to award her the fame that is her due.

As is well known, there was at that time in the Forum Boarium 2 of the city of Rome, near the round temple of Hercules, a famous shrine consecrated not long since by the noblewomen to Pudicitia Patricia. During the fifth consulate of Quintus Fabius and the 3 fourth of Publius Decius Mus, the Senate decreed that supplications should be made in this shrine, as in the other temples, to avert certain divine portents. While a gathering consisting solely of patrician women was devoutly engaged in performing the sacred rites according to ancient custom, Virginia and other women happened to come for this purpose to the shrine of Pudicitia Patricia. There a brief quarrel broke out among them when Virginia was haughtily removed from the temple by order of the patrician ladies. This was because she was the wife of Lucius Volumnius, a plebeian who had, however, been consul the previous year. Eventually the quarrel, feeding on female indignation, burst into flame.

4 morum incendium sese extulit. Ceterum cum se dixisset Virginea
et pudicam esse et patritiam, et ex templo patritie Pudicitie arceri
minime deberi eo quod plebeio homini virgo nupsisset, et gesta
viri miris extulisset laudibus, relictis patritiis, domum indignans
repetiit verbisque opus superadiecit egregium.

5 Nam cum sibi multum edium esset in vico Longo, in quibus
tunc una cum viro habitabat, quantum ex eis ex parte una sufficere
sacello modico arbitrata est, seclusit a ceteris et ibidem aram instituit accersitisque matronis plebeis arrogantiam patritiarum exposuit et questa ex suscepta ab illis iniuria subdidit: 'Vos ergo
deprecor hortorque ut, uti cernitis huius urbis viros habere conti-
nuum de virtute certamen, sic et inter vos solius decoris pudicitie matronalis certamen summatis, operam dantes ut hec ara,
quam ego plebeie Pudicitie presentibus vobis dico, si in aliquo potest, sanctius illa et a castioribus coli credatur appareatque, agentibus vobis, non solum celestes animas pectoribus patritiarum in-
fundi.'

6 O digna atque sanctissima matrone verba! O indignatio laudanda et inventum in astra leto plausu extollendum! Non in virorum substantias, non ad ornamenta lascivie capessenda a Virginea
coniuratum est, quin imo in lascivos petulantesque iuvenum oculos atque concupiscentias et ad suam promerendam castimonie
gloriam optimo instituto sanctisque viribus itum est, adeo ut tunc
inceptum et diu post hec actum sit ut, cum nulla, nisi spectate pudicitie et que uni tantum viro nupsisset, sacrificandi ius eo presta-

Virginia declared that she was a good woman and a patrician, and 4
that she should not be barred from the temple of Pudicitia Patricia
on the grounds that she had married a plebeian. After extolling
her husband's deeds in a magnificent eulogy, she left the patrician
women and returned home in anger. Here she followed up her
words with a remarkable deed.

Virginia owned many houses in the Vicus Longus where she 5
and her husband lived at the time. On one side of this street,
she separated from the other buildings a group of houses which
she thought would be enough for a modest shrine. There she
erected an altar. Then Virginia summoned the married plebeian
women and told them about the arrogance of the patrician ladies.
Complaining of the insult she had received from the latter, she
added: "I beg and implore you to compete with each other in the
single virtue of wifely modesty, just as you see the men of this city
vie continuously with each other in valor. Thus, this altar, which
in your presence I consecrate to Pudicitia Plebeia, will be thought
venerated, if possible, in a holier manner and by chaster women
than is the shrine of Pudicitia Patricia. Your mode of conduct will
also show that god-like souls are not implanted only in the breasts
of patrician women."

How fitting and how holy were the words of this woman! How 6
laudable her anger, how deserving of applause and exaltation her
foundation! Virginia did not conspire against husbands' wealth or
aim to acquire the trappings of wantonness. Rather, she attacked
the lascivious, impertinent eyes and sexual appetites of young
men, and her plan was to acquire a lasting reputation for purity
through this excellent foundation and through the power of
sanctity. It was the rule at the beginning, and for a long time afterwards, that the right to offer sacrifice in the temple would be given
only to women of proven goodness and to those who had been
married just once. The effect was to shatter the hopes of lewd persons who watched the sacrifices with impious eyes. Hence the al-

retur in templo, et, spectantium incestuosis oculis fracta libidinosa
spe, sanctitate patritie equaretur are.

7 Nec dubitem multis ob glorie cupidinem et effugiendam ignominiam, si a sacrificio arcerentur, servande castimonie causam
atque studium iniecisse.

: LXIV :

De Flora meretrice dea florum et Zephiri coniuge

1 Floram romanam fuisse mulierem testari videtur antiquitas: cui
quantum decoris ignominiosus questus subtraxit, tantum fame
fortuna fautrix ausit.

2 Hec autem, ut omnes asserunt, ditissima fuit mulier, sed de
questu divitiarum discrepant. Nam alii dicunt hanc omnem iuventutis sue ac formositatis corporee florem, inter fornices et lenones
scelestosque iuvenes, meretricio publico consumpsisse; et nunc
hos, nunc illos stolidos lasciviis blanditiisque — ut talim moris
est — substantiarum denudans et undique corradens et excerpens,
in eas tam amplissimas devenisse divitias.

3 Alii vero honestius arbitrati, lepidam et ridiculam ex ea referunt
hystoriam, asserentes Rome edituum Herculis ociosum tesseris ludum inchoasse manibus alternis, quarum cum Herculi dextram
statuisset, et sinistram sibi, dicunt fecisse periculum ut, si vincere-
tur Hercules, ipse sibi de stipe templi cenam et amicam pararet; si
vero Hercules victor evaderet, tunc illi de pecunia propria illud
idem facturum se dixit.

4 Verum cum vicisset Hercules, monstra etiam solitus superare,

tar of Pudicitia Plebeia came to equal in holiness that of Pudicitia Patricia.

I am confident that Virginia gave to many women eager for a good reputation and embarrassed at being excluded from sacrifice the motive and desire to preserve their virginity. 7

: LXIV :

Flora the Prostitute, Goddess of Flowers and Wife of Zephyrus

The ancients seem to say that Flora was a Roman woman to whom kindly Fortune gave a fame equal to the good name she lost through her disgraceful occupation. 1

Our sources state unanimously that she was very wealthy, but there is a difference of opinion as to how Flora acquired this wealth. Some say that she squandered the flower of her youth and expended her physical beauty as a common prostitute amid panderers and degenerate young men in the brothels. With the wanton enticements customarily employed by such women, she stripped (they say) this or that simpleton of his riches, and by gnawing and picking everywhere she eventually became immensely wealthy. 2

Others, however, have judged her in a better light and tell the following witty and droll story. One day the custodian of the temple of Hercules in Rome was idle and began to play with dice, throwing them first with one hand and then with the other. He decided that the right hand would play for Hercules and the left for himself under these conditions: if Hercules lost, the custodian would get dinner and a girlfriend for himself with the temple's money; and, if Hercules were victorious, the custodian would do the same for the god with his own money. 3

Hercules, accustomed to beating monsters, won the game, and 4

ei cenam et nobilem meretricem Floram preparasse confirmant. Cui dormienti in templo visum aiunt cum Hercule concubuisse eique ab eodem dictum se suscepturam mercedem concubitus ab
5 eo quem, primo mane, templum exiens, inveniret. Que cum Fanitio, ditissimo iuveni, templum exiens occurrisset, ab eo amata atque deducta est; et, cum secum fuisset diu, ab eodem moriente heres relicta; et sic ditata.

6 Verum sunt qui dicant hanc non Floram, sed Accam Laurentiam fuisse, que Romulum Remumque seu nutriverat, seu nutrivit postea. Sane huius discordantie ego non curo, dummodo constet Floram meretricem et divitem extitisse.

7 Hec autem, ut eo tendam quo cupio, adveniente mortalis vite termino, cum nullus illi filius esset et nominis perpetuandi cupido, ut reor, femineo astu, in futuram sui nominis gloriam, romanum populum substantiarum suarum sibi dixit heredem; in hoc tamen parte divitiarum servata, ut, quod ex ea annuum susciperetur fenus, in anniversarium natalis sui, ludis publice factis, erogaretur omne.

8 Nec eam fefellit opinio. Nam cum gratiam romane plebis ex hereditate suscepta captasset, annuos in memoriam sui nominis fieri ludos obtinuit facile: in quibus, spectante vulgo, ad eius puto questum posteris ostendendum, inter alia turpia, nude meretrices mimorum officium, summa cum inspicientium voluptate, gesticula-
9 tionibus impudicis et variis exercebant. Qua illecebri ostentatione actum est ut, seu ex fenore suscepto, seu ex ere publico, annis singulis cum instantia ludi huiusmodi, tanquam sanctissimi, a plebe, in libidinem prona, peterentur; et florales ab institutrice etiam dicerentur.

the custodian is said to have supplied him with dinner and with Flora, a celebrated courtesan. While Flora was asleep in the temple, she dreamed of having lain with Hercules who told her that she would receive payment for her services from a man she would encounter on leaving the temple in the early morning. In fact, as she was going out of the temple, she met Fanitius, a very wealthy youth, who fell in love with her and took her to his house. Flora stayed with him for a long time and, when he died, he made her his heir. That was how she acquired her money.

But there are some authorities who claim that the woman was not Flora but Acca Larentia, who had nursed (or who later nursed) Romulus and Remus. This disagreement does not matter to me as long as it is clear that Flora was rich and a prostitute.

To proceed with my story: Flora was childless. When her life was drawing to a close, she desired, I think, to perpetuate her name. So she employed womanly cunning and named, with a view to her own future renown, the Roman people as heir to her fortune. But she set aside part of this wealth, stipulating that the total yearly interest from the sum should be used for public games to be held on her birthday.

Flora was not disappointed in her expectation. She gained the people's favor through the inheritance she had left them and easily succeeded in having annual games celebrated in memory of her name. During these events, among other lewd enactments before the crowd, there was a pantomime by naked prostitutes; to the great delight of the viewers, they practiced their art with various bawdy gestures for the purpose (in my opinion) of reminding posterity of Flora's profession. The masses, given as ever to lust, liked the steamy spectacle and insisted religiously on the repetition of similar games each year, with the expenses paid from the interest accumulated on Flora's bequest or from the public fisc. They were called the "Floral Games" after the woman who had established them.

10   Sane tractu temporis cum senatus, originis eorum conscius, erubesceret, urbem, iam rerum dominam, tam obscena maculari nota, ut in meretricis laudes concurreret omnis, adverteretque illam facile deleri non posse, ad ignominiam subtrahendam, turpitudini detestabilem atque ridiculum superiniunxit errorem.

11   Finxit quippe in splendorem Flore, inclite testatricis, fabulam, et ignaro iam populo recitavit: illam asserens iamdudum mire pulchritudinis indigenam fuisse nynpham, nomine Cloram, et a Zephyro vento, quem latine Favonium dicimus, ardentissime amatam et postremo in coniugem sumptam; eique, ab eodem quem, stultitia sua, inter deos nominabant, dotalitio quodam munere, seu propter nuptias, ut fit, deitatem fuisse concessam: hoc cum officio, ut vere primo arbores colles et prata floribus exornaret eisque preesset; et inde ex Clora Flora etiam diceretur; et quoniam fructus ex floribus sequerentur, ut, deitate eius placata ludis, illos ampla quadam liberalitate concederet et in fructum deduceret, eidem dee sacrum aras ludosque a vetustate fuisse concessos.

12   Qua seducti fallacia, eam, que vivens fornices coluerat, a quibuscunque etiam pro minima stipe prostrata, quasi suis alis Zephyrus illam in celum detulerit, cum Iunone regina deabusque aliis sedere arbitrati sunt. Et sic ingenio suo Flora et fortune munere ex male quesita pecunia, ex meretrice nynpha facta est Zephyrique lucrata coniugium et deitatis numen, apud mortales, in templis residens, divinis honoribus celebrata, adeo ut, non solum ex Clora Flora, sed clara ubique locorum, ex insigni sui temporis scorto, facta sit.

In the course of time the Senate, aware of the origin of these   10
games, was embarrassed to have their city, now mistress of the
world, tarnished by so foul a blot, namely, the general rush to celebrate a prostitute. Realizing, however, that the obscenity could not
easily be removed, it superimposed on the shameful spectacle a
disgusting and laughable fiction with the aim of removing the disgrace.

A story was invented in honor of Flora, the illustrious bene-   11
factor, and recited to the now ignorant populace. The tale goes as
follows. Once there had dwelt in that place a nymph of wondrous beauty called Clora. The wind Zephyrus (in Latin known
as Favonius) loved her ardently and finally married her. From
Zephyrus, whom they believed in their foolishness to be one of
the gods, she received as a dowry or wedding gift the privilege of
divinity, with the office of adorning trees, hills, and meadows with
flowers in the early spring. As she was to be in charge of flowers,
she was henceforth to be known as Flora instead of Clora. Since
flowers are followed by fruit, the ancients accorded Flora a sanctuary, altars, and games so that, once the goddess had been propiti-
ated by the games, she would grant blossoms in great profusion
and fruit in due season.

The general public was misled by this deception. Flora, who   12
during her lifetime had lived in brothels and had debased herself
with any and everyone for even the smallest fee, was now thought
to sit with Queen Juno and the other goddesses, as if Zephyrus
had borne her on his wings to heaven. And so, through her
shrewdness and the gift of her ill-gotten fortune, Flora was transformed from a prostitute into a nymph. Profiting from her marriage to Zephyrus and her divinity, she dwelt in temples and received divine honors from mortal beings. Thus not only did she
become Flora instead of Clora, but from a notorious prostitute of
her own day she was made into a world-famous celebrity.

: LXV :

De romana iuvencula

1 Romana fuit iuvencula, nec ex fece plebeia, ni fallor, traxit originem; cuius deperditum malignitate fortune nomen et parentum coniugisque notitia forsan aliquantulum meriti decoris surripuisse
2 videbitur. Sed, ne per me subtractum videatur, si illi inter claras locum non dedero, apponere mens est et innominate mulieris pietatem inclitam referre.

3 Fuit ergo iuvencule huic honesti generis mater, sed infelix; nam Rome apud pretoris tribunal, ob quod demeritum nescio, capitali supplicio damnata; et a pretore triumviro, ut illi iam indictam sententia penam inferret, tradita; a triumviro autem, in hoc idem, publici carceris custodi exhibita. Verum, quoniam nobilis esset, ut
4 nocte necaretur iniunctum est. Custos autem humanitate quadam inpulsus, dum ingenuitati mulieris compateretur, in eam sevire manibus noluit, sed vivam clausamque, ut inedia consumeretur, omisit.

5 Ad quam visendam filia venit et excussa prius egregie, ne quid cibi deferret introrsum, intrare carcerem a custode obtinuit esurientique iam matri lacte, quo recenti habundabat partu, opitulata est; demum, continuatis diebus plusculis, cepit mirari custos quod tam diu damnata mulier absque cibo traxisset spiritum; et clam quid cum matre ageret nata prospectans, advertit quoniam, eductis mammis, illas sugiendas ori matris admoveret; miratusque pietatem et inusitatum nutriendi matrem nate compertum, triumviro retulit; triumvir autem pretori; pretor publico nuntiavit consilio.

: LXV :

A Young Roman Woman

There was a young Roman woman who, if I am not mistaken, was 1
of noble origin. Her name, as well as all knowledge of her ancestors and her husband, has been lost through the malice of Fortune. This may appear to have deprived her of some of the honor
that is her due. Lest it seem, however, that it is I who have taken it 2
away by not giving her a place among famous women, I intend to
give an account of the renowned filial devotion of this anonymous
woman.

Now the young lady's mother was of honorable parentage, but 3
ill-starred. She was condemned to death in Rome before the tribunal of the praetor for a crime unknown to me. The praetor handed
her over to a triumvir to carry out the punishment already determined in the sentence, and the latter delivered her to the city
gaoler for this same purpose. Since she was of noble rank, it was
ordered that she be executed at night. The gaoler, however, was 4
moved by some human impulse and felt compassion for the noblewoman; rather than kill her outright, he left her locked up to die
of hunger.

When her daughter came to visit, the guards allowed her to en- 5
ter the prison only after a careful search to prevent her from bringing in any food. But she had recently given birth and so had plenty
of milk to give to her now starving mother. This continued for a
number of days, and the gaoler began to marvel that the condemned woman could live for so long without food. Secretly
watching what transpired between mother and daughter, he saw
the daughter uncover her breasts and place them at her mother's
mouth so that the latter could suck them. The gaoler was aston-
ished at this filial affection and the unusual way the daughter had

Ex quo comuni consensu factum est ut pietati filie dono daretur meritum matri supplicium.

6   Si servanti in pugna viribus civem, querneam coronam largiebatur antiquitas, qua, lacte servantem in carcere matrem, genitam decorabimus? Non equidem tam pio facinori satis dignum sertum

7 comperies inter frondes. Hec pietas non solum sancta, sed admirabilis fuit; nec tantum equanda, quin imo preferenda nature muneri, quo docemur parvulos natos lacte in firmiorem etatem deducere ac[1] parentes morti subtrahere.

8   Mirabiles ergo pietatis sunt vires; nam nedum feminea corda, que facile in compassionem trahuntur et lacrimas, sed nonnunquam in efferata et adamantina, obstinatione durata, penetrat pectora; et, posita circa precordia sede, primo humanitate flexibili durum emollit omne, et oportunitatum indagatrix atque compertrix optima, agit ut lacrimas cum infelicibus misceant, egritudines atque pericula saltem desiderio subeant et nonnunquam, si desint remedia, vicarias subeant mortes.

9   Qui tam grandes effectus agunt ut minus miremur si quid pium filii in parentes agamus, cum eo potius videamur vices reddere et quod alias sumpsimus debita restitutione persolvere.

found to feed her mother. He told the triumvir; the triumvir told the praetor, who told the city council. The result was a general agreement to annul the mother's deserved punishment as a reward for the daughter's devotion.

If the ancients bestowed an oak crown on a man who with his 6 strength saved a citizen in battle, with what crown shall we adorn a daughter who with her milk saved her imprisoned mother? Indeed, one could not find a plant from whose leaves one could fashion a garland worthy of so pious an action. This filial love was not 7 only holy but admirable; it equals — nay, it is superior to — that natural instinct by which we are taught to raise our small children with milk until they are older and stronger and by which we learn to save our parents from death.

A wonderful thing, then, is the power of filial devotion. Not 8 surprisingly, it pierces the hearts of women, who are easily moved to compassion and tears; but sometimes it makes its way even into cruel breasts of steel that have been deliberately hardened. Seated in the heart, filial devotion first softens every harsh act with supple kindness. Then, knowing well how to look for and find opportunities, it drives us to mingle our tears with those of the unfortunate and take (at least in sympathy) others' sickness and danger upon ourselves, and sometimes, if there are no remedies, death in their stead.

So great are the effects of filial devotion that we hardly wonder 9 when we, as children, perform some pious deed for our parents; by so doing, we seem simply to do our duty and to repay fittingly what we have received from them.

: LXVI :

De Martia Varronis

1 Martia Varronis perpetua virgo Rome iamdudum reperta est; cuius tamen Varronis invenisse non memini, nec etiam qua etate. Hanc ego, ob servatam virginitatem, tanto egregiori laude extollendam puto, quanto sui iuris femina, sua sponte, non superioris coactione, integriorem servaverit.

2 Non enim aut Veste sacerdotio alligatam aut Dyane voto obnoxiam seu alterius professionis implicitam, quibus plurime aut cohercentur aut retinentur, invenio; sed sola mentis integritate, superato carnis aculeo, cui etiam prestantissimi nonnunquam succubuere viri, illibatum a contagione hominis corpus in mortem usque servasse.

3 Verum etsi hac tam commendabili constantia plurimum hec laudanda sit Martia, non minus tamen ingenii viribus et artificio

4 manuum commendanda est. Hec equidem, seu sub magistro didicerit, seu monstrante natura habuerit, nobis incertum est, cum hoc videatur esse certissimum, quod, aspernatis muliebribus ministeriis, ne ocio tabesceret, in studium se picture atque sculpture dederit omnem; et tandem tam artificiose tanque polite pinniculo pinxisse atque ex ebore sculpsisse ymagines, ut Sopolim et Dyonisium, sue etatis pictores famosissimos, superarit; eiusque rei fuit notissimum argumentum, tabulas a se pictas ceteris preciosiores

5 fuisse. Et, quod longe mirabilius, asserunt eam non tantum eximie pinxisse, quod et nonnullis contigit aliquando, verum adeo veloces ad pingendum habuisse manus, ut nemo usquam similes habuerit.

6 Fuerunt insuper diu eius artis insignia, sed, inter alia, eius effi-

: LXVI :

Marcia, Daughter of Varro

It has long been known that in Rome there was a woman named 1
Marcia, daughter of Varro, who remained a virgin all her life. But
I do not remember having found out which Varro it was or even
when she lived.

I believe that this woman should be extolled all the more be- 2
cause she was legally independent and preserved her virginity in its
full integrity of her own free will, not because of the coercion of a
higher authority. As a matter of fact, I do not find that she was
bound by holy orders to Vesta or subject to a vow made to Diana
or entangled in another commitment—all reasons which curb and
restrain many women. I believe it was through purity of mind
alone that she conquered the sting of the flesh, which occasionally
overcomes even the most illustrious men, and she kept her body
unblemished by any relations with men until her death.

Although Marcia deserves great commendation for her laudable 3
constancy, she is to be praised no less for her intellectual ability
and her manual dexterity. We do not know if she learned from a 4
teacher or was naturally gifted. What appears certain, however, is
that, scorning womanly occupations and not wanting to waste her
time in idleness, Marcia devoted herself completely to the study of
painting and sculpture; in the end, she was able to carve ivory figures and to paint with such skill and finesse that she surpassed
Sopolis and Dionysius, the most famous painters of her day. Clear
proof of this is the fact that the pictures she painted were sold for
better prices than those of other artists. And what is still more ex- 5
traordinary, our sources say that, not only did Marcia paint extremely well (a fairly common accomplishment), but she could
paint more quickly than anyone else.

Specimens of Marcia's art survived for a long time. Among 6

gies, quam adeo integre, lineaturis coloribusque servatis et oris habitu, in tabula, speculo consulente, protraxit, ut nemini coetaneo
quenam foret, ea visa, verteretur in dubium.

7   Et inter ceteras, ut ad singulares eius mores deveniamus, ei
fuisse mos precipue asserunt, seu pinniculo pingeret seu sculperet
celte, mulierum ymagines sepissime facere, cum raro vel nunquam,
homines designaret. Arbitror huic mori pudicus rubor[1] causam
dederit; nam, cum antiquitas, ut plurimum, nudas aut seminudas
effigiaretur ymagines, visum illi sit oportunum aut imperfectos viros facere, aut, si perfectos fecerit, virginei videatur oblita pudoris.

8   Que, ne in alterum incideret, ab utroque abstinuisse satius arbitrata est.

: LXVII :

De Sulpitia Fulvii Flacci coniuge

1   Sulpitia, olim venerandissima mulier, non minus, matronarum ro-
manarum testimonio, laudis ob servatam castimoniam quam cul-
2   tro se perimens Lucretia consecuta est. Hec enim Servii Patriculi
filia et Fulvii Flacci coniunx fuit, nobiles ambo viri.

Et cum senatus, visis a decemviris more veteri sybillinis libris,
decrevisset ut Veneris Verticordie simulacrum consacraretur in
urbe, ut virgines cetereque mulieres non solum a libidine abstine-
rent, sed etiam facilius in laudabilem pudicitiam verterentur, peti-
vissetque, iuxta decemvirorum mandatum, quo cavebatur ut ca-
stior ex romanis matronis dedicaret illud, ex ingenti multitudine
qua tunc habundabat Roma, castiorem, feminarum iudicio, actum
est ut, primo, eis agentibus, centum ex omni cetu que pudicitia

them was a self-portrait which she painted on a panel with the aid of a mirror. She rendered the color, features, and expression of the face so faithfully that none of her contemporaries who saw it had trouble identifying the subject of the painting.

As regards her unique moral sensitivity, we are told among 7 other things that, whether she was painting or sculpting, it was her practice to reproduce especially images of women, and those of men rarely if ever. This was occasioned, I think, by her purity and modesty. In antiquity figures were, for the most part, rendered as nude or half nude, and it seemed to her necessary either to portray the men in an unfinished state or, by adding all the details, to forget maidenly delicacy. To avoid either alternative, she deemed it 8 better to abstain from both.

: LXVII :

Sulpicia, Wife of Fulvius Flaccus

According to the testimony of Roman matrons, Sulpicia, who in 1 former times was a much revered woman, won no less praise for preserving her chastity than did Lucretia for killing herself with a knife.[a] She was the daughter of Servius Paterculus and the wife of 2 Fulvius Flaccus, both of whom were nobles.

Once, after a ritual consultation by the decemvirs of the Sibylline Books,[b] the Senate decreed the consecration of a statue in Rome to Venus Verticordia for the dual purpose of encouraging virgins and other women to abstain from wantonness and to turn more readily to a laudable modesty. The decemvirs had prescribed that this statue should be consecrated by the woman regarded as the most chaste of Roman matrons. So the Senate sought her who in the judgment of her sex was the chastest of the enormous number of women abounding in Rome at that time. The ladies first decided to present a hundred women from every class who were

clariores existimate essent selecte traderentur; inter quas una Sul-

3 pitia sumpta est. Demum, senatus iussu, earundem mulierum iudicio, ex centum decem etiam lucidiores subtracte; quas inter et Sulpitia numerata. Postremo, cum ex decem peteretur una, summo omnium consensu Sulpitia data est.

4 Cui etsi pulchrum fuit ea tempestate Veneris Verticordie dicasse simulacrum, longe tamen pulchrius tam ingentis multitudinis existimatione fuit quod castimonia prelata sit ceteris, eo quod non tantum assistentium oculis, tanquam quoddam celeste pudicitie numen, omnium admiratione conspecta sit, sed futurorum omni evo etiam veneratione fere in inmarcescibilem gloriam nomen eius videatur esse delatum.

5 Sed queso, inquiet aliqua, si centum pudice electe sunt, quid huic uni aliarum magis pudicitie superaddi potuit ut ceteris merito preferatur? Palam est: hi vel he videant que arbitrantur solum ab alieno quam viri concubitu abstinuisse pudicitiam. Que quidem, si intueri saniori velimus oculo, non solum consistit ab amplexibus exterorum virorum abstinere, quod multe, etiam invite, faciunt.

6 Equidem oportet matronam, ut pudica integre dici possit, ante alia cupidos vagosque frenare oculos eosque intra vestimentorum suorum fimbrias coercere, verba non solum honesta sed pauca et pro tempore effundere, ocium, tanquam certissimum et perniciosissimum pudicitie hostem, effugere, a comesationibus abstinere cum absque Libero et Cerere frigeat Venus, cantus atque saltationes, tanquam luxurie spicula, evitare, parsimonie ac sobrietati vacare, domesticam rem curare, aures obscenis confabulationibus obturatas habere, a circuitionibus abstinere, pigmenta et supervacaneos odores abicere, ornatus[1] superfluos respuere, cogitationes appetitusque noxios totis calcare viribus, meditationibus sacris insistere atque vigilare; et, ne per cuncta discurram pudoris integri

well known for their virtue. Sulpicia was included in this group.
Then, by order of the Senate, ten were selected from the hundred 3
who in the judgment of the same women were the most illustrious, and Sulpicia was among the ten. Finally, when it came down
to choosing one of the ten, Sulpicia was put forward by unanimous consent.

Granted that at the time it was a great honor for her to conse- 4
crate the statue of Venus Verticordia, it was still more glorious for
Sulpicia to have gained, in the opinion of this large crowd of
women, preeminence for her modesty: not only was she regarded
and admired by all present as a kind of goddess of chastity, but,
thanks to the reverence that would be accorded her by future generations, her name seemed destined for almost imperishable glory.

Someone, however, will ask: if a hundred virtuous women were 5
selected, what greater degree of virtue could have been superadded
to this one woman alone to justify her preeminence? The answer
is clear. Let those men or women reconsider who think that chastity is constituted only by abstention from extramarital relations.
If we examine the matter from a sounder perspective, chastity does
not consist merely in abstaining from adulterous relations. This
many women do, sometimes unwillingly.

Indeed, for a woman to be considered completely chaste, she 6
must first curb her wanton and wandering eyes, keeping them lowered and fixed on the hem of her dress. Her words must be not
only respectable but brief and uttered at the right moment. She
must avoid idleness as a sure and deadly enemy of chastity, and
she must abstain from feasting, for Venus is cooled in the absence
of food and wine. She must avoid singing and dancing as the
weapons of lasciviousness and attend to temperance and sobriety.
She must take care of her house, close her ears to shameful conversation, and avoid gadding about. She must reject make-up, useless perfumes, and superfluous ornaments. Trampling with all her
strength on harmful thoughts and desires, she must be vigilant

testimonia, virum solum summa dilectione colere, ceteros, nisi fraterna diligas caritate, negligere et viri etiam, non absque frontis
animique rubore, in amplexus ad prolem suscipiendam accedere.

7   Que cum forsan omnia in ceteris non invenirentur explicita, et
in sola Sulpitia comperta, merito eam ceteris pretulere.

: LXVIII :

De Armonia Gelonis syculi filia

1   Armonia sycula iuvenis, Gelonis, fratris Yeronis, regis Syragusa-
rum, fuit filia. Que, quanquam regio genere fuerit insignis, longe
2 tamen magis pietate sua digna memoratu facta est. Hanc quidam
virginem occubuisse volunt; alii vero Themistii cuiusdam coniugem. Utrum horum magis placet summatur, cum nil ob diversita-
tem opinionum ex eius pia fortitudine subtrahatur.

3   Cum igitur, Syragusanorum ceca atque repentina seditione, in
omnem regiam prolem seviretur a populo, et iam, trucidato Iero-
nimo rege adolescentulo, atque Andronodoro et Themistio regiis
generibus, et in Damaratam et Heracliam, Yeronis filias, et Armoniam Gelonis multitudinis expeditis gladiis fieret incursus, actum
est sagacitate nutricis Armonie ut, regio exornata cultu, virgo que-
4 dam Armonie coeva pro Armonia interfectoribus pararetur. Que
quidem voto preparantis in nullo fuit adversa, quin imo, cum in se
infestis mucronum cuspidibus irruere multitudinem cerneret, nec
illam exterrita aufugit, nec conditionem suam ferientibus professa

and persistent in holy meditation. In short, so as not to rehearse all the signs of real chastity, she must give all her love to her husband alone and take no notice of other men, unless it is to love them like brothers. Even to her husband's embraces she must go with a modest face and heart and for the sake of procreation.

Perhaps it was because all these qualities were not found fully 7 in the other women and because Sulpicia alone was discovered to have them that she was justly given precedence over everyone else.

: LXVIII :

Harmonia, Daughter of Gelon of Sicily

The young Sicilian woman Harmonia was the daughter of Gelon, 1 who was the brother of King Hiero of Syracuse. Although she was distinguished for her royal lineage, she became much more worthy of remembrance because of her sense of duty. Some sources say 2 that she died a virgin; others report that she was the wife of a certain Themistius. Of these alternatives one may choose whichever one prefers since the divergence of opinion does not detract in the least from Harmonia's courage and loyalty.

The story begins at the time when the people of Syracuse had 3 exploded into senseless rebellion against the royal family. Young King Hieronymus had been murdered along with Andronodorus and Themistius, sons-in-law of Hiero and Gelon, and the mob was now, with swords drawn, assailing Damarata and Heraclia, daughters of Hiero, and Harmonia, daughter of Gelon. Through the shrewdness of Harmonia's nurse, a girl of the same age was dressed in royal robes and made ready to face the assassins in Harmonia's place. The girl was not opposed in any way to the strata- 4 gem. In fact, when she saw the crowd of hostile rebels rushing towards her with their sharp-pointed swords, she did not flee in

est, nec latitantem etiam Armoniam, loco cuius occidebatur, accusavit, verum tacita et immota, suscipiens letiferos ictus, occubuit.

5   Felix pariter et infelix Armonia: felix fide, infelix perditione fidelis. Attamen cum ex oculto innocue puelle perseverantiam et fortem in mortem animum ac manantem ex vulneribus virgineum sanguinem cerneret Armonia stupens, cum, virgine cesa iamque abeuntibus percussoribus, posset evadere, toto pectore admirari fidem cepit et, inclita pietate capta, effusis lacrimis, passa non est impune cruorem innocuum prospectare et vitam, tantopere ac aliena fide servatam, in evum protelare longius, satius ducens ad inferos cum tam fida iuvene immatura morte descendere, quam canos cum infidis civibus expectare.

6   O pietas, o prisca fides! Que evaserat, in medium prodiens, revocatis in se cruentis gladiis, fraudem nutricis et occise fidem suamque conditionem confessa, sanguinem suum ultro inferias occise concessit et crebris lacessita vulneribus, in quantum potuit, secus cadaver premortue corruit.

7   Cui quod pietas evi abstulit, dignissimum literis restituisse fuit; verum difficile cernere cuius maior, an premortue fides an superviventis pietas fuerit: illa virtutem prime, hec secunde nomen facit eternum.

terror. Nor did she reveal her identity to her attackers and accuse Harmonia, who was in hiding, and for whose sake she was being killed. Silent and motionless, she received the mortal blows and died.

Harmonia was both happy and unhappy: happy in the loyalty 5 of her retainer, but unhappy in her loss. From her hiding place she looked on in amazement at the perseverance of the innocent girl, her bravery in the face of death, and the blood flowing from her wounds. When the murderers had left after killing the girl and Harmonia could have escaped, she began to admire with all her heart the girl's constancy. Overcome by this extraordinary devotion, Harmonia burst into tears and could not bear to look on in safety at the shedding of innocent blood, nor to prolong her own life when it had been saved at such great cost by another's allegiance. Thus Harmonia decided it was better to die an untimely death and accompany this faithful girl down to the underworld than to await grey hairs in the company of her faithless countrymen.

What devotion! What old-fashioned loyalty! Harmonia, who 6 had escaped death, now showed herself in public. Summoning back the bloody swords, she confessed her nurse's scheme, the fidelity of the girl who had died, and her own identity. Voluntarily she shed her blood as a sacrifice to the slain girl and, stricken with many wounds, she fell as close as she could to the body of the girl who had preceded her in death.

The years taken from Harmonia by a sense of duty have been 7 justly restored by literature. It is difficult to decide which is greater: the fidelity of the first victim or the piety of the survivor. The former quality immortalizes the virtue of the retainer, the latter the name of Harmonia.

: LXIX :

De Busa canusina apula muliere

1 Busa quam, quasi Busa cognationis sit nomen, quidam Paulinam vocant, mulier fuit apula, origine canusina, quam ut ex generoso sanguine natam credam et aliis meritis pluribus splendidam, facit magnificum illud facinus quod unicum de ea posteritati reliquit antiquitas.

2 Aiunt enim, Hanibale peno infesto bello adversus Romanos agente, atque igne ferroque omnem Ytaliam populante et sanguine plurimo fedante, cum apud Cannas, apulum vicum, magno certamine non solum hostes superasset, sed fere ytalicas omnes confregisset vires, actum est ut ex eo conflictu cedeque ingenti noctu per devia ex multis dispersis vagisque circa decem milia Canusium devenirent, que tunc civitas fidem romane societatis servabat.

3 Quos omnes exangues fessos inopes inermes nudos affectosque vulneribus, non exterrita casu nec victoris potentia, comiter propriis in edibus Busa suscepit hospitio, eosque ante alia bono esse animo iussit et, adhibitis medicis, vulneratos materna affectione curari fecit, nudis vestimenta, imo cunctis, mira liberalitate concessit et inde inermibus arma, cotidianos omnibus sumptus ex bonis exhibuit suis refocillatisque comi pietate miseris et in spem revocatis abire volentibus, ultro viaticum cunctis concessit, nec ulla ex parte circa oportunitates continue affluentium manum retraxit: equidem mirabile dictu et in muliere longe laudabilius quam si homini contigisset.

: LXIX :

Busa of Canosa di Puglia

Busa, whom some people call Paulina as if Busa were a family   1
name, was an Apulian woman of Canosa. A single magnificent
deed—all that antiquity has transmitted to posterity about her—
induces me to believe that she was born of noble blood and renowned for many other meritorious actions.

Our sources relate that when Hannibal the Carthaginian was   2
waging bitter war against the Romans, laying waste the entire
country with fire and sword and soaking its soil in blood, he not
only defeated his enemy in a great battle near the Apulian village
of Cannae but practically shattered the Italian forces. Of the many
who survived the terrible slaughter of that contest and were now
scattered and wandering, about ten thousand came during the
night via back roads to Canosa, a city which at that time maintained an alliance with the Romans.

The fugitives were weak, exhausted, needy, unarmed, naked,   3
and covered with wounds. Busa, undaunted either by the disaster
or by the victor's power, graciously received these men into her
own house and gave them shelter. First she bade them take heart.
Then she summoned doctors and, with maternal affection, arranged for the wounded to be tended. Her generosity was amazing: she clothed the naked (indeed, she clothed all the fugitives);
she provided weapons for those who were unarmed; she paid the
cost of keeping them from her own resources. When these poor
men had regained their strength and hope through her kindness
and compassion and wanted to leave, Busa voluntarily gave each of
them money for the journey, nor did she ever refuse to take care of
the needs of the continuous stream of new arrivals. Certainly, this
is an astonishing story, and it is still more laudable in that it concerns a woman and not a man.

4　　Alexandrum enim Macedonum regem et universi orbis invaso-
rem, inter alia eius decora, precipua magnificentia extollere prisci
consuevere, asserentes eum, nedum iocalia pretiosa, pecunias ingentes et munera huiusmodi permaxima munificentiis aliorum
principum fere largiri consuetum, verum principatus eximios, regna splendida et amplissima imperia amicis et nonnunquam victis
regibus exhibere.

5　　Pulchrum quidem et magnificum et totis extollendum preconiis est, sed minime — ut reor — Buse magnificentie adequandum.

6　　Nam Alexander vir fuit, femina Busa, quibus familiaris, imo in-
nata tenacitas est et animositatis perminimum; rex ille, et maximus, hec privata mulier; ille, quod violentia surripuerat sua, hec,
quod iure hereditario, possidebat; ille, quod sibi forsan commode
servare nequibat, hec, quod diu servaverat et servasse volens adhuc
poterat; ille bene meritis et amicis, hec extraneis et incognitis; ille
rebus florentibus suis, hec suis nutantibus et periclitantibus amicorum; ille apud exteras nationes, hec sub patrio celo in presentia inter suos; ille ut gloriam munificentie lucraretur, hec ut indigenti-
bus auxilium inpenderet.

7　　Quid multum? Si mentem, si sexum, si qualitatem prospectemus amborum, non dubitem quin sub equo iudice longe plus
Busa ex liberalitate sua quam Alexander ex sua munificentia glorie
consequatur.

8　　Sed cui vult candidior cedat laus; mea sententia, Busa suis
substantiis optime usa est. Non enim natura parens e penetralibus
terre in publicum eduxit aurum, ut ex matris utero deferretur in
tumulum, quod avari faciunt dum archivo sepeliunt et custodia nimia incubant, quasi iterum nascituro; verum ante omnia ut com-
muni exhiberetur comodo, inde honesto fulgori nostro et amico-

The ancients were accustomed to extoll Alexander, king of   4
Macedonia and conqueror of the whole world, for (among his
other excellent qualities) his extraordinary generosity. They tell us
that, like other munificent princes, he was not only accustomed to
bestow precious gems, large sums of money, and similar gifts: he
also gave away great domains, splendid kingdoms, and vast empires
to his friends and sometimes even to the kings he had defeated.

Such actions are indeed fine and noble and deserve all possible   5
praise. But, in my view, they should not be reckoned equal to
Busa's magnanimity. Alexander was a man; Busa, a woman, and   6
stinginess is as habitual, or rather innate, to women as is their lack
of boldness. He was a great king and she a private individual. He
possessed what he had taken by force; she, what she had received
through lawful inheritance. He gave away what perhaps he could
not easily keep for himself; she, what she had kept for a long time
and could have continued to keep had she so wished. He gave to
friends and to men who had deserved well of him; she, to outsiders and to strangers. He gave when his affairs were prospering;
she, when hers were in doubt and her friends in danger. He bestowed his gifts in foreign lands; she, in her own country and
among her own people. He gave to acquire a reputation for generosity; she, to aid those who were in need.

Do I need to continue? If we consider the character, the sex,   7
and the condition of both, I have no doubt that under a just judge
Busa would acquire far more glory by her liberality than Alexander by his munificence.

Nonetheless, let the more splendid praise accrue to whomever   8
of the two you prefer; in my opinion Busa made the best use of
her wealth. Mother Nature did not bring gold to light from the secret places of the earth for it to be borne from its mother's womb
into the tomb. This is what misers do when they bury their wealth
in a casket and brood over it with excessive vigilance as if they
were expecting a rebirth. Rather, gold exists above all to be used

rum convictui, et, si supersit, prostratis fortune iniuria, ira celi
fatigatis, paupertate minus digne pressis, carceri alieno crimine
clausis et quibuscunque attritis egestate anxia ministremus suffragia liberali animo; non equidem ut appareamus, verum ut proficia-
mus; non ut lucremur, sed ut largiamur, huiusmodi inpendenda
sunt comoda, eo adhibito rationis moderamine, ne, dum aliis opi-
tulamur, nobis procuremus inopiam, qua cogamur alienis, nedum
dicam manus violentas inicere, sed nec etiam oculis inhiare.

: LXX :

De Sophonisba regina Numidie

1 Sophonisba quidem, posito splendens Numidarum regina inces-
serit, austeritate mortis intrepide a se sumpte longe luculentior
2 facta est. Hec enim filia fuit Hasdrubalis, Gisgonis filii maximique
Cartaginensium principis, Hanibale vexante Ytaliam.

Que cum esset etate florens et forma satis egregia, a patre Sy-
phaci, potentissimo Numidie regi, in coniugium virgo copulata
est; nec equidem desiderio regie affinitatis tantum; sed optabat vir
sagax, instante Romanorum bello, non solum barbarum regem
Romanis subtrahere, sed opere filie blandientis in partes Cartaginensium adversus Romanos convertere; nec a precogitata fallacia
deceptus est.

3 Nam cum nuptias Syfax celebrasset, a premonita adolescentula,
formositate favente, in tantum sue dilectionis ardorem tractus est,

for the common good, then to gain due respect for ourselves and to serve our friends. If anything is left over, let us give generously to people who are laid low by the blows of Fortune, burdened by the wrath of heaven, unfairly oppressed by poverty, imprisoned for someone else's crime, and, finally, to all who are worn down by worry and need. Expenditures of this kind are proper when they actually benefit others, not when they merely appear to do so; when our purpose is philanthropy, not profit. In such activity a reasonable criterion should be applied: while we are helping others we should not bring upon ourselves a poverty that would force us to covet the property of others, much less steal it.

: LXX :

Sophonisba, Queen of Numidia

Although Sophonisba was already famous as the queen of Numidia, she gained considerably more glory through the harshness of the death which she brought boldly upon herself. Her father was Hasdrubal, son of Gisgo and the greatest prince in Carthage, and she lived during the time when Hannibal was disturbing Italy.

When Sophonisba was in the flower of her youth and certainly quite beautiful, her father married her to Syphax, a powerful king of Numidia. In doing so Hasdrubal's motive was not only his desire to have royal kin. A shrewd man, he wanted, in view of the continuing war with Rome, to use his daughter's charms so as to detach the barbarian king from his Roman allies and win him over to the side of the Carthaginians. Nor was he disappointed in his cleverly planned scheme.

After the wedding Syphax fell so ardently in love with the girl, who had been coached beforehand and was helped by her

ut nil preter illam sibi carum aut delectabile arbitraretur Syphax; et sic, dum ureretur infelix et appareret Cornelium Scipionem ex Sycilia in Affricam cum exercitibus traiecturum, Hasdrubalis monitu, Sophonisba blanditiis precibusque adeo Syphacis animum in desiderium suum traxit, ut, non solum Romanos relinqueret, quibus amicitie fidem prestiterat, et Cartaginensibus iungeretur, verum ultro alieni belli principatum assummeret; quam ob rem perfidia calcata fide, quam pridie Scipioni hospiti suo promiserat, ei per literas, nondum transfretanti, in Affricam interdixit ingressum.

4   Ceterum Scipio, ingentis animi iuvenis, damnata barbari regis nequitia, depositis haud longe a Cartagine copiis, illum ante alia expugnavit per Massinissam regem sotium et Lelium legatum suum; per quos, exercitu fuso, captus vinctusque deductus est Cyrtam, regiam Numidie civitatem, nec ante catenis onustus civibus ostensus est quam Massinisse civitatis deditio facta.

5   Qui, cum nondum Lelius appulisset, eam intrans, motu rerum repentino tumultuantibus omnibus, regiam, ut erat armatus, intrans, obviam habuit Sophonisbam; que fortunarum suarum conscia, cum eum intrantem vestibulum ultra alios armis insignem cerneret, ut erat, regem auspicata, ad eius proclivis genua, pristine fortune animum retinens, inquit:

    'Sic, rex inclite, deo visum est et felicitati tue ut in nos, qui

6 paulo ante reges eramus, que velis possis omnia. Verum si permissum est captive <ut>[1] coram victore et vite mortisque sue domino supplices voces emictere possit eiusque genua atque dexteram victricem contingere, deiecta precor per maiestatem tuam, in qua et ego paulo ante eram, perque genus regium et comune numidicum nomen, etsi meliori suscipiaris omine, quam hinc abierit Syphax, in me, quam tui iuris noviter adversa fecit fortuna, agas quod in

beauty, that he thought nothing was dear or delightful except his Sophonisba. While the unfortunate man was in the grip of this burning passion, it became clear that Cornelius Scipio would cross with his army from Sicily into Africa. At Hasdrubal's instigation, Sophonisba coaxed and pleaded with Syphax to accede to her wishes. The result was that, not only did he join the Carthaginians and abandon the Romans to whom he had given a pledge of friendship, but he voluntarily assumed leadership in a war that was not even his own. And so, with a treacherous disregard for the fidelity which shortly before he had sworn to his guest Scipio, Syphax forbade him by letter to enter Africa before Scipio had even begun the crossing.

But Scipio, a young man of high spirit, condemned the villainy 4 of the barbarian king and landed his forces not far from Carthage. His first action was to defeat Syphax, sending King Masinissa, a Roman ally, and his own lieutenant Laelius against him. They routed Syphax's army, captured the king, and took him shackled to Cirta, the capital of Numidia. But the city did not surrender until Syphax was displayed, in chains, to his people.

Laelius had not yet arrived when Masinissa entered the city, 5 now in total uproar at the sudden turn of events. He was still wearing his armor as he went into the royal palace, and Sophonisba came to meet him. Aware that her fortunes hung in the balance, Sophonisba saw at the entrance a figure whose military attire distinguished him from the others, and she realized that he was the king. She knelt down before him as a suppliant and said, still in a queenly fashion:

"Mighty king, it has pleased the gods and your fortune that you can now do whatever you please with Us, who but a short time ago were also sovereign. If, however, a prisoner may be permitted 6 to utter suppliant words in the presence of her conqueror and the master of her life and death and to touch his knees and victorious right hand, I humbly implore you to do to me—I who am newly

oculis tuis pium bonumque visum sit, dummodo insolenti et fa-
7   stidioso, potissime Penis, Romanorum arbitrio viva non tradar.
Facile enim potes advertere quid romana hostis, cartaginensis et
Hasdrubalis filia — sino quod Syphacis coniunx — timere possim;
et, si omnis in hoc alius tollitur modus, ut tua manu potius moriar
facito, quam hostium in potestatem viva deveniam, precor et obsecro.'

8   Massinissa qui et ipse numida erat et, uti omnes sunt, in libidinem pronus, venustatem oris orantis inspiciens — addiderat quippe
infortunium, pium quoddam et insolitum decus suplici — motus et
humanitate et libidine tractus, cum nondum adventasset Lelius,
uti erat in armis, dextera data, inter feminarum querulos ululatus et tumultum discurrentium undique militum, levavit orantem
eamque sibi extemplo iunxit in coniugem, medio in strepitu armorum nuptiis celebratis; puto hac via arbitratus et libidini² sue et
precibus Sophonisbe invenisse modum.

9   Die demum sequenti Lelium venientem suscepit et, eo sic iubente, cum omni ornatu regio et preda cetera ac nova coniuge redeuntes in castra, primo a Scipione ob rem bene gestam comiter
suscepti sunt; deinde cum ab eo, ob celebratas cum captiva romani
populi nuptias, amicabiliter redargutus esset et in tabernaculum
secessisset arbitrisque remotis³ suspiriis lacrimisque oppletus diu
ingemuisset, adeo ut a circumstantibus audiretur, urgente Sophonisbe fato, accersiri ad se iussit quem ex servis fidelissimum habebat, cui commiserat servandum venenum ad incertos fortune casus, eique precepit ut illud, poculo dilutum, Sophonisbe deferret
diceretque libenter se illi, quam sponte dederat, fidem servaturum

placed in your power by a hostile fortune—whatever in your eyes seems right and good, so long as I am not handed over alive to the Romans, a power that is arrogant and hateful, especially to Carthaginians. I beg this in the name of your royal rank, which not long ago I too held; I beg it by the royal blood and the Numidian origin which you share with Syphax, although you are received here with better omens than Syphax had when he left. You 7 can easily understand what I, a Carthaginian, an enemy of the Romans and Hasdrubal's daughter, would have to fear even if I were not Syphax's wife. And if there is for me no other way of escape, I beseech you to let me die at your hands rather than let me fall alive into the power of the enemy."

Himself a Numidian, Masinissa was, like all his countrymen, 8 inclined to lust. When he observed the beauty of his suppliant's face, to which misfortune had added a certain rare and gentle grace, he was moved by both kindness and passion. Since Laelius had not yet arrived, Masinissa, still armed for combat, extended his right hand to Sophonisba. In the midst of the women's plaintive wailing and the tumult of soldiers running in every direction, he lifted her up while she was still pleading and married her on the spot. The wedding celebration was held amidst the clamor of arms. I believe that by doing this he thought he had found a way to satisfy both his own desire and Sophonisba's entreaties.

The next day Masinissa received Laelius when he arrived. At 9 Laelius' bidding they returned to the Roman camp with all the royal trappings, the rest of the booty, and Masinissa's new wife. There they were graciously received by Scipio and congratulated on their success. Then, in a friendly way, he reproached Masinissa for having married a captive of the Roman people. The king withdrew into his tent. When all the witnesses were gone, he wept for a long time, with sighs and moans that were audible to anyone standing outside. Sophonisba's fate was now a pressing issue, and Masinissa sent for his most faithful servant, to whom he had en-

si posset; verum, quoniam a quibus poterat arbitrium subtraheba-
tur suum, quam ipsa petierat, non absque merore suo, prestabat
fidem, si uti velit, scilicet ne in potestatem viva veniat Romanorum; ipsa tamen patris patrieque et duorum regum, quibus paulo
ante nupserit, memor, sibi quod videretur consilium summeret.

10   Que quidem audito, constanti vultu, nuntio dixit: 'Accipio nuptiale munus et, si nil aliud a viro coniugi dari poterat, gratum habeo; sed refer satius me morituram fuisse si non in funere meo
nupsissem.' Nec acrius dicta dedit quam poculum sumpserit et,
nullo signo trepidationis ostenso, confestim hauxit omne; nec diu
tumescens in mortem, quam petierat, miserabunda collapsa est.

11   Edepol annoso homini, cui iam vita tedium, nec spes alia preter
mortem, nedum puellule regie, tunc, habito ad notitiam rerum respectu, vitam intranti et quid in ea dulcedinis sit percipere inci-
pienti, magnum et admirabile fuisset, et nota dignum, morti certe
adeo impavide occurrisse.

trusted a poison to be kept for emergencies. He ordered the servant to dissolve the poison in a cup and to bring it to Sophonisba with this message: gladly would Masinissa have kept, if at all possible, the pledge which he had willingly sworn to her; but, since his freedom to choose was being taken away by those who had the power to do so, he was keeping, not without sadness, the pledge (if she wished to take advantage of it) which she herself had sought, namely, that she should not fall alive into the power of the Romans; nevertheless, mindful of her father, her country, and the two kings whom she had recently married, she should take whatever decision seemed best to her.

Sophonisba listened to this with no change of expression on her face and said to the messenger: "I willingly accept this wedding gift and, if my husband can give me no other, I am grateful for it. But tell him that I would have had a better death had I not married on the very day I was to die." Taking the cup with a sharpness equal to that of her words, she quickly drained it without a trace of fear. Not long after she swelled up and fell piteously to the ground in the death she had sought. 10

By heaven! To have faced certain death so boldly would have been a great and admirable deed worthy of notice even in the case of an old man, tired of life and with nothing to hope for except his demise. It was far more so for a young queen who, so far as knowledge of the world is concerned, was just entering upon life and beginning to see what joys it held. 11

: LXXI :

De Theosena Herodici principis filia

1 Theosena thessala ac nobilis origine mulier, hinc dulci pietate inde atrocitate severa inclitum de se futuris testimonium liquit.

2 Hec enim Herodici Thessalorum principis, Phylippo, Demetrii filio, Macedonibus imperante, filia fuit eique soror ex eisdem parentibus extitit, Archo nomine; quibus cum primo eiusdem Phylippi nequitia pater occisus esset, temporis tractu, eadem suadente perfidia, ab eodem nepharia morte viris private sunt, unicuique ex viro filio unico relicto superstite.

3 Eis igitur viduis, Archo primo Poridi cuidam, gentis eorum principi, nupsit multosque ex eo filios peperit. Theosena autem constantiori animo a multis proceribus frustra in coniugium expetita, longius viduitatem servavit.

4 Verum cum morte subtracta fuisset Archo, compassa nepotibus ne ad manus noverce alterius venirent, seu alias minus accurate alerentur a patre, ut eos tanquam proprios educaret, eidem Poridi sese connubio iunxit, nulla lege illis temporibus prohibente, cepitque, non aliter quam si ipsa foret enixa, pia cum diligentia illos alere, ut satis appareret eorum magis obsequio quam suum ob comodum nupsisse Poridi.

5 Quibus sic se habentibus, contigit ut Phylippus Macedonum rex, eo quod inquieti esset ingenii, iterum adversus Romanos, tunc orbe clara felicitate florentes, bellum moliretur animo; et ob id cum evacuasset, maximo regni sui motu, veteribus colonis fere omnes Thessalie maritimas civitates eosque in Peoniam, que postea Emathia dicta est, mediterraneam regionem turmatim transmigrare iussisset Tracibusque eius ore, tanquam futuro bello aptioribus atque fidelibus, oppida concessisset vacua audissetque abeuntium execrationes in se, ratus est nil sibi tutum fore ni filios eorum, quos dudum truculentus occiderat, eque perimeret omnes;

: LXXI :

Theoxena, Daughter of Prince Herodicus

Theoxena of Thessaly was a woman of noble birth who left pos- 1
terity a glorious remembrance of herself for tender devotion on
the one hand and for stern harshness on the other.

The daughter of Herodicus, a prince of Thessaly, Theoxena 2
lived when Philip, son of Demetrius, ruled Macedonia. She had a
sister called Archo, born of the same parents. First their father was
killed through Philip's villainy, and afterwards the same treachery
of the same man robbed them of their husbands, who were put to
death in defiance of divine law. The two sisters were left each with
an only child.

Of the two widows, Archo was the first to remarry; her hus- 3
band was a man named Poris, head of their own clan, and she
bore him numerous children. But Theoxena long remained firm in
her resolve to preserve her widowhood, and she was wooed in vain
by many princes.

When Archo died, Theoxena felt great sympathy for her neph- 4
ews. Since no law at that time prohibited it, she married Poris, her
late sister's husband. In this way she could raise the children as her
own and avoid the danger of their falling into the hands of another stepmother or receiving an indifferent upbringing from their
father. Thus Theoxena began to look after her nephews with as
much devotion as she would have shown had she given birth to
them herself. It became quite clear that she had married Poris
more to care for his offspring than for her own benefit.

At this point King Philip of Macedonia, a man of restless tem- 5
perament, planned another war against the Romans, who then
were enjoying great success throughout the world. To further his
design, Philip introduced great upheaval into his kingdom by evac-
uating almost all the coastal cities of Thessaly and ordering their

quos cum capi iussisset et in custodiam servari, ut non uno cun-
ctos ictu occideret, sed vicissim successu temporum aboleret, actum est ut Theosena scelesti regis edictum audiret et, memor sui
sororisque virorum necis, filium nepotesque peti arbitrata est; et
existimans, si in regis devenirent manus, non solum sevitie eius
eos ludibrio futuros, sed etiam custodum, necessitate cogente, libidinem et fastidia subituros; ad quod evitandum, confestim in atrox
facinus iniecit animum ausaque dicere viro patrique eorum est se
potius, si aliter non daretur, occisuram omnes propria manu quam
pateretur in Phylippi potestatem deduci.

6   Poris autem execratus tam scelestum crimen, in solatium uxoris
natorumque salutem deportaturum se eos et apud fidos hospites
positurum fugeque futurum comitem spopondit.

7   Nec mora; nam cum finxisset se a Thessalonica Eneam ad sta-
tutum quotannis Enee conditori sacrificium profecturum ibique
inter solemnes cerimonias epulasque diem consumpsisset, una
cum natis et coniuge, clam, soporatis omnibus, noctis vigilia tertia,
tanquam in patriam rediturus, preparatam navim[1] conscendit, eo
proposito ut Euboeam, non Thessalonicam peteret.

8   Ceterum longe illi aliter contigit. Vixdum litus Enee reliquerat,
et ecce per noctis tenebras ventus ex adverso surrexit, eum non
quo cupiebat, sed unde discesserat invitum retrahens. Cui cum
frustra remis in contrarium niterentur navales sotii, dies eluxit li-
torique propinquos ostendit; regii vero custodes ex portu laboran-
tem navem cernentes eamque fugam moliri existimantes, ad eam

former inhabitants to emigrate in small bands to Paeonia, an inland region later called Emathia. These abandoned towns were then bestowed upon the Thracians as better and more reliable allies in the coming war. When Philip heard the curses hurled against himself by the people who were forced to leave, he reasoned that he would not be safe unless he could also destroy all the sons of the men he had butchered earlier. Consequently he ordered them to be seized and kept under guard so that he could kill them, not all at once, but in small numbers over a period of time. Notice of the wicked king's edict reached Theoxena. Remembering the death of her own as well as her sister's husband, she concluded that her son and her nephews would be sought out; moreover, if they fell into the king's hands, they would not only become an object of sport for the king's cruelty but would also be subjected necessarily to the scorn and the lust of the prison guards. To avoid this, she immediately devised a terrible scheme. Boldly she told her husband, the children's father, that, if nothing else could be done, she would kill them with her own hands rather than allow them to come under Philip's control.

Poris, however, abominated so wicked a plan of action. To comfort his wife and protect his family, he promised to take the children away, leave them with some trusted foreigners, and himself accompany them in flight. 6

No time was lost. Poris pretended that he was leaving Thessalonica to go to Aenea for the sacrifices celebrated annually in honor of the eponymous founder of that city. He spent a day there attending solemn ceremonies and banquets. At midnight, when everyone else was asleep, Poris, along with his wife and children, secretly boarded a waiting ship under the pretext of returning home. But the real destination was Euboea, not Thessalonica. 7

Things, however, turned out very differently. Scarcely had the ship left the shores of Aenea when in the darkness of the night there arose a contrary wind; this took Poris not where he wanted 8

retrahendam confestim armatum misere lembum, gravi imperantes edicto ne qui mictebantur absque navi reverterentur in portum.

9 Poris quidem, instantis periculi conscius, dum lembum cernit venientem, nunc remiges nautasque, ut totis insisterent viribus, nunc deos, ut periclitantibus prestarent suffragium, intentus orabat.

10 Quod Theosena[2] conspiciens, nec ignara periculi, quasi sibi a superis tempus prestitum foret, dum Poridem orantem cernit, ad precogitatum revoluta facinus, evestigio venenum poculo diluit et expedivit gladios et filio atque nepotibus in conspectu ponit et ait: 'Mors sola vindictam salutemque nobis omnibus prestare potest. Ad mortem poculum gladiusque sunt vie; qua quenque delectat, regia superbia fugienda est. Mei ergo iuvenes generosos excitate animos et qui maiores estis viriliter agite: capite ferrum, aut poculum haurite, si mors sevior fortasse delectat, et in eam liberam confugite, postquam in vitam tendere estuosi maris impetus prohibet.'

11 Aderant iam hostes et atrox femina mortis autor instabat urgebatque iuvenes hesitantes. Quam ob rem alii alio leto absumpti semianimes et palpitantes adhuc, Theosena iubente, precipitantur e navi.

12 Que cum quos pie educaverat ob libertatem egisset in mortem, ne sibi, quam dissuaserat aliis, servitutem servasse videretur, egregio animo virum adhuc orantem in mortis comitem complexa est secumque in procellosum mare precipitem traxit, satius libere

to go but back, against his wishes, to the place he had just left. The rowers labored in vain against the unfavorable wind. Day broke and revealed that they were near the shore. From their position in the harbor, the royal guardsmen noticed the struggling ship and thought that it was trying to escape. At once they sent out an armed cutter to bring it back, with the stern order not to return to port without the ship. Poris saw the approaching boat and, realizing the imminent danger, alternately exhorted the sailors to row with all their might and implored the gods to help them in their time of peril.

Theoxena observed all this and was fully aware of the danger. When she saw Poris beseeching the gods, she went back to her earlier plan, as if the gods were now giving her the opportunity to execute it. Immediately she dissolved poison in a cup and unsheathed swords. Placing these things before her son and her nephews, Theoxena said, "Only death can bring protection and safety to us all. The cup and dagger are our means of death; we must flee the king's arrogance in whatever way each of us chooses. Therefore, my children, rouse your noble spirit, and let the eldest among you act in a manly fashion. Take the sword, or drink from the cup if you prefer a crueler death; find refuge in an end that is freely chosen since the force of the raging sea does not allow us to set a course towards life."

The enemy was now near, and this terrifying woman was urging death upon the youths who were as yet hesitating. The rest, still half alive and twitching from the effects of the poison or the sword, she ordered to be thrown overboard.

Nor would Theoxena reserve for herself the servitude from which she had dissuaded others. When for the sake of liberty she had driven to their deaths the children she had so devotedly reared, her noble spirit made her husband, still praying, her companion in death. Embracing him, Theoxena pulled Poris with herself headlong into the stormy sea. She thought it better to die in

9

10

11

12

mori rata quam vivens feda servitute tabescere; et sic, hostibus
nave relicta vacua, solatium sevitie sue Phylippo abstulit et sibi dignum memoria mulier austera monimentum peperit.

: LXXII :

De Beronice Capadocie regina

1 Beronices pontica, cui et Laodices nomen fuit, etsi sanguinis fulgore locum inter claras mulieres quesisse forsitan videatur, longe
magis non ob fervidum amorem in filium—quo, ut plurimum,
matres uruntur—sed ob meritum insignis eius audacie in vindi-
2 ctam eius summendam, occupasse censetur. Quod, ne videatur a
calamo surreptum, paucis explicandum est.

Hec Mitridatis, regis Ponti, eius, qui adversus Aristonicum
cum Romanis paulo ante bellum gesserat et repentina demum
subtractus morte fuerat, filia fuit et Mitridatis, superioris Mitridatis filii, et hostis diuturno bello Romanorum, soror, Ariaracti Ca-
padocie regi nupsit.

3 Cui, per insidias agente Mitridate, Beronicis fratre, a Gordio
quodam occiso, filii duo fuere superstites. Verum cum Nicomedes,
ea tempestate Bithinie rex, Capadociam occupasset, quasi cede regis vacuam, regni avidus Mitridates pietatem finxit seque recupe-
raturum nepotibus regnum aiens arma sumpsit in Nicomedem.

4 Sane cum comperisset Laodicem viduam Nicomedi nuptam, ficta
pietas in veram conversa: pulso armorum viribus ex Capadocia Ni-
comede, Ariaracti, natu ex fratribus grandiori, patrium restituit regnum. Quem cum postea facti penitens per fraudem occidisset, et
iunior alter, cui et Ariaractes nomen erat, ex Asya ab amicis revo-

freedom than live to languish in vile slavery. Thus the enemy found an empty ship, Philip was deprived of the solace of cruelty, and the austere Theoxena acquired for herself a memorable place in history.

: LXXII :

Berenice, Queen of Cappadocia

Berenice of Pontus, known also as Laodice, may seem to have 1 gained a place among famous women by reason of her noble birth. Yet she is thought to deserve it much more, not for the fervent love she had for her son (for this is something most mothers experience), but for her remarkable audacity in avenging him. I shall 2 speak of this briefly lest it seem to have escaped my pen.

Berenice was the daughter of that Mithridates, king of Pontus, who a short while before had waged war with the Romans against Aristonicus and then died suddenly. She was the sister of another Mithridates, son of the aforesaid Mithridates and an inveterate enemy of the Romans in war. Her husband was Ariarathes, king of Cappadocia.

Aided by the treachery of Berenice's brother Mithridates, 3 Ariarathes died at the hands of Gordius. He was survived by two sons. Nicomedes was king of Bithynia at the time, and he seized Cappadocia whose throne had been left vacant by the king's death. Mithridates, who coveted the kingdom, put on a show of false piety; saying that he would recover this realm for his nephews, he took up arms against Nicomedes. But when he learned that the 4 widowed Laodice had married Nicomedes, Mithridates' pretended familial devotion became real. After driving Nicomedes out of Cappadocia by force of arms, he restored Ariarathes, the elder son, to his ancestral throne. Later, however, Mithridates repented of this action: he employed deception to kill Ariarathes and engi-

catus regnare videretur, ut placet aliquibus, opere Mitridatis eiusdem per insidias etiam trucidatus est.

5   Quod adeo egre tulit infelix genitrix, gemina orbata prole, ut
dolore coercita, sexus oblita, furens arma corriperet et, iunctis iu-
galibus equis, currum conscenderet, nec fugientem cursu precipiti
Ceneum satellitem regium, scelesti facinoris executorem, sequi
primo desisteret quam eum, cum hasta nequisset, saxo ictum pro-
strasset superque iacentis cadaver indignabunda currum ageret et
inter hostilia tela nullo fratris, tunc hostis, pavore perculsa, domum usque, in qua cesi pueri corpus servari existimabat, perveniret eique maternas lacrimas miseranda concederet et officium per-
solveret funerale.

6   O bone deus, o inexpugnabiles nature vires et amoris invicti
fortitudo, quid maius, quid mirabilius egisse potuistis? Quos omnis Asya et forsan iam Ytalia tremebat exercitus, egistis ut impavida mulier et armis induta, inpulsu penetraret vestro et, formidabilis regis despectis viribus odioque, ad eum perimendum, cui
victoris munus et gratia servabatur, audaciam ingenium prestitistis
et robur.

7   Attamen hunc alii egritudine fatigatum puerum nature solvisse
debitum volunt et eum, quem a Mitridate cesum diximus, fuisse
quem mater, eo quo potuit conatu, ulta est.

neered, according to some sources, the murder of the younger
brother, also named Ariarathes, who, it seems, had been recalled
from Asia by friends in order to rule the kingdom.

The unhappy mother took the loss of both her sons very badly. 5
In her grief Berenice forgot her sex; in her rage she took up arms.
The horses were harnessed; she mounted a chariot and set off
in pursuit of Caeneus, a courtier and the perpetrator of the terrible deed, who was now fleeing headlong. The chase came to an
end only when, after an unsuccessful attempt with her lance, she
knocked him to the ground with a rock. Furiously she drove the
chariot over his dead body as it lay there. Then, unfraid of her
brother, who was now her foe, Berenice passed through a hail of
enemy darts until she reached the house where she reckoned the
body of her slain son had been placed. The wretched woman shed
a mother's tears for him and performed his funeral rites.

Good lord, how invincible are the forces of Nature, how in- 6
domitable is the strength of Love! What greater, what more marvelous deed could they have done? At their instigation, a woman,
intrepid and armed, drove her way through those armies feared
throughout Asia—perhaps even in Italy. Scorning the power and
hatred of a dreaded king, they gave her the daring, intelligence,
and strength to kill a man for whom a conqueror's gifts and favors
were reserved.

Some sources, however, report that this son died a natural 7
death through illness, and that the son whom the mother avenged
as best she could was the one killed by Mithridates.

: LXXIII :

De coniuge Orgiagontis gallogreci

1 Orgiagontis Gallogrecorum reguli coniugis meritum decus et claritatis precipue premium videbatur posse subtrahere ignoratum nomen quod barbaries, ydiomatis incogniti invidia, nostris laudibus,
reor, inter mediterraneos Asye saltus et speleas obruit Latinisque

2 clausum subtraxit. Sed absit ut hoc infortunii crimen egisse potuerit quin illi, sub mariti titulo, quod nostre possunt literule splendoris meriti inpendatur.

3 Superato igitur a Romanis, sub duce Scipione Asyatico,
Anthioco magno, Syrie Asyeque rege, Gneus Manlius Torquatus
consul, Asyam sortitus provinciam, ne frustra transtulisse videretur copias, seu ociosum haberet militem, purgatis hostium reliquiis circa maritimas oras, suo ex arbitrio in montanas abditasque
regiones evectus Asye, adversus Gallogrecos, efferatos barbarie populos, quoniam Anthiocum adversus romana arma subsidiis iuvis-
sent et nonnunquam omnem turbarent discursionibus Asyam,
acre bellum intulit.

4 Verum cum iam diffiderent Gallogreci, oppidis relictis, in verti-
ces montium, natura loci munitos, cum coniugibus filiisque et reliquis fortunis suis abiere et se armis a circumsidentibus hostibus,

5 quibus poterant, tutabantur et viribus. Attamen, duro militum romanorum robore superati ac per decliva montium deiecti cesique,
qui superfuerant, deditione facta, victoriam Manlii confessi sunt.

6 Erat captivorum utriusque sexus et etatis multitudo ingens;
custodie quorum prepositus centurio, cum Orgiagontis reguli coniugem vidisset, etate valentem et corporis formositate conspicuam,
in eius lapsus concupiscentiam, romane honestatis immemor, as-

: LXXIII :

The Wife of Orgiago the Galatian

The fact that we do not know the name of the wife of Orgiago, 1
chieftain of the Galatians, could have withheld from her the honor
and special distinction to which she has a right. I believe that the
barbarians' hatred of an unknown tongue kept it hidden from our
praise amidst the mountains and caves of Asia, and so prevented
its becoming known to the Latins. But God forbid that this unfor- 2
tunate accident should impede her from receiving, under her husband's title, whatever deserved glory my humble words can bestow.

After Antiochus the Great, king of Syria and Asia, had been 3
defeated by the Romans under the command of Scipio Asiaticus,
the consul Gnaeus Manlius Torquatus was allotted the province of
Asia. He first destroyed the remnants of the enemy near the shore.
Then, in order to avoid the appearance of having transported his
army in vain or of not keeping his soldiers busy, he proceeded on
his own initiative to the remote mountainous regions of Asia.
There Manlius waged a bitter war against the Galatians, a savage
and barbarous people, on the pretext that they had sent help to
Antiochus against the Romans and were disturbing all of Asia
with their intermittent raids.

Despairing of victory, the Galatians abandoned their towns and 4
withdrew with their wives, children, and possessions to mountain
peaks whose natural situation afforded them protection. There
they defended themselves against the besieging enemy by strength
of arms as best they could. But the Galatians were overcome 5
by the hardened strength of the Roman army, driven down the
mountain slopes, and slaughtered; the survivors surrendered and
acknowledged Manlius as the victor.

Making up the large number of captives were men and women 6
of all ages, and they were placed in the custody of a centurion.

7 pernanti quibus poterat viribus stuprum intulit. Quod mulier adeo grandi pertulit indignatione ut non magis libertatem cuperet quam vindictam; sed cauta in tempus votum silentio texit.

8 Cum autem venisset pro redimendis captivis, pecunia pacta, excanduit innovata ira caste sub pectore mulieris; que, premeditata quid sibi faciendum instaret, soluta vinculis, cum suis se traxit in
9 partem iussitque centurioni poscenti ponderari aurum. Cui operi dum centurio intentos animum tenebat et oculos, hec, ydiomate suo, Romanis incognito, servis imperavit ut centurionem percuterent et caput evestigio preciderent mortuo; quod sinu servatum il-
10 lesa remeavit ad suos. Et cum in conspectu pervenisset viri recitassetque quid captive illatum sit, quod detulerat ad pedes eius deiecit, quasi pretium illati dedecoris et ruboris feminei, quod potuerat, purgamentum tulisset.

11 Quis hanc, non dicam solum romanam, sed ex acie Lucretie unam, potius quam barbaram mulierem, non dicat? Stabant adhuc in conspectu carcer cathene et circumstrepebant victricia arma et sevi vindicis superimminebant secures, necdum satis erat mulieris libertas reddita, cum labefactati corporis indignatio in tam grandes vires honestum pectus inpelleret ut nec iterum, si oportuerit, subire cathenas, tetrum intrare carcerem et cervicem prebere securibus expaverit animosa femina, inclita scelesti facinoris ultrix, quin servorum gladios constanti iussu in caput infausti stupratoris adigeret.

12 Quonam acriorem hominem, animosiorem ducem, severiorem in male meritos imperatorem comperies? Quonam sagaciorem audacioremque mulierem adeas, aut matronalis honestatis magis pervigilem servatricem? Videbat mirabili mentis perspicacia femina

When this guard caught sight of the young and beautiful wife of the chieftain Orgiago, he yearned to possess her. Forgetting his honor as a Roman, he ravished her though she resisted with all her strength. The victim's indignation at this outrage reached such a pitch that she longed for vengeance as much as freedom, but for the moment she prudently kept her desire secret.

When, however, the centurion came to ransom the prisoners at the price agreed upon, wrath burned anew in the woman's chaste breast. She had already decided on a plan. Freed of her chains, she moved to one side with her retinue and ordered that the gold be weighed out to pay the centurion. While the latter's attention was absorbed in this task, she ordered the servants in her own tongue (unknown to the Romans) to knock the man down and decapitate him forthwith. This done, the woman returned unharmed to her people with the centurion's head under her dress. Once in the presence of her husband, she told him of the shame inflicted upon her in prison and threw at his feet the parcel she was carrying, as if to pay the price of the dishonor she had suffered and to purge the shame she had endured as a woman.

Shouldn't we say that this woman was no barbarian, but a Roman—indeed, a Roman woman who ranks with Lucretia? The prison, the chains were still in full view; around her resounded still the clanging of victorious arms; the ax of the cruel executioner still threatened, for she had not yet completely regained her freedom. Nonetheless, anger at the violation of her body moved her chaste breast with such force that this spirited woman, this glorious avenger of wickedness, was not afraid, should it prove necessary, to feel again the weight of the chains, to enter once more the loathsome prison, and to offer her neck to the executioner's ax. What is more, she unhesitatingly ordered her servants to strike off the head of her unfortunate ravisher.

Where will you find a fiercer person, a braver leader, or a general stricter with regard to the undeserving? Where will you meet

hec quoniam satius foret in mortem ire certam quam cum incerto
dedecore domum viri repetere nec, nisi per maximos ausus et discrimen, posse testari in corpore violato illibatam fuisse mentem.

13   Sic ergo decus servatur femineum, sic sublatum recuperatur, sic
pudici cordis testimonium redditur. Et ideo prospectent, quibus
inclite pudicitie cura insidet animo, quoniam non satis sit, ad cordis sinceritatem testandam, lacrimis et querelis se violentiam pas-
sam dicere nisi, dum possit, quis in vindictam egregio processerit
opere.

: LXXIV :

De Tertia Emilia primi Africani coniuge

1   Tertia Emilia, etsi tam ex claritate familie Emiliorum, ex qua
splendidam originem duxerat, quam ex coniugio strenuissimi viri
Scipionis primi Affricani perlucida sit, longe tamen ampliori lumine facinore emicuit suo.

2   Nam cum is qui iunior quondam Luteio[1] principi sponsam virginem, primo iuventutis flore ac spetiosissimi decoris spectabilem,
cum thesauris a parentibus pro eiusdem virginis redemptione obla-
tis, intactam restituit, senior factus se ipsum a damnate concupiscentie illecebris nequisset surripere, sed in dilectionem ancillule
sue et concubitum incidisset; quod cum difficillimum sit honesti
amoris animadvertentiam fallere, Tertiam latere non potuit; quin
imo temporis tractu cuncta cognovit.

3   Et quis dubitet quin egerrime tulerit? Asserunt enim nonnulle,
omni oris rubore seposito, nil iniuriosius, nil intollerabilius[2] nupte
mulieri fieri posse quam quod iure thori suum dicunt a viro extere

a cleverer and bolder woman, or a more watchful guardian of conjugal honor? With remarkable clarity this woman saw that it would be better to encounter certain death than to return to her husband's house with her honor in doubt; she knew that only great daring and great risk could prove the purity of intention in her defiled body.

Thus is a woman's honor saved; thus is it regained when lost; 13 and thus is proof of an innocent heart given. Let those women who really care about preserving their precious virtue see that, in order to demonstrate purity of heart, it is not enough to complain tearfully that one has been violated; within the limits of possibility one must go on to avenge the outrage with a noble action.

: LXXIV :

Tertia Aemilia, Wife of the Elder Africanus

Tertia Aemilia was distinguished much more for her own accomplishments than for the renown of the Aemilian family, from which she took her noble lineage, or for her marriage to the valiant Scipio Africanus the Elder.

As a young man, Scipio had once restored unharmed to Prince 2 Allucius the latter's fiancée, an extraordinarily beautiful woman in the first flower of youth, along with the treasure offered by her parents for her ransom. But, now that he was old, Scipio could no longer pull himself away from the snares of accursed concupiscence. In fact, he fell in love and committed adultery with one of his young maidservants. Since it is almost impossible for something like this to escape the notice of an honorable love, he could not deceive Tertia, who eventually learned everything.

Doubtless she was very much hurt. Some women claim that 3 nothing more offensive or intolerable (to say nothing of the

4   concedi femine; et ego edepol facile credam. Nam seu fragilitate sexus eveniat, seu minus bona de se opinione faciente, suspitiosissimum animal est femina. Arbitrantur enim evestigio, si quid in alteram a viro agitur, in detrimentum amoris sibi debiti operetur.

5   Sed quantumcunque difficile visum sit, constanti tamen pectore mulier inclita tulit tantoque cognitum viri crimen oppressit silentio ut, nedum alter, sed nec vir ipse perpenderit eam sensisse quid

6   ageret. Existimabat autem discreta uxor indecens nimium in propatulo sciri quod is qui virtute inclita reges nationesque validas

7   subegerat, ipse amori ancillule subiaceret. Nec sanctissime mulieri satis visum hoc, Scipione vivente, archanum servasse; quin imo, eo iam defuncto, ad auferendam a viri memoria illecebrem notam, si, quomodo crimen, alicunde expirasse potuisset et causa[3], ne ea que tam celebris viri fuerat usa concubitu, aut a quoquam servitutis improperio deturpari posset, aut minus decenti lascivia cuiquam misceretur de cetero, qua labefactari videretur amplissimi viri concupiscentia, primo illam manumisit liberali animo, deinde liberto suo in coniugem dedit.

8   O sacris in celum extollenda laudibus mulier, hinc equo atque tacito patiens iniurias animo, inde liberali in rivalem sibi ancillulam defuncti viri persolvens debita! Quod quanto rarius contigisse

9   vidimus, tanto debemus arbitrari splendidius. Conclamasset altera et in concilium vocasset affines vicinas et quascunque cognitas mulieres easque longa dicacitate complesset onerassetque querelis innumeris se omissam, se relictam, se vilipensam, se in nullo pretio a

shame) can happen to a wife than for her husband to take another woman into his bed, to which, they say, only the wife has a right. I can well believe this. The female is a very suspicious creature, either because of the weakness of her sex or because she does not have a good opinion of herself. If a husband is attentive to another woman, a wife immediately thinks that this works to the detriment of the love that is her due. 4

But however difficult the situation may have seemed, the illustrious Tertia steadfastly endured and concealed so quietly her knowledge of her husband's fault that no one else, not even Scipio himself, realized that she knew what he was doing. Moreover, as a discreet wife she thought it most unbecoming for the public to learn that the brave conqueror of kings and powerful nations was himself conquered by his love for a maidservant. Nor did it seem sufficient to this saintly woman that she keep the matter secret only while Scipio was alive. Quite the contrary: after his death, Tertia generously freed the slave and married her to one of her own freedmen. This she did so as to remove an infamous stain from her husband's memory in case his fault and the cause behind it should somehow be exposed. By this action she prevented the woman who had shared the bed of so eminent a man from being disgraced by references to her servile condition. Tertia also kept her from satisfying in the future the unseemly lust of another man, something that might have made the passion of her distinguished husband seem vile. 5 6 7

Surely Tertia is a woman who should be praised to the skies with reverent homage. On the one hand she endured the affront in patient silence, while on the other she generously paid her late husband's debt to her rival, the maidservant—a gesture we see so rarely that we must deem it all the more splendid. Another woman would have shouted and called a council of her relatives, neighbors, and sundry female acquaintances. She would have filled their ears with slander and burdened them with endless com- 8 9

viro habitam eoque vivente viduam et ancillule servule et deiecte
sortis meretricule postpositam; abiecisset extemplo, imo sub corona vendidisset ancillam, virum etiam publice infestasset lacrimis
et questibus, nec curasset, dum ius suum garrulitate defenderet,
numquid honestissimi alias viri famam inclitam macularet.

: LXXV :

De Dripetrua Laodocie regina

1 Dripetruam Laodocie fuisse reginam et magni Mitridatis filiam legimus. Quam etsi commendabilem fecerit ea fides qua parentibus
sumus obnoxii, plus satis, me iudice, illam inaudito quodam opere
memorabilem fecit natura parens.

2   Nam, si codicibus veterum adhibenda fides est, hec, cum gemino dentium ordine nata, monstruosum de se spectaculum Asya-

3 ticis omnibus tribuit evo suo. Que etsi nullum in mandendo a tam
inusitata dentium quantitate susceperit impedimentum, insigni tamen deformitate non caruit quam, ut iam pretactum[1] est, laudabili

4 fide compescuit. Nam superatum a Pompeo magno Mitridatem
genitorem suum, nullis periculis aut laboribus indulgendo, semper
secuta est et obsequio tam fideli testata nature crimina imputari
parentibus non deberi.

plaints that she had been deserted, abandoned, scorned, and reckoned worthless by her husband, that she was a widow in his lifetime, and that she had had to take second place to a slave and a common trollop. She would have sent the girl away at once — no, she would have sold her at auction. She would have harassed her husband in public with tearful protests, and, so long as she could defend her rights with her chatter, she would not have cared that she was staining the glowing reputation of her husband, who in all other respects was a man of spotless honor.

: LXXV :

Dripetrua, Queen of Laodicea

Dripetrua, we read, was the queen of Laodicea and daughter of   1
Mithridates the Great. Although she should be commended for that fidelity which binds us to our parents, it seems to me that the unprecedented handiwork of Mother Nature made her still more memorable.

If we can trust the accounts of ancient authors, Dripetrua, who   2
was born with a double row of teeth, presented a monstrous spectacle in her day to all the people of Asia. So unusual a quantity of   3
teeth gave her no difficulty in eating, but they did constitute a notable deformity. This, as I have already indicated, she mitigated by a loyalty deserving of praise. For, after Mithridates' defeat by   4
Pompey the Great, Dripetrua showed total disregard for danger and toil and always accompanied her father. By such faithful service she demonstrated that natural deformities should not be held against one's parents.

: LXXVI :

De Sempronia Gracci

1 Sempronia filia fuit Titi Sempronii Gracci, suo tempore clarissimi viri, suscepta ex Cornelia, olim maioris Scipionis Africani filia. Fuit et insuper coniunx splendidi viri Scipionis Emiliani qui et avi cognomen ob deletam Cartaginem postea consecutus est, et soror insuper Tyberii et Gaii Graccorum, amplitudine et constantia animi a maioribus non degenerans suis.

2 Huic enim post cesos fratres ob seditiones suas aiunt contigisse ut a tribuno plebis coram populo in iudicium traheretur, non qui-
3 dem absque maxima consternatione mentis. Ibi autem favente multitudine et potestate tribunitia omni instante, ut deoscularetur Equitium, ex Firmo piceno hominem, tanquam nepotem suum et Tyberii Gracci fratris sui filium, eumque ex Sempronia familia susciperet cogebatur.

4 Que quidem, etsi eo in loco consisteret in quo etiam principes tremere consueverant, et hinc inde dissonis clamoribus imperite multitudinis ageretur minareturve, ex adverso torva facie sublimis tribunorum autoritas, in nichilo muliebris constantia fracta est; quin imo memor Tyberio fratri preter tres filios non fuisse, quorum alter iuvenis, dum in Sardinia stipendia mereretur, obierat et alter adolescentulus paulo ante patris ruinam Rome diem clauserat, et tertius infantulus, post genitoris cedem postumus natus, apud nutricem aleretur adhuc, constantissimo pectore et acri vultu nulla ex parte territa, extraneum temerariumque Equitium, clarum genus Graccorum mendaci demonstratione fedare conantem, a se ignominiose reiecit, nec ad id agendum quod iubebatur ullis imperiis aut minis induci potuit aut flecti.

: LXXVI :

Sempronia, Daughter of Gracchus

Sempronia was the daughter of Titus Sempronius Gracchus, who   1
was quite a famous personage in his day; her mother was Cornelia, daughter of the late Scipio Africanus the Elder. In addition,
Sempronia was the wife of Scipio Aemilianus, a distinguished man
who later acquired his grandfather's nickname because of his own
role in the destruction of Carthage. She was also the sister of
Tiberius and Gaius Gracchus. In greatness and perseverance of
spirit, Sempronia was certainly the equal of her ancestors.

It is said that, after the slaying of her brothers in the wake of   2
the insurrections they had provoked, to her great dismay Sempronia was brought to trial before the people by a tribune of the
plebs. There the tribunes, with the backing of the mob, pressed   3
her to kiss Equitius, a man from Fermo in the district of Piceno,
and to accept him into the Sempronian family as the son of her
brother Tiberius Gracchus and hence as her nephew.

But this woman did not move an inch in her resolve, even   4
though, standing in a place where even princes are wont to tremble, she was alternately shoved by a noisy, ignorant crowd and
threatened by the lofty authority of the tribunes who glared
harshly at her. Instead, Sempronia kept in mind that her brother
Tiberius had had only three children: one had died young while
serving as a soldier in Sardinia, another had died in Rome shortly
before his father's downfall, and the third, who was born after his
father's death, was an infant still in the care of a nurse. With firmness of spirit and a stern expression on her face, she fearlessly and
contemptuously thrust Equitius aside as a presumptuous stranger
who was making a fraudulent attempt to stain the family honor of
the Gracchi. Neither threats nor commands could make Sempronia do what was ordered.

5   Qua[1] tam animose Equitio data repulsa, et insani hominis pro-
tervia frustrata, et a tribunis accuratius exquisito negocio, cognita
et generosi animi mulieris perseverantia laudata est.

6   Erunt forte qui dicant, esto iure maiorum suorum Sempronia
meruerit, non tamen hanc ob constantiam inter claras fuisse ponendam, eo quod, quodam innato sibi more, mulieres in quocunque proposito obstinate opinionis atque inflexibilis pertinacie

7   sint. Ego autem dato non inficiar, eas tamen, si veritati innitantur,
arbitror laudandas; cui profecto Sempronia insistebat.

8   Sunt preterea qui velint hanc tam indomite fuisse cervicis ut nil
adversus iudicium suum factum quod reliquerit, si daretur facul-
tas, inultum; et ob id arbitrantur eam in mortem Scipionis viri sui
prestitisse consensum eo quod, diruta Numantia, rogatus sententiam dicere numquid iuste cesum existimaret Tyberium, nullo habito ad affinitatem respectu, seditiosi hominis truculentam lauda-
verit mortem.

: LXXVII :

De Claudia Quinta muliere romana

1   Claudia Quinta romana fuit mulier; quibus tamen orta parentibus, non satis patet; verum insigni quadam audacia perpetuam sibi
claritatem peperit.

2   Hec cum assiduo ac vario et accurate plurimum uteretur ornatu
ac oris cultu nimio incederet splendida, a gravioribus matronis non
tantum minus honesta, verum et minus pudica arbitrata est.

3   Sane, Marco Cornelio et Publio Sempronio consulibus, anno
scilicet quintodecimo belli punici secundi, factum est ut e Pesi-

CHAPTER LXXVII

After her courageous rejection of Equitius and the frustration 5
of his mad impudence, a more careful investigation of the matter
by the tribunes resulted in recognition and praise for the constancy of this woman's noble spirit.

Perhaps some will object that, although Sempronia deserved it 6
by right of ancestry, nonetheless she should not have been included among famous women on the grounds of constancy since
women are instinctively obstinate and unbending in their opinions
about everything. I do not deny this, but I believe that women 7
ought to be praised if they rely, as Sempronia certainly did, upon
the truth.

She is also reported by some sources to have been so unbending 8
that, when she had the means, no slight to her wishes was left
unavenged. Hence certain authorities believe that Sempronia consented to the death of her husband Scipio for the following reason: after destroying Numantia, he was asked to give his views on
the justice of Tiberius Gracchus' murder, and Scipio endorsed the
rebel's brutal death without regard for family ties.

: LXXVII :

Claudia Quinta, a Roman Woman

Claudia Quinta was a Roman woman. We do not know the name 1
of her parents, but through her extraordinary boldness she gained
everlasting fame for herself.

As she was always beautifully dressed, had an extensive ward- 2
robe, and appeared in public with too much make-up, the more
serious matrons decided that Claudia was not only dishonorable
but also unchaste.

Now during the consulate of Marcus Cornelius and Publius 3
Sempronius, that is, in the fifteenth year of the Second Punic

4 munte deum mater Romam in faucibus Tyberis applicaret. Ad quam suscipiendam e navi, cum iuxta responsum oraculi Nausica, ab universo senatu totius urbis vir optimus iudicatus, cum matronis omnibus eo usque concederet ubi propinqua navis, contigit ut, volentibus nautis litori propinquare, hereret vado fluminis ratis qua vehebatur simulacrum.

5 Et cum nec trahente iuvenum multitudine posse moveri videretur, Claudia aliis matronis immixta, sue virtutis conscia, palam summissis genibus deam supplex deprecata est ut, si se castam arbitraretur, cingulum sequeretur suum.

6 Et illico fidenter consurgens, id futurum sperans quod prece quesiverat, navim alligari cingulo iussit et ab ea iuvenes amoveri omnes; nec ante factum est quam, trahente Claudia, facillime navem a vado evelleret et, mirantibus cunctis, eam in partem quam cupiebat traheret; ex quo tam mirabili successu secutum est evestigio ut omnium de minus servata pudicitia, maxima Claudie laude, in contrarium verteretur opinio. Et sic que ad litus turpi lascivie nota maculata processerat, decorata insigni pudicitie splendore patriam reintravit.

7 Verum etsi pro voto Claudie cesserit, absit ut existimem sane mentis esse, quantumcunque innocue, similia audere. Velle enim, ut se quis ostendat insontem, id agere quod preter naturam sit, Deum potius temptare est quam obiecti criminis purgare labem.

8 Sancte nobis agendum est, sancte vivendum; et si minus boni existimemur, non absque bono nostro patitur Deus; vult quippe nostra firmetur patientia, auferatur elatio, exerceatur virtus et ut nobiscum ipsi letemur, dum alios noscit indignos.

9 Satis nobis est, multum est, imo permaximum, si Deo teste

War, the statue of the mother of the gods left Pessinus and was approaching Rome at the mouth of the Tiber.[1] In accord with an oracle's response, Scipio Nasica, whom the entire Senate had judged to be the best man in the city, went with all the married women to receive the statue when it disembarked. The ship drew near and the sailors wanted to bring it to shore, but the vessel transporting the statue happened to run aground. 4

When the efforts of a crowd of young men dragging on the ropes seemed of no avail, Claudia, who had joined the other women, knelt in the presence of all the onlookers. Conscious of her own virtue, she humbly implored the goddess to be led by her sash if she judged Claudia to be chaste. 5

Thereupon Claudia arose with confidence and, trusting that her prayer would be answered, she ordered the ship to be tied to her sash and all the young men moved out of the way. No sooner was this done than Claudia easily drew the ship out of the shallows. To everyone's astonishment, she pulled it to the place where she wanted it to go. This wonderful success immediately converted the general belief in her unchaste conduct to the opposite view, and Claudia received great praise. Thus the woman who had gone in procession to the shore, stained by a reputation for loose conduct, returned home adorned with glorious purity. 6

Although everything turned out as Claudia had wished, I am far from thinking that it is the sign of a rational mind, however innocent, to risk similar undertakings. To want to do something supernatural in order to show that one is blameless is rather to tempt God than to purge the blot of an imputed crime. We must live and act in a holy manner; if we are thought to be flawed, God does not allow this except for our own good. He wants our patience to be strengthened, our pride to be put aside, and our virtue to be exercised. He wants for us to be happy within ourselves; He knows the unworthiness of others. 7 8

For us it is sufficient, in fact it is much — nay, it is the greatest 9

bene vivimus; et idcirco, si minus bene de nobis sentiunt homines,
dum bene fecerimus, non curemus, dum male, ut emendemur totis
viribus instandum est, ut eos potius male opinantes sinamus quam
male agentes simus.

: LXXVIII :

De Hypsicratea regina Ponti

1 Hypsicrathea, quamvis eius originem ignoremus, magni tamen
Mitridatis coniunx et Ponti grandis regina fuit, forma spectabilis
et invicti amoris in virum adeo commendanda ut ex eo suo nomini
fulgorem perpetuum meruerit.

2 Mitridati quippe, diuturno atque sumptuoso et discriminibus
variis pendulo adversus Romanos bello laboranti, esto illi barba-
rico more coniuges alie et concubine plurime forent, amoris eximii
facibus incensa, seu regiones amplissimas peragranti, seu certamina ineunti, seu transfretationes paranti, semper fuit fidissima et
inseparata comes.

3 Hec equidem, egre ipsius absentiam patiens atque existimans
neminem posse preter se rite obsequia inpendere viro et, ut plurimum, infida ministeria fore servorum, ut ipsa dilectissimo sibi
posset oportuna prestare, etsi difficillimum videretur, sumpsit tamen prosequendi consilium; et quoniam tanto operi muliebris habitus videbatur incongruus et indecens lateri bellicosissimi regis
incedere feminam, ut marem fingeret, ante alia aureos crines, quibus plurimum gloriantur mulieres, forcipibus secuit et syderei vultus sui precipuum decus, non solum una cum crinibus galea tegere

thing of all—to live well in the sight of God. Therefore, so long as we act well, we must not care if men do not have a good opinion of us. If we act badly, then we must strive with all our strength to mend our ways so that we leave others to their evil assumptions rather than act ourselves like evildoers.

: LXXVIII :

Hypsicratea, Queen of Pontus

Although we are ignorant of her parentage, we do know that 1 Hypsicratea was a noble queen of Pontus and the wife of Mithridates the Great. She was remarkably beautiful, and her steadfast love for her husband was so deserving of praise as to impart perpetual luster to her own name.

Even while Mithridates was burdened with a long, costly, and 2 unpredictable war against the Romans, Hypsicratea's passion for him was such that she always remained his faithful and inseparable companion: on his travels across vast territories or at the onset of battle or on his journeys across the sea—and this despite the fact that, in accordance with barbaric custom, he had other wives and many concubines.

Simply put, Hypsicratea could hardly bear to be apart from 3 Mithridates. She also thought that no one but herself could serve him properly and that, for the most part, the care provided by his servants could not be trusted. So, even though she realized the great difficulties involved, she decided to follow him in order to attend personally to the needs of her beloved husband. Female attire did not seem appropriate for so important a job, nor did it seem right for a woman to march alongside a warlike king. Hence, to make herself look like a man, Hypsicratea first scissored off those golden locks in which most women would have gloried. Then she

passa est, verum pulvere et sudoribus ac armorum deturpare rubigine, armillas aureas et iocalia vestesque purpureas et in pedes
fluxas ponere aut genutenus resecare et eburneum pectus lorica tegere atque tibias ocreis devincire, abicere anulos et digitorum pre-
ciosissima ornamenta et eorum vice parmam hastasque gestare
fraxineas et parthicos arcus et pharetras, loco monilium, cingere et
adeo apte omnia, ut ex petulanti regina veteranum factum militem
credas.

4   Sed forsan facilia hec. Assueta quidem regiis in thalamis ocio et
molliciei et celum spectare perraro cum, eis omissis, animo virili
predita, equis insidere didicisset invicta et armorum onusta, post
virum per aspreta montium et lubrica vallium die nocteque algores
estusque superans, citato discurrere cursu persepe comperta est re-
galisque thori loco nudum quandoque solum et lustra ferarum,
corpore durato, cogente somno, premebat impavida, victori viro
seu profugo semper comes adiutrixque laborum et consiliorum
particeps incedens ubique.

5   Quid multa? Pios oculos vulnera cedes sanguinem, quem et
ipsa pugnans spiculis fundebat, aliquando posse absque horrore
conspicere docuit; et aures, cantibus assuetas, equorum fremitum
militares tumultus et classica audire absque mentis obstupefa-
ctione coegit.

6   Tandem cum multa pertulisset, etiam robusto militi gravia, Mitridatem, a Gneo Pompeio superatum atque fatigatum, per Armenos saltus Pontique latebras et efferatas quascunque nationes cum
paucis ex amicis secuta est, nunc afflictum spe meliori recreans,

not only suffered a helmet to cover her starry countenance (which was particularly beautiful) and her hair, but allowed that face to be disfigured with sweat, dust, and the rust of armor. She discarded her golden bracelets, jewels, and dresses of purple flowing down to her feet, or she cut them at the knee, and she covered her ivory breast with a cuirass and fastened greaves to her legs. She cast aside her rings and the other precious ornaments on her hands, and in their place she carried a shield and ashwood lances; instead of her necklaces she hung Parthian bows and quivers about her neck. So well did Hypsicratea accomplish all this that you might well believe she had been transformed from a haughty queen into a seasoned soldier.

Such changes may seem easy. Yet the woman who once was ac- 4 customed to ease and softness in the royal bedchamber and only rarely went outdoors now abandoned her former ways. Endowed with a manly spirit, Hypsicratea became a matchless horsewoman. She was often sighted, heavily armed, indifferent to heat and cold, galloping day and night after her husband over rough mountains and through treacherous valleys. Her body now toughened, she was not afraid when she needed sleep to exchange the royal bed for the bare earth and sometimes the lairs of wild beasts. Hypsicratea followed Mithridates everywhere: she was his constant companion in victory or in flight, his helper in work, his partner in counsel.

In short, Hypsicratea eventually taught her gentle eyes to wit- 5 ness without horror the wounds, the slaughter, and the blood that her own arrows too spilled in battle. She forced her ears, once accustomed to the sound of songs, to listen without amazement to the neighing of horses, the tumult of soldiers, and the blare of trumpets.

Finally, when she had endured much that would have been hard 6 even for a stout soldier, Hypsicratea followed the weary Mithridates after his defeat by Pompey. Accompanied by a few friends,

nunc solatiis, quorum cupidum noverat, demulcens adeo ut illi tantum consolationis attulerit ut, in quascunque solitudines ageretur, coniugali sibi videretur in thalamo refoveri.

7   O pectus coniugalis dulcedinis sacrarium, o inexhausta amicitie virtus, quibus quamque sanctis viribus muliebrem animum roborastis! Nulla profecto usquam uxor pro viro similia, nedum graviora, pertulit. Quo merito, si in eius perpetuam laudem antiquitas versata est, minimum admirari iure posteritas poterit.

8   Ceterum ex tot laboribus tantaque tanque inclita fide benemerita mulier a viro non satis dignum retulit premium. Nam cum is senex iam filium ex ea susceptum iratus occidisset et, urgentibus Romanorum viribus, non solum in regnum sed in regiam se recepisset, esto animo moliretur ingentia et legationibus varias atque longinquas nationes in bellum adversus Romanos suscitare conaretur, a Pharnace filio, ob eius sevitiam in filios amicosque rebellante, obsessus est.

9   Quod cum cerneret et eum inexorabilem invenisset, postremam rerum suarum arbitratus ruinam, cum reliquis tam coniugibus quam pellicibus ac filiabus, Hypsicratheam, que tot vite sue subsidia laborando prestiterat, ne illi superviveret, veneno assumpsit.

10   Sane ingratum Mitridatis opus Hypsicrathee meritam gloriam minuisse non potuit; corpus mortale veneno immatura morte sublatum est, nomen eius monimentis venerandarum literarum ad

they passed through the woods of Armenia and the recesses of Pontus in the midst of savage peoples. Sometimes she refreshed her despondent husband with hope of better things to come, and at times she soothed him with the pleasures she knew he longed for. Hypsicratea brought him so much comfort that, no matter where he had been driven to take refuge in the wilderness, it seemed to the king that he had returned to the gentle care of their chamber at home.

O loving breast, temple of conjugal tenderness! O inextinguish- 7 able power of friendship, with what holy strength did you fortify that woman's soul! Never did any wife endure greater (or even similar) hardships for her husband's sake. Posterity should not be surprised if for these merits antiquity accorded Hypsicratea ever- lasting praise.

But this deserving woman did not receive from her husband a 8 reward worthy of her many exertions and splendid loyalty. When Mithridates reached old age, he killed in a fit of anger the son she had borne him. Then, hard pressed by Roman forces, the king re- treated not only within the boundaries of his kingdom but into the royal palace itself. There he hatched great schemes and sent le- gations to various peoples, including some far away, in an effort to incite them to war against the Romans. Eventually he was be- sieged by his son Pharnaces, who rebelled because of the cruelty Mithridates had shown towards his own children and friends.

The king saw that he was surrounded and that Pharnaces could 9 not be moved by entreaty. Thinking that his final ruin was at hand, he did not wish Hypsicratea to survive him. So, together with his other wives, concubines, and daughters, he poisoned her—she whose labors had given him so much support while she was alive.

This ungrateful action of Mithridates could not lessen, of 10 course, the glory that Hypsicratea deserved. Her mortal body was

nos usque et in perpetuum fama celebri vivet et longa quidem po-
steritate fraudari non poterit.

: LXXIX :

De Sempronia romana

1 Semproniam, alteram a superiori, fuisse celebris ingenii feminam
sepius legisse meminimus, sed, ut plurimum, ad nephanda procli-
vem. Hec, maiorum testimonio, genere inter romanas et formosi-
2 tate splendida fuit et tam viro quam liberis fortunata satis. Quorum cum nomina minime teneam, in id veniamus ut que in femina
laudari forte possunt seu ex quibus nomen eius effulsit, locum primum occupent.

3   Fuit igitur hec ingenii tam prompti atque versatilis ut et intelli-
geret illico et exequeretur etiam imitando quicquid aliquem dicentem aut facientem vidisset aliquando. Hinc cum non solum latinas
sed et grecas literas didicisset, ausa est, nec muliebriter, quin imo
adeo perspicaciter, versus, dum vellet, componere, ut in admirationem etiam traheret qui legissent: egregium quippe et laudabile
4 docto viro. Fuit insuper tante tanque elegantis facundie ut modestiam suadere, iocos movere, risum elicere, molliciem atque proca-
citatem excitare volens posset et, quod maius est, tam lepidi moris
in loquendo fuit ut, in quocunque sermonis genere verteretur, illud
5 facetie atque leporis plenum audientium auribus inferret. Preterea
psallere eleganter et eque etiam saltare novit: que quidem, si sane
utantur, forsan commendande plurimum in femina dotes sunt.

6   Ceterum pessimis imbuta facinoribus longe aliter usa est. Nam

destroyed by an untimely death through poison; but her glorious
name, through the testimony of venerable books, will live forever
among us, and it cannot be cheated of lasting fame.

: LXXIX :

Sempronia, a Roman Woman

I remember often having read that Sempronia (who is different 1
from the Sempronia discussed above[a]) was a woman of celebrated
intellect but inclined to wickedness. Ancient sources tell us that
she was famous among the Romans for her ancestry and her
beauty, and very fortunate in both her husband and her children.
Since I do not recall who they are, let us come to those things that 2
ought to occupy the first place in our discussion because they
make a woman worthy of praise or render her name illustrious.

Sempronia, then, was so versatile and quick-witted that she im- 3
mediately comprehended and could imitate whatever she happened to hear or see others do. Knowledgeable in both Latin and
Greek, she did not hesitate to compose verses when she wished,
and these she wrote, not in the way women usually do, but with
such discernment as to elicit the admiration of all her readers —
a feat that would have been notable and praiseworthy for a man
of learning. Her eloquence was so powerful and attractive that at 4
will she could encourage modesty, start the play of wit, draw a
laugh, or arouse wanton and shameful conduct. What is more,
Sempronia spoke so engagingly that, no matter what the topic
was, she presented her audience with a discourse full of wit and
charm. She also knew how to sing elegantly and to dance equally 5
well; these accomplishments, if used properly, are perhaps the
most commendable in a woman.

But Sempronia, who was thoroughly acquainted with the worst

audacia nimia percita, nonnunquam in viriles damnandos nimium ausus evasit; et dum psallere et saltare, instrumenta profecto luxurie, in lasciviam uteretur, urens libidine, ad eam exaturandam, fama pudoris matronalis omnino neglecta, homines sepius requisivit quam requireretur ab eis.

7 Cuius huius mali, quod in nonnullis tam validum cernimus, existimes fuisse radices? Ego naturam absit ut damnem cuius, quantumcunque magne sint vires, circa rerum principia flexibiles adeo sunt, ut eo fere quo velis parvo labore ducas quod natum est; et sic, neglectum, semper vergit in peius.

8 Nimia enim, ut arbitror, in adolescentulas maiorum indulgentia, virginum sepe depravata sunt ingenia; quibus licentiose, ut sepius fit, declinantibus in lasciviam, paulatim feminea cedit tepiditas et insurgit illico audacia, aucta a stolida quadam opinione qua asserunt id decere quod libet; et postquam semel eo itum est ut infectum sit virginale decus et frontis rubor abiectus, ut retrahamus labantes in vacuum labores inpendimus. Hinc non solum libidini hominum mulieres occurrunt, sed provocant.

9 Post hec Sempronie fuit auri cupido permaxima et, uti ad adipiscendum turpi questui se avida ingerebat, sic in quibuscunque sceleribus erat in expendendo profusa, in tantum ut nullus illi esset in avaritia et prodigalitate modus.

10 Exitiale malum est auri desiderium in femina et manifestissimum vitiati pectoris testimonium. Sic et detestanda prodigalitas que, quotiens mentem sibi natura adversam intrat, uti muliebris est, cui infixa tenacitas, nulla preter inopiam salutis spes haberi de cetero potest; de honestate eius deque suis substantiis actum est.

11 Non enim ante subsistunt quam in extremum dedecus et miseriam[1] venerint.

kinds of wrongdoing, made a far different use of the last-named skills. Stimulated by her reckless nature, she sometimes ended up 6 doing things that have to be condemned even in a man. Dancing and singing are tools of sensuality, and Sempronia used them for lascivious purposes. To satisfy her burning lust, she completely discarded any kind of reputation as a chaste woman and was not so much men's prey as their hunter.

What do you think is the root of this evil which we see to be so 7 strong in certain people? Far be it from me to blame Nature! However robust our tendencies, at the outset they are so pliable that, with a little effort, every creature can be guided almost at will. If, however, no notice is taken in the early stages, the situation will always tend to deteriorate.

I believe that too much parental indulgence ruins the character 8 of young girls. As they slide all too freely towards wantonness (as often happens), little by little feminine reserve gives way, and in its place there arises a cheekiness nourished by the foolish opinion that whatever they want is right. Once virginal honor has been stained and the blush of shame cast aside, vain are our efforts to save women from falling. From this time on, not only do women rush to meet a man's lust: they provoke it.

Sempronia, moreover, craved wealth. To acquire it, she eagerly 9 took up disreputable ways of making money and lavished her earnings on all kinds of wicked extravagances. The result was that she had no control over her avarice and her prodigality.

This yearning for money is a fatal evil in a woman, and the sur- 10 est sign of a heart that has gone wrong. And prodigality should be equally detested. When it enters into a mind naturally opposed to it—like the female mind, which is innately frugal—there can be no hope of salvation afterwards except in poverty. Otherwise, it is all over so far as their honor and their means are concerned. Such 11 women will not stop until they have plumbed the depths of shame and misery.

12 Mulierum parsimonia est: ad eas spectat intra limen cum fide servare quod quesitum defertur a viris. Hec, quantum auri damnanda cupido et immoderata profusio, tantum laudanda est, cum ipsa sit sensim substantiarum auctrix egregia, domestice rei salus, integre mentis testis, laborum solatium et inconcussa splendide posteritatis basis.

13 Porro, ut in unum eius et extremum, ut arbitror, facinus omnia eius concludamus scelera, flagrante illa pestifera face seditiosissimi hominis Lucii Catiline et se iniquis consiliis et coniuratorum numero ad desolationem perpetuam romane reipublice in ampliores vires assidue extollente, facinorosa mulier ad pleniorem suarum libidinum captandam licentiam, id appetens quod etiam perditis hominibus fuisset horrori, coniuratis se immiscuit ultro; domus 14 etiam sue penetralia sevis colloquiis patuere semper. Verum nequitiis obsistente Deo, et Ciceronis studio coniuratorum detectis insidiis, cum iam Catilina Fesulas secessisset, in aliorum excidium frustratam arbitror corruisse.

15 Ex quo, esto eius ingenium laudare possimus et ob id illam extollere, turpe exercitium ut damnemus necesse est. Nam matronalis stola labefactata lasciviis pluribus egit ut in suum dedecus evaderet nota Sempronia, ubi, si modestia<m>[2] conservasset, evasisse poterat gloriosa.

Frugality is a virtue proper to women. It is their task to save faithfully at home what their husbands have earned. Frugality, in 12 fact, is to be praised as much as greed and reckless spending are to be condemned: the former facilitates in a notable way the gradual accumulation of wealth, safeguards the domestic patrimony, testifies to one's integrity, is the comfort of one's work, and forms a solid foundation for an illustrious posterity.

Let us sum up all of Sempronia's crimes in the one wicked deed 13 that was, so I believe, also her last. It took place when the deadly revolution of the rebellious Lucius Catiline was at fever pitch. In an effort to destroy forever the Roman Republic, he was steadily increasing his power through his wicked stratagems and the growing number of his co-conspirators. This nefarious woman wanted something that would have inspired horror even in the most dissolute of men. In order to enjoy a wider field for satisfying her lusts, she voluntarily joined the conspirators; the innermost recesses of her house were always available to host their angry plottings. But 14 God opposes evil, and through Cicero's zeal the treachery of the conspirators was revealed. It was, I believe, when Catiline retreated to Fiesole that Sempronia, whose scheming had come to naught, perished along with the others.

Hence, while we may praise her intellect and even extoll her for 15 it, we must condemn the vile use she made of it. The many instances of lewdness that stained her matronly dress made Sempronia notorious for disgrace; if she had maintained discretion, she could have become glorious.

: LXXX :

De coniugibus <Cymbrorum>[1]

1 Cymbrorum a Gaio Mario acri certamine superatorum pregrandis
coniugum fuit numerus, pudicitie sacro et constanti proposito lau-
2 dandus, quin imo extollendus precipue. Nam quanto fuit quanti-
tas amplior, tanto videtur honoribus sublimanda maioribus; et hoc
ideo, quia in castitatis observantiam devenisse paucas persepe legimus, multas convenisse nunquam audivimus, aut rarissime.

3 Romanis ergo rebus florentibus, Theotones Cymbrique et quedam alie barbare nationes ab Arthoo in romanum coniuraverunt
nomen et in unum primo convenientes, ut eos in fugam verti posse
nemo speraret, coniuges natos et supellectilem omnem secum ma-
4 gno agmine traxere vehiculis. Inde, ut omnem Ytaliam uno et eodem concuterent impetu, tripartito illam intrare agmine triplici itinere statuere.

5 Quibus a consternatis tumultu Romanis, Gaius Marius consul,
in quem inniti omnis reipublice spes ea tempestate videbatur, obvius missus, primos obiectos habuit Theutonum insolentes duces;
adversus quos in nichilo declinantes, certamen cum conseruisset et
longa pugna partium aliquandiu nutasset fortuna, postremo multo
sanguine fuso terga dedere Theutones. Deinde in Cimbros[2] itum
est et, ut Theutones[3] apud Aquas Sextias, sic illos in campo Rau-
dio duplici fudit certamine, facta hominum strage permaxima.

6 Quod advertentes cum ceteris impedimentis seposite coniuges,
non virorum secute sunt fugam, sed plaustris, quorum pregrandis
erat illis copia, in formam valli redactis, stulto sed animoso consi-

: LXXX :

The Wives of the Cimbrians

Very large indeed was the number of wives who survived the bitter   1
struggle in which Gaius Marius defeated the Cimbrians. These
women are to be praised—nay, they merit special commendation—for their holy and steadfast determination to preserve their
virtue. The greater their number, the loftier the honor they would   2
seem to deserve. And this is why: I have read often of the occasional woman who succeeded in retaining her chastity, but I have
never, or only very rarely, heard of many women banding together
for such a purpose.

The story begins when the Teutons, Cimbrians, and certain   3
other barbarian peoples from the north plotted against the Romans during a period of prosperity for the city. First they assembled in one place, transporting en masse their wives, children, and
all their household goods on a great line of carts. By this action
they took away any hope that they could be put to flight. Then, so   4
as to strike at all of Italy with a single simultaneous blow, they decided to divide their forces into three parts and to enter that country by three different routes.

Dismayed by the sudden tumult, the Romans sent against   5
them the consul Gaius Marius, on whom rested at that moment
all the hope of the republic. First he faced the arrogant leaders of
the Teutons, and when they stood their ground, he joined battle.
The struggle was a long one, and for some time its outcome was in
doubt, but finally, after much bloodshed, the Teutons were put to
flight. Then Marius moved against the Cimbrians. He had routed
the Teutons at Aquae Sextiae, and at Campi Raudii he did the
same to the Cimbrians in two battles with a terrible loss of life.

The Cimbrian women had remained in a separate place along   6
with the baggage train. Upon learning the outcome of the battles,

lio, preustis fustibus lapidibus gladiisque libertatem suam castimo-
7 niamque tutare quam longius possent disposuere. Sed acie facta,
advenientibus marianis militibus, cum non diu obstitissent, sensere quoniam in vacuum conatus disponerent et ob id, si possent,
8 inire cum imperatore concordiam petiere. Erat enim illis infixum
animo si viros[4], si sedes avitas, si substantias omnes pugna perdi-
dissent, una saltem, qua possent via, libertatem et pudicitiam servare suam.

Et idcirco postulavere unanimes non fugientium virorum pacem, non in patriam redire suam, non ut sua resarcirentur auro
damna, sed ut omnes Romam virginibus Vestalibus iungerentur.
9 Quod cum honestissimum visum foret et sincere mentis testimonium, nec impetrassent, succense furore in obstinatam voti sui
10 perseverantiam per sevum ivere facinus. Nam ante omnia, collisis
in terram parvis filiis atque peremptis, ut illos, qua poterant via,
turpi servituti subtraherent, nocte eadem intra vallum a se confe-
ctum, ne et ipse in dedecus sue castitatis et victorum ludibrium
traherentur, laqueis omnes lorisque mortem conscivere sibi nec
prede aliud ex se, preter pendentia cadavera, avidis liquere militibus.

11 Ivissent fractis hominum viribus alie, nonnulle supplices victori-
bus obviam soluto crine, tensis manibus precibus et ululatu com-
plentes omnia, et — quod fuisset obscenius — nonnulle blanditiis et
amplexibus impetrassent, si potuissent, supellectilis conservatio-
nem, reditum in patriam, nulla honestatis feminee habita men-
12 tione, aut se permisissent a quocunque, more pecudum, trahi. Ast
Cimbre[5] constanti pectore meliori[6] fortune servavere animos nec

336

they did not follow their husbands in flight but constructed a stockade out of their large supply of carts for the mad but brave purpose of defending their freedom and their virtue as long as they could with burnt staves, stones, and swords. A battle line was 7 formed; Marius' soldiers arrived; but after brief resistance the women realized that their efforts were futile. Hence they sought to come to terms, if possible, with the Roman general. They had al- 8 ready resolved that, if they should lose their husbands in battle, along with their ancestral homes and all their property, they would save in the only way possible at least their freedom and their virtue.

Thus the women were unanimous in not asking for peace on behalf of their fleeing husbands, nor did they ask to return to their own country or to receive monetary compensation for their losses. Instead they asked only to be taken to Rome and to be included among the Vestal Virgins. This was a most honorable request and 9 proof of their purity of heart, but it was not granted. Burning with rage, the women then committed a terrible crime in their inflexible determination to keep their vow. First they killed their lit- 10 tle children by dashing them against the ground — the only possible way to save their offspring from a life of degrading servitude. That same night, in the confines of the stockade they had built, the women hanged themselves with ropes and bridle reins so as to avoid dishonor to their virtue and the mockery of their conquerors. Dangling bodies were the only plunder left for the greedy soldiers.

Some women, once their protectors had been routed, would 11 have gone as suppliants to meet the victors, their hair loosened, their hands raised, and the air filled with moans and entreaties. Others — even more to their shame — would have forgotten their feminine dignity and tried to obtain with flattery and caresses permission to retain their goods and return to their own country, or they would have let anyone, no matter whom, drive them away like cattle. But the Cimbrian women resolutely kept themselves for 12

ulla passe sunt ignominia maiestatis gentis sue gloriam fedare;
dumque servitutem et turpitudinem laqueo obstinate fugerent,
non viribus, sed fortune crimine suos homines superatos osten-
dunt et castimonie sue, paucis abiectis annis, quibus suspendio
supervivere potuissent, vitam longissimam quesiverunt, et unde
miraretur posteritati liquerunt, tam grandem scilicet mulierum
multitudinem, non ex conventione, non ex consulto publico, infra
noctis unice spatium, non aliter quam si spiritus idem omnibus
fuisset, in eandem mortis sententiam devenisse.

: LXXXI :

De Iulia Gaii Cesaris dictatoris filia

1 Iulia et genere et coniugio forsan totius orbis fuit clarissima mulierum; sed longe clarior amore sanctissimo et fato repentino.

2 Nam a Gaio Iulio Cesare ex Cornelia coniuge, Cynne quater
consulis filia, unica progenita est. Qui Iulius ab Enea, inclito
Troianorum duce, per multos reges et alios medios paternam duxit
originem, maternam vero ab Anco, quondam Romanorum rege;
gloria bellorum atque triunphorum et dictatura perpetua insignis
plurimum homo fuit.

3 Nupsit preterea Pompeio magno, ea tempestate Romanorum
clarissimo viro, qui in vincendis regibus, deponendis eisque de
novo faciendis, nationibus subigendis, pyrratis extinguendis, favorem romane plebis obtinendo, et regum orbis totius clientelas ac-
4 quirendo, non terras tantum, sed celum omne fatigavit diu. Quem

a better destiny and did not allow the glorious dignity of their race to be stained by ignominy. Their resolution in escaping slavery and shame by means of the rope showed that their people had been overcome, not by might, but by the fault of fortune. Scorning the few years they could have lived had they not hanged themselves, they sought a much longer life for their chastity. To posterity they left reason to be amazed at the fact that in one night such a large number of women chose to die in the same way, not through a covenant nor by public decree, but as if they had all been moved by the same spirit.

: LXXXI :

Julia, Daughter of the Dictator Julius Caesar

Her ancestry and her marriage made Julia perhaps the most fa- 1 mous woman in the world, but her inviolable love and sudden death added much more luster to her reputation.

She was the only child of Julius Caesar and his wife Cornelia, 2 whose father Cinna had been consul four times. On his father's side, Julius was descended through many kings and other inter-mediaries from Aeneas, renowned leader of the Trojans; on his mother's side, from Ancus Marcius, a former king of the Romans. Caesar was especially famous for the glory attached to his military campaigns and triumphs and also for his permanent dictatorship.

Julia married Pompey the Great, one of the most distinguished 3 Romans of the time, who for many years gave heaven and earth no rest as he vanquished kings, deposed and created new ones, sub-dued nations, destroyed pirates, gained the favor of the Roman populace, and became the patron of kings throughout the world. Pompey was much older than Julia, who was still a mere girl, but 4

adeo illustris mulier, esto iuvencula et ille provectus etate, ardenter amavit, ut ob id immaturam mortem quesierit.

5 Nam cum Pompeius in comitiis edilitiis sacrificaturus ab hostia, quam tenebat, ex suscepto vulnere se in varia agitante, plurimo respergeretur sanguine, et ob id, vestibus illis exutus, domum alias induturus remicteret, contigit ut deferens ante alios Iuliam

6 pregnantem haberet obviam. Que cum vidisset viri cruentas vestes, ante quam causam exquireret, suspicata non forsan Pompeio fuisset violenta manus iniecta, quasi non illi dilectissimo sibi viro occiso supervivendum foret, in sinistrum repente delapsa timorem, oculis in tenebras revolutis, manibus clausis, concidit et evestigio expiravit: non solum viri atque civium romanorum, sed maximo totius orbis ea etate incomodo.

: LXXXII :

De Portia Catonis Uticensis filia

1 Portia eius Marci Catonis fuit filia qui, post eductas ex Egypto per ardentes solitudines Lybie in Affricam pompeiani exercitus reli-

2 quias, victorie Cesaris inpatiens apud Uticam se occidit. Nec equidem insignis mulier a patria fortitudine atque perseverantia degenerasse in aliquo visa est.

3 Hec autem — ut alia eius virtutis preclara[1] postponamus — cum, etiam vivente patre, Decio Bruto nupsisset, adeo eum dilexit integre atque caste ut, inter ceteras muliebres curas, is esset longe prima atque precipua; nec oportuno tempore potuit honestas amoris flammas casto occuluisse pectore.

4 Que, quoniam eius in perpetuam evasere laudem, ad eius ampliandam claritatem se offerunt ultro.

340

she loved him ardently. This love caused her to seek an untimely death.

One day, as Pompey was engaged in sacrifice at the aedilician elections, the animal he was holding jerked in all directions after it was wounded, spattering him with a great deal of blood. Pompey then took off his clothes and sent them back to his house to be exchanged for other garments. The first person this courier happened to meet was Julia, who was pregnant. She saw her husband's bloody clothing and, without asking the reason, assumed that Pompey had been murdered. Ominous fear overcame her. Almost as if she could not bear to survive her beloved husband, Julia fell to the ground, her eyes shrouded in darkness and her hands clenched. She died immediately, to the great distress not only of her husband and her compatriots but of the whole world at that time.

: LXXXII :

Portia, Daughter of Cato Uticensis

Portia was the daughter of that Marcus Cato who, unable to endure Caesar's victory, killed himself near Utica after leading the remains of Pompey's army from Egypt through the burning deserts of Libya to the province of Africa. An extraordinary woman, she fully inherited her father's bravery and perseverance.

I shall pass over other famous incidents that illustrate her virtue and mention here that her father was still alive when she married Decius Brutus. Her love for her husband was so complete and so pure that he was by far the first and most important of her wifely concerns. Nor, when the moment of crisis came, could she hide in her chaste breast the flames of her noble love.

These demonstrations of her love brought Portia everlasting praise, and they afford us also a means of increasing her fame.

5 Quieverat iam pestifer tumultus bellorum civilium, oppressis a Cesare ubique pompeianis, cum in eum dictatorem perpetuum — ut satis animadversum est — regnum affectantem senatus pars sa-

6 nior coniuravit; quos inter fuit et ipse Brutus. Qui integritatis Portie conscius, cum eidem scelesti facinoris aperuisset archanum, factum est ut, ea nocte cui dies illuxit qua Cesar humanis rebus coniuratorum opere subtractus est, exeunte Bruto cubiculum, Portia tonsoris novaculam summeret, quasi unguium superflua resectura; fingensque illam sibi casu cecidisse, se ex animo vulneravit.

7 Sane astantes ancillule cum manare vidissent sanguinem, suspicate aliquid gravius, clamore sublato, abiens Brutus in cubiculum revocatus est et ab eo obiurgata Portia quoniam tonsoris preripuisset

8 officium. Portia autem, semotis ancillulis, inquit: 'Minime temerarie factum quod putas est; tentatura autem quo animo me ipsam gladio perimere et mortem perpeti possem, si minus tibi pro votis cepta succederent, feci.'

9 O inexhausti vigoris amor et vir tali coniuge felix! Sed quid ultra?

In scelus a coniuratis itum est et occisores, occiso Cesare, evasere. Non tamen impune; sed cum preter extimatum omnia responderent, a senatu reliquo damnati patricide in diversa abierunt. Brutus autem et Cassius in orientem tendentes non parvas copias adversus Octavianum Cesarem et Antonium, Cesaris heredes, col-

10 legere. Adversus quos cum Octavianus et Antonius eduxisse<n>t[2] exercitum, apud Phylippos pugnatum est; et cum victe fugateque Cassii Brutique partes essent, et ipse Brutus etiam occisus est.

11 Quod cum audisset Portia nil sibi, subtracto viro, letum futurum existimans, arbitrata non alio animo mortem passuram quam olim cultri tonsorii vulnus, confestim in vetus propositum venit; et cum ad voluntariam necem nullum sibi adeo cito, ut impetus ex-

After Caesar's crushing defeat of Pompey's followers, the ruin- 5
ous turmoil of the civil wars ceased. Then the more rational senators plotted against Caesar, who as permanent dictator was obviously aspiring to kingship. Among this group was the said Brutus.
Knowing well Portia's integrity, he disclosed to her the secret of 6
the infamous conspiracy. Thus on the night preceding the day of
Caesar's death at the hands of the conspirators, just as Brutus was
leaving the bedroom, Portia took a barber's razor as if she wanted
to trim her nails. Pretending that it was an accident, she purposely
cut herself. At the sight of the spurting blood, the maids who were 7
present feared that the wound was quite serious, and they began
to shout. Brutus, on the point of departure, was summoned back
to the bedroom, and he upbraided Portia for usurping the barber's
duties. Once the servants had been dismissed, she replied: "What 8
I did was not done, as you think, in some ill-considered fashion,
but to see if I would have the courage to kill myself with a sword
and endure death if your enterprise should not succeed as you
wish."

How inexhaustible is the force of love! How lucky the man 9
with such a wife! But what happened next?

The conspirators proceeded with their crime and became assassins after the murder of Caesar. But they did not escape punishment. The outcome was not in accord with their expectations:
condemned as parricides by the rest of the Senate, they fled in various directions. Brutus and Cassius went towards the East and assembled a large host against Octavian and Antony, Caesar's heirs.
Octavian and Antony led their armies against them, and a battle 10
took place at Philippi. The partisans of Brutus and Cassius were
defeated and put to flight, and Brutus himself was killed.

When Portia heard the news, she felt that the future held no 11
happiness for her now that her husband was gone. Immediately
she reverted to her earlier plan and decided to face death in the

poscebat, prestari videbatur instrumentum, ignitos carbones, quos forte propinquos habebat, indubitanter manibus gucturi iniectos exhauxit; a quibus precordia exurentibus spiritus vitalis abire in mortem coactus est.

12 Nec dubium quin, quanto magis inusitatum mortis genus intulere, tanto occumbenti plus fulgoris coniugalis diligentie ingessere. Cuius etiam fortitudini patris reseratum manibus vulnus nil merite laudis potuit auferre.

: LXXXIII :

De Curia Quinti Lucretii coniuge

1 Curia romana fuit mulier et, si nomini fidem dabimus, ex prosapia Curionum, si operibus, mire constantie atque integerrime fidei vetustatis splendidum specimen.

2 Nam <cum>[1] ea[2] in turbine rerum, qua[3] triumvirorum iussu nove proscriptorum in urbe apposite tabule sunt, Quintus Lucretius eiusdem coniunx inveniretur proscriptus una cum pluribus, ceteris fuga celeri patrium solum linquentibus, et vix tutam, inter ferarum speleas et solitudines montium, seu apud hostes romani nominis, latebram invenientibus, solus ipse, amantissime uxoris usus consilio, intra romana menia, intra domestici laris parietes, intra coniugalis cubiculi secretum, in sinu coniugis intrepidus latuit; et tanta uxoris solertia, tanta sagaci industria, tanta fidei inte-

same courageous way that she had once endured the wound from the barber's razor. But she had to hand no means of effecting her suicide with the speed required by her violent impulse. So, without hesitation, she seized some live coals which happened to be nearby, put them in her mouth, and swallowed them. The coals burned through her entrails and compelled her vital spirit to depart in death.

There is no doubt that the unusual manner of her death heaped 12 upon the fallen woman an even greater measure of fame for conjugal devotion. Even her father's self-inflicted wound could take nothing away from the praise she deserved for her courage.

: LXXXIII :

Curia, Wife of Quintus Lucretius

Curia was a Roman woman. If we can put any stock in her name, 1 then she belonged to the Curio family; if we believe in her deeds, she was a splendid example in the ancient world of extraordinary constancy and absolute fidelity.

During that time of political upheaval when, by order of the 2 triumvirs, new lists of outlawed persons were posted in Rome, among the many names was that of Curia's husband Quintus Lucretius. The others swiftly fled their native soil and found insecure hiding places in the dens of wild animals and lonely mountain regions or with the enemies of Rome. Only Lucretius, following the advice of his loving wife, hid fearlessly within the walls of Rome itself, inside the confines of his own house, in the secrecy of the marriage chamber, indeed, in the bosom of his wife. Curia protected him so cleverly and zealously and faithfully that, with the exception of a servant girl who was part of the plan, not one of

gritate servatus est ut, preter ancillulam[4] unam consciam, nemo
etiam ex necessariis arbitrari, nedum scire, potuerit.

3   Quotiens ad contegendum facinus arte credere possumus mulierem hanc, exoleta veste, habitu sordido, mesta facie, flentibus
oculis, neglecto crine, nullis comptam de more velamentis, anxio
suspiriis pectore, ficto quodam amentis stupore, in medium pro-
diisse et, quasi sui inscia, discurrisse patriam, intrasse templa, pla-
teas ambisse et tremula ac fracta voce, dum videretur deos precibus votisque onerasse, percontasse obvios amicosque numquid
Lucretium vidissent suum, an scirent nu<m>quid[5] viveret, quor-
sum fugam ceperit, quibus sociis, qua spe; preterea se summopere desiderare fuge exiliique et incommodorum comitem fieri; et
huiusmodi plura factitasse que infelices consuevere facere, latebris
4   quidem viri integumenta prevalida; quibus insuper blanditiis, quibus delinimentis, quibus suggestionibus ancillule secreti conscie
firmasse animum saxeumque fecisse? quibus demum consolationi-
bus spem erexisse viri trepidantis, pectus anxium animasse et me-
stum in aliqualem traxisse letitiam?

5   Et sic, reliquis eadem peste laborantibus, et inter aspreta montium, maris estus, celi procellas, barbarorum perfidias, odia hostium infesta et manus quandoque persequentium misere periclitantibus, solus Lucretius, in gremio piissime coniugis tutus,
servatus est. Quo sanctissimo opere Curia non immeritam sibi claritatem quesivit eternam.

their friends and relatives even suspected, much less knew, the situation.

We can imagine how often Curia, in order to provide an artful   3
disguise for the true state of affairs, appeared in public wearing an
old dress and exhibiting an unkept appearance, a sad face, tearful
eyes, disheveled hair, her veils disordered, a heart wracked with
sighs, and a kind of simulated mad stupor. We can visualize her,
as if in a daze, running through the city, going into the temples,
drifting around the squares, and, in a cracked and trembling voice
(so as to seem already to have burdened the gods with vows and
petitions), inquiring of friends and passersby if they had seen her
Lucretius or knew if he were alive, whither he had fled, with
whom, and with what hope — adding that she wished above all to
share his flight and exile and misfortune. She must have done
many things characteristic of sorrowful persons that served well to
cloak her husband's hiding-place. With what flattery and cajolery   4
and admonishments, we wonder, did Curia harden, until it was as
firm as a rock, the spirit of the servant girl who was in on the secret? Finally, with what consolation did she rouse the hope of her
fearful husband, lighten his anxiety, and give the despondent man
some happiness?

Thus, while the others who endured the identical ruin of pro-   5
scription faced their misery amid the dangers of wild mountains,
raging seas, storms, barbarian treachery, fierce hatred from the enemy, and imminent persecution, only Lucretius, protected in the
arms of his devoted wife, was safe. With this holy deed Curia
achieved — and deserved — eternal fame.

: LXXXIV :

De Hortensia Quinti Hortensii filia

1   Hortensia Quinti Hortensii egregii oratoris filia dignis extollenda
laudibus est, cum non solum Hortensii patris facundiam vivaci
pectore amplexa sit, sed eum etiam pronuntiandi vigorem servaverit quem oportunitas exquisivit, et qui sepissime in viris doctissi-
mis deficere consuevit.

2   Hec autem triumvirorum tempore, cum matronarum multitudo, exigente reipublice necessitate, intolerabili fere onere pecunie
exolvende[1] gravata videretur, nec hominum inveniretur aliquis qui
in rem tam incongruam prestare patrocinium auderet, sola ausa
est constanti animo coram triumviris rem feminarum assummere
eamque perorando tam efficaciter inexhausta facundia agere, ut
maxima audientium admiratione mutato sexu redivivus Hortensius crederetur.

3   Nec infeliciter opus tam egregium a femina sumptum aut executum est; nam, uti nulla in parte fracta oratione aut laudabili sui
iuris demonstratione defecerat, sic nec exoptato aliquid a triumviris diminutum est, quin imo concessum libere ut longe amplior
pars iniuncte pecunie demeretur, arbitrati quantum sub matronali
stola in publicum taciturnitas laudanda videatur, tantum, oportunitate exigente, ornatu suo decora sit extollenda loquacitas. Quo
tandem facto, non absque maximo Hortensie fulgore, reliquum,
quod minimum erat, a matronis facile exactum est.

4   Quid dicam vidisse tantum veteris prosapie spiritus in Hortensia afflavisse femina, nisi eam merito nomen Hortensie consecutam?

: LXXXIV :

Hortensia, Daughter of Quintus Hortensius

Hortensia, daughter of the distinguished orator Quintus Horten- 1
sius, should be exalted with fitting praise. Not only did she enthu-
siastically embrace her father's eloquence: she also retained the
forceful delivery demanded by certain situations but often lacking
in highly learned men.

During the time of the triumvirs, the needs of the state ap- 2
peared to require women to shoulder an almost intolerably heavy
burden of taxation. No man could be found who would dare to
lend the ladies his advocacy against a measure so unjust; only
Hortensia was bold and courageous enough to bring the female
cause before the triumvirs. She pleaded so effectively and with
such tireless eloquence that, to the great admiration of the audience, she seemed to have changed her sex and was Hortensius
come back to life.

Hortensia did not undertake or execute this noble enterprise 3
fruitlessly. In every part of the oration she gave a smooth and admirable proof of the justice of her case, and so the triumvirs
granted everything she desired. In fact, it was freely conceded that
the greater part of the taxes imposed should be revoked. The triumvirs were of the view that, as much as silence in public was a
praiseworthy quality in a woman, still, when the occasion required
it, an elegant and seemly flow of language deserved to be extolled.
When everything was over, the remaining taxes, which did not
amount to much, were easily exacted from the women, and Hortensia came away with much glory.

Now that we have seen how the spirit of her ancient family 4
flourished in this woman, what is there to say but that she deserved to bear the name of Hortensia?

: LXXXV :

De Sulpitia Truscellionis coniuge

1 Sulpitia Lentuli Truscellionis coniunx equa fere benivolentia sibi adinvenit indelebilem famam. Fuit enim hac eadem, qua supra,
2 procella proscriptus a triumviris Lentulus. Qui cum esset volucri fuga tutatus in Syciliam et ibidem exul moraretur et inops, facta eius rei Sulpitia certior, in sententiam ivit labores una velle cum coniuge pati, rata indecens esse letos honores et fortunam candidam ferre cum viris has que eorundem erumnas, si oportunum ferre sit, fuga renuerent.

3 Verum nec ad virum pergere facile Sulpitia consecuta est: summa quippe diligentia, ne exilium sequeretur viri, servabatur a matre Iulia. Sed quas non ludit verus amor custodias? Captato igitur tempore, servili sumpta veste, matre custodiisque deceptis reliquis, duabus tantum ancillulis et servulis totidem sociata splendida mulier, natale solum patriosque penates linquens, exulem virum secuta est: cum posset, lege non prohibente, infelici abdi-
4 cato marito, novas celebrare nuptias. Nec expavit, mulier inclita, per subterfugia et maris estus atque montana ytala incerta viri sequi vestigia eumque per incognitas regiones exquirere, donec comperto se iunxerit: honestius rata per mille discrimina vite virum sequi a fortuna deiectum quam, eo exule laborante, in patria vacare delitiis et quiete.

5 Inclite profecto mentis et prudentem virum potius quam feminam redolentis, tale iudicium est. Non enim semper auro et gemmis splendendum, non semper indulgendum cultui, non semper estivus fugiendus est sol aut hyemis pluvie, non semper colendi sunt thalami, non semper sibi parcendum; sed cum viris, exigente

: LXXXV :

Sulpicia, Wife of Truscellio

Sulpicia, wife of Lentulus Truscellio, won for herself undying fame   1
because of a love that was almost equal to that of Curia. Lentulus
had been proscribed by the triumvirs in the same disturbance I
mentioned above.[a] He quickly fled to safety in Sicily, where he   2
lived in exile and poverty. Once Sulpicia had been informed of
this, she decided to endure these sufferings alongside her husband.
To her way of thinking, it was improper for wives to share pleasant honors and bright fortune with their husbands and then recoil
from bearing adversity with them if necessary.

But it was not easy for Sulpicia to join her husband. Indeed,   3
her mother Julia kept very careful watch to prevent her daughter
from following Lentulus into exile. True love, however, eludes all
sentinels. Sulpicia seized the right moment, dressed herself as a
slave, and tricked her mother and her other guards. Accompanied
only by two little servant girls and two little slaves, this noble
woman left her native soil and her household gods and followed
her exiled husband, even though the law would have allowed her
to divorce the unfortunate man and marry again. Nor was she   4
afraid, glorious woman that she was, to follow her husband's faint
trail in secret flight through raging seas and over the mountains of
Italy to look for him in unknown regions until she found him and
took her place at his side. Sulpicia thought it was more honorable
to follow her unfortunate husband through the innumerable perils
of his life than to remain at home in comfort and peace while he
struggled in exile.

Surely her decision showed a noble mind and savored more of a   5
wise man than of a woman. For women should not always be resplendent with gold and jewels; they should not always be ad-
dicted to fashion; they should not always flee the sun in summer

fatorum serie, subeundi labores, exilia perpeti, pauperiem tolerare, pericula forti ferre animo: que hec renuit, coniugem esse non novit. Hec uxorum spectanda militia, hec sunt bella, he victorie et victoriarum triunphi conspicui. Molliciem luxumque et angustias domesticas honestate et constantia ac pudica mente superasse, hinc illis est fama perennis et gloria.

6   Erubescant igitur, non que solum felicitatis umbreculam totis sequuntur pedibus, sed et he magis que pro comuni coniugii commodo, nauseam timent, levi solvuntur labore, nationes exteras horrent et expavent bovis forsan audito mugitu, cum in sectandis mechis fugam laudent, maria placeant fortemque animum quibuscunque oportunitatibus scelestissime prestent.

: LXXXVI :

De Cornificia poeta

1   Cornificia, utrum romana fuerit mulier, an potius extera, comperisse non memini; verum, testimonio veterum, memoratu fuit dignissima.

   Imperante autem Octaviano Cesare, tanto poetico effulsit dogmate, ut non ytalico lacte nutrita, sed Castalio videretur latice et Cornificio germano fratri, eiusdem evi poete insigni, eque esset il-
2   lustris in gloria. Nec contenta tantum tam fulgida facultate valuisse verbis, reor sacris inpellentibus musis, ad describendum heliconicum carmen sepissime calamo doctas apposuit manus, colo reiecto, et plurima ac insignia descripsit epygramata que Ieronimi

and rain in winter; they should not always dwell within their bed-rooms; they should not always spare themselves. When changed circumstances demand it, they must, alongside their husbands, en-dure toil, suffer exile, bear poverty, and face danger bravely: the woman who refuses does not know how to be a wife. This is the military service that brings distinction to women; these are their battles, these their victories and their glorious triumphs. To have overcome ease and luxury and petty domesticity with virtue, con-stancy, and purity of heart: this is how women win perpetual fame and glory.

Shame, then, not only on those women who pursue relentlessly 6 the mirage of happiness but even more on women who, in ques-tions of marital convenience, fear seasickness, are worn out by light work, tremble at the sight of foreign lands, and blanch to hear an ox bellow — yet, when it comes to following their adulter-ous lovers, they are all in favor of flight, are delighted by the sea, and in their wickedness are ready to face courageously any and all adventures.

: LXXXVI :

Cornificia, a Poetess

I do not remember having read whether Cornificia was a Roman 1 woman or from another country. Nevertheless, ancient testimony shows that she deserves very much to be remembered.

During Octavian's reign, Cornificia radiated such poetical learning that she seemed to have been nourished not by the milk of Italy but by the Castalian spring, and to have been just as cele-brated as her brother Cornificius, a renowned poet of the same pe-riod. She was not satisfied with having, thanks to her splendid tal- 2 ent, merely a way with words. I think that the sacred Muses inspired her to use her learned pen in the composition of verses

presbiteri, viri sanctissimi, temporibus — ut ipse testatur — stabant
in pretio. Numquid autem in posteriora devenerint secula, non satis certum habeo.

3   O femineum decus neglexisse muliebria et studiis maximorum
vatum applicuisse ingenium! Verecundentur segnes et de se ipsis
misere diffidentes; que, quasi in ocium et thalamis nate sint, sibi
ipsis suadent se, nisi ad amplexus hominum et filios concipiendos
alendosque utiles esse, cum omnia que gloriosos homines faciunt,
si studiis insudare velint, habeant cum eis comunia.

4   Potuit hec nature non abiectis viribus, ingenio et vigiliis femineum superasse sexum, et sibi honesto labore perpetuum quesisse
nomen: nec quippe gregarium, sed quod estat paucis etiam viris
rarissimum et excellens.

: LXXXVII :

De Marianne Iudeorum regina

1   Mariannes hebrea femina, genere quam viro felicior, Aristoboli Iudeorum regis, ex Alexandra regina, Hyrcani regis filia, genita fuit,
tante tanque invise pulcritudinis[1] clara ut non solum eo tempore
ceteras formositate feminas anteire crederetur, sed celestis arbitraretur ymago potius quam mortalis. Nec credulitati huic Marci
Antonii triumviri testimonium defuit.

2   Erat autem Marianni frater ex eisdem parentibus, nomine Ari-
stobolus, eque secum pulchritudinis[2] et etatis. Cui cum Alexandra

worthy of Helicon. Rejecting the distaff, Cornificia wrote many notable epigrams still held in esteem at the time of St. Jerome, as he himself attests.[a] But I do not know for certain if these poems reached later ages.

How glorious it is for a woman to scorn womanish concerns 3
and to turn her mind to the study of the great poets! Shame on slothful women and on those pitiful creatures who lack self-confidence! As if they were born for idleness and for the marriage bed, they convince themselves that they are useful only for the embraces of men, for giving birth, and for raising children. Yet, if women are willing to apply themselves to study, they share with men the ability to do everything that makes men famous.

Cornificia did not waste the powers Nature had given her. By 4
means of talent and hard work she succeeded in rising above her sex, and with her splendid effort she acquired for herself fame that is perpetual and rare precisely because it stands for an excellence few men have equalled.

: LXXXVII :

Mariamme, Queen of Judaea

Mariamme, a Hebrew woman more fortunate in her ancestry than 1
in her marriage, was the daughter of Aristobulus, king of the Jews, and Queen Alexandra, daughter of King Hyrcanus. She was famous for such great and unusual beauty that in her day she was believed to be fairer than all other women and judged of divine rather than human likeness. Concurring in this opinion was the triumvir Mark Antony.

Mariamme's brother, whose name was Aristobulus, had the 2
same parents and was her equal in beauty and age. After their fa-

mater, defuncto Aristobolo genitore, principatum dari sacerdotii
ab Herode, Mariannis viro atque rege, summopere cuperet atque
procuraret, Gellii amici suasione, amborum effigies optimi pictoris
artificio in tabula delinitas, ad Antonium triumvirum, extreme
luxurie hominem, ad eius in se excitandam libidinem et per consequens in desiderium suum trahendum, in Egyptum usque trans-
missas aiunt.

3   Quas[3] cum vidisset Antonius, primo in admirationem longiusculam constitit, deinde dixisse asserunt hos, quantum ad formositatem, profecto dei filios esse et subsequenter iuramento firmasse,
se nunquam aut usquam, nedum pulchriores, sed nec similes as-
pexisse.

4   Sed ad Mariannem solam redeundum. Hec quidem, etsi inaudita pulchritudine fuerit insignis, animi tamen ingenti fortitudine
longe magis emicuit. Que cum ad nubilem devenisset etatem,
infausto omine Herodi Antipatris Iudeorum regi nupta est; et
maximo infortunio suo, summe ob eius venustatem ab eode<m>[4]
dilecta.

5   Qui cum gloriaretur plurimum se solum orbe toto possessorem
pulchritudinis divine, in tam grandem animi curam lapsus est, ne
quis alter in hoc sibi posset equari, ut timere ceperit ne sibi superstes evaderet Mariannes. Ad quod evitandum, primo dum vocatus
in Egyptum ad Antonium esset iturus, causam dicturus super
morte Aristoboli, fratris Mariannis a se occisi, et demum, Antonio
mortuo, accessurus ad Octavianum Cesarem et purgaturus, si posset, quod amicus Antonii adversus eum auxilia prestitisset, Cy-
prinne matri amicisque liquit ut, si quid in eum quod in mortem
tenderet ab Antonio vel Cesare seu casu alio ageretur, Mariannem
confestim occiderent.

ther Aristobulus died, Mariamme's mother Alexandra was very eager to obtain from King Herod, Mariamme's husband, the office of chief priest for her son. It is said that Alexandra was persuaded by her friend Gellius to send to the triumvir Antony, then in Egypt, portraits of her children painted on a panel by a skilled artist. Since Antony was an extremely sensual man, the plan was to rouse his desire for Mariamme and Aristobulus and consequently make him accede to Alexandra's wishes.

When he saw the pictures, Antony first stood a long while in 3 admiration. Then he is reported to have declared that, so far as beauty was concerned, they were surely the children of a god. Next he swore that he had never seen anyone anywhere who was their equal, much less more beautiful.

But let us concentrate on Mariamme. Although she was cele- 4 brated for unheard-of beauty, she was far more distinguished for her strength of character. When she reached marriageable age, she wed, with unlucky omens, Herod, son of Antipater and king of the Jews; to her great misfortune, he loved her very much on account of her beauty.

In fact, Herod took enormous pride in the fact that he alone in 5 the whole world was the owner of such divine beauty. He became quite preoccupied lest someone else should equal him in this good fortune, with the result that he began to fear that Mariamme would survive him. Twice he tried to prevent this: once when he was summoned to Egypt by Antony to defend himself in connection with the death of Aristobulus, Mariamme's brother, whom he had killed; and again, after Antony's death, when he had to go to the Emperor Octavian to excuse himself, if he could, for having provided his friend Antony with auxiliary troops to fight Octavian. On both occasions he ordered his mother Cyprinna and his friends to kill Mariamme immediately if he should die at the hands of Antony or Octavian or by some accident.

6   O ridenda, alias sagacissimi, regis insania ob alienum incer-
tumque commodum ante vexari et invidere post fatum!

Quod occultissime factum fuerat rescivit tractu temporis Mariannes et cum iam ob Aristoboli indignam cedem in Herodem
concepisset execrabile odium, arbitrata se ab Herode non, nisi
propter pulchritudinis usum, diligi, cumulavit iras, vitam suam bis
immerito ab eo damnatam egerrime ferens; et quamvis Alexandrum et Aristobolum, conspicuos pulchritudine pueros, ex eo
enixa foret, in nullo potuit moderasse conceptum eoque, ferente
impetu, delapsa est ut amanti viro suum negaret concubitum et
dum sperneret, quasi veteris regie prosapie omnis in se resurgeret
indoles, gestu quodam elato illius calcare conabatur potentiam,
non verita persepe dicere palam Herodem alienigenam non iu-
deum, nec regie prolis hominem; quin imo ignobilem et ydu-
meum, nec regia coniuge dignum, trucem insolentem infidum sce-
lestumque et immanem beluam.

7   Que etsi Herodes cum difficultate pateretur, tamen, amore prohibente, nil sevum audebat in illam. Tandem in peius procedenti-
bus rebus, ut placet aliquibus, a Cyprinna Herodis matre et Salo-
mine sorore, quibus summe gravis erat Mariannes, actum est ut a
subornato ab eisdem pincerna Herodi accusaretur, quod eum conata sit exorare ut illi amatorium poculum, quod ipsa paraverat,
propinaret, seu—ut volunt alii—quod effigiem suam speciosissimam, non eo tempore quo premonstratum est, nec matris opere,
sed motu suo, post conceptum in Herodem odium, ad Antonium,
ut illum in sui desiderium provocaret, et in Herodis odium trans-

8   misisset. Que cum crederet Herodes et Mariannis in se malivolen-
tia fidem faceret, irritatus et anxio furore succensus, cum amicis

How ridiculous was this madness of an otherwise astute   6
king—first to torment himself over the chance that someone else
might enjoy her and then to carry jealousy beyond the grave!

Eventually Mariamme found out about these secret arrangements. She had already conceived a deadly hatred for Herod because of the undeserved death of her brother Aristobulus, and the
thought that Herod loved her only for the enjoyment of her
beauty increased her anger. Mariamme found it intolerable that he
had unjustly condemned her to death twice. Although she had
borne him two very handsome boys, Alexander and Aristobulus,
she could not restrain her feelings. In time her anger drove her to
refuse to sleep with her loving husband. She spurned him and, as
if all the spirit of her ancient royal lineage were revived in her person, she strove with a certain proud demeanor to trample upon his
power. She was not afraid to state, often and publicly, that Herod
was a foreigner and not a Jew; that he was a man not of royal but
of lowly birth and an Idumean; that he was unworthy of a royal
consort, being cruel, proud, disloyal, wicked, and altogether a savage beast.

Herod found it hard to endure these attacks, but his love   7
forbade him to retaliate with cruelty. Finally the situation wors-
ened. According to some sources, Herod's mother Cyprinna and
his sister Salome, both of whom detested Mariamme, bribed a
cupbearer to accuse Mariamme before Herod. Mariamme, he
claimed, had tried to persuade him to offer Herod a love potion
of her own making. Others, however, say that Mariamme was
charged with having sent on her own initiative, once she had begun to hate Herod (hence not at the time mentioned above and
not as a result of her mother's handiwork), a beautiful portrait
of herself to Antony for the purpose of arousing his desire for
her and hatred for Herod. Herod believed the allegations and   8
Mariamme's hostility towards himself substantiated them. Ex-
asperated and burning with anguished fury, he complained long

longa oratione conquestus est; eoque, eis suadentibus et Alexandra, Mariannis matre, ad eius gratiam promerendam, deductus est
ut eam, tanquam in regiam maiestatem excidium molientem, capitali damnatam supplicio iuberet occidi.

9   Que quidem tantum in se excitavit generosi animi ut, vilipensa
morte, integro vultus sui servato decore, nec ulla ex parte femineo
ritu flexa et obiurgantem matrem tacita audiret et flentes ceteros,
genis siccis, aspiceret et uti in triunphum letissimum non solum
intrepida sed aspectu alacri, nullis pro salute sua porrectis precibus, iret in mortem eamque a carnifice, ut optatam, susciperet.

10   Qua quidem tam immota securitate non solum efferati regis
tristavit invidiam, sed et plura suo nomini secula ausit quam mor-
talitati sue menses concessisse, lacrimis precibusque suis flexus,
potuisset Herodes.

: LXXXVIII :

De Cleopatra regina Egyptiorum

1   Cleopatra egyptia femina, totius orbis fabula, etsi per multos medios reges a Ptholomeo macedone rege et Lagi filio, originem traheret et Ptholomei Dyonisii seu — ut aliis placet — Minei regis
filia, ad imperandum, per nephas tamen, ipsi regno pervenerit,
nulla fere, nisi hac et oris formositate, vere claritatis nota refulsit,
cum e contrario avaritia crudelitate atque luxuria omni mundo
conspicua facta sit.

2   Nam, ut placet aliquibus, ut ab eiusdem dominii initio summamus exordium, Dyonisius seu Mineus, romani populi amicis-

360

and bitterly to his friends. He was persuaded by them and by Mariamme's mother Alexandra, who was trying to gain his favor, to order the condemnation and execution of his wife. The pretext was that she was plotting to commit *lèse majesté*.

Mariamme for her part called up from within great nobility of spirit. Scorning death, she did not give way at all, as women are wont to do, but with a dignified expression on her face listened silently to her mother's reproaches and looked dry-eyed at the weeping bystanders. Fearlessly, even eagerly, she went to her death as if to a joyful triumph; she did not beg for her life but accepted death from the executioner as though it were something for which she longed. 9

With her remarkable composure, Mariamme not only turned to misery the jealousy of a cruel king. She also earned centuries of fame more numerous than the months of life Herod could have granted her, had he been moved by tears and entreaties. 10

: LXXXVIII :

Cleopatra, Queen of Egypt

Cleopatra was an Egyptian woman who became the subject of talk the world over. The daughter of Ptolemy Dionysius or, as some authorities prefer, of King Mineus, she was, it is true, through a long line of intermediate kings, a descendant of Ptolemy of Macedonia, son of Lagus and king of Egypt, but she succeeded to the rule of the kingdom only through wickedness. Cleopatra had no true marks of glory except her ancestry and her attractive appearance; on the other hand, she acquired a universal reputation for her greed, cruelty, and lust. 1

Let us start at the beginning of her reign. Some sources say that when Dionysius or Mineus, a great friend of the Roman peo- 2

simus, Iulii Cesaris consulatu primo in mortem veniens, signatis
tabulis liquit ut filiorum natu maior, quem aliqui Lysaniam nomi-
natum arbitrantur, sumpta in coniuge Cleopatra, ex filiabus etiam

3 natu maiore, una, se mortuo, regnarent. Quod, eo quod familia-
rissima esset apud Egyptios turpitudo matres filiasque tantum a

4 coniugiis exclusisse, executum est. Porro exurente Cleopatra regni
libidine, ut nonnullis visum est, innocuum adolescentulum eun-
demque fratrem et virum suum, quindecimum etatis annum agen-
tem, veneno assumpsit et sola regno potita est.

5 Hinc asserunt, cum iam Pompeius magnus Asyam fere omnem
occupasset armis, in Egyptum tendens, superstitem puerum mor-

6 tuo subrogasse fratri eumque regem fecisse Egypti. Ex quo indignata Cleopatra adversus eum arma corripuit et, sic se rebus habentibus, fuso apud Thesaliam Pompeio et a puero, rege a se facto,
litore in egyptiaco ceso, adveniente post eum Cesare, ibidem bellum inter se gerentes invenit.

7 Quos dum ad causam dicendam se coram accersiri iussisset —
ut de Ptholomeo iuvene sileamus — ultro erenata malitiis mulier
Cleopatra, de se plurimum fidens, regiis insignita notis, accessit et
auspicata sibi regnum si in suam lasciviam domitorem orbis con-
traheret, cum formosissima esset et oculorum scintillantium arte
atque oris facundia fere quos vellet caperet, parvo labore suo libidi-
nosum principem in suum contubernium traxit pluresque noctes,
medio Alexandrinorum in tumultu, cum eo comunes habuit,
concepitque — ut fere omnibus placet — filium quem postmodum
ex patris nomine Cesareonem nuncupavit.

8 Tandem cum et Ptholomeus puer a Cesare dimissus in liberato-
rem suum inpulsu suorum bella vertisset et ad Deltam Mitridati

ple, was near death during the first consulship of Julius Caesar, he
left a will instructing his oldest son, who appears as Lysanias in
certain sources, to marry Cleopatra, his oldest daughter; at their
father's death they were to reign together. His wishes were carried out because it was the common (though disgraceful) practice 3
among the Eygptians to prohibit marriage only with mothers and
daughters. Then Cleopatra, burning with the desire to rule, re- 4
portedly poisoned the innocent fifteen-year-old boy who was both
her brother and her husband, thus gaining sole control of the
kingdom.

Our sources tell us that Pompey the Great, who had conquered 5
almost all of Asia, later went to Egypt and substituted for Cleopatra's dead brother another brother still living and made him king
of Egypt. Angered by this, Cleopatra took up arms against the lat- 6
ter. That is how matters stood after Pompey had been routed in
Thessaly and killed on the Egyptian coast by the boy he had made
king. Thus Caesar, when he came to Egypt after Pompey, found
the two royal siblings at war with each other.

Caesar ordered them to appear before him to plead their case. I 7
shall not speak of young Ptolemy here, but Cleopatra, naturally
malicious and extremely self-confident, was happy to comply and
arrived in royal splendor. She thought she had a good chance of
getting the kingdom for herself if she could entice Caesar, the conqueror of the world, to desire her. As she was very beautiful indeed and could captivate almost anyone she wished with her sparkling eyes and her powers of conversation, Cleopatra had little
trouble bringing the lusty prince to her bed. In the midst of the
Alexandrian revolt she stayed with him for many nights and, as
practically everyone agrees, conceived a son, whom she later called
Caesarion after his father.

Eventually young Ptolemy, after Caesar had released him, 8
yielded to the urging of his followers and attacked his liberator.

pergameno, in auxilium Cesaris venienti, cum exercitu occurrisset ibique a Cesare, qui itinere alio illum prevenerat, superatus, fugam schapha[1] temptaret et plurium irruentium pressa pondere mergeretur; et sic pacatis rebus, facta Alexandrinorum deditione, cum Cesar esset iturus in Pharnacem Ponti regem, qui Pompeio faverat, quasi noctium exhibiturus Cleopatre premium ac eo etiam quod in fide mansisset, eidem nil aliud optanti regnum concessit Egypti, Arsinoe sorore deducta, ne forsan, ea duce, novi aliquid moliretur in eum.

9   Sic iam scelere gemino adepta regnum Cleopatra, in voluptates effusa suas, quasi scortum orientalium regum facta, auri et iocalium avida, non solum contubernales suos talium nudos arte sua liquit, verum et templa sacrasque Egyptiorum edes vasis statuis thesaurisque ceteris vacuas liquisse traditum est.

10   Hinc occiso iam Cesare, et Bruto et Cassio superatis, eunti in Syriam Antonio obvia facta, impurum hominem pulchritudine sua et lascivientibus oculis facile cepit et in amorem suum detinuit misere eoque deduxit ut, que fratrem veneno necaverat, Antonii manu Arsinoem sororem, ad suspitionem regiminis amovendam omnem, in templo Dyane ephesie, quo salutem queritans infelix aufugerat, trucidari faceret, id adulteriorum suorum a novo amasio loco primi muneris assumptura.

11   Et cum iam scelesta mulier Antonii mores novisset, verita non est eidem postulare Syrie regnum et Arabie. Sane cum permaximum videretur illi et incongruum nimis, ad satisfaciendum tamen desiderio amate mulieris, sortiunculas ei ex utroque dedit, super-

He hurried with his army to the Delta to face Mithridates of Pergamum, who was coming to Caesar's aid. There Ptolemy was defeated by Caesar, who had arrived earlier by another route. When Ptolemy tried to escape in a small boat, it sank, weighed down by the great number of men rushing on board. With the quelling of the uprising and the surrender of the Alexandrians, Caesar was on the point of moving against Pharnaces, king of Pontus, who had taken Pompey's side. As a kind of recompense for the nights they had spent together and for her loyalty, Caesar gave Cleopatra, who desired nothing else, the kingdom of Egypt. Then he took with him her sister Arsinoë to prevent Cleopatra from leading new uprisings against him.

Cleopatra, who had acquired her kingdom through a double 9 crime, now abandoned herself to sensuous pleasure. She became, so to speak, the whore of the Eastern kings: greedy for gold and jewels, she not only stripped her lovers of these things by means of her artfulness, but she allegedly emptied the temples and the sacred places of the Egyptians of their vessels, statues, and other treasures.

Later, after Caesar's murder and the defeat of Brutus and 10 Cassius, Cleopatra went to meet Antony who was advancing towards Syria. Her beauty and her wanton eyes ensured an easy conquest of this vile man, and she kept him miserably enthralled. In order to remove all threats to her rule, Cleopatra, who had already poisoned her brother, persuaded Antony to kill her sister Arsinoë in the temple of Diana at Ephesus, where the unfortunate girl had fled in search of safety. This crime she received from her new lover as the first fruits of her adultery.

Next the wicked woman, aware by this time of Antony's character, made bold to ask him for the kingdom of Syria and Arabia. 11 This seemed to him an excessive and quite inappropriate request. Yet to satisfy the desire of the woman he loved, he gave her a small piece of both countries and added as well all the cities located on

additis etiam civitatibus omnibus que intra Eleuterum flumen et Egyptum syriaco litori apposite sunt, Sydone et Tyro retentis.

12   Que cum obtinuisset, Antonium in Armenos seu, ut volunt alii, in Parthos euntem, ad Eufratem usque prosecuta, dum Egyptum per Syriam repeteret, ab Herode Antipatris, tunc Iudeorum rege[2], magnifice suscepta, non erubuit eidem per intermedios suum suadere concubitum, sibi, si annuisset, muneris loco, Iudee subtractura regnum, quod ipse, Antonii opere, non diu ante susceperat.

13   Verum Herodes advertens non solum ob Antonii reverentiam abstinuit, quin imo ut illum a nota tam incestuose femine liberaret, ni dissuasissent amici, eam gladio occidere disposuerat. Cleopatra autem frustrata, quasi ob hoc moram traxisset, eidem locavit redditus Iericuntis, quo balsamum nascebatur, quod et ipsa postmodum in Babiloniam egyptiam transtulit, quo viget usque in hodiernum, et inde, amplis ab Herode susceptis muneribus, in Egyptum rediit.

14   Inde vero in fugam ex Parthis redeunti Antonio accersita occurrit. Qui quidem Antonius cum fraude Arthabarzanem[3] Armenie regem olim Tygranis filium cum filiis et satrapibus cepisset et thesauris permaximis spoliasset atque argentea catena vinctum traheret, ut avidam in suos amplexus provocaret, effeminatus venienti captivum regem cum omni regio ornatu atque preda deiecit in gremium. Quo leta munere cupidissima mulier adeo blande flagran-

15   tem complexa est, ut, repudiata Octavia, Octaviani Cesaris sorore, illam totis affectibus sibi uxorem iungeret.

Et ut arabicas unctiones et odoratos Sabee fumos et crapulas sinam, cum magnificis assidue saginaretur ingluviosus homo epulis,

the Syrian shore between Egypt and the Eleutherus River, reserving only Tyre and Sidon for himself.

After she had obtained these lands, Cleopatra followed Antony all the way to the Euphrates in his campaign against the Armenians, or, according to some authorities, against the Parthians. Returning to Egypt through Syria, she was lavishly received by Herod, son of Antipater and then king of Judaea. Cleopatra did not blush to urge him, through panderers, to sleep with her; if he accepted, she would take as a gift the kingdom of Judaea which he had regained not long ago, thanks to Antony. 12

Herod, however, was aware of her scheme. Not only did he refuse out of respect for Antony but, to free his benefactor from the shame of such a lewd woman, was ready to kill her with his sword. His friends, however, dissuaded him. Having failed in her real purpose, Cleopatra pretended she had stopped in order to lease to Herod the revenue from Jericho, where balsam grew. (This plant she afterwards transported to Babylon of Egypt, and it still flourishes there to this day). After receiving handsome gifts from Herod, she left Syria and went back to Egypt. 13

When Antony, in flight from the Parthians, returned to Egypt, he sent for Cleopatra, and she went to meet him. Antony had employed treachery in his capture of Artavasdes, king of Armenia and son of the late Tigranes, together with his children and satraps; he had despoiled the king of vast treasures and was now dragging him along shackled in silver chains. To bring the avaricious Cleopatra to his embraces, the weakling hurled into her arms, as she approached, the captive king in all his regalia as well as all the booty. Delighted with the gift, the greedy woman embraced her ardent lover with such seductive power that he divorced Octavia, sister of Octavius Caesar, and gave all his love to Cleopatra, making her his wife. 14 15

I shall pass over the Arabian ointments, the perfumes of Sheba, and the carousing that ensued while this gluttonous fellow steadily

in verba venit, quasi Cleopatre convivia extollere vellet, quid ma-
16 gnificentie cotidianis cenis posset apponi. Cui respondit lasciva
mulier se cena una centies, si velit, sextertium absumpturam.
17 Quod cu<m>⁴ minime fieri posse arbitraretur Antonius, tamen videndi avidus atque ligurriendi, fecere periculum, sumpto Lucio
Planco iudicis loco.

Que postero die dum non excessisset eduliorum consuetudinem
et iam sponsionem irrideret Antonius, iussit Cleopatra ministris
ut secundam mensam afferrent illico. Qui premoniti nil aliud
18 quam vas unum aceti acerrimi attulere. Ipsa autem confestim ex altera aurium unionem inexcogitati pretii, quem, ornamenti loco,
orientalium more, gestabat, summens, aceto dissolvit et liquefa-
ctum absorbuit; et cum ad alium, quem altera in auricula eque carum gerebat, iam manus apponeret, illud idem factura, extemplo
Lucius Plancus victum esse Antonium protulit; et sic secundus
19 servatus est, victrice regina. Qui quidem postea divisus Romam in
Pantheonem delatus, auribus Veneris appositus est, diu postmodum dimidie Cleopatre cene perhibens testimonium prospectantibus.

20 Ceterum cum insatiabilis mulieris in dies regnorum aviditas augeretur, ut omnia complecterentur in unum, temulento Antonio,
et forsan a tam egregia cena surgenti, romanum postulavit imperium, quasi in manibus posse concedere fuisset Antonii; quod
ipse, minime sui compos, minus oportune suis romanisque pensatis viribus, se daturum spopondit.

21 O bone Deus, quam grandis poscentis audacia nec minor spon-
dentis stultitia! O liberalis homo! Tot seculis, tanta cum difficultate, sanguine fuso et in morte tot insignium virorum, tot etiam
populorum, tot egregiis operibus, tot bellis vixdum quesitum im-

fattened himself with sumptuous delicacies. One day, as though he wanted to make Cleopatra's dinners more splendid, Antony asked what refinements could be added to their daily meals. She 16 playfully replied that, if he wished, she could spend ten million sesterces on a single dinner. Antony thought this was impossible, 17 but he was eager to see as well as to salivate. They conducted the experiment, calling in Lucius Plancus to act as judge.

The next day the food did not exceed the customary fare and Antony began to ridicule her promises. Thereupon Cleopatra ordered her attendants to serve the second course. Acting on previous instructions, they brought only a goblet of strong vinegar. Cleopatra then took from one of her ears a pearl of inestimable value which she wore as an ornament in the fashion of Oriental women, dissolved it in the vinegar, and drank the mixture. As she was taking an equally valuable pearl from her other ear with the intention of doing the same thing, Lucius Plancus hastily declared Antony the loser. And so the second pearl was saved thanks to the queen's victory. This pearl was later divided in two, brought to Rome, and 19 placed on the ears of Venus in the Pantheon where for a long time it gave onlookers testimony to half of Cleopatra's supper.

The craving of this insatiable woman for other kingdoms increased daily. So, to encompass all her desires into one, she asked Antony, when he was drunk and perhaps just getting up from that famous dinner, for the Roman Empire — as if such a gift were in his power. Antony was not in full possession of his mental faculties and vowed to give it to her, but without taking into consideration either his own powers or those of the Romans.

Good God! The audacity of the woman who requested this 21 was as great as the stupidity of the man who promised it. And what a liberal fellow Antony was! Without a moment's thought he bestowed on this demanding woman — as if he could give it away on the spot like the ownership of some cottage — the empire, so recently acquired after so many centuries with such great difficulty

perium, postulanti mulieri, non aliter quam domuncule unius dominium, inconsulte, quasi evestigio daturus, concessit.

22   Sed quid? Iam ob repudium Octavie belli seminarium inter
Octavianum et Antonium videbatur iniectum et ob id actum est
ut, congregatis ex utraque parte copiis, iretur in illud.

Verum Antonius cum Cleopatra, ornata purpureis velis et auro
classe, processere in Epyrum, ubi, cum obviis hostibus inita pugna
terrestri, cessere victi et in classem se recipientes Antoniani in

23   Actium rediere, experturi navalis belli fortunam. Adversus quos
Octavianus, cum Agrippa genero factus obvius, ingenti cum classe
mira audacia eos aggressus est et susceptus acriter tenuit aliquandiu mars dubius pugnam in pendulo. Tandem cum subcumbere
viderentur Antoniani, prima omnium insolens Cleopatra, cum au-

24   rea qua vehebatur navi et sexaginta aliis fugam cepit. Quam extemplo Antonius, deiectis ex⁵ pretoriana insignibus, secutus est; et
in Egyptum redeuntes incassum vires suas ad defensionem regni,
transmissis comunibus filiis ad Rubrum mare, disposuerunt.

25   Nam victor Octavianus secutus eos pluribus secundis preliis vires exinanivit eorum. A quibus cum sere pacis conditiones peterentur nec obtinerentur, desperans Antonius, ut nonnulli volunt,
mausoleum regum intrans, sese gladio interemit.

26   Capta vero Alexandria, cum Cleopatra ingenio veteri in vanum
tentasset, uti iamdudum Cesarem et Antonium illexerat in concupiscentiam suam, sic et iuvenem Octavianum illicere, indignans
cum audisset se servari triunpho atque de salute desperans, regiis
ornata, Antonium suum secuta est; et secus eum posita, adapertis
brachiorum venis ypnales serpentes vulneribus moritura apposuit.

27   Aiunt quidem hos somno mortem inferre. In quo resoluta, avaritie

and bloodshed, with the death of so many great men and even entire nations, with so many noble deeds and so many wars.

What happened next? The seeds of war between Octavian and Antony already appeared to be sown by the latter's divorce from Octavia. So both sides gathered their troops and hostilities commenced. 22

Antony and Cleopatra proceeded to Epirus, their gilded fleet adorned with purple sails. Here, in a land battle with the enemy, they were defeated and withdrew. Retreating to their ships, Antony's men went to Actium where they were to test their fortunes in a naval battle. Octavian moved against them with his son-in-law Agrippa and made a daring attack with his enormous fleet. The outcome of this fierce battle remained doubtful for some time. Finally, when Antony's forces seemed on the point of surrender, proud Cleopatra was the first to flee on her golden ship, taking with her sixty other vessels. Antony immediately lowered the ensign of his flagship and followed her. Upon returning to Egypt, they sent away the children they had had together to the Red Sea and in vain prepared their troops to defend the kingdom. 23 24

Octavian, their conqueror, pursued Antony and Cleopatra and depleted their forces in numerous successful battles. Their request for last-minute peace terms was refused. Some sources report that Antony, in despair, entered the royal mausoleum and killed himself with his sword. 25

After the fall of Alexandria, Cleopatra tried to seduce the young Octavian with the old wiles she had used on Caesar and Antony, but this time it was useless. Angered by the news that she was being reserved for a triumphal procession, she gave up any hope of deliverance, put on her royal insignia, and followed her Antony. Cleopatra lay down next to him and determined to die; she opened the veins in her arms and placed asps on the wounds. These snakes, so it is claimed, bring death with slumber. While 26 27

lascivie atque vite finem sumpsit infelix, Octaviano conante, Psillis vulneribus venenatis admotis, illam in vitam reservare si posset.

28   Sunt tamen alii eam ante premortuam et alio mortis genere dicentes. Aiunt enim Antonium timuisse apparatu attici belli gratificationem Cleopatre et ob id nec pocula nec cibos, nisi pregustatos,

29   assummere assuevisse. Quod cum advertisset Cleopatra, ad fidem suam erga eum purgandam pridianis floribus, quibus coronas ornaverat, veneno perlitis capitique suo impositis, in ludum traxit Antonium et procedente hilaritate invitavit eundem ut coronas biberent; et in sciphum dimissis floribus cum haurire voluisset Antonius, manu a Cleopatra prohibitus est, ea dicente: 'Antoni dilectissime, ego illa sum Cleopatra quam novis et insuetis pregustationibus tibi suspectam ostendis; et ob id, si pati possem, ut bi-

30   beres et occasio data et ratio est.' Tandem cum fraudem, ea monstrante, novisset Antonius, eam in custodiam deductam, poculum, quod ne biberet prohibuerat, exhaurire coegit et sic illam exanimatam volunt.

31   Prior vulgatior est opinio, cui additur ab Octaviano compleri iussum monumentum quod Antonius incipi fecerat et Cleopatra, eosque simul in eodem tumulari.

drowned in sleep, the wretched woman put an end to her greed, her concupiscence, and her life. Octavian tried to keep her alive, if possible, by calling in the Psyllians to tend to the wounds that were already filled with poison.[a]

Other authorities, however, speak of an earlier and a different 28 kind of death for Cleopatra. They say that Antony, in preparing for the battle of Actium, grew fearful that he had lost Cleopatra's favor and consequently adopted the practice of taking neither food nor drink without having it tasted beforehand. When Cleopatra 29 realized this, she devised a plan for removing any doubt about her fidelity. Poison was sprinkled on the flowers with which, the day before, she had adorned their crowns. Placing these flowers on her head, she then began to banter with Antony. As their merriment increased, she invited him to drink the garlands with her. The flowers had been put into the cup, and Antony was about to drain it, when Cleopatra restrained him with her hand, saying, "My beloved Antony, I am that Cleopatra whom you show you no longer trust by employing these novel precautionary tastings of your food. I had the opportunity and the motive to poison you just now, had I been cruel enough to let you drink." When he under- 30 stood the deception which she herself disclosed to him, Antony had her taken into custody and forced her to drink the same cup that she had prevented him from imbibing. And this is said to have been the manner of Cleopatra's death.

The first version is the more common. To this I must add that 31 Octavian ordered the completion of the tomb begun by Antony and Cleopatra and had them buried in it together.

: LXXXIX :

De Antonia Antonii filia

1 Antonia minor clarissime viduitatis exemplum indelebile posteritati reliquit. Hec etenim Marci Antonii triumviri ex Octavia — ut creditur — filia fuit et ideo minor cognominata quia illi soror esset natu maior et eodem nomine nuncupata.

2 Nupsit quidem Druso (Tyberii Neronis fratri et Octaviani Augusti privigno, et ex eo peperit Germanicum atque Claudium, postea Augustum, et Livillam), qui dum germanice expeditioni vacaret — ut quidam arbitrantur — Tyberii fratris sui opere veneno

3 periit. Cuius post mortem cum etate florida atque conspicua formositate vireret, rata satis honeste mulieri nupsisse semel, a nemine potuit ad secundas nuptias provocari, quin imo reliquum vite spatium sub Livia socru intra limites cubiculi viri sui adeo caste, adeo sancte transegit, ut preteritarum omnium matronarum laudes viduitate celebri superaret.

4 Equidem inter Cincinnatos Fabritios Curiosque et Lucretias atque Sulpitias sanctissimum splendidumque est, etiam provectis etate mulieribus et Catonum filiabus, absque lascivie nota duxisse

5 vitam et laude plurima extollendam. Quod si sic est, quibus prosequemur preconiis iuvenem pulcritudine insignem et Marci Antonii, spurcissimi hominis filiam, non in silvis et solitudinibus, sed inter imperialia ocia atque delicias, inter Iuliam Octaviani filiam et Iuliam Marci Agrippe, libidinis et lascivie ferventissimos ignes, inter Marci Antonii genitoris sui atque Tyberii, postea principis, obscenitates et dedecora in patria, olim frugi, nunc turpitudinibus omnibus dedita, inter mille concupiscientiarum exempla, constanti

: LXXXIX :

Antonia, Daughter of Antony

Antonia the Younger left posterity a lasting example of outstand- 1
ing widowhood. The daughter of the triumvir Mark Antony by
(so it is believed) Octavia, she was called the Younger because she
had an older sister of the same name.

Her husband was Drusus, brother of Tiberius Nero and step- 2
son of Octavian Augustus, and Antonia bore him Germanicus,
Claudius (who later became emperor), and Livilla. Drusus died
in Germany on a military expedition, allegedly poisoned through
the agency of his brother Tiberius. After his death, Antonia, 3
though still beautiful and in her prime, thought that an honorable
woman should wed only once, and no one could persuade her to
enter into a second marriage. Indeed, she spent the rest of her life
with her mother-in-law Livia. Antonia lived so chastely and modestly within the confines of her husband's chamber that, by reason
of her renowned widowhood, she surpassed in praise all the Roman matrons of earlier times.

To be sure, it is a high and holy thing to live an irreproachable 4
and eminently praiseworthy life when one is of mature years, a
daughter of Cato, a contemporary of Cincinnatus, Fabricius, and
Curius, or a companion of Lucretia and Sulpicia. But if this is 5
true, how then shall we praise this young woman of remarkable
beauty who through love of virtue was brave and steadfast in the
practice of celibacy, not for a little while and in hope of a future
marriage, but even to old age and death? The daughter of Mark
Antony, a man of the vilest character, she did not live in rustic
isolation but amidst imperial ease and luxury; in the company
of Julia, Octavian's daughter, and Julia, Marcus Agrippa's daughter,
who were raging fires of passion and concupiscence; surrounded
by the depravities of her father Mark Antony and the future em-

animo et forti pectore castimoniam, non per tempusculum et in spem futuri coniugii, sed virtuti obsequentem, in senectutem et mortem usque, servantem?

6   Edepol nil dignum satis relictum est verbis, considerationi forsan aliquid superextat; quod quidem, quia vires excedit scribentium, considerandum et merita consideratione extollendum satis sit sacris ingeniis reliquisse.

: XC :

De Agrippina Germanici coniuge

1   Agrippina Marci Agrippe ex Iulia, Octaviani Cesaris filia, genita fuit, esto Gaius Caligula, eiusdem Agrippine filius, iam orbis princeps, abhorrens Agrippe avi materni rusticitatem, diceret eam non ex Agrippa, sed ex stupro Octaviani, in Iuliam filiam perpetrato, fuisse progenitam; stolide credi cupiens se nobiliorem ex tam incestuose concepta matre natum, quam ex ignobili patre, sacrata lege suscepta.

2   Sed cuiuscunque fuerit filia, Germanico sue etati insigni iuveni et plurimum rei publice oportuno ac Tyberii Cesaris Augusti filio adoptivo, nupta est; satis ob hoc fulgida, sed fulgidior quod insolentissimi principis obstinato proposito retudisset perfidiam.

3   Hec cum ex Germanico viro suo tres iam enixa fuisset mares, ex quibus unus Gaius Caligula, qui postmodum rebus prefuit, et totidem eque femellas, ex quibus Agrippina Neronis Cesaris mater, cum opere Tyberii patris — ut pro comperto habitum est — veneno sublatum egre ferret et femineo ritu plangore plurimo celeberrimi iuvenis viri sui necem defleret, in Tyberii odium incidit

peror Tiberius; in a country once virtuous but now abandoned to every kind of infamy; with a thousand examples of lust all around her.

Alas, we have no written accounts that are at all worthy of 6 Antonia, yet there remains, perhaps, the possibility of reflecting on her example. But as even this is beyond the power of literature, it is enough to have left to lofty intellects matter for thought and, after due thought, for praise.

: XC :

Agrippina, Wife of Germanicus

Agrippina was the daughter of Marcus Agrippa and Julia, whose 1 father was Octavian Caesar. Nonetheless, Agrippina's son Caligula, once he became the ruler of the world, began to hate the humble origin of his maternal grandfather Agrippa and asserted that his mother had been born, not of Agrippa, but of Octavian, who had ravished his own daughter Julia. Caligula's foolish wish was to be thought more noble as the son of a mother begotten in incest than as the offspring of a legitimate daughter of a baseborn father.

Whoever her father may have been, Agrippina was married to 2 Germanicus, adopted son of Tiberius Caesar and an eminent young man of her own age who had rendered great service to the state. For this reason she was famous, but even more so because she resolutely curbed the perfidy of an arrogant prince.

Agrippina bore Germanicus three sons (one of whom was the 3 future emperor Gaius Caligula) and as many daughters (including Agrippina, mother of the emperor Nero). When Germanicus' father Tiberius — and we may regard this as proven fact — engineered her husband's death by poison, Agrippina could hardly bear the loss. She observed feminine custom and mourned with

adeo ut ab eodem, eam brachio tenente et obiurgationibus in fletum usque infestante, quod nimium ferret inpatienter se rebus principari non posse; et pluribus deinde in processu lacessitam apud senatum criminationibus custodiri iussit insontem.

4   Porro egregia mulier indignum rata quod in se agebatur a Cesare, morte fastidia stomachosi principis effugere aut finire disposuit. Que cum aliter satis commode non daretur, fame generoso animo accersire statuit et confestim a quocunque cibo abstinere ce-

5   pit. Quod cum esset relatum Tyberio et advertisset ignavus homo quo ieiunium tenderet mulieris, ne tam certa via tanque brevi spatio sese suis subtraheret iniuriis, nil proficientibus minis aut verberibus ut cibum caperet, eo usque, ne sibi auferretur seviendi in eam materia, deductus est ut cibum gucturi eius violenter impingi faceret, ut quocunque modo stomacho fuisset iniectus, alimenta nolenti prestaret.

6   Agrippina vero, quanto magis exacerbabatur[1] iniuriis, tanto acrioris efficiebatur propositi; et incepto perseverans scelesti principis insolentiam moriens superavit, ostendens, cum multos posset facile, dum vellet, occidere, unum solum mori volentem totis sui dominii viribus vivum servare non posse[2].

7   Qua quidem morte, etsi plurimum glorie sibi apud suos quesiverit Agrippina, Tyberio tamen longe amplius ignominie liquit.

loud laments the death of her young and illustrious husband. By so doing she incurred the hatred of Tiberius. He seized her by the arm and scolded her until she wept, charging that what she found unbearable was the prospect of not becoming empress. Later Tiberius attacked Agrippina with many accusations brought before the Senate and ordered her, innocent though she was, to be placed under guard.

But this extraordinary woman, knowing that she did not de- 4 serve what the emperor was doing to her, decided upon suicide as the means to escape or put an end to the angry ruler's loathing. With no other means readily available, she nobly decided to seek death by starvation and immediately began to refuse all food. When this was reported to Tiberius, the wicked man realized the 5 purpose of her fasting. Lest Agrippina evade his acts of injustice so surely and swiftly — for neither threats nor floggings availed to make her eat —, the emperor was reduced to the practice of forcing food down her throat. However the food reached her stomach, it would provide nourishment against her will, and hence Tiberius would not be deprived of the object of his cruelty.

The more Agrippina was provoked by these indignities, the 6 firmer her purpose became. By persevering in her resolve, she overcame through death the insolence of the infamous emperor. She also demonstrated that, although he could easily kill many people if he so desired, yet with all the power of his empire he could not keep alive someone who wished to die.

With her death Agrippina acquired great glory among her 7 countrymen for herself, but far greater was the dishonor in which she left Tiberius.

: XCI :

De Paulina romana femina

1   Paulina romana mulier quadam ridicula simplicitate sua fere indelebile nomen consecuta est. Hec, Tyberio Cesare Augusto imperante, uti pre ceteris matronis formositate oris et corporis venustate habebatur insignis, sic nupta inclite pudicitie specimen reputabatur a cunctis nec aliud, preter virum, studio curabat precipuo, quam ut Anubi Egyptiorum deo, quem tota veneratione colebat, obsequi posset et eius promereri gratiam.

2   Sane cum ubique a iuvenibus speciose amentur et he potissime quibus est solers castimonie cura, pulchritudinis huius iuvenis unus romanus, cui Mundus nomen erat, eam inpense, nunc oculis gestibus facetiis, nunc promissionibus atque muneribus, nunc precibus et blanditiis sollicitare ceperat, si forte posset obtinere quod

3   ardenter optabat. Sed omnia frustra: castissima mulier soli viro dicata, amantis cuncta sinebat in auras. Qui dum ceptis insisteret adverteretque aperto calle sibi mulieris constantia viam preripi, in fraudes vertit ingenium.

4   Consueverat autem Paulina Ysidis templum singulis diebus visitare sacrisque continuis placare Anubem. Quod cum novisset iuvenis, amore ostendente, dolum inauditum excogitavit; et ratus Anubis sacerdotes votis suis plurimum posse conferre, eos adivit illosque amplissimis donis in suam deduxit sententiam; actumque est, eo premonstrante, ut ex eis senectute venerabilior, venienti more solito Pauline placida voce diceret noctu ad se venisse Anubem eique iussisse ut eidem diceret se devotione sua delectatum plurimum seque eo in templo per quietem eius desiderare colloquium.

: XCI :

Paulina, a Roman Woman

Paulina, a Roman woman, gained practically indelible fame for 1
a certain ridiculous naïveté. During the reign of the emperor
Tiberius, she was considered particularly striking for the beauty of
her face and figure; after her marriage, everyone also regarded her
as a distinguished model of virtue. Besides her husband, her only
concern was to serve and win the favor of Anubis, an Egyptian
god whom she worshipped with the utmost reverence.

Young men everywhere love beautiful women, especially those 2
who are careful to preserve their virtue, and a youthful Roman
named Mundus was captivated by Paulina's beauty. He began to
court her zealously, first with glances, gestures, and pleasantries,
then with promises, gifts, pleas, and flattery, to see whether he
might perhaps obtain what he so ardently desired. But absolutely 3
nothing worked: this woman, so eminently pure and devoted to
her husband alone, let all her lover's devices pass her by. Mundus
persisted in his efforts but, observing that the high road was
blocked by her fidelity, turned his wits to deception.

Now it was Paulina's daily practice to visit the temple of Isis 4
and to try to gain the favor of Anubis with continual sacrifice.
When Mundus learned of this, love showed the young man how
to contrive a novel trick. Certain that the priests of Anubis could
be very helpful in the attainment of his desires, Mundus approached them and with magnificent gifts won them over to his
purpose. On his instructions it was arranged that one of the
priests, whose advanced years made him the most venerable,
would say in a soothing tone to Paulina, when she made her usual
visit, that Anubis had come to him at night and ordered him to
tell her of his pleasure at her devotion and of his wish to speak to
her in that temple during the night.

5　　Que cum audisset Paulina ob sanctitatem suam hoc contingere
arbitrata, in immensum ex dictis gloriata secum est; adeoque vera
credidit uti a deo Anube auribus suis percepisset ipsa mandata vi-
6　roque suo retulit omnia. Qui stolidior coniuge, annuit petenti ut
pernoctaret in templo.

　　Stratur ergo ede in sacra, ignaris omnibus preter eam et sacerdotes, lectus deo dignus; et tenebris in terram obumbrantibus, intrat Paulina locum arbitrisque remotis, post orationem et sacra,
7　deum expectatura lectum adit. Cui iam soporate Mundus, a sacerdotibus intromissus et ex composito ornatu Anubis tectus, affuit;
et cupidus amate a se mulieris ruit in oscula iubetque excusse
somno atque obstupescenti bono animo esse; se Anubem a se tam
diu veneratum fore, e celo suis precibus atque devotione lapsum et
in eius venisse concubitum ut ex se eaque similis gigneretur deus.

8　　Que ante alia petiit ab amasio deo numquid superi aut possent
aut consuevissent misceri mortalibus. Cui evestigio Mundus respondit posse, Iovemque per tegulas in gremium Danis lapsum,
dedit exemplum, et <ex>[1] eo accubitu genuisse Perseum, qui post-
9　modum in celum assumptus est. Quibus auditis Paulina letabunda
petito annuit: intrat Mundus nudus pro Anube lectum et amplexu
coituque fruitur optato. Sed cum iam nox iret in diem, abiens luse
dixit eam filium concepisse.

　　Mane autem facto, sublato e templo a sacerdotibus lecto, Paulina viro que acta sunt retulit. Credidit insulsus homo et applausit
coniugi enixure deum; nec dubium quin ab ambobus fuisset ex-
pectatum pariendi tempus, ni iuvenis ardens nimium minus caute

When Paulina heard this, she attributed it to her own sanctity 5 and felt within herself great pride at the priest's words. She believed the message to be as true as if she had heard it from the god Anubis with her own ears, and she told her husband of the divine command. Even more foolish than his wife, he consented to her 6 request to spend the night in the temple.

Accordingly a bed worthy of the god was made up in the sacred place, with no one the wiser except for the priests and Paulina. She entered the temple just as the shadows were darkening the earth. When all the spectators had left and she had finished her prayers and sacrifices, Paulina got into bed to wait for the god. She 7 fell asleep, and Mundus was then brought in by the priests; he came dressed (as previously agreed) in the regalia of Anubis. The passionate young man rushed to kiss the woman he loved. When she awoke in amazement, he told her to be of good cheer, for he was Anubis, whom she had so long revered; thanks to her prayers and devotion, he had come down from heaven to sleep with her so that together they could beget another god.

Paulina, however, first asked her divine lover if the gods were 8 able or accustomed to have intercourse with mortals. Mundus answered immediately that they could, citing as an example Jupiter's descent from the roof into Danae's lap and the result of their union, namely, the birth of Perseus who later was taken up into heaven. Upon hearing this, Paulina joyfully granted his wish. 9 Mundus, in the guise of Anubis, entered the bed naked and enjoyed the embraces and physical union he had longed for. But when night was already passing into day, he left, telling the duped woman that she had conceived a son.

In the morning the priests removed the bed from the temple, and Paulina reported to her husband what had happened. The silly man believed the story and congratulated his wife that she was to give birth to a god. Doubtless they would both have awaited the moment of birth if the overly ardent youth had not

10 dolum aperuisset. Is quidem forte conscius eam avide in amplexus et coitum venisse, arbitratus, si prostratam a se ingenio
suo eius ostendisset pudicitiam, flexibilem magis et avidam eque
noctis futuram; et sic faciliori via iterum et sepius in concupitos
posse redire amplexus, eunti ad templum Pauline factus est obvius
dixitque voce submissa: 'Beata, inquam, es Paulina, cum ex me
Anube deo conceperis.'

11 Verum longe aliter quam arbitraretur successit ex verbo. Nam
cum obstupuisset Paulina et in mentem ex gestis auditisque revocasset plurima, confestim fraudem sensit et turbata se ad virum retulit eique Mundi atque sacerdotum dolum, ut ipsa percipiebat,

12 aperuit. Ex quo subsecutum est ut vir conquereretur Tyberio; a
quo, comperta fraude, actum est ut sacerdotes afficerentur supplicio et Mundus multaretur exilio et lusa Paulina in romani vulgi
verteretur fabulam: clarior simplicitate sua et Mundi fraude facta,
quam ex Anubis devotione et servata castimonia tam solerter.

: XCII :

De Agrippina Neronis Cesaris matre

1 Agrippina Neronis Cesaris mater genere, consanguinitate, imperio
et monstruositate filii ac sua non minus quam claris facinoribus
emicuit.

2 Hec etenim Germanici Cesaris, optimi atque laudande indolis
iuvenis, ex Agrippina superiori filia fuit, vocata Iulia Agrippina et
Gaii Caligule principis soror nupsitque Gneo Domitio, homini ex

imprudently disclosed the trick. Knowing how eagerly Paulina had 10
accepted his caresses and his lovemaking, Mundus thought that, if
he explained how cleverly he had ravished her virtue, she would
be more pliable and eager for similar nights in the future. Thus he
might return by an easier route, again and again, to the arms
he yearned for. Approaching Paulina on her way to the temple,
Mundus said in a low voice, "Lucky you, Paulina, for you have
conceived a child by me, the god Anubis."

What happened, however, after he had finished speaking was 11
quite different from what he was expecting. Paulina was stunned.
Recalling much of what had been done and said, she immediately
understood the imposition. In distress she returned to her husband and gave him her version of the trick played by Mundus and
the priests. The husband then complained to Tiberius who, once 12
the fraud was established, had the priests executed while Mundus
was condemned to exile. How Paulina had been fooled became
a topic of common gossip at Rome; she emerged more famous for
her naïveté and Mundus' stratagem than for her devotion to
Anubis and her carefully guarded virtue.

ː XCII ː

Agrippina, Mother of the Emperor Nero

Agrippina, mother of the emperor Nero, attracted attention for 1
her noble birth, lineage, power, and for the monstrous character of
her son — and herself — as well as for famous actions.

Named Julia Agrippina, she was the daughter of Germanicus 2
Caesar, an excellent young man of praiseworthy character, by the
Agrippina we have already discussed.[a] She was also the sister of
the emperor Caligula. Her husband was Gnaeus Domitius, an

Enobardorum familia fastidiosissimo atque gravi, ex quo Neronem, insignem toto orbi beluam, premissis ex materno[1] utero pedibus, peperit.

3   Verum Domitio intercutis morbo assumpto, Nerone adhuc parvulo, cum formosissima[2] esset, Gaius frater eius, homo spurcissimus, turpi stupro ea abusus est; et sublimatus in principem, seu minus eius mores approbans, eo quod se Lepido dominii spe miscuerit, seu emuli alicuius inpulsu, eam fere bonis omnibus privatam, relegavit in insulam. Quo tandem a militibus suis trucidato 4 eique Claudio substituto, ab eodem revocata est.

Que tractu temporis, cum audisset Valeriam Messalinam, variis agentibus meritis, confossam, spem evestigio intravit sibi natoque potiundi orbis imperii; et celibem principem, esto Germanici patris sui fuisset frater, decora pulchritudine sua, adversus Lolliam Paulinam, opitulante Calixto liberto, et Eliam Petinam, Narcisso favente, opere Pallantis, Claudium in pregrande nuptiarum suarum desiderium traxit. Sed obstare voto videbatur honestas eo 5 quod illi neptis esset ex fratre. Verum oratione Vitellii subornati, actum est ut in desiderium suum cogeretur precibus senatorum, eoque orante fieret a senatu decretum quo prestaretur patruos posse neptes inducere.

6   Et sic Agrippina, volente Claudio et orante senatu, eius venit in nuptias. Que tandem Augusta dicta est et carpento in Capitolium ferebatur, solis sacerdotibus ante concessum, et in adversos sibi se- 7 vire cepit suppliciis. Demum cum astutissima esset mulier, tempore captato, quanquam utriusque sexus filii essent Claudio, eum induxit, suadente illi Memmio Pollione, tunc consule, et urgente plurimum Pallante liberto, qui ob stuprum Agrippine summe fau-

austere and haughty member of the Ahenobarbus family, to whom she bore a son, Nero. The child emerged from her womb feet first and was known the world over as a wild beast.

While Nero was still a child, Domitius died of dropsy. There- 3 upon her brother Caligula, a disgusting man, foully raped Agrippina, who was very beautiful. When he became emperor, he despoiled her of almost all her wealth and exiled her to an island, either because he disapproved of her conduct (she had slept with Lepidus in the hope of gaining power) or because he was influenced by some enemy of hers. Caligula in due course was killed by 4 his soldiers, and his successor Claudius recalled Agrippina.

Eventually Agrippina learned that Valeria Messalina had been stabbed to death for her various misdeeds.[b] At once she began to hope that she could gain control of the empire for herself and her son. Claudius was the brother of her father Germanicus but, with her magnificent beauty and the help of Pallas, Agrippina induced in the widowed emperor an overwhelming desire to marry her rather than her rivals Lollia Paulina and Aelia Paetina (who were favored by the freedmen Calixtus and Narcissus respectively). Sheer decency appeared to be an obstacle to Agrippina's wishes, as 5 she was Claudius' niece on his brother's side. But Vitellius, who had been recruited for this purpose, gave a speech whose result was that Claudius was compelled by the pleas of the Senate to acquiesce in his own desire. At the latter's request, the Senate issued a decree allowing paternal uncles to marry their nieces.

Thus Agrippina married Claudius, thanks to his own willing- 6 ness and the entreaties of the Senate. At last she had the title of *Augusta,* and she was taken to the Capitol by carriage, an honor formerly accorded only to priests. Then Agrippina began to inflict cruel punishments on her opponents. A very shrewd woman in- 7 deed, she seized a golden opportunity. Claudius had children of his own of both sexes; but, under coaxing by Memmius Pollio, who was then consul, and at the strong urging of Pallas, a freed-

tor erat, ut Neronem privignum in filium adoptaret, quod ante in familia Claudiorum factum nemo meminerat; eique Octaviam, quam ex Messalina susceperat, et que Lucio Sylano nobili iuveni desponsata fuerat, sponderet in coniugem.

8   Quibus obtentis, rata in casses beluam incidisse, non tantum Claudii assiduarum ingurgitationum affecta tedio, quantum ne ante patris mortem Britannicus Claudii filius in etatem solidam deveniret exterrita, Narcisso etiam pro Britannico multa perorante, quasi proposito suo futurum obicem arbitrata, in mortem Claudii facinus exitiale commenta est.

9   Delectabatur quidem Claudius boletis plurimum illosque cibum dicebat deorum et ideo absque semine sua nasci sponte. Quod cum advertisset Agrippina, studiose coctos infecit veneno
10   eosque, secundum quosdam, ipsa apposuit temulento. Alii vero dicunt epulanti in arce cum sacerdotibus per Alotum spadonem pregustatorem suum ab Agrippina corruptum appositos. Verum cum vomitu et alvi solutione videretur salus Claudii secutura, opere Xenophontis medici illitis veneno pennis ad vomitum continuandum porrectis, eo itum est quo cupiebat uxor.

11   Ipse tandem in cubiculum reductus, ignaris omnibus preter Agrippinam, mortuus est. Cuius quidem mors non ante ab Agrippina palam nuntiata est quam, amicorum suffragio, omisso Britannico tanquam iuniore, Nero iam pubescens sublimaretur in princi-
12   pem. Quod adeo gratum fuit Neroni ut matrem illico, tanquam

man (and Agrippina's great supporter by reason of their adulterous liaison), she persuaded Claudius to adopt his stepson Nero as his own. This was something that had never in living memory been done before in the Claudian family. Moreover, she induced Claudius to promise Nero in marriage his and Messalina's daughter Octavia, who had been engaged to the young nobleman Lucius Silanus.

Once these favors were obtained, Agrippina thought that the 8 beast had fallen into the trap. She now devised a deadly plan against Claudius. In this she was influenced not so much by disgust at Claudius' incessant acts of gluttony as by fear that his son Britannicus, on whose behalf Narcissus was making many solicitations, would reach the age of maturity before his father's death and obstruct, so she thought, her scheme.

Now Claudius loved mushrooms and used to say that they 9 were the food of the gods because they were generated without seeds. Aware of her husband's preferences, Agrippina had some mushrooms cooked and sprinkled them carefully with poison; some sources tell us that she herself placed this dish before Claudius while he was intoxicated. Others say, however, that the eu- 10 nuch Halotus, Claudius' taster, who had been bribed by Agrippina, brought the mushrooms to the emperor as he was eating in the temple with the priests. After vomiting and a bowel movement, Claudius seemed on the point of recovery. But his wife achieved her desire through the agency of Xenophon, Claudius' doctor: to maintain constant vomiting, he tendered the emperor feathers — first smearing them with poison.

Finally Claudius was brought back to his room where he died, 11 but no one except Agrippina knew it. She did not announce his death publicly until her friends had helped her to make the adolescent Nero emperor; Britannicus was passed over on the grounds that he was younger still. This turn of events so pleased Nero that 12

bene meritam, in cunctis, tam publicis quam privatis, preponeret videreturque sibi titulum, matri vero principatum sumpsisse.

13   Et sic e specula romani principatus Agrippina toto effulsit orbi. Ceterum splendor iste tam grandis turpi macula labefactatus est; 14   nam cede plurium atque exiliis aliquandiu debachata est. Preterea creditum fuit, ea patiente, preter naturalem et debitam dilectionem in matrem, amore illecebri a filio fuisse dilectam, cum is meretricem ei persimilem inter pellices assumpsisset et concubitum testarentur persepe macule vestibus iniecte, quotiens cum eo lectica delata est; dato velint alii eam in facinus hoc filium attraxisse, desiderio recuperandi dominii a quo deiecta videbatur, eo quod in Neronem quibusdam ex causis multum oblocuta fuerat; quod firmari volunt ob id quod de cetero Nero sit assuetus fugere eius contubernium et solitudines collocutionum.

15   Attamen que patruum in coniugium suum allexerat, boleto peremerat, ineptum iuvenem fraudibus et violentia sublimarat imperio, in detestabilem, quanquam meritam, mortem deducta est. Nam cum in multis filio gravis esset, eius meruit odium ex quo 16   omni honore et augustali maiestate ab eo privata est. Que indignans et femineo irritata furore, eidem, uti procuraverat, sic se subrepturam imperium minata est. Quibus exterritus Nero, cum eam et oculatam nimium nosceret et ob memoriam Germanici patris amicorum subsidiis plenam, veneno ter illam surripere conatus 17   est. Sed discreta mulier antidotis offensam vitavit.

Demum cum et laqueos ceteros, quos in necem eius tetenderat, vitasset, intellexit Nero cautiori fraude agendum fore eique expo-

he at once gave his mother, in return for her good offices, the place of honor on all public and private occasions. In fact, he seemed to have taken the title for himself and the power for his mother.

Thus Agrippina, atop the pinnacle of Roman dominion, shone   13
radiant throughout the world. But this great splendor was marred by an ugly stain: she had long fits of rage in which she killed and exiled many people. It was also believed that Agrippina allowed   14
Nero to show her an illicit love exceeding the natural affection owed to a mother. Indeed, he had included among his concubines a prostitute who resembled his mother and, every time he and Agrippina rode together in a litter, the stains on their clothes testified to their relationship. According to other accounts she enticed her son to commit incest, desiring to recover the power she had apparently lost when, for various reasons, she would subject Nero to bitter reproaches. As proof of this they allege the fact that Nero thereafter would usually avoid her company and private conversations.

An abominable but deserved death awaited this woman who   15
had seduced her uncle into marrying her, killed him with mushrooms, and elevated an incompetent youth to the rank of emperor by means of violence and fraud. In many ways she was strict with regard to her son; he hated her for this and stripped her of every honor and imperial majesty. Angry and driven by female fury,   16
Agrippina threatened to take away the empire she had procured for him. Nero was frightened by her words. He knew how extremely shrewd she was and that she could rely on the help of many friends thanks to the fact that her father Germanicus was still remembered. Three times he tried to poison Agrippina. But   17
she was cunning and escaped harm with antidotes.

Agrippina having evaded all the other traps he had set to kill her, Nero finally realized that a more subtle form of deception was necessary. He sought the advice of Anicetus, prefect of the fleet near Misenum and his own childhood tutor. Anicetus showed

scenti ab Aniceto prefecto classis apud Misenum olim a pueritia nutritore suo, ostensum est navim posse componi fragilem in qua suscepta Agrippina doli ignara periclitari posset.

18   Quod cum Neroni placuisset, eam ab Ancio[3] venientem, quasi preteritorum odiorum penitens, ficta filiali affectione, suscepit in ulnis et usque domum prosecutus est. Inde apparata navi in suam pernitiem, ad cenam itura illam conscendit, comitantibus Creperio Gallo et Acerronia libertis; eisque per noctem navigantibus dato signo a consciis, cecidit tectum navis plurimo plumbo grave et op-

19   pressit Creperium. Deinde nautis agentibus ut tranquillo mari navis verteretur in latus, auxilia Acerronia invocante, contis remisque occisa est et Agrippina, humero saucia et in mare tandem deiecta, a litoralibus suffragantibus in Lucrinum lacum villamque suam deducta est.

20   Inde, ea iubente, ab Agerino liberto Neroni quoniam evasisset nuntiatum est; qui detineri illum iussit, quasi saluti sue insidiaturus venisset, missique sunt Anicetus et Herculius tetrarcus et

21   Obarius centurio classiarius ut illam perimerent. Et cum esset ab Aniceto circundata domus et ancillula, qua sola sotiata erat Agrippina, fugisset, introgressi ministri ad eam, primus Herculeus caput eius fuste percussit; inde cum ipsa cerneret centurionem ferrum in mortem eius expedientem, protenso utero clamavit ut ventrem ferirent.

22   Et sic occisa nocte eadem cremata est et vilibus obsequiis[4] terra contecta, levem demum tumulum sui<s[5]> in via prope Misenum et Cesaris Iulii villam eidem apponentibus.

23   Alii volunt a Nerone conspectam post cedem et ex membris aliqua ab eodem damnata, aliqua laudata, et demum sepultam.

the emperor how a collapsible ship could be assembled; once on board, the unsuspecting Agrippina would be at risk.

This idea appealed to Nero. Feigning filial affection, as though 18 he were repenting of his past hatred, he embraced his mother on her arrival from Antium and escorted her to her residence. Then, to go to dinner, Agrippina boarded the ship prepared for her own destruction. She was accompanied by the freedman Crepereius Gallus and the freedwoman Acerronia. As they sailed through the night, a signal was given by the accomplices; the heavy lead roof fell down and crushed Crepereius. Since the sea was calm, the sail- 19 ors then tried to capsize the vessel. Acerronia shouted for help and was killed with oars and poles. Agrippina was wounded in the shoulder and finally hurled into the sea; she was rescued by people on the shore and taken to her villa on the Lucrine Lake.

At her orders, the freedman Agerinus informed Nero that 20 Agrippina had been saved. Nero ordered his arrest on the pretext that the freedman had come to make an attempt on the emperor's life. Then Anicetus, the tetrarch Herculeius, and Obarius, a centurion of the marine soldiers, were dispatched to kill Agrippina. Anicetus surrounded the house, and the little maidservant who 21 was Agrippina's only companion fled. Nero's henchmen entered. First Herculeius hit her on the head with his club. When Agrippina saw the centurion drawing his sword to kill her, she thrust out her belly and cried that they should strike her womb.

This was how she died. That same night she was cremated and 22 given an ignominious burial. Finally her friends erected a modest tomb near Julius Caesar's villa on the road to Misenum.

Other sources, however, say that after her death Nero inspected 23 the corpse, criticizing some parts of her body and praising others; only then was Agrippina buried.

: XCIII :

De Epycari libertina

1 Epycaris extera potius quam romana creditur femina, nec tantum
ullo generis fulgore conspicua, sed a liberto genita patre libertina
mulier fuit; et, quod longe turpius est, nullis delectata bonis artibus; circa tamen vite exitum, sibi generosum fuisse animum patefecit virili robore.

2 Crescentibus quidem apud Romanos et Ytalos omnes Neronis,
Romanorum principis, insolentiis lasciviisque, eo itum est ut, Lucio Pisone principe, in eum nonnulli senatorum aliorumque civium conspirarent, dumque rem in finem trahere variis temptarent
colloquiis, quo pacto nescio, sed in notitiam Epycaris predicte venere[1] omnia et coniuratorum nomina.

3 Verum cum iudicio suo nimium protraheretur opus, quasi tedio
affecta, in Campaniam secessit; et dum apud Puteelos[2] forte resi-
deret, ne tempus sineret abire vacuum, Volusium Proculum chy-
nolarcem classisque romane prefectum et olim Agrippine interfe-
ctorem convenit, rata[3] multum emolumenti addere coniurationi si
eum trahere posset in partes; et ostensis longo ordine Neronis flagitiis fastidiis ineptisque moribus et insolentiis et inde eius in eum
ingratitudine, quod ob tam grande facinus, Agrippine scilicet cedis, in re nulla, tanquam bene de se meritum promovisset, coniu-
rationem aperuit totisque viribus conata est eum coniuratis addere
sotium.

4 Sed longe aliter quam arbitraretur Epycaris secutum est. Nam
Volusius experturus numquid obsequiis in se principis gratiam
flectere posset, quam cito illi Cesaris copia concessa est, Epycaris

: XCIII :

Epicharis, a Freedwoman

Epicharis is thought to have been a foreigner rather than a Ro- 1
man. Not only was she not famous for any distinction of lineage
but, as the daughter of a freedman, she was herself a freedwoman.
More shameful still is the fact that she lacked any taste for good
literature. Nonetheless, at the end of her life she revealed manly
fortitude and a noble spirit.

During the reign of Nero, the Romans and the Italic peoples 2
observed a constant increase in his insolence and debauchery. It
reached the point where, under the leadership of Lucius Piso,
some senators and other citizens began to conspire against him.
While they were trying to complete their arrangements in various
meetings, the plot and the conspirators' names somehow came to
the knowledge of the above-mentioned Epicharis.

In her opinion, however, the whole business was being dragged 3
out far too long and so she went off in disgust to Campania.
While she happened to be staying at Pozzuoli, not to let time go
to waste, she met with the chiliarch Volusius Proculus, commander of the Roman fleet and murderer of Agrippina. It was her
belief that the conspiracy would be greatly strengthened if she
could win him over to their side. Accordingly, Epicharis dwelt at
length on Nero's crimes, haughtiness, unseemly conduct, insolence, and, finally, ingratitude towards Volusius himself as someone who had rendered Nero a great service, namely, by killing
Agrippina, but who had never received any kind of promotion.
Then she revealed the conspiracy and tried her best to add him to
the ranks of the conspirators.

The outcome, however, was very different from what Epicharis 4
had expected. Volusius wanted to see if his allegiance would gain
for him the imperial favor; consequently, as soon as he was

dicta reservavit omnia, esto non egerit quod rebatur; nam ambiguo adhuc homini astuta mulier nullum conspirantium⁴ nomen edide-
5 rat. Ea autem accita, fieri non potuit ut ex rogatis quicquam aperi-ret rogantibus.

6 Tandem cum servaretur sub custode, coniuratione per coniura-tos ipsos casu patefacta, iterum in examen revocata, quasi sup-pliciorum hominibus inpatientior, facilius ab ea quod optabatur extorqueri posset, post longos cruciatus, carnificibus etiam infe-rentibus ultro, ne superari viderentur a femina, nullum constantis-simi pectoris reservavit archanum. Tandem in diem reservata poste-rum, cum pedibus ire non posset, timens si tertio vocaretur non posse subsistere, solutam pectori fasciam arcui selle, qua vehebatur, implicuit et facto laqueo gucturi iniecit suo et, cum omnem illi corporis dimisisset molem, ne conspiratis obesset, violentam sibi mortem conscivit, veteri frustrato proverbio, quo docemur tacere quod nesciunt mulieres; et sic Neronem vacuum trepidumque reli-quit.

7 Quod quidem, etsi maximum videatur in femina, longe tamen spectabilius est, si spectetur eiusdem coniurationis egregiorum ho-minum inconstantia, quorum, aliunde quam ab Epycari cognito-rum, nemo tam robuste iuventutis fuit qui, nedum pati pro salute propria, quod pro aliena femina passa est, sed nec audire tormen-torum nomina pateretur, quin imo percontanti confestim que no-verat de conspiratione narraret. Et sic nemo sibi amicisque peper-cit, cum cunctis, nisi sibi, femina pepercisset inclita.

granted an audience by the emperor, he reported everything that Epicharis had said. But Volusius did not accomplish thereby what he thought he would because she was clever enough not to have mentioned the names of the conspirators while he was still undecided. Then Epicharis was summoned; it proved impossible, however, to make her answer any of her inquisitors' questions. 5

Finally, while she was being held in custody, the conspiracy was 6 accidentally revealed by the conspirators themselves, and Epicharis was recalled for questioning. On the grounds that it would be easier to extract from her what they wanted because, as a woman, she would not be able to stand up to torture in the way that men do, her tormentors on their own initiative added to her long sufferings in order to avoid the appearance of being beaten by a woman. But she would not unlock any of the secrets kept in her stout heart. At last she was remanded to the next day. Epicharis was now unable to walk and fearful that she could not hold out if they called her a third time. She tore off her breastband, tied it to the arched canopy of the chair in which she was being carried, and made a noose which she put around her neck. Letting all the weight of her body fall, she inflicted a violent death upon herself so as not to bring harm to the conspirators. Thus she proved false the old proverb that women keep silent only about what they do not know,[a] and she left Nero empty-handed and terrified.

This seems a great thing for a woman to do, but it is even more 7 striking if we consider the weakness of the eminent men who were involved in the same conspiracy. After the revelation of their identities from another source, not one of them was strong enough to endure for his own sake what Epicharis had endured for the sake of others. They could not bear even to hear the description of the tortures without immediately telling their inquisitors what they knew of the conspiracy. Thus they spared neither themselves nor their friends, whereas that glorious woman had spared everyone but herself.

8   Oberrare crederem naturam rerum aliquando, dum mentem mortalium corporibus nectit, illam scilicet pectori infundendo femineo quam virili immisisse crediderat. Sed cum Deus ipse dator talium sit, eum circa opus suum dormitari nephas est credere. Summamus ergo perfectas omnes arbitrandum est; numquid tamen servemus, ipsum indicat opus.

9   Erubescendum nempe hominibus reor dum, nedum a lasciva femina, sed etiam a constantissima quacunque laborum tolerantia

10 vincuntur. Nam si prevalemus sexu, cur non ut et fortitudine prevaleamus decens est? Quod si non sit, cum ipsis effeminati, iure de moribus transegisse videmur.

: XCIV :

De Pompeia Paulina Senece coniuge

1   Pompeia Paulina Lucii Annei Senece, preceptoris Neronis, inclita fuit coniunx; utrum autem romana an alienigena fuerit, legisse non recolo. Attamen, dum spiritus eius generositatem intueor, cre-

2 didisse malim romanam fuisse potius quam forensem. Cuius etsi certa careamus origine, certissimo tamen piissimi eius amoris in virum exemplo illustrium virorum testimonio non caremus.

3   Credidere quidem ex honestissimis illius evi hominibus quam plurimi sevitia Neronis potius quam crimine Senece eum Senecam, senem atque celeberrimum virum, pisoniane coniurationis labe notatum, si labes iure dici potest in tyramnum agere quid adversum. Qua sub umbra, ob vetus, imo ob innatum in virtutes odium, ab ipso Nerone seviendi in Senecam via comperta est; esto

I am inclined to think that Nature sometimes errs when she 8
unites souls with mortal bodies, namely, when she gives to a
woman a soul which she intended to give to a man. But since God
Himself is the giver of such things, it is sacrilegious to believe that
He might nod at his work. Therefore we must believe that we all
receive perfect souls; our actions show whether we keep them so.

In my view, men should be ashamed to be defeated, not so 9
much by a wanton female, but by a woman who had steeled herself to endure any difficulty. If, in fact, we are the stronger sex, is it 10
not fitting for us to have the stronger resolve? If this is not the
case, we are as effeminate as the conspirators and appear with as
good reason to have deviated from sound morals.

: XCIV :

Pompeia Paulina, Wife of Seneca

Pompeia Paulina was the distinguished spouse of Lucius Annaeus 1
Seneca, Nero's tutor. I do not remember reading whether she was
a Roman or foreign-born. When I consider, however, her nobility
of spirit, I would prefer to believe that she was Roman rather than
foreign. Nonetheless, even if we do not know Paulina's exact ori- 2
gin, we do not lack, thanks to the testimony of illustrious authors,
a well-documented example of the devoted love she felt for her
husband.

In his old age, the celebrated Seneca was branded with disgrace 3
in the Pisonian conspiracy, more through Nero's savagery (as many
of the most honorable men of the age believed) than because of
any guilt of his own — if one can be called guilty for acting against
a tyrant. On that pretext Nero himself, because of his inveterate
or, better, his innate hatred of virtue, found a way of lashing out
against Seneca. Certain authorities, however, claimed it was at the

arbitrati quidam sint, inpulsu Poppee atque Tigillini, unicum imperatori crudelitatis consilium, eo itum sit ut indiceretur per centurionem Senece ut sibi mortem deligeret.

4   Quem cum se ad executionem accingentem vidisset Paulina, sepositis consolatoriis viri ad vitam blanditiis quibus hortabatur, castissimi amoris inpulsu mortem, et illud idem mortis genus, forti animo capessere una cum coniuge disposuit, ut quos iunctos honesta vita tenuerat, iunctos mors una dissolveret.

5   Et cum impavida tepentem intrasset aquam, et eadem hora cum viro, ad effundendum spiritum, venas aperuisset, iussu principis, cuius in eam nullum erat particulare odium, ad opprimendam paululum infamiam innate crudelitatis, renitens a servis morti subtracta est. Verum non adeo cito sanguis consistere coactus est,

6   quin pallore perpetuo testaretur mulier optima plurimum vitalis spiritus emisisse cum viro. Tandem, cum paucis annis viri memoriam[1] laudabili viduitate servasset, cum aliter non posset, nomine saltem Senece coniunx clausit diem.

7   Quid, preter amoris dulcedinem et conspicuum pietatis insigne ac venerabile sacrum coniugii, suasisse potuisset mulieri optime malle honeste, si potuisset, cum sene coniuge mori, quam vitam, ut plurimum faciunt femine, secundis nuptiis non absque erubescentia ineundis, servare?

8   Etenim, in maximum matronalis pudicitie dedecus, nonnullis his diebus, non dicam secundum aut tertium — quod omnibus fere comune est — sed sextum, septimum et octavum, si casus emerserit, inire connubium adeo familiare est et novorum virorum thalamis inferre faces, ut videantur morem meretriculis abstulisse,

instigation of Poppaea and Tigellinus that the emperor came to a singularly cruel decision: that Seneca should be ordered, through a centurion, to choose the manner of his own death.

When Paulina saw him preparing to commit suicide, she paid   4
no attention to the consolatory caresses with which her husband encouraged her to go on living. Moved by the purest love, she courageously decided to die together with her husband and in the same way. Hence a single death would undo the bonds of two people who had been joined together in an honorable life.

Fearlessly, at the same moment as her husband, Paulina stepped   5
into the warm water and opened her veins to pour out her spirit. But the emperor did not have any particular hatred for her and wanted to lessen in some small way the infamy of his natural cruelty; consequently, at his orders (and despite her resistance) she was saved from death by the intervention of her slaves. The flow   6
of blood, however, could not be stopped quickly enough to prevent the excellent woman from showing by her constant pallor that she had lost both her husband and the greater part of her vital spirit. Paulina survived for a few years and by exemplary widowhood kept alive her husband's memory. She died at least in name as Seneca's wife, since she could not die otherwise.

What, if not the sweetness of love, the clear sign of devotion,   7
and the venerable sacrament of marriage could have persuaded that fine woman to prefer, if possible, to die honorably with her aged husband rather than to save her life, as most women do, by submitting to a shameful second marriage?

Nowadays, most unfortunately for matronly virtue, it is the   8
practice for women to marry, I will not say two or three times (for that is almost universal), but six, seven, or eight times if the opportunity presents itself. It is so normal for them to bring wedding torches to the chambers of new husbands that they seem to have stolen the custom from prostitutes, whose habit it is to change

quibus consuetudo est \<per>noctando² novos sepissime mutare
concubitus, nec alio subeunt vultu iugalia sepius iterata iura, quam
si persanctissimum honestati prestarent obsequium.

9   Equidem non satis certum est an ex lupanari cellula an ex pre-
mortui viri thalamo tales exire dicende sint; nec dubitem suspican-
dum quis agat aut inhonestius intrans, aut stultius introducens.

10   Heu miseri, quo nostri corruere mores? Consuevere veteres,
quibus erat pronus in sanctitatem animus, ignominiosum arbitrari,
nedum septimas, sed secundas inisse nuptias; nec posse de cetero
11 tales honestis iure misceri matronis. Hodierne longe aliter; nam li-
bidinosam pruriginem reticentes suam, formosiores carioresque se
existimantes, quoniam crebris sponsalitiis, viduitatis superata fortuna, totiens placuerint maritis variis.

<h2 style="text-align:center">: XCV :</h2>

<h3 style="text-align:center">De Sabina Poppea Neronis coniuge</h3>

1   Sabina Poppea romana et illustris fuit femina, T. Ollii, non equidem extreme nobilitatis viri, filia, quanquam non ex eo nomen
sumpserit, sed a materno avo Poppeo Sabino viro inclito, atque
triunphalis decoris et consulatu¹ insigni; nec ille cetere muliebres
defuissent dotes si honestus affuisset animus.

2   Fuit enim formositatis invise et matri, suis annis ceteras Romanas pulchritudine excedenti, persimilis. Preterea erat illi sermo
blandus et laudabili sonorus dulcedine, ingenium egregium atque
versatile, si eo honestis artibus fuisset usa; mosque illi fuit assi-
duus palam modestiam preferre, clam autem uti lascivia, comune

partners frequently during the night. They enter into their too-often repeated marriage vows with the same expression they would use to make some perfervid vow of honor.

Certainly it is not at all plain whether such women can be said 9 to leave the chamber of a dead husband or the cell of a brothel. Someone might well wonder whether the husband was more stupid for bringing her to his bed or the wife more shameless for entering it.

Alas, what wretches we are! To what depths have our morals 10 plunged! The ancients, who were naturally inclined to purity, used to regard a second marriage as disgraceful, much less a seventh; they also held that after remarriage it was wrong to permit such women to mingle with respectable wives. The women of our day 11 are quite different. They conceal their itching lust and think they are more beautiful and beloved for having pleased so often the various husbands of their frequent marriages and for having overcome the misfortune of widowhood.

: XCV :

Sabina Poppaea, Wife of Nero

Sabina Poppaea, an eminent Roman woman, was the daughter of 1 Titus Ollius, a man not quite of the highest nobility. She took her name not from him but from Poppaeus Sabinus, her famous maternal grandfather, who had enjoyed a distinguished consulship and triumphal honors. If she had been of good moral character, she would not have lacked other womanly attributes.

In fact, Poppaea was unusually attractive and resembled her 2 mother, who in her own day was the most beautiful of all the Roman women. Moreover, Poppaea's voice was gentle and resonant with laudable sweetness; her intellect would have been considered

mulierum crimen; et cum illi rarus esset in publicum egressus, arte

3 tamen non caruit. Nam, cum intellexisset callida mulier intuitu oris sui multitudinem et primores potissime delectari, semper eius parte velata egressa est, non quidem ut absconderet quod concupisci desiderabat, verum ne intuentium oculos liberali nimium demonstratione satiaret, sed potius quod occultaverat velo videndi desiderium linqueret.

4 Et ne per mores omnes suos discurram, cum nunquam fame parceret, eo libidinem flectebat suam quo paratior ostendebatur

5 utilitas, nullum faciens inter maritos mechosque discrimen. His insignita notis femina obsequentem satis fortunam habuit. Nam, cum sibi abunde facultates ad gloriam generis sustinendam suppeterent, primo Rufo Crispo romano equiti nupsit. Et cum iam ex eo peperisset filium, suggestu Othonis, iuventute luxuque valentis, potentisque Neronis contubernio, eidem adhesit adultera, nec diu et coniunx effecta est.

6 Sane is, seu amoris fervore minus cautus, seu iam nequiens petulce mulieris tolerare mores et ob id eam in Neronis concupiscentiam trahere conaretur, seu, sic exigente fortuna Poppee, e[2] convivio Cesaris surgens auditus dictitare consueverat se ad illam rediturum cui a superis omnis penitus fuisset concessa nobilitas elegantia morum et divina formositas, in qua consisterent omnium

7 vota mortalium atque gaudia voluptatesque felicium. Quibus facile irritata Neronis libido, adinventa non longa cunctatione per intermedios adeundi via, in amplexus principis volens cupiensque devenit.

Nec multum distulit, et artificiosis femine delinimentis adeo irretitus est Nero, ut arbitraretur ea esse verissima que dictitare

excellent and versatile, if she had used it for honest purposes. It was always her custom to appear modest, but in private she practiced lasciviousness, that common feminine vice. Although she seldom went out in public, Poppaea was not without cunning. The clever woman realized that the multitude and especially the leading citizens took pleasure in seeing her face, and so she always went out partially veiled. She did this not to shield herself from lust (for that she welcomed), but rather so as not to satiate the eyes of the onlookers by showing herself too freely; instead she preferred to leave them with a desire to see what she hid behind her veil. 3

I will not go into detail about her behavior but say only that, since Poppaea never spared her reputation, she bent her passion wherever the advantage seemed greater, making no distinction between husbands and lovers. Though known for these infamous actions, she nonetheless enjoyed Fortune's favor. Poppaea had abundant wealth, sufficient to maintain the splendor of her lineage, and so first married the Roman knight Rufus Crispus. After bearing him a son, she was wooed by Otho, a robust and sensuous youth who was powerful because he was a companion of Nero. She joined Otho in adultery and not long after became his wife. 4 5

Perhaps the ardor of his love made him less cautious; or he may have been unable to endure the ways of his headstrong wife and for that reason tried to make her an object of desire to Nero; or Poppaea's destiny may have willed it so—at any rate, Otho, on rising from the emperor's dinner table, was commonly overheard saying that he was returning to the woman to whom the gods had given every possible nobility, elegance of manner, and divine beauty, and in whom dwelt the desires of all mortal men and the delights and joys of the blessed. Nero's lust was easily aroused by these remarks. Intermediaries quickly found a way, and Poppaea came willingly and ardently to the emperor's embraces. 6 7

It was not long before Nero was so enmeshed by the artful wiles of this woman that he regarded as absolutely true the things

8 consueverat Otho. Quod cum nosceret sagacissima mulier, dissimulans quod optabat, captato tempore, fictis perfusa lacrimis, aiebat aliquando se amorem suum omnino quo cupiebat inferre non posse, cum et ipsa Othoni coniugali iure obnoxia esset et principem teneri gratia Attis ancillule pelicis advertebat.

9 Ex quibus secutum est ut Otho, sub specie honoris amotus, prefectus Lusitanie provincie micteretur et Attis excluderetur omnino. Inde in Agrippinam principis matrem invehi cepit Poppea, dicens aliquando principem, nedum imperio, sed nec libertate gau-

10 dere, eum esse pupillum, et tutricis arbitrio trahi. Quibus obstante nemine, ob odium fere omnium in superbiam Agrippine, actum est ut Neronis iussu misera mater violenta morte subtraheretur et paulatim subtraherentur emuli plures, Tigillino opitulante castrorum prefecto.

11 Tandem cum principem in sui dilectionem ardentissimum cerneret, et obstacula desiderii sui cuncta fore sublata, in coniugium Neronis explicare retia cepit; et cum illi iam peperisset filiam unicam, Memmio Regulo et Virginio Rufo consulibus, quam summo cum gaudio Nero susceperat, eamque Augustam Poppeam nuncuparat, iam audaci oratione instare cepit, dicens nemini geminam concessisse noctem quin evestigio sequeretur connubium, neque se fore degenerem, et fecunditate uteri atque formositate corporis imperatoris mereri nuptias; et cum iam flagrantem principem in desiderium traxisset connubii, primo Octavia coniunx, olim Claudii Cesaris filia, in Pandateriam insulam innocua relegata est; et demum, vigesimo etatis sue anno, inpulsu Poppee, Nerone mandante, occisa, et Poppea Cesari iuncta coniugio.

Otho had repeatedly asserted. Poppaea, who was very shrewd, recognized this and concealed what she wanted. At an opportune moment she would often say, her face drenched with false tears, that she could not give her love as completely as she wished, for she was bound to Otho by the law of marriage and she realized that the emperor was bound by the tender regard he showed his concubine, the slave Acte. 8

These tactics effected the total rejection of Acte as well as the removal of Otho who was sent, under the guise of the conferral of an honor, as prefect to the province of Lusitania. Then Poppaea began to assail Agrippina, the emperor's mother. The former declared any number of times that Nero did not enjoy liberty, much less power, and that he was just a ward, ruled by the will of his guardian. No one gainsaid these accusations owing to the almost universal hatred of Agrippina's haughtiness, and thus, at Nero's order, there came about the violent death of his wretched mother[a] and, with the aid of the praetorian prefect Tigellinus, the gradual elimination of many rivals. 9

Finally, when Poppaea saw that the emperor was passionately in love with her and that all obstacles to her goal had been removed, she began to spread her nets for marriage with Nero. Already she had presented the emperor with a daughter during the consulship of Memmius Regulus and Virginius Rufus, and Nero had welcomed the child with great joy and named her Augusta Poppaea. Now Poppaea began to insist brazenly that she had never given herself to anyone for two successive nights without marrying him immediately; that she would not become a degenerate; and that she deserved to marry the emperor because of her beauty and her fertility. When she had filled the prince with a burning desire to marry her, his innocent wife Octavia, daughter of the late emperor Claudius, was first exiled to the island of Pandateria, and then, in the twentieth year of her age, executed by order of Nero at Poppaea's instigation. And so Poppaea married Nero. 11

12   Sed non diu longis artibus quesito atque potito culmine gavisa est. Nam, pregnans iterum facta, fortuita Neronis ira calce percussa, diem obiit. Cuius aboleri corpus igne romano more Nero prohibuit, sed exterorum regum ritu magnifica exequiarum pompa deferri publice iussit, illudque refertum odoribus Iuliorum tumulo

13   condi. Ipse autem pro rostris illam, et potissime formositatis precipue, longa et accurata oratione laudavit, nonnulla fortune seu nature dona, quibus insignita erat, loco clarissimarum virtutum illi attribuens.

14   Erat michi inter has Poppee fortunas quid dicerem in molliciem nimiam, in blanditias petulantiam lacrimasque mulierum, certissimum atque perniciosissimum virus credentium animorum. Sed ne viderer satyram potius quam hystoriam recitasse, omictendum censui.

: XCVI :

De Triaria Lucii Vitellii coniuge

1   Triaria, mulier nullo alio sui generis splendore cognita, nisi quia Lucii Vitellii, fratris Auli Vitellii, Romanorum principis, coniunx fuit. Cuius seu ob fervidum in virum amorem, seu ob insitam animo natura atrocitatem, tanta fuit ferocitas, quod ob adversum muliebribus morem memoratu digna visa sit.

2   Discordantibus igitur ob principatum Vitellio Cesare atque Vespasiano, actum est ut, cum intrassent Tarracinam, Volscorum oppidum, nonnulli gladiatores sub Iuliano quodam duce, et remiges etiam plures romane classis, haud longe a Circeo monte sub Apollenario prefecto morantis, et ab his, cum Vespasiano sentientibus, per negligentiam et socordiam teneretur, servi cuiusdam in-

Poppaea did not long enjoy the summit she had sought and at- 12
tained by means of her deeply laid schemes. She died during her
second pregnancy when Nero kicked her in a fit of anger. The emperor refused to have her body cremated according to Roman custom; instead he ordered the corpse to be embalmed, publicly con-
veyed with a magnificent funeral in the manner of foreign kings,
and placed in the sepulcher of the Julii. Before the Rostra he deliv- 13
ered a long and elaborate panegyric, with special praise of her
marvelous beauty, and credited her with certain gifts of fortune or
nature rather than with the most illustrious virtues.

With respect to Poppaea's fortunes, I could have spoken at 14
length against the excessive softness, flattery, petulance, and tears
of women—a sure and deadly poison for credulous souls. But I
have decided to leave out these matters lest I seem to be writing
satire rather than history.

: XCVI :

Triaria, Wife of Lucius Vitellius

Triaria is a woman known for no other familial luster apart from 1
the fact that she was the wife of Lucius Vitellius, brother of the
Roman emperor Aulus Vitellius. Such was her ferocity—owing
either to her passionate love for her husband or to a cruelty naturally implanted in her soul—that she seems worthy of mention
precisely for this non-feminine characteristic.

Now, Vespasian and Emperor Vitellius were at odds over the 2
empire. A number of gladiators, led by a certain Julianus, entered
the Volscian city of Terracina; they were accompanied by many
sailors from the Roman fleet which lay at anchor not far from
Monte Circeo under the command of the prefect Apollinaris. Partisans of Vespasian, these men occupied the city, but in a careless

3   dicio factum est ut nocte illam Lucius intraret. Qui dum in semi-
     sopitos arma arripientes hostes atque oppidanos infestos ferro
     seviret, Triaria, que per noctem secuta virum civitatem intraverat,
     in coniugis victoriam avida, accinta gladio et vitellianis immixta
     militibus, nunc huc nunc illuc, per medias noctis tenebras, inter
     clamores dissonos et discurrentia tela sanguinem morientiumque
     singultus extremos, nil militaris severitatis omictendo, irruebat in
     miseros adeo ut, recuperato oppido[1], crudeliter nimium atque su-
     perbe in hostes egisse relatum sit.

4   <I>ngentes[2] in sano pectore coniugalis amoris sunt vires: nulla
     illis, dummodo viri gloria extollatur, formido, nulla pietatis memo-
     ria, nulla feminei sexus erubescentia, nulla temporum qualitatis
     existimatio. Potuit Triaria in decus viri, omnia facili labore subire,
     que, nedum feminas, quibus, ut plurimum, mos est etiam diurno
     muris murmure in sinu coniugis exanimari, sed robustos iuve-
5   nes atque bellicosos horrore <solent>[3] quandoque corripere. Et si
     tanto cum impetu se tulit hec in arma nocturna mulier, quis credet
     eam hoc tantum facinore fuisse conspicuam, cum non consueve-
     rint, seu exitiose sint seu celebres, sole mortalium pectora subire
     virtutes?

6   Ego quidem reor, quanquam a memoria sublata sint, longe aliis
     meritis spectabilem fuisse Triariam.

: XCVII :

De Proba Adelphi coniuge

1   Proba, facto et nomine, literarum notitia, memoratu dignissima
     fuit femina; et, cum eius ignoretur nobilitas et origo, placet non-
     nullis—et ex coniectura, credo—eam fuisse romanam (alii vero

and lazy manner. Lucius Vitellius, acting on a slave's instructions, entered the place at night. Sword in hand he launched a furious 3 attack on the drowsy enemy and the hostile inhabitants as they seized their arms. Triaria, who had followed her husband that night and entered the city, was eager to secure his victory. Armed with a sword, she mingled with Vitellius' soldiers, falling upon the poor wretches, now here, now there in the darkness of the night, in the midst of shrieks and cries, flying weapons, blood, and the last gasps of the dying. Triaria indulged in all the atrocities of war, so much so, in fact, that after the capture of the town she was charged with excessive cruelty and arrogance towards the enemy.

Great is the power of conjugal love in a pure heart. Women like 4 Triaria fear nothing provided that their husband's glory is extolled; they forget pity and womanly shame; they pay no heed to the nature of the circumstances. For the sake of her husband's honor Triaria could endure with little effort things that usually terrify not only women, who even in broad daylight are accustomed to faint on their husbands' bosom at the slightest noise of a mouse, but also strong and warlike young men. Moreover, if this woman 5 threw herself so forcefully into a nocturnal fray, who will believe that she was famous only for this deed? Virtues, whether for good or ill, do not usually dwell singly within the breast of mortals.

For my part, I believe that Triaria was long renowned for other 6 meritorious actions, but all record of them has been lost.

: XCVII :

Proba, Wife of Adelphus

Proba, an excellent woman in reality as well as name, is worthy of 1 remembrance for her knowledge of literature. Her lineage and origin are unknown, but some writers maintain — on the basis of

clarissimi viri asserunt eam ex oppido Orti oriundam) et cuiusdam Adelphi coniugem et christianam religione.

2   Hec igitur — sub quocunque preceptore factum sit — liberalibus artibus valuisse liquido potest percipi. Verum, inter alia eius studia, adeo pervigili cura virgiliani carminis docta atque familiaris effecta est, ut, fere omne opere a se confecto teste, in conspectu et

3   memoria semper habuisse videatur. Que dum forsan aliquando perspicaciori animadvertentia legeret, in existimationem incidit ex illis omnem Testamenti Veteris hystoriam et Novi seriem placido atque expedito et succipleno versu posse describi.

4   Non equidem admiratione caret tam sublimem considerationem muliebre subintrasse cerebrum, sed longe mirabile fuit executioni mandasse.

5   Operam igitur pio conceptui prestans, nunc huc nunc illuc per buccolicum georgicumque atque eneidum saltim discurrendo carmen, nunc hac ex parte versus integros, nunc ex illa metrorum particulas carpens, miro artificio in suum redegit propositum, adeo apte integros collocans et fragmenta connectens, servata lege pedum et carminis dignitate, ut, nisi expertissimus, compages possit advertere; et his ab orbis exordio principium faciens, quicquid hystorie in veteribus atque novis legitur literis, usque ad immissionem Sacri Spiritus tam compte composuit, ut huius compositi ignarus homo prophetam pariter et evangelistam facile credat fuisse Virgilium.

6   Ex quibus non minus commendabile summitur, huic scilicet mulieri sacrorum voluminum integram, seu satis plenam fuisse notitiam; quod quam raris etiam hominibus nostro contingat evo dolentes novimus.

7   Voluit insuper egregia femina labore suo compositum <opus>[1] vocari *Centonam*; quod ipsi persepe vidimus. Et quanto magis illud

conjecture, I believe—that she was Roman (other famous authors claim that she came from the town of Orte), and that she was the wife of a certain Adelphus, and a Christian.

Whoever her teacher may have been, it is quite clear that Proba   2
was trained in the liberal arts. Indeed, among other studies she gained such expertise and familiarity with Virgil's poems through her attentive reading that she seems to have had them memorized, as is attested by almost all her own works. The idea came to   3
Proba, perhaps while she was reading Virgil one day with more than usual insight, that from his poems one could compile the history of the Old and New Testaments in pleasing, easy, and delectable verse.

Certainly it is no small wonder that such a lofty design made its   4
way into a woman's mind, but more wondrous still is the fact of its fulfillment.

Proba devoted herself to her pious scheme, searching here and   5
there through the *Bucolics*, the *Georgics*, and the *Aeneid*; sometimes she took entire lines from one passage, and at other times parts of lines from elsewhere. These texts she adapted with great skill to her purpose. So expertly did she place whole lines together and combine fragments, always in observance of the rules of meter and the dignity of the verse, that no one except a real connoisseur could detect the sutures. Beginning with the creation of the world, she put into verse the history of the Old and New Testaments, up to the coming of the Holy Spirit,ᵃ and so neatly was it done that a person unacquainted with this work would easily believe Virgil to have been both prophet and evangelist.

From her efforts we can draw another conclusion no less praise-   6
worthy, namely, that Proba had a complete or at least a very full knowledge of the Bible. How rarely this is true of even the men of our own day we know to our regret.

This distinguished woman, moreover, wanted the text she had   7
labored to put together to be called the *Cento*, and I have consulted

memoratu perpetuo dignum putamus, tanto minus credimus tam celebre mulieris huius <ingenium>[2] huic tantum acquievisse labori; quin imo reor, si in annos ampliores vite protracta est, eam alia insuper condidisse laudabilia, que librariorum desidia, nostro tamen incommodo, ad nos usque devenisse nequivere.

8   Que inter—ut nonnullis placet—fuit Omeri centona, eadem arte et ex eadem materia qua<m>[3] ex Virgilio sumpserat, ex Omero sumptis carminibus edita. Ex quo, si sic est, summitur, eius cum ampliori laude, eam doctissime grecas novisse literas ut latinas.

9   Sed queso nunc: quid optabilius audisse feminam Maronis et Homeri scandentem carmina, et apta suo operi seponentem? Selecta artificioso contextu nectentem eruditissimi prospectent viri, quibus, cum sit sacrarum literarum insignis professio, arduum tamen est et difficile ex amplissimo sacri voluminis gremio, nunc hinc nunc inde, partes elicere et ad seriem vite Christi passis verbis prosaque cogere, ut hec fecit ex gentilitio carmine.

10   Erat huic satis—si femineos consideremus mores—colus et acus atque textrina, si, more plurium, torpere voluisset; sed quoniam sedula studiis sacris ab ingenio segniciei rubiginem absterxit omnem, in lumen evasit eternum. Quod utinam bono intuerentur animo voluptatibus obsequentes et ocio, quibus pregrande est cubiculo insidere, fabellis frivolis irreparabile tempus terere et a summo diei mane in noctem usque totam persepe sermones aut nocuos aut inanes blaterando deducere, seu sibi tantum lasci-

11   viendo vacare! Adverterent edepol quantum differentie sit inter fa-

it quite often. The more we think the work worthy of being remembered forever, the less can we believe that so intellectually gifted a person would have been satisfied with only this effort. In fact, I think that, if Proba lived for many years, she must have written other praiseworthy works which have not reached us, to our loss, because of scribal laziness.

Among these, according to some sources, was a Homeric *cento* 8 consisting of verses taken from Homer in which she displayed the same skill and used the same subject matter she had employed for Virgil.[b] If this is the case, we can infer (and it redounds even more to her credit) that she was deeply learned in Greek as well as Latin literature.

But now I ask you: what more could one wish than to hear of a 9 woman scanning the poems of Virgil and Homer and choosing those apt for her purpose? Let learned men consider how artistically she wove together her selected passages. Though they themselves belong to the honorable calling of sacred letters, they find it difficult and challenging enough to pluck passages here and there from the vast corpus of Holy Scripture and to press them into an ordered prose narration of the life of Christ—something Proba did from a pagan poem.

If we reflect on normal feminine practice, the distaff, the needle, 10 and the loom would have been sufficient for Proba, had she wanted to lead an idle life like the majority of her sex. But she achieved eternal fame by taking her sacred studies seriously and scraping off completely the rust of intellectual sloth. Would that her example was favorably regarded by those women who yield to pleasure and idleness, who think it wonderful to stay in their rooms and waste irrevocable time in frivolous stories, who often drag out their hours from dawn to late at night in harmful or useless gossip and save time only for the pursuit of wantonness! Then 11 they would see how much difference there is between seeking fame

mam laudandis operibus querere, et nomen una cum cadavere se-
pelire, et, tanquam non vixerint, e vita discedere.

: XCVIII :

De Faustina Augusta

1 Faustina Augusta, que et inter divos postea relata est, glorie plurimum vivens moriensque, viri sui magis benignitate quam opere
suo, consecuta est.

Fuit quippe Antonini Pii Cesaris Augusti, ex Faustina coniuge,
filia et Marco Antonino, iam ab Antonino Pio adoptato in filium,
connubio iuncta; eoque, patre mortuo, imperavit una cum viro et
consulto senatus Augusta appellata est, non parva eo tempore gloria mulieri. Nam etsi precedentibus ab Augustis viris Augustarum
cognomen esset, nulli ante hanc senatus consulto fuisse concessum
invenio.

2 Fuit preterea tam exquisiti decoris ut aliquid divinum mortali-
tati eius crederetur admixtum quod, ne consumeretur senio aut
morte, actum est ut iuvencula et etate provectior aureis argen-
teisque ac ereis numis eius effigies sculpperetur[1]; et in hodiernum
3 usque perdurat. In quibus etsi oris habitus, oculorum motus, color
vividus et hilaritas faciei desint, illud tamen lineamenta testantur
permax<i>mum[2]. Sane quantum totius orbis fama celebratum est
tantum turpi impudicitie nota pollutum.

4 Creditum quidem est hanc non uno, preter virum, contentam
fuisse amasio, quin imo in amplexus plurium devenisse ex quibus

for praiseworthy works and burying one's name together with one's body — in effect, dying as if one had never lived.

: XCVIII :

Faustina Augusta

Faustina Augusta, who was later deified, acquired considerable 1
glory in life and death more through her husband's generosity than
through her own deeds.

She was the daughter of the emperor Antoninus Pius and his
wife Faustina, and the wife of Marcus Antoninus, whom Antoninus Pius had previously adopted as his son. When the younger Faustina's father died, she ruled alongside her husband and by
a decree of the Senate was called *Augusta*, no small honor for a
woman at that time. Although previous empresses were entitled
Augusta from their husbands who were each known as *Augustus*, I
do not find that this name was granted by senatorial decree to any
other imperial wife before Faustina.

Faustina possessed such exquisite grace as to make it credible 2
that something divine had been infused into her mortal body. To
prevent her beauty from being consumed by old age or death, it
was decreed that her portrait as a young girl and then as a mature
woman should be engraved on gold, silver, and copper coins, and
thus it still survives today. Even though the expression of the 3
mouth, the movement of the eyes, the vivid complexion, and the
cheerfulness of her countenance are missing from such likenesses,
the features nonetheless attest to extraordinary beauty. And yet
the fame that her beauty had throughout the world was defiled in
equal measure by the shameful stamp of indecency.

Indeed, it was believed that, besides her husband, Faustina was 4
not satisfied with just one lover but enjoyed the embraces of many.

quorundam nomina detexit infamia. Nam Vetilus quidam inter eius adulteros habitus est; sic et Orphitus et post hunc Moderatius; sed qui ceteros anteivit, Tertullus nominatus est, quem etiam

5 aiunt ab Antoni<n>o³ secum in cena compertum. Et his superadditus Marcus Verus, non obstante quod eius esset ex Lucilla filia gener.

Et, quod omnium horum turpius est, aiunt eam gladiatorem quendam adeo amasse ut ob desiderium eius incurreret egritudinem fere letalem et sanitatis desiderio Antonino concupiscentiam detexisse suam eumque, medici consilio usum, ad fervorem sedandum languentis gladiatorem occidi fecisse et eius adhuc tepenti sanguine omne delinisse corpus egrote et sic ab impetuoso amoris estu ac etiam morbo liberasse coniugem.

6 Quod quidem remedium fictum credidere prudentes, cum temporis in processu Commodus Antoninus ea tempestate conceptus, non deliniti sanguinis, sed habiti potius cum gladiatore concubitus, scelestis⁴ operibus suis, quibus potius gladiatoris quam Antonini credebatur filius, testimonium veritati prestaret.

7 Quibus in Faustine ignominiam personantibus, Antonino ab amicis suasum est ut illam occideret seu saltem, quod humanius

8 videbatur, abdicaret. Verum Antoninus cum esset mitis ingenii homo, esto egre ferret adulteria coniugis, recusavit in consilium ire et ne in maius evaderet dedecus perpeti maluit. Nec aliud suadentibus respondit amicis quam oportere repudiatis dotes restitui, volens⁵ ob id intelligi quod ob Faustinam teneret imperium.

Sed ista sinenda sunt (sepissime quidem etiam intuitu minimo, minus etiam advertenter facto, labefactari honestiores consuevere) et e nebulis redeamus in lucem.

9 Antonino autem apud orientales reges magnifice rem publicam curante, actum est ut Faustina in vico Alalee, in radicibus

Infamy has made known some of their names. These adulterers
included a certain Vetilus, Orfitus, and later Moderatus, but the
one who was preferred to all the others was called Tertullus,
whom Antoninus allegedly found dining with her. To these must   5
be added Marcus Verus, despite the fact that he was her son-in-
law, [i.e.] the husband of her daughter Lucilla.

Most shameful of all, she is reported to have loved a certain
gladiator so much that out of desire for him she fell dangerously
ill; longing to be cured, she told Antoninus of her lust. To quench
Faustina's ardor, he followed the doctor's advice and had the gladiator killed and his sick wife's body smeared all over with the man's
blood while it was still warm. And so her fiery passion as well as
her sickness was cured.

Sensible men, however, regarded this cure as a mere fiction. For   6
in due course, the wicked deeds of Commodus Antoninus, who
had been conceived at the time, bore witness to the truth: that he
was the son of a gladiator, not Antoninus, and had been conceived, not by the smearing of blood, but by his mother's sexual
congress with the gladiator.

With these stories trumpeting Faustina's ignominy, his friends   7
urged Antoninus to kill her, or at least (and this seemed more humane) to repudiate her. But the emperor was a man of gentle   8
character. Despite his distress at his wife's adultery, he refused to
follow their counsel and preferred to bear with her shame rather
than to incur more of it. In answer to the friends who were advis-
ing him, he said only that dowries had to be returned to divorced
wives, wanting them to understand by this that he owed his position as emperor to Faustina.

But enough of such things. To be sure, often a mere glance,
even one made inadvertently, can cause honorable women to slip.
Now let us return from obscure matters to certainties.

While Antoninus was caring brilliantly for public affairs among   9
the Eastern kings, Faustina fell ill and died in the village of Halala

Tauri montis, egritudine diem clauderet extremum. Quam Antonini precibus senatus inter divos extulit et de cetero diva Faustina appellata est: quod apud Romanos mulieri nulle ante contigerat.

10 Et cum eam iam castrorum matrem appellasset Antoninus, ei templum eo in loco in quo decesserat construi fecit insigne et eidem statuas iussit apponi sui nominis conspicuas instituitque puellas sacerdotes templo quas faustinianas vocitari precepit; et sic loco dee per tempus ibidem celebris habita est Faustina ut quod subtraxisse claritatis videbatur luxuria, deitas resarciret.

: XCIX :

De Semiamira muliere messana

1 Semiamira greca fuit mulier, ex civitate Messana; quo tamen patre[1] genita, non constat, cum clarum sit Variam quandam messanam, Iulie stiline, coniugis olim Severi Pertinacis imperatoris, feminam eius fuisse matrem. Inhonesta quidem aliquandiu fuit mulier, sed post hec, filii claritate et senatus etiam principatu, conspicua facta est.

2 Hec, ut prisca sinamus probra, mater fuit Varii Helyogabali primo Phebi sacerdotis, inde romani principis. Quem ex Antonino Caracalla imperatore, cuius aliquando contubernio usa fuerat, affirmabat genitum, tantaque vulgati corporis laboravit infamia, ut Helyogabalus adhuc puer, non ab avia Varia, ut putaverunt aliqui, sed eo a condiscipulis vocaretur Varius, quia ex variorum hominum concubitu, quibus continue miscebatur mater, videretur genitus.

at the foot of Mount Taurus. At Antoninus' request the Senate elevated her to a place among the gods, and thereafter she was known as the deified Faustina. This had never before happened to a Roman woman. Antoninus had already given her the title 10
"Mother of the Camp"; now he had an imposing temple built for her in the place where she died, and in her honor he ordered a number of splendid statues to be placed in it. Furthermore, he established an order of young priestesses in the temple and ordered them to be known as Faustinians. Hence for a time Faustina achieved the celebrity of a goddess, so that divinity restored the glory lost through profligacy.

: XCIX :

Symiamira, Woman of Emesa

Symiamira, who was Greek, came from the city of Emesa. We do 1
not know her father's name, but it is clear that her mother was Varia of Emesa, sister[a] of Julia whose late husband was the emperor Severus Pertinax. For some time Symiamira was a dishonorable woman, but she later became famous by reason of her son's distinction and her own leading role in the Senate.

Let us pass over in silence her earlier shameful actions. Symi- 2
amira was the mother of Varius Elagabalus, initially a priest of Phoebus and then emperor of Rome. She claimed that Elagabalus was the son of Emperor Antoninus Caracalla, whose concubine she had been for some time. Symiamira, however, suffered such infamy for having prostituted herself that as a boy Elagabalus was called Varius by his fellow students — not after his grandmother Varia, as some authorities have thought, but because he looked as if he had been conceived in the course of his mother's incessant copulations with 'various' men.

3   Ceterum cum is esset spectabilis forma et ob sacerdotium plurimum cognitus et creditus assertione matris a milititibus provincia-
libus Caracalle filius, factum est, avie pecunia, quam plurimam
penes Iuliam imperatricem sagacitate cumulaverat sua, ut, conque-
rentibus de Macrino imperatore militibus, eorum in eum, si quid
4   in Macrinum attentaretur, deveniret consensus. Nec difficulter:
erat enim eo tempore tante autoritatis apud romanos exercitus
Antoninorum nomen atque familia, ut nil magis quam ut ex eis
aliquis principatum teneret optaretur a cunctis. Nec diu, cum in
Macrinum coniurassent, Helyogabalus haud longe Anthiochiam[2]
imperator salutatus est et Antoninus nominatus.

5   Quod cum in Anthiochia[3] audisset Macrinus, miratus Varie
mulieris audaciam, cuius opus hoc, ut erat, ratus est, dum Helyogabalum obsideri curat, Iulianus, in hoc missus, occiditur et eius
milites in fidem Helyogabali transitum fecere et cum ipse Macrinus adversus Helyogabalum descendisset in pugnam, victus atque
fugatus est; et post paululum in Bithinie vico, una cum Dyadu-
6   meno filio, occisus. Ex quo Helyogabalus, quasi Caracalle patris mortem ultus, opere Varie avie sue indubitanter principatum
adeptus est; et Romam veniens a cuncto senatu, maximo cum desiderio, expectatus atque susceptus est.

7   Ex qua repentina provectione Semiamira usque ad astra fere delata est et, Augusta nuncupata, ex fornicibus, romani principis
aule dominium consecuta refulsit, hac una fulgidior causa. Nam
dato scelestus esset Helyogabalus, cognoscens se avie facto principem et per consequens filie genitricis sue, in tantum illam, quasi
loco retributionis, honoribus pretulit, ut nil fere, nisi ea dispo-
nente, perageret; et cum eadem die, qua Romam intraverat, sena-

Elagabalus was handsome, and his priesthood brought him 3
considerable fame. On the basis of his mother's claim, the soldiers
in the provinces thought that he was Caracalla's son. Hence,
thanks also to the large amount of money that his grandmother
had shrewdly accumulated at the court of the empress Julia, it
transpired that, as the soldiers became discontented with the emperor Macrinus, their choice would fall upon Elagabalus, should
there be an attempt made to overthrow Macrinus. Nor would it 4
have been difficult: at that time the name and family of the
Antonines carried such weight among the Roman armies that they
asked of their emperor only that he belong to this house. Shortly
afterwards they organized a conspiracy against Macrinus; Elagabalus was hailed as emperor near Antioch and named Antoninus.

When Macrinus heard this in Antioch, he was surprised at 5
Varia's audacity, to whose handiwork he rightly attributed these
developments. He laid plans to besiege Elagabalus. But Julianus,
who had been dispatched for this purpose, was killed and his soldiers went over to Elagabalus' side. When Macrinus himself came
to attack Elagabalus, he was defeated, put to flight, and shortly
thereafter killed along with his son Diadumenus in a town in
Bithynia. Thus did Elagabalus appear to have avenged the death of 6
his father Caracalla by gaining, with the help of his grandmother
Varia, undisputed possession of the empire. He came to Rome,
where he was awaited and received by the entire Senate with great
enthusiasm.

Her son's rapid rise led to Symiamira's own elevation practically 7
to the stars. Now called *Augusta*, she shone the more radiantly by
reason of having come from the brothels to the power of the Roman imperial court. Elagabalus, though wicked, realized that he
was emperor because of the service rendered by his grandmother
and, consequently, by her daughter, who was his mother. As a
kind of recompense, he heaped such honors upon Symiamira that
he did almost nothing without her consent. The same day he en-

8 tum habuisset, iussit matrem rogari ut in senatum accederet. Que a consule rogata concessit; eique, ibidem ubi reliquis senatoribus, apparato subsellio, more ceterorum, de agendis sententiam dixit; quod mulieri alteri contigisse, memoria nulla est.

9 O ignominiosum spectaculum, inter gravissimos viros vidisse, e lupanari pridie evulsam, meretriculam sedisse; et ubi de regibus agebatur, inter lenones assuetam, dicentem audisse sententiam! O libertas vetus, o prisca sanctitas, o maiorum indignatio veneranda, qua minus graves homines ex tam celebri collegio pellebantur, nota deturpati censoria, ubi es? Spectasne infamem mulierculam Curionum Fabritiorum Scipionum Catonumque loca fedantem?

10 Sed quid mulierem senatoriam queror, cum hostes reipublice et illecebres iuvenes exteri atque incogniti urbis et orbis teneant principatum?

Quid tandem? Nunquam postea senatum Helyogabalus intravit

11 quin una secum intraret sanctissima mater. Cui hoc insuper fecit ceca felicitas ut tam grandis existimationis haberetur vulgo ut[4] Sybillis etiam preponeretur omnibus.

Preterea, cum fastidienda sint dicta, quod sequitur ridiculum est. Tante enim fuit hec mulier apud ignavum filium dignationis, ut in Quirinali colle, facto ab eo loco quem *senaculum* appellavit, ubi iamdudum solemnibus diebus matronarum quandoque consueverat esse conventus, ordinatis mulieribus que eum convenirent statutis diebus in locum, iussit eas senatorio more de moribus et agendis circa statum matronarum consulta facerent legesque instituerent; et huic tam discreto senatui Semiamiram principissam constituit, a qua senatus consulta plurima, quanquam ridenda, manasse compertum est.

tered Rome, Elagabalus convened the Senate and ordered that his mother be summoned. Symiamira agreed to the consul's request. 8 A seat was prepared for her among the other senators, and she, like the rest, gave her views on the affairs of the day. There is no record that any other woman ever achieved this.

O what a shameful spectacle to see a little prostitute, who had 9 been pulled the day before from the brothel, seated in the midst of such eminent men! How shameful to hear a woman accustomed to the company of panderers expressing her views in a place where the fate of kings was settled! O ancient liberty, o time-honored sanctity, o righteous indignation of our forefathers by which unworthy men, whom the censors had judged unfit, were expelled from so distinguished a body—where are you? Do you not see this infamous little woman soiling the place of the Curii, the Fabricii, the Scipios, and the Catos?

But why do I complain of a woman senator when enemies of 10 the state and pleasure-seeking young men, foreign and unknown, rule Rome and the world?

Well, then, Elagabalus from that time on never entered the Senate unless he was accompanied by this purest of mothers. And 11 blind good luck presented her with this added boon: Symiamira was held in such high regard by the populace that she was given precedence over all the Sibyls.

If what has already been said is disgusting, what follows is ridiculous. This woman was so highly esteemed by her good-for-nothing son that he selected a place on the Quirinal Hill which he called the *senaculum* (where in the past women had sometimes been accustomed to meet on holy days). Elagabalus chose some women to assemble here on appointed days and ordered them, just like senators, to enact decrees and pass laws on feminine mores and affairs. He designated Symiamira as president of this wise Senate, and she is known to have issued many decrees, although they were absurd.

12 Sancitum quippe eo in collegio fuit quo vestitu uti et quibus ornamentis fas esset unicuique; cui etiam cedere, cui assurgere, cuius
etiam ad osculum venire unaqueque matrona deberet; insuper et
que pilento et que equo aut carpento mulari seu sella vehi deberet;
13 et huiusmodi. Que etsi potius, uti erant, viderentur inania et ludo
quam veritati similia, et potissime muliebri vanitate pensata, et
inepto vulgi iudicio, eo tamen tempore permaxima visa sunt.
14 Sane cum nil violentum durabile, hec facile dissoluta periere in
auras. Nam cum potius meretricio quam matronali ritu in principis aula sese haberet Semiamira, vacante etiam filio obscenis atque
profusis libidinibus, eo usque itum est ut Helyogabalus pro meritis occideretur a suis et cum eo Semiamira, umbratili splendore relicto, cesa in cloaca iaceretur et inde una cum cadavere filii traheretur in Tyberim, ne cursus iuventutis eius differre videretur ab
exitu, quod et nos, viventes misere, minime cogitamus.

: C :

De Zenobia Palmirenorum regina

1 Zenobia Palmirenorum fuit regina, tam eximie virtutis femina,
priscis testantibus literis, ut ceteris gentilibus inclita fama preponenda sit.

Hec ante alia genere fuit insignis. Nam a Ptholomeis Egyptio-

For example, it was ordained in that assembly how women 12
should dress and what ornaments were appropriate for each, to
whom each woman should give precedence, in whose presence
each should rise, and whom each should advance to kiss. Moreover, they decreed who should ride in a carriage or on horseback
or in a coach drawn by mules or in a litter, and other things of this
kind. Even though these matters may seem foolish, as indeed they 13
were, and more like a joke than reality (especially since they were
subject to deliberation by vain females and the witless rabble),
nonetheless they were taken very seriously at the time.

Still, nothing imposed by arbitrary force can endure. All this 14
was easily dissolved and vanished into thin air. Symiamira behaved
in the royal palace more like a prostitute than a lady, and her son
indulged in obscene and extravagant acts of debauchery. Finally it
reached the point that Elagabalus for his just deserts was killed by
his soldiers. Symiamira, forsaking her illegitimate splendor, was
slain and thrown into a sewer with him; from there both bodies
were cast into the Tiber. Thus her demise matched her early career. This is something to which we who lead contemptible lives
give too little thought.

: C :

Zenobia, Queen of Palmyra

Zenobia was the queen of Palmyra and a woman so remarkably 1
virtuous, according to our ancient sources, that she ought to receive precedence over other pagan ladies for her illustrious reputation.

She was eminent, first of all, because of her lineage. In fact,
Zenobia is said to have been descended from the famous

rum regibus claram volunt originem habuisse, parentibus tamen memorie non concessis.

2   Dicunt autem hanc a pueritia sua, spretis omnino muliebribus offitiis, cum iam corpusculum eduxisset in robur, silvas et nemora coluisse plurimum et accinctam pharetra, cervis capriisque cursu

3   atque sagittis fuisse infestam. Inde cum in acriores devenisset vires, ursos amplecti ausam, pardos leonesque insequi, obvios expectare, capere et occidere ac in predam trahere; et impavidam, nunc hos nunc illos saltus et prerupta montium discurrere, lustra perscrutari ferarum et sub divo somnos etiam per noctem capere, imbres, estus et frigora mira tolerantia superare, <amores hominum et contubernia spernere>[1] assuetam et virginitatem summopere colere.

4   Quibus fugata muliebri mollicie adeo eam in virile robur duratam aiunt ut coetaneos iuvenes luctis palestricisque ludis omnibus viribus superaret.

5   Tandem, instante etate nubili, amicorum consilio, Odenato, iuveni equis studiis durato et longe Palmirenorum nobiliori principi, nuptam volunt. Erat hec speciosa corpore, esto paululum fusca colore; sic enim, urente sole, regionis illius omnes sunt incole; preterea nigris oculis niveisque dentibus decora.

6   Que cum cerneret Odenatum, capto a Sapore rege Persarum Valeriano Augusto turpique servitio damnato et Galieno filio effeminate torpescente, ad orientale occupandum imperium intentum, non immemor duriciei pristine armis formositatem tegere et sub viro militare disposuit; et cum eo, sumpto regio nomine et ornatu, atque cum Herode privigno, collectis copiis, in Saporem, late iam Mesopotamiam occupantem, animose progressa est; et, nullis parcens laboribus, nunc ducis, nunc militis officia peragens, non so-

Ptolemies, the rulers of Egypt, although there is no record of her parents.

We are also told that from childhood she scorned all womanly 2 occupations and, having toughened her young body, she generally lived in forests and groves; girded with the quiver, she hunted and killed goats and stags with her arrows. Then, after her strength 3 had developed, Zenobia dared to confront bears and to pursue, lie in wait for, capture, and kill leopards and lions, dragging them away as booty. Fearlessly she wandered hither and yon through ravines and rugged mountain slopes, exploring the lairs of wild beasts, sleeping in the open at night, and enduring rain, heat, and cold with admirable fortitude. It was her practice to scorn the love and companionship of men and to place great store by her virginity.

By such means did Zenobia rid herself of feminine weakness. 4 Reportedly she acquired such hard, masculine vigor that sheer strength enabled her to subdue her young male contemporaries in wrestling and gymnastic contests.

At last she arrived at marriageable age. Our sources say that, on 5 the advice of her friends, Zenobia married Odaenathus, a young man toughened by similar pursuits who was by far the noblest of Palmyra's princes. She had a beautiful body despite being somewhat dark-skinned, as are all the inhabitants of that region of the burning sun. Her dark eyes and white teeth also contributed to her attractiveness.

At this time the emperor Valerian had been captured by Sapor, 6 king of the Persians, and condemned to disgraceful servitude, while his son Gallienus was living a life of effete idleness. Zenobia saw that Odaenathus was determined to conquer the Eastern Empire; and so, remembering her earlier austerity, she decided to conceal her beauty with armor and serve under her husband. With him she assumed the royal title and insignia, and with her stepson Herodes she gathered an army and marched courageously

lum acerrimum virum et bellorum expertum virtute armorum superavit, sed creditum eius opere Mesopotamiam in iurisdictionem
venisse et Saporem, castris eius cum concubinis et ingenti preda
captis, usque Thesiphontem pulsum atque secutum.

7   Nec multo post Quietum, Macriani filium, qui patrio sub nomine orientis imperium intraverat, ut opprimeretur curavit vigilanti studio.

Et cum iam omnem orientem ad Romanos spectantem una
cum viro pacatum obtineret, et ecce a Meonio consobrino suo
Odenatus una cum Herode filio occisus est; et, ut quidam asserunt, ob invidiam, existimantibus aliis, Zenobiam in mortem
Herodis prestitisse consensum, eo quod sepius eius damnasset
molliciem et ut filiis Herenniano et Thimolao, quos ex Odenato
susceperat, successio cederet regni.

8   Et imperante Meonio aliquandiu quievit. Verum Meonio brevi
a militibus suis trucidato, quasi possessione vacua derelicta, generosi animi mulier in predesideratum imperium intravit continuo
et, filiis eius adhuc parvulis, imperiali sagulo humeris perfusa et
regiis ornata comparuit, filiorumque nomine, longe magis quam
9   sexui conveniret, gubernavit imperium. Nec segniter; nam in eam
nec Galienus, nec post illum Claudius imperator aliquid attem-
ptare ausi sunt. Similiter nec orientales Egyptii neque Arabes aut
Saraceni, vel etiam Armeni populi, quin imo eius timentes potentiam suos posse servare terminos fuere contenti.

10   Fuit enim illi tanta bellorum industria et adeo acris militie di-

against Sapor, who was already occupying much of Mesopotamia. Zenobia spared herself no toil, sometimes performing the duties of a general and at other times those of an ordinary soldier. Not only did she conquer by force of arms a tough foe experienced in war, but it was believed that through her actions Mesopotamia came under her jurisdiction. After capturing Sapor's camp with his concubines and a large amount of booty, she drove him back and pursued him as far as Ctesiphon.

Shortly thereafter, Zenobia attended very ably to the task of 7 crushing Quietus, son of Macrianus, who in his father's name had taken possession of the Eastern empire.

Now she and her husband controlled all the Eastern empire which bordered on Roman territory. Then suddenly Odaenathus and his son Herodes were killed by a cousin named Maeonius. According to some accounts, envy was the cause, but others report that Zenobia had consented to Herodes' death because she had often condemned his softness and wanted to ensure that the succession of the kingdom would fall to Herennianus and Timolaus, the sons she had borne to Odaenathus.

For some time Zenobia remained quiet during Maeonius' reign. 8 But Maeonius was soon murdered by his soldiers. With the throne left vacant, as it were, this noble-minded woman immediately entered into possession of the empire she had long desired. Since her children were still young, she draped the imperial mantle around her own shoulders, put on the royal insignia, and ruled the empire in her sons' name longer than was suitable to her sex. Nor was Zenobia a weak ruler: neither the emperor Gallienus nor 9 the emperor Claudius after him dared make any attempt against her. Nor did the Eastern peoples: neither the Egyptians, the Arabs, the Saracens, nor even the Armenians. Indeed, they feared her power and were happy to be able to maintain their own borders.

So great was Zenobia's zeal in fighting and so strict was the 10

sciplina, ut eque illam magni penderent sui exercitus et timerent. Apud quos nunquam concionata est nisi galeata; et in expeditionibus vehiculo carpentario perrarissime utebatur, equo sepius incedebat et nonnunquam tribus vel quatuor[2] milibus passuum cum militibus pedes signa precedebat: nec fastidivit cum ducibus suis quandoque bibisse, cum esset alias sobria; sic cum persis et armenis principibus ut illos urbanitate et facetia superaret.

11 Fuit tamen adeo pudicitie severa servatrix ut nedum ab aliis abstineret omnino, sed etiam Odenato viro suo, dum viveret, se nunquam exhibere, preter ad filios procreandos, voluisse legimus; hac in hoc semper habita diligentia, ut post concubitum unum, tam diu abstineret ab altero, donec adverteret utrum concepisset ex illo; quod si contigerat, nunquam preter post partus purgationes a viro tangi patiebatur ulterius; si autem non concepisse perceperat, se ultro poscenti viro consentiebat.

12 O laudabile iudicium mulieris! Satis quidem apparet arbitratam nil ob aliud a natura mortalibus immissam libidinem quam ut prolis innovatione continua conservetur posteritas et reliquum, tan-
13 quam supervacaneum, viciosum. Perrarissimas quidem huiuscemodi moris comperies mulieres.

Hec tamen ne a mente differrent ministeria, ad oportuna domestica preter eunuchos, etate atque moribus graves, neminem unquam, vel perraro, admicti voluit. Vixit preterea ritu regio et magnifico sumptu usa, ea qua reges utuntur pompa; persicoque more voluit adorari et ad instar romanorum imperatorum convivia celebravit, in eis vasis usa aureis gemmatisque quibus olim usam Cleopatram acceperat; et quanquam servatrix thesaurorum per-

discipline of her campaigns that the troops accorded her fear and respect in equal measure. She never addressed the soldiers without wearing her helmet; while on expeditions, she rarely used a carriage, went often on horseback, and sometimes would walk ahead of the standards for three or four miles with the infantry. Zenobia did not shrink from occasional drinking with her generals, though at other times she refrained. She also drank with the Persian and Armenian princes for the purpose of besting them in wit and affability.

Nevertheless, she guarded her virtue so jealously that not only 11 did she shun relations with other men but also, as we have read, she never gave herself to her husband Odaenathus, while he was alive, except for the purpose of procreation. Zenobia was so careful about this that, after sleeping with her husband once, she would abstain long enough before the next time to see whether she had conceived, and, if she had, she would not let him touch her again until the purification after the birth. If, however, she found that she was not pregnant, she would give herself willingly to her husband at his request.

How praiseworthy was this woman's attitude! Clearly she 12 thought that nature had instilled sexual drive in human beings for no other reason than to preserve the species by a continuous replenishment of offspring; beyond this, the instinct was apparently superfluous and therefore a vice. Very rarely indeed will you find 13 women of this stamp.

Moreover, so that the servants would not distract her from her purpose, Zenobia never, or very rarely, let anyone perform the necessary household tasks unless they were eunuchs of sound morals and advanced age. She lived royally and sumptuously, with a sovereign's pomp. She wanted to be worshipped in the Persian manner and gave banquets like those of the Roman emperors, using jewelled and golden vessels which she believed had once been used by Cleopatra. Although she guarded her treasuries very carefully, no

maxima esset, nemo, ubi oportunum visum est, ea magnificentior aut profusior visus est.

14 Et si plurimum venationibus armisque vacasset, non obstitere hec quin literas egyptias nosceret et sub Longino philosopho preceptore grecas etiam disceret. Quarum suffragio hystorias omnes latinas grecas et barbaras summo cum studio vidit et memorie commendavit. Nec hoc tantum; quin imo creditum est illas etiam sub epythomatis brevitate traxisse et preter suum ydioma novit egyptium eoque, cum syriacum sciret, usa est.

15 Quid multa? Tanti profecto fuit hec ut, Gallieno atque Aureolo et Claudio Augusto sublatis, et Aureliano, integre virtutis homine, in principatu suffecto, ad ignominiam romani nominis expiandam

16 et³ ingentem gloriam consequendam, in se traxerit. Nam, marcomannico bello peracto, et Rome rebus compositis, Aurelianus cum omni cura zenobianam expeditionem assumpsit, et multis egregie, adversus barbaras nationes eundo, confectis, cum legionibus tandem haud⁴ longe Emessam civitatem devenit, quam penes Zenobia, in nullo perterrita, una cum Zaba quodam, quem belli susceperat sotium, cum exercitu suo consederat.

17 Ibi inter Aureli<an>um⁵ et Zenobiam de summa rerum acriter et diu pugnatum est. Ad ultimum, cum romana virtus videretur superior, Zenobia cum suis in fugam versa Palmira sese recepit. In qua evestigio a victore obsessa est. Quam cum aliquandiu, nullas volens conditiones deditionis audire, mira solertia defendisset, in

18 penuriam oportunarum rerum deducta est. Hinc nequeuntibus Palmirenis Aurelianorum obsistere viribus, interceptis etiam ab eodem Persis Armenisque et Saracenis auxilio Zenobie venienti-

19 bus, armorum vi civitas a Romanis capta est. Ex qua cum Zenobia vecta dromonibus cum filiis in Persas aufugeret, ab aurelianis militibus secuta et capta cum filiis, Aureliano viva presentata est. Ex

one was more grand or lavish than Zenobia when she thought it proper.

She spent most of her time in hunting and fighting, but these 14 pursuits did not prevent her from learning Egyptian, and she also learned Greek from the philosopher Longinus. Zenobia's knowledge of these languages enabled her to read voraciously and commit to memory all the Latin, Greek, and barbarian histories. Moreover, she is believed to have composed epitomes of these works. Besides her own language, she knew Egyptian and spoke it although she also knew Syriac.

In short, Zenobia's greatness was such that, after the death of 15 the emperors Gallienus, Aureolus, and Claudius, it induced their successor Aurelian, who was a thoroughly upright man, to move against her for the purpose of redeeming the dishonored Roman name and acquiring immense glory. When the war with the Mar- 16 comanni had ended and everything was under control in Rome, Aurelian mounted a carefully prepared expedition against Zenobia. He successfully attacked many barbarian nations and finally drew near with his legions to the city of Emesa. There Zenobia, who was not at all afraid, had encamped along with Zaba, whom she had taken as an ally in the war.

A long and bitter struggle ensued between Zenobia and 17 Aurelian. Finally, when the Roman forces appeared to gain the upper hand, Zenobia was forced to retreat in flight with her men to Palmyra, where she was immediately besieged by the conqueror. For some time she refused to hear of any terms of surrender and defended the city with great skill. Then she reached a point where she lacked the necessary supplies. The people of Palmyra could 18 not withstand Aurelian's mighty forces and, after intercepting the Persians, Armenians, and Saracens who were coming to Zenobia's assistance, the Romans took the city by storm. Zenobia and her 19 children left the city on camels and fled towards Persia, but they were pursued and captured by Aurelian's soldiers and she was pre-

quo non aliter quam si permaximum[6] superasset ducem et acerrimum reipublice hostem, Aurelianus gloriatus est eamque triunpho
servavit et adduxit cum filiis Romam.

20   Inde ab Aureliano celebratus <triunphus>,[7] spectaculo Zenobie
admirandus, in quo, inter alia egregia et memoratu dignissima,
currum duxit, quem sibi ex auro gemmisque preciosissimum Zenobia fabricari fecerat, sperans se Romam venturam, non quidem
captivam, sed rerum dominam atque triunphaturam et romanum
21   possessuram imperium; quem et ipsa cum filiis precessit. Verum
ipsa catenis aureis collo manibus pedibusque iniectis corona et vestimentis regiis ac margaritis et lapidibus pretiosis honusta, adeo
ut, cum roboris inexhausti esset, pondere fessa persepe subsisteret.

22   Sane consumato triunpho thesauro et virtute spectabili, aiunt
illam privato in habitu inter romanas matronas cum filiis senuisse,
concessa sibi a senatu possessione apud Tiburtum, que zenobiana
diu postmodum ab ea denominata est, haud longe a divi Adriani
palatio, quod eo in loco est cui Conche ab incolis dicebatur.

:   CI   :

De Iohanna anglica papa

1   Iohannes,[1] esto vir nomine videatur, sexu tamen femina fuit.
Cuius inaudita temeritas ut orbi toto notissima fieret et in posterum nosceretur effecit.

Huius etsi patriam Maguntium quidam fuisse dicant, quod
proprium fuerit nomen vix cognitum est, esto sint qui dicant, ante
2   pontificatus assumptionem, fuisse Gilibertum. Hoc constat, as-

sented alive to the emperor. Aurelian prided himself on this as if he had conquered a great leader and a bitter enemy of the state. He reserved her for his triumph and took her to Rome with her children.

There the triumph was celebrated, Zenobia's presence making 20 it a marvelous sight. Among other outstanding things worthy of remembrance, he brought the precious chariot adorned with gold and gems which Zenobia had had built for herself when she hoped to come to Rome, not as a prisoner, but as a triumphant conqueror arriving to take possession of the Roman Empire. Now she walked in front of the chariot with her children. Fettered with 21 gold chains around her neck, hands, and feet and burdened by her crown and royal robes and pearls and precious stones, she was exhausted by their weight and often had to stop, despite her inexhaustible vigor.

At the conclusion of this triumph, conspicuous for its treasure 22 and its valor, Zenobia is said to have lived privately with her children amidst the women of Rome until she reached old age. The Senate granted her an estate near Tivoli; long called Zenobia after her own name, it was not far from the palace of the emperor Hadrian, in the place which the inhabitants called Conca.

: CI :

Joan, an Englishwoman and Pope

From her name John would seem to be a man, but in reality she 1 was a woman. Her unprecedented audacity made her known to the whole world and to posterity.

Some authorities claim she was from Mainz. There is little evidence for her real name, but it is said to have been Gilbertus before she became pope. This much is known according to some 2

sertione quorundam, eam virginem a scolastico iuvene dilectam, quem adeo dilexisse ferunt ut, posita verecundia virginali atque pavore femineo, clam e domo patris effugeret, et amasium adolescentis in habitu et mutato sequeretur nomine; apud quem, in Anglia studentem, clericus ex<is>timatus[2] ab omnibus et Veneri et literarum militavit studiis.

3   Inde iuvene morte subtracto, cum se cognosceret ingenio valere et dulcedine traheretur scientie, retento habitu nec adherere voluit alteri, nec se feminam profiteri, quin imo studiis vigilanter insistens, adeo in liberalibus et sacris literis profecit ut pre ceteris excellens haberetur.

4   Et sic, scientia mirabili predita, iam etate provecta, ex Anglia se Romam contulit; et ibidem aliquibus annis in trivio legens insignes habuit auditores; et cum, preter scientiam, singulari honestate ac sanctitate polleret, homo ab omnibus creditus. Et ideo

5 notus a multis, solvente Leone quinto pontifice summo carnis debitum, a venerandissimis patribus comuni consensu premortuo in papatu suffectus est nominatusque Iohannes; cui, si vir fuisset, ut octavus esset in numero contigisset.

6   Que tamen non verita ascendere Piscatoris cathedram et sacra ministeria omnia, nulli mulierum a christiana religione concessum, tractare agere et aliis exhibere, apostolatus culmen aliquibus annis

7 obtinuit Christique vicariatum femina gessit in terris. Sane ex alto Deus, plebi sue misertus, tam insignem locum teneri, tanto presideri populo tanque infausto errore decipi a femina passus non est et illam indebita audentem nec sinentem suis in manibus liquit.

sources: while still a maiden, she became the sweetheart of a youthful student. Reportedly she loved him so much that, casting aside virginal modesty and feminine timidity, she fled in secret from her father's house. Changing her name and dressing as a young man, she followed her lover. For the duration of his studies in England she remained in his company and was universally taken for a cleric while serving in the armies of Love and Literature.

Then her lover died. Joan, realizing that she had a good mind 3 and drawn by the charms of learning, retained her masculine dress and refused to attach herself to anyone else or admit that she was a woman. She persisted diligently in her studies and made such progress in liberal and sacred letters that she was deemed to excel everyone.

And so, equipped with an admirable array of knowledge, Joan 4 left England and went to Rome. She was no longer young. In Rome she lectured for a number of years on the trivium and had distinguished students. Besides her erudition, Joan was esteemed for her outstanding virtue and holiness, and thus was believed by everyone to be a man. In this way she became widely known, and, 5 when Pope Leo V died, she was elected to succeed him as pontiff by the unanimous vote of the cardinals and was called John. If she had been a man, she would have had the title of John VIII.

This woman was not afraid to mount the Fisherman's throne, 6 to perform all the sacred offices, and to administer them to others (something that the Christian religion does not permit any woman to do). For a few years she occupied the highest apostolate and a woman acted as Christ's Vicar on earth. Then from on high 7 God took pity on his people. He did not suffer a woman to hold so eminent an office, govern so great a people, and deceive them with so inauspicious a misapprehension. He abandoned to her own devices this person who boldly persisted in doing what should not have been done.

8   Quam ob rem suadente diabolo[3] qui eam in tam scelestam deduxerat atque detinebat audaciam, <actum est>[4] ut, que privata precipuam honestatem servaverat, in tam sublimi evecta pontificatu in ardorem deveniret libidinis. Nec ei, que sexum diu fingere noverat, artes ad explendam defuere lasciviam. Nam adinvento qui clam Petri successorem conscenderet et exurentem pruriginem defricaret, actum est ut papa conciperet.

9   O scelus indignum, o invicta patientia Dei! Quid tandem? Ei que fascinare diu oculos potuerat hominum, ad incestuosum par-
10   tum occultandum defecit ingenium. Nam cum is preter spem propinquior esset termino, dum ex Ianiculo, amburbale sacrum celebrans, Lateranum peteret inter Coloseum et Clementis pontificis edem, obstetrice non vocata, enixa publice patuit qua fraude tam diu, preter amasium, ceteros decepisset homines. Et hinc a patribus in tenebras exteriores abiecta, cum fetu misella abiit.

11   Ad cuius detestandam spurcitiem et nominis continuandam memoriam, in hodiernum usque summi pontifices rogationum cum clero et populo sacrum agentes, cum locum partus, medio eius in itinere positum, abominentur, eo omisso, declinant per diverticula vicosque et sic, loco detestabili postergato, reintrantes iter perficiunt quod cepere.

In private life, Joan had been remarkably virtuous. But at the 8
instigation of the devil, who had led her into this wicked act of audacity and caused her to continue in it, she fell prey to burning
lust once she had risen to the lofty pontificate. Nor did Joan, who
had long been able to hide her sex, lack the wiles necessary to
quench her desire. She found someone who would secretly mount
Peter's successor and scratch her uncontrollable itch; and so it
happened that the pope became pregnant.

What a shameful crime! How invincible is God's patience! 9
But what followed? This woman, who had been able for so long
to bewitch men's eyes, lacked the wit to conceal the shameful
birth. When Joan celebrated the Rogation Days[a] in a procession 10
from the Janiculum Hill to the Lateran Palace, she was nearer the
end of her pregnancy than she had thought. Between the Colos-
seum and the church of Pope Clement, she gave birth in public
and without the help of a midwife, showing how long she had deceived everyone except her lover. The cardinals then cast her out,[b]
and the wretched woman departed with her child.

Even today the popes, when they celebrate the Rogation Days 11
with the clergy and the people, condemn her foul actions and perpetuate her infamy. The place where Joan gave birth is located at
the halfway point of the procession; they abominate this site and
avoid it by turning away and taking side streets. When they have
bypassed the hated place, they return to the main road and complete the initial route.

: CII :

De Yrene const<ant>inopolitana[1] imperatrice

1 Yrenes atheniensis nobilissima mulier fuit et insignis decoris conspicua; quam cum a patria Constantinopolim Constantinus imperator vocasset, eam Leoni, seu Leocazario, filio dedit in coniugem et, post dicti Constantini mortem, Romanorum imperatrix effecta, ex viro filium peperit Constantinum nomine.

2 Demum, rebus humanis[2] Leone subtracto, cum Constantino parvulo admodum adolescentulo per decennium egregie imperio 3 presedit. Sed eo iam grandiusculo asserenteque sibi dominium soli deberi, eam octo annis — ut placet aliquibus — a societate removit.

4 Tandem ingentis animi mulier et imperandi avida, cum in discordiam devenisset cum filio, femineo quodam astu iuvenem, fidentem viribus[3] suis, cepit et depositum ab imperio servari iussit in carcere; soliumque a quo universus orbis olim iura susceperat sola conscendit et pre ceteris mortalibus clara imperatrix annis quinque ingenti cum gloria imperavit.

5 Porro amicorum Constantini opere actum est ut, Armeniorum auxiliis, e culmine deponeretur Yrenes et Constantinus, solutus a vinculis, patrio reassumeretur in throno; qui in matrem mitior, quam eam in se comperisset, et plurimum in amicorum viribus spei habens non illam carceri tradidit, sed in palatio Eleutherii, quod ipsamet construi fecerat, cum omni rerum copia fuit seposuisse contentus, amicis eius omnibus inde relegatis exilio.

6 Attamen cum is infeliciter adversus Bulgaros bellum inisset tenptassentque[4] ob id primates eum ab imperio movere eiusque loco Nycephorum quendam patruum suum substituere, exasperatus ira in turpem prorupit sevitiam: nam Nycephoro et Christophoro fratribus linguas evulsit. Hinc Alexium Armenie patritium

: CII :

Irene, Empress of Constantinople

Irene was an Athenian and a noblewoman of outstanding beauty. 1
The emperor Constantine summoned her to Constantinople from
Greece and gave her in marriage to his son Leo, also called Leo the
Chazar. When Constantine died, she became empress of the Ro-
mans and bore her husband a son named Constantine.

After Leo's death, Irene and the young Constantine governed 2
the empire well for ten years. Upon reaching manhood, her son as- 3
serted his right to rule alone and for eight years (according to
some sources) he excluded Irene from their joint rulership. Finally 4
this woman of great spirit, who thirsted for power, quarreled with
Constantine. He was confident of his own strength but with feminine cunning Irene seized him, removed him from the throne, and
had him imprisoned. Thus she alone occupied the throne from
which the whole world had once received its laws. She became the
most famous person in the world and ruled gloriously as empress
for five years.

Then Constantine's supporters managed, with help from the 5
Armenians, to pull Irene down from her lofty place. Constantine
himself was freed from prison and placed once again on the throne
of his fathers. He showed his mother greater kindness than he had
experienced at her hands; placing great trust in his adherents'
strength, he did not incarcerate Irene. With all her friends in exile,
he was content to send her away to live in the Eleutherian Palace
which she herself had built.

But Constantine entered into a war against the Bulgarians with 6
unfortunate results, and this prompted an attempt by the nobles
to depose and replace him with a certain Nicephorus, his uncle.
Goaded by anger, Constantine exploded into a black fury and tore
out the tongues of Nicephorus and his brother Christopher. Then

orbavit luminibus et Mariam coniugem suam monasticum habitum summere coegit, superinducta Theodote cubicularia quam
evestigio coronavit.

7   Quibus enormitatibus oculata mulier Yrenes que, esto coacta
fortunam deposuisset imperii, egregium tamen servaverat animum, spe sumpta reassummendi principatus, si aurum largiretur
optimatibus, profuse reseratis thesauris quos, dum imperaret, eo
in palatio, in quo seposita habitabat, absconderat, clam animos
principum imperii sibi fecit accommodos; cumque eos amplis muneribus in suam deduxisset sententiam, egit ut qui illam deposue-
rant Constanti<n>um[5] filium caperent lumi<ni>busque[6] privarent;
et sic animosa mulier sublatum olim sibi reassumpsit imperium;
Constantinus autem morbo correptus interiit.

8   Tandem cum quinque iterum imperasset annis, a Nycepharo[7]
rebellante in palatio Eleuterii obsessa est. Qui cum ab Acharisio
patriarcha constantinopolitano dyadema suscepisset imperii, fa-
ventibus Leone et Triphylo patritiis atque Sycopeo[8] sacellario, nu-
per ab Yrene ditatis, actum est ut[9] ad Yrenem cum humilitate intraret blanditiisque ageret, ea tamen advertente nec aliud preter id
palatium in quo erat ex imperio postulante, ut, obtenta petitorum
promissione, aperiret omnes illi thesauros. Quibus obtentis nepha-
rius homo, fide fraudata, illam Lesbos relegavit in exilium, in qua
iam senex vitam clara terminavit mulier.

9   Alii tamen de fine huius aliter sentire videntur. Dicunt quidem,
matre et filio discordantibus, et vicissim sese imperio privantibus,
Romanos ab eis descivisse et in Karolum magnum, Francorum
tunc regem, suum imperium transtulisse eumque tenptasse[10] ut in
unum, quod dividi videbatur, imperium redigeret Yrenis nuptiis
eique Yrenes hesisse. Quod cum advertisset Eutitius patritius,

he blinded Alexius (an Armenian patrician), forced his own wife Maria to take the veil, and married in her stead the chambermaid Theodote, whom he immediately crowned.

Irene was an astute woman who had maintained her noble 7 spirit despite the fact that she had been compelled to lay down her power. Having witnessed Constantine's atrocities, she began to hope that she might regain her rule by showering the aristocrats with gold. Thanks to extravagant gifts from the treasure she had hidden during her reign in the very palace where she later lived in banishment, Irene secretly gained the good will of the princes of the empire. When she had won them over to her side with lavish presents, she arranged that the men who had deposed her from the throne should seize her son Constantine and blind him. And so this courageous woman recovered the empire which had once been taken from her. Constantine, however, took ill and died.

After ruling for another five years, Irene was besieged in the 8 Eleutherian Palace by the rebel Nicephorus. He had received the imperial crown from Acarisius, Patriarch of Constantinople. With the support of the patricians Leo and Triphilus and the chaplain Sycopeus, all of whom Irene had recently made rich, Nicephorus approached the empress in a humble and flattering manner. Irene, however, took note of this and asked for nothing from her empire except the palace where she lived; she agreed, if this were promised her, to reveal to him all her treasure. Once he had obtained her money, the wicked man went back on his word and exiled her to Lesbos where, now in her old age, this famous woman died.

Other authorities, however, give a different version of her 9 death. They say that when mother and son were at odds and had deprived each other by turns of the empire, the Romans broke away from them and gave the empire to Charlemagne, then king of the Franks. He tried to unite the divided empire by proposing marriage to Irene, and she consented. When this came to the no-

confestim sublimavit Nycephorum et obsidione Yrenem ad intrandum monasterium, dimisso imperio, coegisse et in eodem demum
eam consenuisse.

: CIII :

De Enguldrada florentina virgine

1   Enguldrada ex Ravennatum olim clarissima civitatis nostre familia
duxit originem. Quam ego, nec immerito, ob insignem eius coram
principe Romanorum, ad defendendam animi sui sinceritatem, audaciam, inter claras ponendam censui.

2   Hec enim cum in templo, olim Marti, postea vero Deo sub Iohannis Baptiste vocabulo dicato, cum pluribus ex florentinis matronis diem celebrem ageret, contigit ut Octo quartus Romanorum
imperator, qui tum[1] forte Florentiam venerat, ad exhilarandum
festum et sua presentia augendum, maxima cum procerum comitiva templum intraret et cum e sublimiore loci sede et ornatu
templi et civium concursum et circumsedentes matronas inspiceret, ut in Enguldradam oculos forte defigeret factum est.

3   Cuius cum aliquandiu formositatem et habitum nulla varietate
distinctum honestatemque eius et gravitatem puellarem admiratus
laudasset, in Bilicionem quendam, unum ex civibus etate atque
nobilitate venerabilem virum et militia eo tunc forsan insignem, ei
assistentem verba convertit inquiens: 'Quenam queso virgo hec
econtra sedens, nostro iudicio honestate et oris decore ceteras an
4   tecedens?' Cui Bilicio subridens, faceta quadam urbanitate respondit: 'Serenissime princeps, qualiscunque sit, talis est ut, dum velis,
te deosculetur, si iussero.'

5   Que verba dum percepisset auribus virgo, confestim indignata
est, egre ferens patrem tam facile de constantia sua et virginei pudoris custodia opinionem ostendisse, nec diu tulisse noxam potuit,

tice of the patrician Eutitius, he immediately elevated Nicephorus to the throne. Irene was besieged and forced to abandon her throne and enter a convent, where she lived to an advanced age.

: CIII :

Gualdrada, a Florentine Maiden

Gualdrada was a descendant of the Ravignani, formerly an illustrious family in our city. I have decided to include her among the famous women for a good reason, namely, her remarkable daring in defending her integrity in the presence of the Roman emperor.

One day she was celebrating a feast day with many other Florentine women in the church formerly dedicated to Mars and later to the true God under the name of St. John the Baptist. The Holy Roman Emperor Otto IV, who had come to Florence by chance, entered the church with a large and princely retinue for the purpose of making the occasion more joyous and splendid by his attendance. From his lofty seat, as he inspected the furnishings of the church, the assembled citizens, and the women sitting all around, he happened to fix his eyes upon Gualdrada.

Admiringly the emperor praised for quite some time the beauty, simplicity of dress, dignity, and earnestness of the young girl. Then he inquired of a bystander named Bellincione, a Florentine citizen revered for his age and nobility and perhaps distinguished at that time also for his military service: "Who, pray, is that girl seated facing us, who in my opinion surpasses all the others in dignity and in the beauty of her face?" Bellincione smiled and answered with a certain witty sophistication, "Your Majesty, whoever she may be, she will kiss you at my bidding if you desire it."

When she heard these words, Gualdrada was immediately indignant and distressed that her father had displayed a frivolous attitude towards her constancy and the protection of her maidenly

1

2

3

4

5

quin imo nil adhuc respondente principe, surgens purpureo respersa colore, elevatis paululum in patrem oculis et inde deiectis in
terram, voce infracta, humili tamen dixit: 'Siste queso, mi pater, ne
dixeris; nam si violentia absit, nemo ecastor, eum preter quem tu
michi legitimo sanctoque coniugio iuncturus es, quod offers tam
profuse habiturus est.'

6   O Deus bone! Nusquam quod ex animo bene eleganterque dictum est ab ingentis animi viro cecidisse permissum est. Stetit Cesar aliquantulum mirabundus; demum, germanica non obsistente
barbarie, ea iam cognita, collegit ex verbis animo virginei pectoris
sanctum castumque propositum; et cum longa dicacitate virginis
indignationem laudasset et verba, Guidonem quendam nobilem
iuvenem accersiri iussit et, ne diu careret virgo cui posset honestum, si vellet, exhibere osculum, presente atque gratias agente
patre, Enguldradam, viro maturam, a se dotatam egregie, antequam moveretur, Guidoni dedit in coniugem; arbitratus quod
dixerat iusti bonique non solum virginis in archano consistere, sed
ab ampliori virtutis fomite vi merite indignationis emissum et ob
id eam cesareo munere fuisse dignissimam.

7   Sic igitur que virgo templum intraverat, ob integritatem pudice
mentis in domum patriam, maxima genitoris et suorum alacritate,
desponsata rediit; et in processu, fecundos enixa partus, ornatam
generosa et in hodiernum usque amplo virorum numero perseverante prosapia, diem claudens, viri splendidam domum liquit.

8   Hec dixisse placuit in dedecus modernarum, quarum tanta
animi levitas est et effrenati sunt mores, ut oculis gestibusque irruere in quorumcunque intuentium videantur amplexus.

modesty. Nor could she long endure the insult. Indeed, the emperor had not yet answered when, blushing, she rose, looked briefly at her father, and then, lowering her eyes to the ground, said in a firm but respectful voice, "Please stop, Father; don't speak. For by Heaven, unless force is used, absolutely no one except the man to whom you will give me in lawful and holy matrimony shall receive what you are offering so freely."

Good God! What is well and elegantly said from the heart is 6 never lost on a man of great spirit. For a little while the emperor remained lost in wonder. Then, though a German and a barbarian, he realized who she was and grasped the depths of her holy and chaste resolve. After a long and voluble speech praising the girl's outspoken indignation, he sent for a certain young nobleman named Guido. Before the emperor departed, he presented Gualdrada, who was of marriageable age, with a fine dowry and gave her in marriage to Guido, so that the girl would not be for long without someone whom she could honorably kiss if so she wished. Gualdrada's father was present and expressed his gratitude. The emperor thought that the good and proper sentiment she had shown not only resided in the secret places of her maidenly heart but sprang also from a more profound impulse to virtue which had emerged under the pressure of righteous indignation; hence she was worthy of an imperial gift.

Thus, thanks to her determination to remain chaste, the girl 7 who had entered the church as a virgin returned betrothed, amid the great joy of her father and her family, to her father's house. In due course she had many children and at her death left her husband's illustrious house adorned by her own noble progeny, whose descendants still survive in great numbers.

I decided to write this account as a reproach to the girls of our 8 own day who are so giddy and of such loose morals that, at the wink of an eye or any gesture, they rush into the arms of whoever looks at them.

: CIV :

De Constantia Romanorum imperatrice et regina Sycilie

1 Constantia e summo orbis cardine terris Romanorum imperatrix effulsit. Verum, quoniam iam multis comune decus admirationem intuentium minuisse videtur, alia claritatis causa nostro evo apparere volentibus querenda est; que huic non defuit. Nam si ullo alio non detur merito, unico saltem partu undique conspicua facta est.

2 Fuit hec Guilielmi, optimi quondam Syculorum regis, filia. Cuius in ortu cum adesset, ut aiunt plurimi, Ioachin quidam calaber abbas, prophetico dotatus spiritu, Guilielmo dixit natam re-

3 gni Sycilie desolationem futuram. Qua prefatione stupefactus rex atque perterritus, cum prestitisset vaticinio fidem, secum cepit anxia meditatione revolvere quo pacto posset contingere istud a femina; nec aliter videns quam a coniuge vel a filio, regno compatiens suo, avertere, si posset, istud consilio statuit; eamque, ut connubii atque prolis auferretur spes, virgunculam monasticis clausam claustris egit ut Deo perpetuam virginitatem voto promicteret.

4 Nec aspernandum, si profuisset consilium. Sed quid adversus Deum, iuste mortalium scelesta facinora expiantem, stolidi imbecillesque conatus exponimus? Minimo equidem et unico frustramur inpulsu.

5 Hec autem cum, sanctissimo patre fratreque extinctis, nemine, se preter, legitimo regni herede superstite, iuventutem omnem peregisset iamque facta videretur anus, sumpsissetque post obitum Guilielmi regni dyadema Tancredus regulus, et post eum Guilielmus filius, iuvenculus adhuc, eoque itum esset, seu crebra seu minus digna regum innovatione, ut, factionibus procerum undique

: CIV :

Constance, Empress of Rome and Queen of Sicily

From her lofty place atop the world the Roman empress Con- 1
stance once shone throughout the lands. But the admiration of
onlookers seems to have lessened since this honor has by now
been shared with many other women. So another cause of renown
must be sought by those who wish her to be conspicuous in our
time, and such a reason is not lacking in the present instance. If
for no other merit, Constance is famous everywhere because of her
only son.

She was the daughter of William, who had been in his day an 2
excellent king of Sicily.[a] Present at her birth, according to many
sources, was a certain Joachim, a Calabrian abbot endowed with a
prophetic spirit;[b] he told William that his daughter would cause
the destruction of the Kingdom of Sicily. William believed this 3
prediction. In amazement and terror, he began anxiously to brood
on how this could be caused by a woman: the only possibilities he
could visualize involved a husband or a child. Out of compassion
for his kingdom, he formed a plan to prevent, if possible, this outcome. To remove all hope of marriage and children, he shut up the
little girl in a monastery and made her promise God eternal virginity.

This would not have been a reprehensible plan if it had suc- 4
ceeded. But why do we powerless fools pit our strength against
God, who justly punishes the wicked deeds of mortals? A single,
tiny blow is enough to frustrate our designs.

After the death of her saintly father and her brother, there was 5
no surviving legitimate heir to the kingdom except Constance. She
was no longer young; indeed, she now looked like an old woman.
When William died, Prince Tancred assumed the kingly crown,
and after him his son William who was still a boy. Whether it was

bellis scaturientibus, ferro igneque regnum omne in exterminium trahi videretur; quam ob rem quibusdam compatientibus infortunio menti incidit quod postmodum subsecutum est, Constantiam scilicet alicui insigni principi in coniugem dari, ut eius opere et potentia pestiferi sedarentur tumultus.

6   Nec absque dolo atque labore ingenti obtentum est, summo consentiente pontifice, ut in eam Constantia deveniret sententiam, scilicet ut nuberet, cum immobilis staret in professionis sue proposito, et annosa etiam videretur etas obsistere. Sed cum, ea etiam renuente, res adeo processissent ut commode nequirent retrahi, Henrico Romanorum imperatori, olim Frederici primi filio, desponsata est.

7   Et sic rugosa anus, sacris omissis claustris positisque sanctimonialium victis, cultu ornata regio, nuptaque et imperatrix devenit in medium; et que Deo virginitatem dicarat perpetuam, thalamum principis intrans nuptialemque conscendens thorum, eam invita deposuit. Ex quo factum est, non absque audientium admiratione, ut quinquagesimum et quintum etatis sue annum agens, annosa conciperet.

8   Et cum tarda penes omnes conceptionis huiusmodi fides esset dolusque crederetur a pluribus, ad auferendam suspitionem provide actum est ut, propinquante partus tempore, edicto Cesaris matrone regni Sycilie vocarentur omnes volentes futuro partui in-

9 teresse. Quibus convenientibus etiam ex longinquo, positis in pratis extra civitatem Panormi tentoriis et, secundum alios, intra urbem, percipientibus cunctis, imperatrix decrepita infantem enixa est, Fredericum scilicet, qui postea in monstruosum evasit hominem et Ytalie totius, nedum regni Sycilie, pestem, ut non evacuaret calabri abbatis vaticinium.

the frequent changes in the royal succession or their unworthy character, wars began to break out everywhere between competing factions of the nobility, and the whole kingdom seemed on the way to destruction by fire and sword. Hence there occurred to some who were distressed by the sad state of affairs an idea which later was realized, namely, that Constance should be married to some great prince so that the deadly tumult might be quelled through his powerful intervention.

With the pope's approval, they managed to convince Constance 6 to wed, but not without great effort and deceit: she held fast to her religious vows, and her advanced age seemed to pose another obstacle. Nonetheless, despite her continuing objections, matters had reached the stage where it was not easy to retreat, and she was given in marriage to Henry, emperor of Rome and son of the late Frederick I.

Thus did a wrinkled crone abandon the sacred cloister, discard 7 her monastic veil, and, royally adorned, marry and emerge in public as empress. She went into the imperial chamber, entered the marriage bed, and against her will lost the eternal virginity she had dedicated to God. And so it happened, to the amazement of everyone who heard of it, that the old woman conceived at the age of fifty-four.[c]

People were slow to accept the truth of Constance's pregnancy, 8 the majority believing it to be a fraud. So, to remove any suspicion as the time for the birth approached, the emperor prudently ordered that all women in Sicily who so desired should be invited to attend the impending delivery. They came, even from far away, 9 and tents were pitched in the meadows outside the city of Palermo and, according to some sources, in the city itself. The aged empress gave birth in the presence of all to a baby, namely, Frederick, who later turned out to be the monster and scourge not only of Sicily but of all Italy. Thus was the prophecy of the Calabrian abbot fulfilled.

10 Quis ergo non conceptum partumque Constantie arbitrabitur
monstruosum? Cum, preter hunc, nullus sit nostris auditus temporibus. Quid nostris dico temporibus? Non ab adventu Enee ad
Ytalos, unum preter, tam annose mulieris compertus, Helisabeth
scilicet coniugis Zacharie, ex qua, Dei singulari opere, Iohannes
natus est cui, inter natos mulierum, secundus non erat in posterum surrecturus.

: CV :

De Cammiola senensi vidua

1 Cammiola vidua mulier decore corporeo, moribus magnificentia ac
honestate et laudabili pudicitia splendida, senensis origine fuit,
Laurentii de Toringo, hominis equestris ordinis, filia; vitam autem
apud Messanam, Sycilie vetustissimam civitatem, non minus commendabilem quam egregiam, cum parentibus et viro unico, dum
vixere, deduxit, Frederico III rege insule imperante.

2 Quibus diem claudentibus, heres fere regias divitias consecuta
est; eaque honestatis decore<m>¹ servante, Frederico iam dicto rebus humanis subtracto eique Petro filio suffecto, factum est ut
Messane, regis iussu, pregrandis pararetur classis sub ducatu Iohannis Clarimontis comitis, ea tempestate bellicosissimi hominis,
Liparitanis obsessis et extrema fere inedia laborantibus, latura sub-

3 sidium. Quam non solum mercede conductus miles, sed et auxilia-
rii plures, et tam litorani quam mediterranei voluntarii, ad armorum gloriam consequendam, consce<n>dere² proceres.

4 Obsederat enim oppidum strenuus vir Goffredus de Squilacio,
Roberti Ierusalem et Sycilie regis, tunc navalis prefectus, qui oppi-
danos oppugnationibus et bellicis machinis atque frequenti circun-

Hence it is evident that Constance's pregnancy and birth were 10
monstrous. Indeed, no other such birth, apart from this one, has
been heard of in our time. Or, for that matter, in times other than
our own. Since Aeneas' arrival in Italy, only one other example involving such an aged woman is known, namely, the case of Eliza-
beth, Zachariah's wife, who through God's wondrous intervention
gave birth to John; and no son born afterwards to any woman
could equal him.

: CV :

Camiola, a Sienese Widow

Camiola, Sienese by birth and a widow renowned for her physical 1
beauty, noble conduct, and praiseworthy modesty, was the daughter of the knight Lawrence of Thuringia. While her parents and
her only husband were alive, she lived with them near Messina, an
ancient city in Sicily, during Frederick III's rule of that island. Her
life was as blameless as it was remarkable.

When these members of her family died, Camiola inherited al- 2
most royal wealth and continued to preserve a dignified virtue.
Then the above-mentioned Frederick died and his son Peter succeeded him. At the latter's order, an enormous fleet was prepared
at Messina; commanded by Count John of Chiaramonte, one of
the most able soldiers of the period, its mission was to bring aid to
the besieged and starving inhabitants of Lipari.[a] Those who em- 3
barked included not only mercenaries but also auxiliary troops as
well as many nobles—both from the coast and inland—who had
volunteered in order to win military glory for themselves.

Godfrey of Squillace, a valiant man who was then fleet com- 4
mander in the service of Robert, king of Jerusalem and Sicily, had
besieged Lipari. The townspeople were so weakened by his as-
saults and war machines and frequent blockades that an imminent

5 datione adeo debilitaverat ut proxima speraretur deditio. Sane cum novisset, exploratoriis referentibus lembis, classem hostium longe sua ampliorem propinquari, revocatis in unum navibus, ex tuto cepit rei expectare fortunam. Hostes autem, occupatis evestigio locis omissis, impediente nemine, que ferebant oppidanis intulere sussidia.

6 Quo rerum successu Iohannes elatus, Goffredum in dimicationem evocavit; quod cum ardentissimi vir ingenii non detrectasset et nocte tabulatis ac turribus roborasset classem, ordinassetque naves et cetera et, apparente aurora, oratione ferventi suos animasset in pugnam, sublatis ancoris et signo dato proras vertit in Syculos.

7 Iohannes vero, cui non erat animus Goffredum sumpturum, sed nec expectaturum Syculorum navigiorum molem, non in certamen, sed ad insequendas fugientium suas composuerat naves; ardorem et apparatum venientium hostium videns, fere destitutus animo timuit penituitque eum petiisse quod minime se obtenturum putarat.

8 Et secum iam rebus diffidens, animo satis tepenti ne omnino videretur exanguis, revoluto rerum repente in prelium ordine, quantum scilicet pro tempore concessum est, signum et ipse dedit certaminis.

9 Aderant iam hostes qui, sublato clamore ingenti, lente venienti Syculorum classi miscuere proras et iniecere ferreas manus, tormentis telisque primo impetu inchoantes certamen; et hesitantibus atque fere torpentibus ob repentinam consilii mutationem Syculis, premoniti atque irruentes ultro goffrediani milites sese hostium intulere navigiis et gladiis manibusque rem agere cepere et sanguine cuncta fedare.

10 Syculi vero iam diffidentes, qui potuere, revolutis proris terga dedere. Attamen cum appareret victoriam Goffridianis[3] cedere, plurime sunt Syculorum demerse naves, plurime capte, pauce tan-

surrender was expected. When Godfrey learned from the scouting   5
vessels of the approach of an enemy fleet much larger than his
own, he gathered all his ships together and in safety awaited future
developments. With no opposition, the enemy immediately occupied the abandoned positions and brought the aid they were carrying to the inhabitants of Lipari.

Elated by his success, John challenged Godfrey to battle, an in-   6
vitation this fiery man did not refuse. During the night Godfrey
fortified the decks, poops, and forecastles of his fleet, set his ships
in battle formation, and made other preparations. At daybreak he
gave a rousing speech, urging his men to fight. The anchor was
raised and, at a given signal, he turned his prows round to face the
Sicilians. John did not believe that Godfrey would attack or even   7
await the mighty Sicilian fleet; consequently he had drawn up his
ships not for battle but for pursuit of the retreating enemy vessels.
When he observed the bold advance and the preparations of the
approaching foe, John all but lost his nerve; in his fear he regretted
seeking an encounter which he had thought would be refused.

Privately John despaired of the situation. But he had enough   8
courage left to avoid the appearance of complete cowardice. So immediately, inasmuch as time permitted, he converted his formation into a battle line and personally gave the signal for combat.
The enemy was already at hand. They raised a great war cry and   9
locked prows with the slow-moving Sicilian ships. Hurling iron
grappling hooks, they commenced the first assault with missiles
and arrows. The Sicilians hesitated, as though stunned by the sudden change in tactics. Godfrey's men were prepared and began to
rush at the foe, boarding their ships and engaging in hand-to-hand
combat with swords; soon all was stained with blood.

By now the Sicilians had lost confidence, and those who could   10
turned their ships around and fled. Victory seemed to be Godfrey's. Many Sicilian vessels had been sunk and many captured; a
few vessels that were maneuverable by oars got away to safety,

11 tum[4] et remigio faciles remigantium virtute incolumes abiere. Eo
vero in conflictu cecidere pauci, vulnerati plures: Iohannes classis
prefectus captus est et cum eo fere proceres omnes, qui voluntarii
classem conscenderant, capti et milites atque remiges plurimi mili-
taria atque navalia signa et regium pregrande vexillum, quod in
pretoria vehebatur navi; et cum in deditionem venisset oppidum
post longos errores, maris tempestatibus circumacti, Neapolim catenis honusti tracti sunt et servati carceribus.

12 Erat hos inter Rolandus quidam, Frederigi regis ex concubina
filius, iuvenis forma valens et probitate corporea; qui, cum ceterorum captivorum[5] redemptio pararetur, solus inrepetitus, abeuntibus aliis redemptione soluta, tristis servabatur captivus. Nam Petrus rex, ad quem fratris spectabat opus, ob rem male gestam et
preter preceptum, tam eum quam ceteros omnes qui in acie navali
fuerant habebat exosos.

13 Eo igitur sic captivo et ab omni libertatis spe fere destituto ac in
compedibus marcescente, contigit ut Cammiole veniret in mentem. Que cum illum a fratribus videret neglectum, infortunio eius
compassa est secumque disposuit, si cum honestate posset, velle
eum in libertatem educere; et cum, decore honestatis sue servato,
nulla alia monstraretur via, ni in maritum summeret, missis qui
clam percontarentur numquid hoc pacto vellet catenas exuere, facile obtinuere.

14 Et sic, omni servata iuris celebritate, eam in personam procura-
toris consensu et anuli sub arratione desponsavit in coniugem.
Nec mora: mictente Cammiola duobus milibus unciarum argenti
solutisque carcere liber Messanam rediit. Nec aliter apud sponsam

15 divertit quam si nullum ex connubio factum verbum. Mirata primum Cammiola, demum cum sensisset hominis ingratitudinem,
indignata est. Verum ne videretur ira inpulsa potius quam iure
agere, ante alia illum placide requiri fecit ut nuptiale sacrum perfi-
ceret; quem, cum omnino nil tale secum esse negasset, apud eccle-

thanks to the prowess of their rowers. Not many men died in that 11
battle, but there was a sizeable number of wounded. John, the admiral of the fleet, was captured along with almost all the princes
who had voluntarily embarked. Also seized were numerous soldiers and oarsmen, military and naval flags, and the great royal ensign, which flew from the admiral's ship. The city surrendered.
After long wanderings during which they were buffeted by storms,
the prisoners were taken in chains to Naples and jailed.

Among them was a certain handsome and robust young man 12
called Roland, a son of King Frederick by a concubine. Ransom
was collected for the other captives, but only in Roland's case was
there no request. His companions left once the money had been
paid; Roland remained gloomily in prison. In fact, King Peter,
whose duty it was to liberate his brother, hated Roland as well as
everyone else who had taken part in the naval engagement because
of their incompetence and their disobedience of his orders.

Camiola, however, happened to remember Roland. He was still 13
incarcerated, languishing in his shackles with practically no hope
of freedom. When she saw that he was neglected by his brothers,
she pitied his misfortune and determined that, if it could be honorably done, she would give him his liberty. As there was no other
way to free Roland and preserve her honor except to marry him,
she sent messengers to ask him secretly if he wanted to be released
from his chains on that condition. They readily obtained his
agreement.

So, all the legal formalities were observed. Roland, through a 14
legal agent, voluntarily pledged his troth with a ring. Camiola immediately sent a ransom of two thousand ounces of silver; Roland
was released from prison and returned to Messina a free man. He
behaved, however, towards his betrothed as if not a word had been
said about marriage. At first Camiola was surprised; then, real- 15
izing the man's ingratitude, she became indignant. But she did
not want to be regarded as acting out of anger rather than from

16 siasticum iudicem convenit; atque signatis tabulis et testimonio probatorum virorum convicit in coniugem. Quod postquam erubescens confessus est et benefitium mulieris in eum cognitum, obiurgatus a fratribus et amicorum inpulsu, eo deductus est ut petitioni annueret mulieris et nuptias postularet.

17 Ast ingentis animi femina petentem, astantibus multis, fere his verbis allocuta est:

'Habeo, Rolande, unde Deo gratias agam; nam antequam, sub pretestu coniugii, integritatem castitatis delibares mee, tue iniquitatis ostendisti perfidiam; et, eodem favente, cuius sanctissimum nomen nephasto periurio ludere conatus es, iure mendacium retudi tuum, quod michi de te deque tuo coniugio permaximum est.

'Putasti, reor, adhuc clausus, me mee conditionis oblitam, temerarie regium optasse sponsum et tuam formositatem muliebri ardere concupiscentia easque, meo ere suscepta libertate, negatione unica purgare ridere atque comprimere et te, pristinis restitutum honoribus, splendidiori servare coniugio; et, quantum in te fuit, obnixe fecisti.

18 'Verum qui ex alto humilia respicit nec sperantes in se deserit, mentis mee sinceritate cognita, egit ut parvo labore meo tuas infringerem fraudes, ingratitudinem tuam detegerem et perfidiam demonstrarem. Nec hoc tantum in detestationem impietatis tue

19 meo feci facinore. Possunt enim de cetero videre fratres, possunt et reliqui quid tue commictendum sit fidei, quid de te amici sperare,

a sense of justice, so she initially arranged that he should receive a polite invitation to go through with the marriage ceremony. When Roland refused to have anything to do with this request, Camiola had him summoned before an ecclesiastical judge. She proved, with the help of legal documents and the testimony of honorable men, that he was her intended husband. Then Roland 16 flushed and admitted the truth. When Camiola's kindness toward him became known, Roland was rebuked by his brothers and persuaded by his friends to consent to her claim and to seek a formal wedding.

Thereupon the magnanimous woman addressed her petitioner 17 in the presence of a large crowd, using almost these very words:

"I have reason, Roland, to thank God that you have demonstrated your treachery and wickedness before taking away my purity under the pretense of marriage. With the help of Him whose holy name you tried to mock with your impious perjury, I have struck down, with the help of the law, your lies about yourself and your marriage, and this was my principal concern.

"You thought, I suppose, while you were still in prison, that I had forgotten my position, longed rashly for a husband of royal lineage, and burned with feminine concupiscence for your good looks. When my money brought you freedom, you believed that with a single denial you could rid yourself of your obligations, mock and suppress them, and then, after regaining your former high station, save yourself for a more splendid marriage. You strove to do this with all your might.

"But He who from on high looks down upon the humble and 18 abandons not those who place their hope in Him — He recognized the sincerity of my intention and saw to it that with little effort on my part I should upset your schemes, reveal your ingratitude, and disclose your perfidy. I did not do this only to make your sinful conduct an object of detestation. From now on, your brothers and 19 everyone else can see how much your word is to be trusted, what

quid hostes timere. Ego aurum perdidi, tu famam; ego spem, tu regis et amicorum gratiam. Sycule matrone magnificentiam mirantur meam et laudibus efferunt, tu ignominiosum ridiculum notis omnibus et incognitis factus es[6].

20   'In hoc tamen aliquandiu decepta sum: rebar stolide, pro terre fece, regium atque illustrem vinculis eripuisse iuvenem, ubi mendacem lixam, infidum ganeonem, immanem beluam liberasse me video.

21   'Nec velim tanti te arbitreris ut credas me scelus in hoc traxisse; movit memoria benefitiorum veterum genitoris tui in patrem meum, si genitor tibi fuit sacre recordationis Fredericus rex; quod ego vix credere queo ex tam celebri principe adeo inhonestum

22   filium fuisse progenitum. Indignum existimasti non regii sanguinis viduam regium habere virum, robustum iuvenem atque oris decore prefulgidum; quod ego confitebor ultro.

23   'Verum velim, si iure potes, respondeas: "Dum ego te meo munere fecisse meum credidi, dum amplissimum aurum in libertatem tuam solvi, ubi splendor tunc regius erat? Ubi inexhaustus vigor, ubi nitens oris decus?" Obscura cavee caligine, qua angebaris, tegebantur hec omnia. Squalor rubigine cathenarum, pallorque lucis invise et tetri carceris pedor, quibus invalidus marcebas fetidus et neglectus ab omnibus, has dotes, quas nunc elatus extollis, represserant.

24   serant. Tunc tu me non solum regio iuvene, sed celesti[7] Deo dignam dicebas.

'O quam facile, quam cito, homo scelestissime, viso preter spem celo patrio, vertisti sententiam, immemor, postquam tui iuris fa-

your friends may hope from you, and what your enemies may have to fear. I have lost my money; you, your reputation. I have lost hope; you, the favor of the king and your friends. The women of Sicily admire my generosity and extoll me with their praise; you have become ridiculous and disgraced in the eyes of all, whether they know you or not.

"For some time I was deceived in this entire affair. I foolishly   20 thought that, for the price of gold,[b] I was delivering from bondage a regal and illustrious young man, but now I see that I have freed a lying parasite, a faithless rake, and a monstrous beast.

"Nor would I have you enjoy such a good opinion of yourself as   21 to believe it was your misfortune that induced me to do this. I was prompted by the memory of your father's kindness of long ago to my own father—that is, if King Frederick of sacred memory was indeed your father. I find it hard to believe that such a disgraceful son could be born of so distinguished a prince. You thought it im-   22 proper for a widow not of royal blood to have a young, strong, handsome husband of royal lineage; this is something that I shall freely admit.

"But I should like you to answer my questions, if you can justly   23 do so: 'When I believed that I had made you mine with my gift, when I paid a great deal of money for your freedom, where then was your royal splendor? Where was your tireless strength? Where were your radiant good looks?' All of these were obscured by the darkness of the cell where you were held. These endow-ments of which you now proudly boast—these were crushed by the filth from your rusty chains, by your pallor from lack of sun-light, by the stench of your gloomy prison, all of which caused you to waste away, weak, fetid, and abandoned by everyone. *Then* you   24 used to say that I was worthy not only of a royal youth, but of a celestial god.

"How easily, how quickly, o wretched man, you changed your mind as soon as you saw the sky of your native land (and this was

ctus es, quoniam ego Cammiola sum, que sola tui memor fui, que sola infortunio tuo miserta sum, que sola pro salute tua substantias exsolvi[8] meas! Ego Cammiola sum que te e manibus capitalis hostis maiorum tuorum, e cathenis, e carcere, ex extrema miseria pecunia mea te eripui, te iam desperatione labantem in spem substuli, te in patriam redegi, te in regiam, te in lucem pristinam revocavi, te ex captivo debili turpique regium robustum spetiosumque iuvenem feci.

25   'Quid ego in mentem tuam revoco que meminisse debes et negare non potes? Tu vero pro benefitiis tam memorandis has rependisti gratias ut ausus sis sponsum negare matrimonium, honestis sanctisque testimoniis tabulisque signatis vallatum et redemptricem tuam despicere ac floccifacere et turpi, si potuisses, suspitione

26   maculare. Erubescebas insane mentis homo viduam ex equestri viro natam habere coniugem. O quam satius erubuisse fuerat evacuasse fidem prestitam, Dei parvipendisse sanctum et terribile nomen, et execrabili ingratitudine tua quam abundans vitiorum sis ostendisse! Fateor me non regiam feminam, sed, cum ab incunabulis apud regias virgines nurus et coniuges versata sim, mores et animum sumpsisse regios mirum non est quod satis est ad nobilitatem assummendam regiam.

'Sed quid multa? Ego tibi in hoc facilis ero in quo tu michi
27   difficilis fuisti pro viribus. Negasti meum esse cum esses. Verum te
28   meum esse cum vicerim, ne meus sis sponte concedo. Tua sit regia claritas, infidelitatis tamen nota fedata; tuum sit iuvenile robur, tua caduca formositas. Ego de cetero mea viduitate contenta

more than you could have hoped for). How soon you forgot, once you were your own master, that I, Camiola, was the only one who remembered you, the only one who felt pity for your misfortune, the only one who spent her substance for your safety. I, Camiola, snatched you, by means of my wealth, from the hands of your ancestors' deadly enemies, from your shackles, from prison, and from utter wretchedness. When you were sinking in despair, I raised you up to hope; I brought you back to your country, to the royal palace, to your former life; I changed you from a weak and ugly prisoner into a regal, robust, and good-looking young man.

"But why do I remind you of what you ought to remember and cannot deny? You should have been grateful for these benefits, but you have thanked me by daring to deny the promised marriage that is confirmed by honest and worthy witnesses and authentic documents. You have despised and vilified me, your rescuer, and stained me with vile allegations when you could. You, a madman, were ashamed to have as your wife a widow who was the daughter of a knight. How much better it would have been if you had been ashamed of breaking your sworn word; of scorning the holy and terrible name of God; of showing through your wretched ingratitude just how abundant are your vices! I admit that I am not a woman of royal blood. But from my childhood I have been in the company of the daughters, daughters-in-law, and wives of kings, so it is not surprising that I have acquired their manners and spirit. And this is sufficient for me to assume the noble state of royalty.

"In short, I will yield to you on that issue in which you have treated me as badly as you could. You denied that you were mine when you were mine. Now that I have proven that you are mine, I concede of my own free will that you are not mine. Let yours be royal renown, but foully branded with your treachery; keep your youthful strength and your fleeting good looks. Henceforth I shall be satisfied with my widowhood, and I shall leave the fortune God

25
26
27
28

consistam; et quas michi prestitit fortunas Deus, quam ex te geni-
tis, honestioribus relinquam heredibus.

29 'Vade igitur, infauste iuvenis; et quoniam me habere te indignum fecisti, tuis disce sumptibus quibus artibus quibus fallaciis
30 alias ludas feminas. Michi sat est quoniam semel a te decepta sum,
ob quod nunquam una tecum esse michi mens est, verum celibem
servare[9] vitam, quam tuis amplexibus longe preponendam censeo.'

Seque his dictis e conspectu subtraxit suo, nec de cetero potuit
precibus aut monitis a laudabili amoveri proposito.

31 Rolandus autem confusus et sero ignavie sue penitens, ab omnibus parvipensus, deiecto vultu non solum fratrum, sed etiam plebeiorum hominum faciem fugiens, in miseram fortunam abiit, non
ausus quam fraude renuerat iure repetere.

32 Generosum autem mulieris animum miratus est rex et proceres
ceteri illumque miris extulere laudibus, incerti quid commendabile
magis: an quod adversus tenacitatem femineam Cammiola tam
grandi pecunia redemerit iuvenem, an quod redemptum atque
convictum, tanquam immeritum animosa spreverit atque reiecerit[10].

: CVI :

De Iohanna Ierusalem et Sycilie regina

1 Iohanna Ierusalem et Sycilie regina preter ceteras mulieres origine
potentia et moribus evo nostro illustris est femina. De qua, ni videretur omisisse odium, satius erat tacuisse quam scripsisse pauca.

2 Fuit ergo hec serenissimi principis Karoli Calabrie ducis incliti

has given me to heirs more honorable than those whom you might have sired.

"Go, then, unhappy youth. You have made yourself unworthy 29 of me; learn at your own expense the arts and deceits you may use to toy with other women. For my part it is enough to have been 30 deceived by you once. For this reason I intend never to be with you; indeed, I think a celibate life is much to be preferred to your embraces."

Camiola withdrew from his sight after this speech, and from that time forward she could be prevailed upon neither by pleas nor by reprimands to alter her praiseworthy resolve.

Roland, confused and repenting too late his vile conduct, was 31 scorned by everyone. With bowed head, he fled not only his brothers' presence but even that of the common people. He went away to face a miserable future, not daring to ask lawfully for the woman whom he had unlawfully rejected.

The king, however, and the other noblemen marveled at the 32 woman's lofty spirit and extolled it with great praise, not knowing which was more commendable: that Camiola, contrary to the usual feminine avarice, had redeemed the young man at such great expense; or that, once he had been ransomed and found to be guilty, she bravely scorned and rejected him as unworthy.

: CVI :

Joanna, Queen of Jerusalem and Sicily

Joanna, queen of Sicily and Jerusalem, is more renowned than any 1 other woman of our time for lineage, power, and character. It would have seemed hateful not to speak of her at all, yet it would have been better to remain silent than to write too little.

She was the eldest daughter of the Most Serene Prince Charles, 2

et primogeniti celebris memorie Roberti, Ierusalem et Sycilie regis,
3 ac Marie, Phylippi regis Francorum sororis, filia prima. Cuius parentum, si velimus avos proavosque in finem usque exquirere, non
subsistemus antequam per innumeros ascendentes reges in Darda-
num, primum Ylionis auctorem, venerimus, cuius patrem Iovem
4 dixere veteres. Ex qua tam antiqua tanque generosa prosapia tot
hinc inde clari[1] manavere principes ut nullus christianorum regum
sit qui huic non veniat consanguineus vel affinis; et sic nulla diebus
patrum nostrorum nec nostris orbe effulsit nobilior.

5 Hec etiam, Karolo patre, ea adhuc infantula, immatura morte
subtracto, cum nulla esset Roberto avo melioris sexus proles altera,
iure factum est, eo etiam sic mandante, ut eidem morienti super-
6 stes regnorum efficeretur heres. Nec equidem ultra torridam zo-
nam aut inter Sauromatas sub glaciali polo illi pregrandis cessit
hereditas, quin imo inter Adriaticum et Tyrrenum mare ab
Umbria et Piceno ac veteri[2] Volscorum patria in syculum usque
fretum sub miti[3] celo; quos inter fines eius parent imperio Cam-
pani veteres, Lucani Brutii[4] Sallentini Calabri Daunique et Vestales ac Samnii Peligni Marsique et alii plures, ut maiora sinam, ut
puta ierosolomitanum[5] regnum, Sycilie insulam et in Cisalpina
Gallia Pedimontis territorium, que illi ab usurpantium quorundam occupantur iniuria; sic et qui septimanam provinciam inter
narbonensem Galliam Rhodanum Alpesque[6] incolunt et Focalche-
rii comitatum, suis eque iussis parent eamque sibi fatentur dominam et reginam.

7 O quot his in regionibus civitates inclite, quot insignia oppida,
quot maris sinus et refugia nautarum, quot navalia, quot lacus,
quot medici fontes, quot silve nemora saltus amenique recessus et
pinguia arva! Necnon quot numerosi populi, quot ingentes sunt

the eminent Duke of Calabria and first-born son of Robert of illustrious memory, king of Sicily and Jerusalem. Her mother was
Mary, sister of King Philip of France. If we trace her parents' an-   3
cestors to the beginning of the dynasty, we will not stop until we
have made our way through many kings to Dardanus, founder of
Troy and (according to the ancients) son of Jupiter. From this old   4
and distinguished family have been born so many famous princes
on both sides that every Christian king is related to it by blood or
by marriage. No dynasty has shone more nobly throughout the
world in our own or our fathers' time.

Joanna was still a small child when her father met a premature   5
death. Since her grandfather Robert had no other male children,[a]
through his directive she became, as the only survivor, the legitimate heir to the kingdom at his death. Her mighty inheritance did   6
not extend beyond the torrid zone or to the North Pole among the
Sarmatians; rather, it fell in a temperate climate, that is, between
the Adriatic and the Tyrrhenian Sea, from Umbria, Piceno, and
the ancient country of the Volscians to the straits of Sicily. Within
these borders her rule is obeyed by the ancient Campanians,
Lucanians, Bruttii, Salentines, Calabrians, Daunians, Vestini,[b]
Samnites, Pelignians, Marsians, and many others — not to mention still greater lands, such as the kingdom of Jerusalem, the island of Sicily, and the territory of Piedmont in Cisalpine Gaul,
all of which certain usurpers now wrongly occupy. In addition,
those who obey her commands and acknowledge her as their sovereign and queen include the inhabitants of Provence between
Narbonian Gaul, the Rhone, and the Alps, as well as those who
live in the county of Forcalquier.

How many famous cities are in these regions, how many re-   7
markable towns, gulfs, havens for sailors, ports, lakes, medicinal
springs, groves, forests, pastures, pleasant retreats, and fruitful
fields! How numerous are the people, how magnificent the

proceres! Quam grandis insuper opulentia et rerum omnium, ad victum spectantium, copia, equidem non esset explicare facile.

8   Quod cum permaximum sit dominium nec id sit a mulieribus possideri consuetum, non minus miraculi quam claritatis affert, si satis inspicimus. Et, quod longe mirabilius est, sufficit illi ad imperium animus: tam perlucidam adhuc avorum indolem servat.

9   Ea enim, postquam regio dyademate insignita est, virtute insurgens valida, adeo purgavit, nedum civitates et domestica loca, verum Alpes, saltus devios, nemora et ferarum lustra scelesta hominum manu, ut aufugeret omnis terrefacta aut se celsis clauderet arcibus; quos, agmine armatorum emisso sub egregio duce, non ante locorum talium obsidionem solveret, quam, captis munitionibus, infandos homines affecisset supplicio, quod precedentium regum aliquis aut noluit aut fecisse nequivit; eoque redegit terras quas possidet, ut non solum inops, sed et opulentus cantando nocte dieque possit quo velit tutus iter arripere; et — quod non minus salubre — insignes viros Regnique proceres tanta frenavit modestia et eorum mores solutos retraxit in melius, ut, posita superbia veteri, qui reges olim parvipendebant, hodie faciem irate mulieris horrescant.

10   Est insuper oculata femina tantum, ut fraude potius quam ingenio illam decipere queas. Est et magnifica, regio potius quam femineo more; sic et grata memorque obsequiorum; longanimis est et constans, ut sacrum propositum eius non leviter flectas in vacuum: quod satis monstravere iamdudum in eam fortune sevientis insultus, quibus persepe acri concussa motu et agitata est atque turbine

11 circunducta vario. Nam perpessa est intestina regulorum fratrum discordia et extera bella, nonnunquam intra regni gremium debachata, sic et alieno crimine fugam exiliumque[7] et coniugum auste-

princes! Certainly it would not be easy to describe the greatness of her kingdom's wealth and the abundance of its provisions.

If we examine her domain closely, our amazement will equal its 8 fame, for it is a mighty realm of the sort not usually ruled by women. Yet far more admirable is the fact that Joanna's spirit is equal to its governance, so well has she preserved the luminous character of her ancestors.

For example, after she was crowned with the royal diadem, 9 Joanna bravely took action and cleansed not only the cities and inhabited areas but also the Alpine regions, remote valleys, forests, and wild places from bands of outlaws, who fled in terror or retreated to lofty fastnesses. Soldiers were then dispatched under the command of a courageous leader, and the siege of these places was not lifted until their strongholds had been captured and the accursed men inside executed. No previous king had been willing or able to do this. Joanna has brought such order to the lands she now possesses that both rich and poor can go safely and joyously by day or night, wherever their road takes them. No less beneficial, with such discretion has she curbed the leading men and princes of the kingdom and reformed their dissolute ways that, discarding their former arrogance, those who earlier had no respect for kings now tremble at the sight of an angry queen.

Moreover, Joanna is so astute that only trickery, not brains, can 10 deceive her. She is generous in the manner of a king rather than of a woman. She values and remembers devoted service. She is so patient and steadfast that she cannot be easily deflected from her righteous path. This was clearly demonstrated some time ago by the blows of hostile fortune which often struck and buffeted her fiercely from every direction. Indeed, Joanna has endured internal 11 struggles between princes of the royal family as well as foreign wars which at times raged within the heart of her kingdom. Through the fault of others, she has had to endure flight, exile, the grim ways of her husbands[c] and the envy of noblemen, undeserved

ros mores, livores nobilium, sinistram nec meritam famam, pontificum minas et alia, que omnia forti[8] pertulit pectore; et tandem erecto invictoque omnia superavit animo: edepol grandia, nedum mulieri, sed robusto ac prevalido regi!

12   Est illi preterea spectabile ac letum decus oris, eloquium mite et cunctis grata facundia. Et uti[9] illi regalis et inflexa maiestas est, ubi oportunitas exigit, sic et familiaris humanitas, pietas, mansuetudo atque benignitas, ut non reginam suis dicas esse, sed sociam[10].

13   Que maiora petas in prudentissimo rege? Esset necnon, si quis de integritate mentis sue omnia explicare velit, sermo longissimus.

14   Quibus agentibus, ego non solum illam reor egregiam et splendida claritate conspicuam, sed singulare decus ytalicum, nullis hactenus nationibus simile visum.

Conclusio

1   In nostras usque feminas, ut satis apparet, devenimus, quas inter adeo perrarus rutilantium numerus est, ut dare ceptis finem honestius credam quam, his ducentibus hodiernis, ad ulteriora progredi; et potissime dum tam preclara regina concluserit quod Eva, prima omnium parens, inchoavit.

2   Scio tamen non defuturos qui dicant multas omissas[1] fore; et hos super, alios qui alia obiciant, que forsan merito redargui possint.

   Ego autem — <ut>[2] primis cum humilitate respondeam — omisisse multas fatebor[3] ultro; non enim ante alia omnes attigisse

3   poteram, quia plurimas fame triunphator tempus assumpsit. Nec michi, ex superstitibus, omnes videre potuisse datum est; et ex cognitis, non semper omnes volenti ministrat memoria. Sane, ne me omnino immemorem putent, credant volo quia non me inadver-

ill-repute, papal threats, and other evils, all of which she has borne with a stout heart. In short, she has overcome everything with her lofty and indomitable spirit. Truly these would have been magnificent accomplishments for a vigorous and mighty king, much less for a woman.

Joanna has besides a wonderfully charming appearance. She is 12 soft-spoken, and her eloquence pleases everyone. When the occasion demands it, she has a regal and unyielding majesty; equally she can be affable, compassionate, gentle, and kind, so that one would describe her as her people's ally rather than as their queen. What greater qualities would one seek in the wisest king? If some- 13 body wanted to give full expression to the integrity of Joanna's character, it would require a very long discourse indeed.

For all these reasons, I think that she is not only remarkable 14 and striking for her splendid fame, but a singular glory of Italy such as has never before been seen by any nation.

Conclusion

As is apparent, I have now come to the women of our own time. 1 But so small is the number of those who are outstanding that I think it more honorable to end here rather than continue with the women of today—all the more so since this work, which began with Eve, mother of the human race, concludes with so illustrious a queen.

I know that some will say I have left out many famous women; 2 besides these detractors, others will raise diverse objections about things arguably deserving of censure.

To reply humbly to the former group, I admit willingly that I have omitted many women. First, I could not mention them all, for Time, which triumphs over Fame, has engulfed the majority. Nor was I able to read about all those whose fame has survived, 3 and memory did not serve me as I wished for all those of whom I

tente[4] plurime, tam barbare quam grece atque latine et Augusto-
4 rum coniuges atque regum, preterierint. Vidi equidem innumeras
et earum facinora novi, sed non michi, arripienti in hoc calamum,
animus fuit omnes velle describere; quin imo—ut ab initio opusculi huius testatus sum—ex multitudine quasdam elicere et apponere. Quod cum satis congrue factum rear, supervacanea restat
obiectio.

5   Reliquis vero sic dictum sit: possibile esse et contigisse facile
credam nonnulla minus recte consistere. Decipit enim persepe non
solum ignorantia rerum, sed circa opus suum nimia laborantis[5]
affectio. Quod si factum sit, doleo quesoque, per venerabile hone-
storum studiorum decus, equo animo quod minus bene factum est
prudentiores ferant; et si quis illis pie caritatis spiritus est, minus
debite scripta augentes minuentesque corrigant et emendent, ut
potius alicuius in bonum vigeat opus, quam in nullius commodum
laceratum dentibus invidorum depereat.

Iohannis Boccaccii de Certaldo
De mulieribus claris liber explicit feliciter

had knowledge. Let people, however, not deem me altogether forgetful: I would have them know that I have deliberately omitted many women, barbarian as well as Greek and Latin, and wives of emperors and kings. In truth, I considered innumerable women 4 and learned of their deeds, but when I took up my pen I did not intend to describe all of them. Rather, as I stated at the beginning of this book, I meant to choose only some from a very large number and to bring these to the reader's attention. I think I have done this suitably and well; hence the objection is unnecessary.

To my other critics, I say that it is possible (and I can easily believe it happened) that some things were improperly included. Certainly, an author is often deceived both by ignorance of events and by an excessive attachment to his own work. If this is the case, I am sorry, and I ask on behalf of the venerable dignity of honorable studies that my readers tolerate with a wise and kindly spirit what has not been skillfully executed. If they are charitably inclined, let them correct and emend the inappropriate passages by addition or deletion: in this way, the work will live for someone's benefit rather than perish, mangled by the teeth of envy, of service to no one.

Here Ends the Book on Famous Women
Written by Giovanni Boccaccio of Certaldo

Note on the Text

Ɓ𝔖𝔭𝔖

The autograph witness (Florence, Biblioteca Medicea Laurenziana 90 sup. 98[1] [Gaddi 593]) dates from the last period of Boccaccio's life and presents the text of the *Famous Women* in its final form. It was this version that Vittorio Zaccaria used as the basis of his edition and Italian translation ([Milan,] 1967, 1970). Our translation of the *Famous Women* is based on Zaccaria's text and so is the first in English to utilize the autograph.

I am much indebted to Zaccaria's outstanding work on the *Famous Women*; his great erudition and knowledge of Boccaccio's Latin and vernacular compositions, together with the numerous informative notes on the text, have clarified many obscurities in Boccaccio's often contorted Latin. Readers who wish to inform themselves more fully regarding the textual tradition and sources of the *Famous Women* are advised to turn first to Zaccaria's edition.

The only other complete translation into English of the *Famous Women* is that of Guido A. Guarino. His rendering (New Brunswick, N.J.: Rutgers University Press, 1963) was based on the 1539 Bern edition, a vulgate text derived from a redaction of the text prior to that which appears in the autograph used by Zaccaria. When Guarino embarked upon his task, the Bern edition was the most widely available; unfortunately, it contains numerous defective readings and much questionable punctuation. Many of the faults of the 1539 edition are reflected in Guarino's translation. Nevertheless, the present translation from time to time gratefully makes use of Guarino's renderings.

The chief principles governing the translation and the accompanying Latin text are as follows:

(1) Zaccaria's Latin text has generally been followed, including the division into chapters and sections and the reproduction of Boccaccio's orthography (except that some separated compound words like *cui nam, non nulli, num quid* and so forth are written as *cuinam, nonnulli, numquid*);

477

(2) occasional departures from Zaccaria's text have been made, mostly in matters of punctuation, but a few readings have also been adjusted in light of a fresh collation of a microfilm of the autograph;

(3) only selected textual variants, making up the ninth and final revision (according to Zaccaria's hypothesis), have been reported in the *apparatus criticus*;

(4) Boccaccio's lengthy and complicated Latin sentences have been broken up in the English translation as seemed required by sense and syntax;

(5) in accord with Zaccaria's practice in his Italian translation, proper names rendered in English generally conform to the Latin spelling, even when the Latin name differs from what is usually regarded as correct (e.g., Pocris instead of Procris), with exceptions made for names involving diphthongs or the letters *h* and *y* (thus Aeneas, Aegisthus, Isis, Rhoeteum) and names exhibiting more profound changes;

(6) the principal entry in the Index is the form of the name as given by Boccaccio, with a secondary entry as needed for the more usual form, e.g., [main entry] Pocris (Procris), [secondary entry] Procris: see Pocris.

Notes

꙾ꙩ꙾

The notes and apparatus below are arranged as follows: under the title of each biography, the first section gives sources and/or parallels, the second (keyed to arabic numerals) the *apparatus criticus*, and the third (keyed to letters of the alphabet) such brief explanations as seemed necessary for the reader to grasp the immediate sense of a passage; such annotations have been limited to matters that could not easily be explained using standard dictionaries of mythology or reference works like the *Oxford Classical Dictionary*.

ABBREVIATIONS

August.	Augustine, *De civitate dei*
Cic., *De inv.*	Cicero, *De inventione*
Cic., *Nat. D.*	Cicero, *De natura deorum*
Euseb.	Eusebius, *Chronicon* (trans. Jerome), ed. R. Helm (Leipzig, 1913)
Hegesip.	Hegesippus, *Historiae*
Isid.	Isidore, *Etymologiae*
Joseph.	Josephus, *Antiquitates iudaicae*
Just.	Justinus, *Epitoma Historiarum philippicarum Pompei Trogi*
Lact.	Lactantius, *Divinae institutiones*
Lact. Plac.	Lactantius Placidus, *Commentarii in Statii Thebaida*
Livy	Livy, *Ab urbe condita libri*
Luc.	Lucan, *Bellum civile*
Macrob.	Macrobius, *Saturnalia*
MS.	Florence, Biblioteca Medicea Laurenziana 90 sup. 98[1] (Gaddi 593)
Oros.	Orosius, *Historiae adversus paganos*
Ov., *Fast.*	Ovid, *Fasti*
——, *Her.*	*Heroides*
——, *Met.*	*Metamorphoses*

· NOTES ·

Pliny	Pliny the Elder, *Historia naturalis*
Pompon.	Pomponius Mela, *De chorographia*
Serv.	Servius, *In Aeneida*
SHA	*Scriptores Historiae Augustae*
Solin.	Solinus, *Collectanea rerum memorabilium*
Stat.	Statius, *Thebais*
Suet.	Suetonius, *De vita Caesarum*
Tac.	Tacitus, *Annales*
Val. Max.	Valerius Maximus, *Factorum et dictorum memorabilium libri IX*
Virg., Aen.	Virgil, *Aeneis*
——, Ecl.	*Eclogae*
——, Georg.	*Georgica*
Zac, Zaccaria	V. Zaccaria, ed., *De mulieribus claris*, 2nd edition ([Milan,] 1970)

DEDICATION

1. solutus *Zac*: -tis MS.   2. <in>firmiori *Zac*

3. professa *Zac*: -fessam (?) MS.

a. The final chapter (CVI) of the *De mulieribus claris* contains a lengthy eulogy of Joanna.

b. Carlo d'Arto, Count of Monteodorisio, was Andrea Acciaiuoli's first husband; he died in 1346. By 1357 she had not yet remarried, to judge from a letter of 14 September 1357 from her brother Niccolò in which she is mentioned as Countess of Monteodorisio (L. Tanfani, *Niccolò Acciaiuoli: Studi storici fatti principalmente sui documenti dell'Archivio fiorentino* [Florence, 1863], p. 119). The *et nunc* ('and now') in the Latin text may suggest that her second marriage was a fairly recent event.

c. In dedicating to Andrea what he has 'thus far' (*hactenus*) written, Boccaccio gives a discreet indication that the text of the *Famous Women* is still a work in progress; see the Introduction for his various revisions.

PREFACE

1. sanguinis *MS.*: sangui<ni>s *Zac*

a. Of the older *De viris illustribus*, Boccaccio knew the anonymous work (fourth century A.D.?) which he and others wrongly ascribed to Pliny. He was also familiar with the *De viris illustribus* of Jerome (continued by Gennadius of Marseilles). Petrarch's work of the same name was begun before he wrote the *Africa* (1338–39) and remained unfinished at his death (1374). Boccaccio, who met Petrarch in 1350, would have been able to see the enlarged version produced by Petrarch during the period 1351–53.

I. EVE, OUR FIRST MOTHER

Genesis II:7–III:23; Paulinus Minorita, *Compendium* (Zaccaria).

1. suas *Zac:* suos *MS.*   2. -bron *seems corrected from* -bror *in the MS.*

II. SEMIRAMIS, QUEEN OF THE ASSYRIANS

Val. Max. IX.3, ext. 4; Just. I.2; Euseb. 20.13–17, 19–26; Oros. I.4, II.2.5, 6.7; Paulinus Minorita, *Compendium* (Zaccaria).

1. erronea *Zac:* erronica *MS.*   2. regendas *Zac:* regendos *MS.*

3. populus *MS.*: popolus *Zac*   4. cuntis *corrected from* cunctis (?) *in the MS.*   5. latere *Zac:* latore *MS.*   6. obsideret *Zac:* obsidoret *MS.*   7. adhuc *MS., om. Zac*   8. explendum *corrected in the margin of the MS. from* -dam

a. According to Just. I.2.9 and Oros. I.4.5 (who are among Boccaccio's sources), only Semiramis herself and Alexander the Great had undertaken an expedition to India.

III. OPIS, WIFE OF SATURN

Livy XXIX.10.4–11.8, 14.5–14; Lact. I.13.2–3, 14.2–5.

1. sacerdotes *corrected from* sacert- *in the MS.*

a. The difficulties connected with bringing the statue of Ops to Rome are described in chapter LXXVII.3–6 below.

IV. JUNO, GODDESS OF KINGDOMS

Lact. I.17.8; Serv. II.225.

1. dictu *MS.*: dictum *Zac*

V. CERES, GODDESS OF THE HARVEST
AND QUEEN OF SICILY

Virg., *Georg.* IV.58; Ov., *Fast.* IV.401–404, VI.285–286 and *Met.* V.341–343, 385 ff.; Euseb. 49.19–26; August. VII.20; Lact. Plac. II.382.

1. agricolationis *MS.*: agricula- *Zac*

a. This is the first of a number of instances in which Boccaccio expresses or implies his preference for the simple, rustic life of the ancients and his distrust of the alleged benefits of civilization.

VI. MINERVA

Cic., *Nat. D.* III.21.53, 23.59; Livy VII.3.7; Luc. IX.350; Lact., I.17.12–13, 18.22–23; Euseb. 30.21–26, 42.11–14; August. XVIII.8–9.

1. et celo *MS.*: et e celo *Zac*   2. largintrix *MS.*: largitrix *Zac*
3. finem *MS.*: finis *Zac*

a. For Arachne of Colophon and her rivalry with Athena vis-à-vis weaving, see chapter XVIII below.

VII. VENUS, QUEEN OF CYPRUS

Cic., *Nat. D.* II.20.53, III.23.59; Ov., *Met.* IV.171–189; Lact. I.17.10; Just. XVIII.5.4, XXI.3.2.

1. extollendam eius *MS.*: eius extollendam *Zac*   2. in terras: in terris *Zac*: intrans (?) *MS.*   3. genitricis *MS.*: gene- *Zac*

a. See below, chapter XLII.6, for another reference to this custom of prostitution among the Cypriots.

VIII. ISIS, QUEEN AND GODDESS OF EGYPT

Ov., *Met.* I.588–747; Euseb. 32.9–13, 40.7, 8–9, 43.12–16.

1. transfretasse *corrected from* transfretrasse *in the* MS.
2. conmictere MS.: commic- *Zac*

IX. EUROPA, QUEEN OF CRETE

Euseb. 47.7–10, 25, 53.16–17, 55.4–5; Ov., *Met.* II.833-III.2, VI.103–107; Isid. XIV.4.1.

1. faciles MS.: facile *Zac*   2. <arbitror> *Zac, om.* MS.
3. ex spectabili *Zac*: expectabili MS.

X. LIBYA, QUEEN OF LIBYA

Euseb. 46.17–18; August. XVIII.12; Lact. Plac. IV.737; Isid. XIV.4.1, 5.1.

XI–XII. MARPESIA AND LAMPEDO, QUEENS OF THE AMAZONS

Just. II.4.1–16; Oros. I.15.1–6.

1. mammille MS.: mamille *Zac*   2. partis *Zac*: parctis MS.

a. Just. II.4.1 gives the name of the youth as 'Plynos'. Boccaccio's *Sylisios* is derived from *Ylynos* (*Ylinos*), the reading in some manuscripts of Justinus.

b. *Cyrii* (= 'Cyrian') appears to be a truncated form of *Themiscyrii* (= 'Themiscyrian') from Themiscyra, a city in Pontus at the mouth of the Thermodon River and the reputed home of the Amazons.

c. 'Amazon' is traditionally (and fancifully) derived from ἀ and μαζός ('without a breast').

XIII. THISBE, A BABYLONIAN MAIDEN

Ov., *Met.* IV.55–166.

1. rata *Zac*: ratam *MS.*   2. sors *MS.*: fors *Zac.*   3. toleranda *MS.*: tolle- *Zac*

XIV. HYPERMNESTRA, QUEEN OF THE ARGIVES AND PRIESTESS OF JUNO

Ov., *Her.* XIV; Euseb. 46.8–12, 47.22–23; Oros. I.ii.1; Lact. Plac. II.222.

1. Quibus . . . servamus *added by Zac*

XV. NIOBE, QUEEN OF THEBES

Ov., *Met.* VI.146–312.

1. clarissimo *Zac*: -mi *MS.*

XVI. HYPSIPYLE, QUEEN OF LEMNOS

Stat. V.28–721; Lact. Plac. IV.717, V.613–675.

1. imperio *MS.*: imp<er>io *Zac*   2. Colcos *Zac*: Colcon (?) *MS.*

a. Archemorus is also known as Opheltes; see § 9 below and Lact. Plac. IV.717.

XVII. MEDEA, QUEEN OF COLCHIS

Ov., *Met.* VII.1–450.

1. antris *MS.*: antro *Zac*   2. arbitr<ar>etur: arbitretur *MS.*
3. eo *Zac*: ea *MS.*

XVIII. ARACHNE OF COLOPHON

Ov., *Met.* VI.1–145; Pliny VII.56.196.

1. suo evo *MS.*: evo suo *Zac*   2. se *MS.*, *om. Zac*   3. satorem *Zac*: satoeem (?) *MS.*   4. omnes *MS.*: omnium *Zac*

XIX–XX. ORITHYA AND ANTIOPE, QUEENS OF THE AMAZONS

Just. II.4.17–30; Oros. I.15.7–9.

XXI. ERYTHRAEA OR HEROPHILE, A SIBYL

Lact. I.6.8, 14; August. XVIII.23; Isid. VIII.8.1, 3, 4.

XXII. MEDUSA, DAUGHTER OF PHORCUS

Ov., *Met.* IV.774–785, 790–801; Luc. IX.624–684; Serv. VI.289; Theodontius (Zaccaria).

XXIII. IOLE, DAUGHTER OF THE KING OF THE AETOLIANS

Ov., *Her.* IX.73–134; Lact. I.9; Serv. VIII.291.

XXIV. DEIANIRA, WIFE OF HERCULES

Ov., *Met.* IX.101–238 and *Her.* IX.

XXV. JOCASTA, QUEEN OF THEBES

Seneca, *Oedipus* 1024–41; Stat. XI.634–644.

1. maxima *MS.*: maximo *Zac*   2. molis *MS.*: malis *Zac*

a. Polynices and Eteocles, sons of Oedipus and Jocasta, had made a compact to alternate the kingship every year. Polynices, who was the first to hold the royal power, stepped down at the expiration of his year in office to make way for his brother. Eteocles, however, refused to give up the throne when his own year was over, and this ultimately led to the war against Thebes.

XXVI. ALMATHEA OR DEIPHEBE, A SIBYL

Virg., *Aen.* VI.268 ff.; Solin. II.16, 17, 18; Lact. I.6.10–11; Serv. VI.72, 321; Isid. VIII.8.5.

1. Deyphebe *Zac*: Deyphile *MS.*

a. See John I:9 "Erat lux vera, quae illuminat omnem hominem venientem in hunc mundum" ("This was the true light which enlightens every man who comes into the world").

b. See Zaccaria, p. 503 n. 8.

XXVII. NICOSTRATA OR CARMENTA, DAUGHTER OF KING IONIUS

Ov., *Fast.* I.461–542; Solin. I.10, 13; Serv. VIII.51; Theodontius (Zaccaria).

1. vates *MS.*: vaste *Zac*   2. multum *MS.*: multa *Zac*
3. gramaticam *MS.*: gramma- *Zac*

XXVIII. POCRIS, WIFE OF CEPHALUS

Ov., *Met.* VII.694–862.

1. Ignoro *Zac*: Egnoro (?) *MS.*   2. dixerim *Zac*: dixrim *MS.*
3. immo- *Zac*

XXIX. ARGIA, WIFE OF POLYNICES AND DAUGHTER OF KING ADRASTUS

Stat. IV.187–213.

1. videatur *Zac*: videan- *MS.*

a. For the agreement between Polynices and Eteocles, see above, XXV.4 and note a.

b. This necklace had been presented to Cadmus and Harmonia by the god Hephaestus as a wedding gift. Dazzling in beauty but fraught with curses, it brought ill-luck to the married couple and to their descendants.

Polynices gave the necklace to Eriphyle (not Eurydice as reported by Boccaccio), the wife of Amphiaraus; in return, Eriphyle betrayed the hiding place of Amphiaraus, who was then compelled to join the expedition known as 'The Seven against Thebes'.

XXX. MANTO, DAUGHTER OF TIRESIAS

Virg., *Ecl.* IX.59–60; Stat. IV.463–468, X.597–603; Pompon. I.88; Isid. XV.1.59.

1. iecinora *Zac*: iocinora (?) *MS.*   2. obsederant *Zac*: obside- *MS.*

XXXI. THE WIVES OF THE MINYANS

Val. Max. IV.6, ext. 3.

1. lucidi *MS.*: perlu- *Zac*   2. eis *MS.*: ei *Zac*

XXXII. PENTHESILEA, QUEEN OF THE AMAZONS

Just. II.4.31–32.

1. eius *added in the margin of the MS.*   2. Hectorem *MS.*: Herculem *Zac*

a. Penthesilea seems to have been confused with Minithya, another Amazon queen, who is reported by Boccaccio's source (Just. II.4.32) to have gone to Alexander's camp and slept with him for thirteen nights for the purpose of conceiving a child.

XXXIII. POLYXENA, DAUGHTER OF KING PRIAM

Ov., *Met.* XIII.441–480; Seneca, *Troades* 1117–61; Serv. III.321.

1. adolescentula *MS.*: adules- *Zac*

XXXIV. HECUBA, QUEEN OF THE TROJANS

Homer, *Iliad* XVI.717–718; Virg., *Aen.* III.19–68; Ov., *Met.* XIII.423–450, 481–571; Pompon. II.26; Solin. X.22; Lact. Plac. I.22; Leontius Pilatus (Zaccaria).

1. eximius *MS.*: eximi\<us\> *Zac*   2. oppressam *MS.*: oppressa *Zac*
3. Cynosema *Zac*: Cynosenia *MS.*

a. For purpose of safekeeping at the outbreak of the Trojan War, Polydorus, the infant son of Priam and Hecuba, had been sent along with much gold to King Polymestor of Thrace and his wife Ilione (who was also Polydorus' sister). Virgil relates that, after the destruction of Troy, Polymestor seized the gold intended for the rearing of Polydorus and killed the boy.

b. Cynossema, a promontory on a peninsula of Thrace, derives its name from κυνὸς σῆμα ('Tomb of the Dog'); in some accounts (e.g., Ov., *Met.* XIII.565 ff.), Hecuba was actually changed into a dog.

XXXV. CASSANDRA, DAUGHTER OF KING PRIAM OF TROY

Virg., *Aen.* II.246–247, 341–346, 403–408; Serv. II.247.

1. promisisse *MS.*: -missi- *Zac*   2. aut\<em\> *Zac*: aut *MS.*

XXXVI. CLYTEMNESTRA, QUEEN OF MYCENAE

Serv. XI.267; Leontius Pilatus (Zaccaria).

1. capiti\<s\> *Zac*: capiti *MS.*

XXXVII. HELEN, WIFE OF KING MENELAUS

Cic., *De inv.* II.1.1–2; Serv. I.526, XI.262; Lact. Plac. I.21; Leontius Pilatus (Zaccaria).

1. precepta *Zac*: per- *MS.*   2. leticiam *MS.*: -titi- *Zac*
3. \<erat\> *Zac, om, Ms.*   4. hec *MS.*: hoc *Zac*
5. Lacedemonam *MS.*: -mona *Zac*

a. Paris was the son of Priam, king of Troy, and his wife Hecuba. While the queen was pregnant, she dreamed that she had given birth to a flaming torch. Priam consulted the oracle of Apollo and was told to put the child to death. A servant was ordered to kill the infant Paris, but in

pity he abandoned the boy on Mount Ida. See § 11 below where the burning of Troy is interpreted as the fulfillment of Hecuba's dream.

b. When Juno, Minerva, and Venus all laid claim to the golden apple thrown by Eris, goddess of Discord, onto the table at the wedding banquet of Peleus and Thetis, Jupiter appointed Paris, then a shepherd on Mount Ida, as judge. Each of the three goddesses offered a different gift if judgment were pronounced in her favor, and Paris accepted the offer of Venus.

c. The exposure of Hesione, daughter of King Laomedon of Troy, to a sea monster was the only way (according to an oracle consulted by her father) to free the land of this menace. Hercules killed the monster and restored Hesione to her father in return for the immortal horses which Laomedon had inherited from Tros. Laomedon, however, substituted other horses and Hercules retaliated by mounting an expedition against Troy. Troy was taken, Laomedon killed, and Hesione given to Telamon as a concubine. The latter took her to Salamis, and Priam made several futile requests for her return.

XXXVIII. CIRCE, DAUGHTER OF THE SUN

Ov., *Met.* XIV.248–308; Serv. VII.190; Leontius Pilatus (Zaccaria).

1. contubernio *MS.*: -turber- *Zac*

XXXIX. CAMILLA, QUEEN OF THE VOLSCIANS

Virg., *Aen.* XI.539–841; Serv. XI.543, 558.

XL. PENELOPE, WIFE OF ULYSSES

Ov., *Her.* I; Leontius Pilatus (Zaccaria).

1. continue *MS.*: -tinuo *Zac*

a. The name of Ulysses' swineherd is Eumeus; here 'sybotes' (= συβώτης, 'swineherd') has been made into a proper name.

XLI. LAVINIA, QUEEN OF LAURENTUM

Virg., *Aen.* VII, XII passim; Livy I.3.1; Euseb. 66.1–7; Serv. IV.620, VI.760.

1. mortesque MS.: -tem- *Zac*

XLII. DIDO OR ELISSA, QUEEN OF CARTHAGE

Virg., *Aen.* I.338–368; Just. XVIII.4.1–6, 8; Serv. I.338.

1. somnis MS.: -niis *Zac*   2. interoganti MS.: interro- *Zac*
3. si *before* exteram *deleted by Zac*   4. et MS., *om. Zac*   5. nonne *Zac*: non MS.   6. carea<n>t *Zac*: careat MS.   7. enim *Zac*: tamen MS.

a. Boccaccio's account of Dido's conduct at Carthage has no mention of Aeneas and so is completely different from that of Virgil (*Aeneid* IV). Instead, Dido is presented as an example of chaste widowhood, and this portrayal serves as the model for subsequent interpretations of Dido in Renaissance Italian literature; see A. Cerbo, "Didone in Boccaccio," *Annali dell'Istituto Universitario Orientale, Napoli,* sezione romanza, 21 (1979) 177–210.

b. The 'customary sacrifice' consisted of prostitution; see above, chapter VII.10 for the Cypriots' practice of this custom.

c. I Corinthians 7:9.

d. For the notorious Valeria Messalina, wife of the emperor Claudius, see note b in chapter XCII.4 below.

XLIII. NICAULA, QUEEN OF ETHIOPIA

Pliny VI.32.154, 35.185–186; Joseph. VIII.6.2.

1. produxit *Zac*: per- MS.   2. Egyptii *Zac* : Egytii MS.

a. III Kings 10:1–13; II Paralipomenon 9:1–12; Matthew XII:42; Luke XI:31.

XLIV. PAMPHILE, DAUGHTER OF PLATEA

Pliny XI.26.76.

a. Pliny reports that Pamphile invented weaving on the island of Cos.

XLV. RHEA ILIA, A VESTAL VIRGIN

Livy I.3–4.

1. Deo added *in the margin of the MS.*
2. incestu *MS.:* -tum *Zac*
3. transcendentes *MS.:* trascen- *Zac*
4. et *Zac, om. MS.*
5. <cogitant> *Zac, om. MS.*

XLVI. GAIA CYRILLA, WIFE OF KING TARQUINIUS PRISCUS

Pliny VIII.74.194.

1. nuptis *MS.:* nuptiis *Zac*

XLVII. SAPPHO, GIRL OF LESBOS AND POETESS

Ov., *Her.* XV; Isid. I.39.7.

1. liram *MS.:* lyram *Zac*

XLVIII. LUCRETIA, WIFE OF COLLATINUS

Livy I.57–58.

1. hoc *MS., om. Zac*   2. occisurum *Zac:* -suram *MS.*

a. Shocked by the circumstances of Lucretia's death, the Romans expelled the Tarquins and established a republic.

XLIX. TAMIRIS, QUEEN OF SCYTHIA

Just. I.8; Oros. II.7.

1. Rypheis *MS.:* Ri- *Zac*

L. LEAENA, A PROSTITUTE

Pliny VII.23.87; Euseb. 106.1–7.

1. pretiosa *MS.*: preci- *Zac*   2. Macedonas *MS.*: -dones *Zac*
3. contubernio *MS.*: conturbenio *Zac*   4. Demosthenes *Zac*:
-thenis *MS.*

a. See above, Preface, §§ 5–6.

b. The same proverb is also cited in chapter XCIII.6 below.

LI. ATHALIAH, QUEEN OF JERUSALEM

IV Kings 8:16–11:16; II Paralipomenon 22:1–23:15; Joseph. VIII–IX.

1. coruscaret *Zac*: -care *MS.*   2. dedecorose *Zac*: -rese *MS.*
3. prophana *MS.*: profana *Zac*

LII. CLOELIA, A ROMAN MAIDEN

Livy II.13; Val. Max. III.2.2.

1. transitu *Zac*: -sita *MS.*

a. See chapter XLVIII above.

LIII. HIPPO, A GREEK WOMAN

Val. Max. VI.1, ext. 1.

LIV. MEGULLIA DOTATA

Val. Max. IV.4.10.

1. quam aliquo *Zac*: quam a aliquo *MS.*   2. inexplebilia *Zac*: -pli-
MS.

LV. VETURIA, A ROMAN MATRON

Livy II.39.1–40.12; Val. Max. V.2.1a.

1. abstulerat *Zac*: -rant *MS.*   2. Volumniam *Zac*: Voluminam *MS.*
3. senatu<s> *Zac*: -tu *MS.*   4. diminutum *MS.*: demi- *Zac*

LVI. TAMARIS, DAUGHTER OF MICON

Pliny XXXV.35.59, 40.147.

1. Miconis MS.: My- Zac   2. virtus MS., Zac

a. Pliny (see above) gives the name of this personage as Timarete (not Tamaris).

LVII. ARTEMISIA, QUEEN OF CARIA

Vitruvius, De architectura II.8.10–11, 14–15; Val. Max. IV.6, ext. 1; Pliny XXXVI.4.30–31; Just. II.12.23–24; Oros. II.10.1–3.

1. monimenta MS.: monu- Zac   2. Arthimisia MS.: Arthe- Zac
3. viri cineres MS.: viri mortui cineres Zac   4. <celaverat> Zac, om. MS.   5. Themistode MS. (the correct form is Themistocle)

a. Boccaccio has turned Pliny's pteron (= 'colonnade') into the name of the fifth artist, who is not identified by Pliny. The translation of this sentence relies, to some extent, on the fuller, clearer sense of Pliny's version (XXXVI.4.31: "Accessit et quintus artifex. Namque supra pteron pyramis altitudinem inferiorem aequat, viginti quattuor gradibus in metae cacumen se contrahens" — "With them was associated a fifth artist. For above the colonnade there is a pyramid as high again as the lower structure and tapering in 24 stages to the top of its peak", trans. D. E. Eichholz, vol. X, Loeb Classical Library [London-Cambridge, Mass., 1962], p. 25).

b. Zaccaria, p. 522 n. 8 suggests that Boccaccio confused stematibus (the reading in the autograph witness) with stigmatibus (the reading in Vitruvius); stigmatibus is understood in our translation of this passage.

LVIII. VIRGINIA, VIRGIN AND DAUGHTER OF VIRGINIUS

Livy III.44–48, 58.

1. conspicui MS.: -cua Zac   2. Claudio Zac: Appio MS.
3. frustra MS., om. Zac   4. in ruinam Zac: in iniuriam MS.
5. sequuntur MS.: secuntur Zac   6. interpretes Zac: -petres MS.

a. The rather free translation of "legum sed lenonum . . . iudicia" as "the counsels of panderers rather than of the *Pandects*" preserves the alliterative effect of the Latin text. The *Pandects* are a digest of Roman civil law, in fifty books, compiled in the sixth century for the emperor Justinian. Here, however, *Pandects* is simply taken in a collective sense as "laws".

LIX. IRENE, DAUGHTER OF CRATINUS

Pliny XXXV.40.140, 147.

1. celebre *Zac*: cebre *MS*.   2. que *MS*., *om. Zac*   3. absque *Zac*: abque *MS*.

LX. LEONTIUM

Cic., *Nat. D.* I.33.93; Pliny, praef. 29.

1. tempestate *Zac*: -tem *MS*.   2. per *Zac*: post *MS*.

3. su<b>lime *Zac*: sulime *MS*.   4. spurcido *MS*.: -cide *Zac*

LXI. OLYMPIAS, QUEEN OF MACEDONIA

Just. VII.6.10, IX.5–7, XIV.5–6; Oros. III.14, 23.30–32.

1. regi<s> *Zac*: regi *MS*.   2. Mistilis *Zac*: Mistalis *MS*.

LXII. CLAUDIA, A VESTAL VIRGIN

Val. Max. V.4.6.

1. ob *MS*., *om. Zac*

LXIII. VIRGINIA, WIFE OF LUCIUS VOLUMNIUS

Livy X.23.1–9.

1. Verginea *MS*.: Vir- *Zac*

a. Virginia, daughter of Aulus Virginius (chapter LVIII above).

LXIV. FLORA THE PROSTITUTE, GODDESS OF FLOWERS AND WIFE OF ZEPHYRUS

Ov., *Fast.* V.193–212; Lact. I.20.6–10; Macrob. I.10.11–14.

LXV. A YOUNG ROMAN WOMAN

Val. Max. V.4.7; Pliny VII.36.121.

1. ac *Zac:* hac *MS.*

LXVI. MARCIA, DAUGHTER OF VARRO

Pliny XXXV.40.147–148.

1. rubor *MS.*: robur *Zac*

LXVII. SULPICIA, WIFE OF FULVIUS FLACCUS

Val. Max. VIII.15.12; Pliny VII.35.120.

1. ornatus *MS.*: -tos *Zac*

a. Lucretia's death is described in chapter XLVIII.6–8 above.

b. For the importance of the Sibylline Books to the Romans, see above, chapter XXVI.5–6 .

LXVIII. HARMONIA, DAUGHTER OF GELON OF SICILY

Livy XXIV.24–25; Val. Max. III.2, ext. 9.

LXIX. BUSA OF CANOSA DI PUGLIA

Livy XXII.52; Val. Max. IV.8.2.

LXX. SOPHONISBA, QUEEN OF NUMIDIA

Livy XXIX.23, XXX.8, 12–15.8.

1. ut *Zac, erased (?) in MS.*   2. libidini *MS.*: -dinis *Zac*
3. remotis *Zac:* remoris *MS.*

LXXI. THEOXENA, DAUGHTER
OF PRINCE HERODICUS

Livy XL.3–4.

1. navim *MS*.: navem *Zac*   2. Theosena *Zac*: -senam *MS*.

LXXII. BERENICE, QUEEN OF CAPPADOCIA

Val. Max. IX.10, ext. 1; Just. XXXVIII.1–2.

LXXIII. THE WIFE OF ORGIAGO THE GALATIAN

Livy XXXVIII.12–14, 24.2–14; Val. Max. VI.1, ext. 2.

LXXIV. TERTIA AEMILIA, WIFE OF
THE ELDER AFRICANUS

Val. Max. VI.7.1.

1. Luteio *Zac*: Luteino (?) *MS*.   2. intollerabilius *MS*.: intolera- *Zac*
3. causa *Zac*: causam *MS*.

LXXV. DRIPETRUA, QUEEN OF LAODICEA

Val. Max. I.8, ext. 13.

1. pretactum *MS*.: per- *Zac*

LXXVI. SEMPRONIA, DAUGHTER OF GRACCHUS

Val. Max. III.8.6, IX.15.1.

1. qua *Zac*: que *MS*.

LXXVII. CLAUDIA QUINTA, A ROMAN WOMAN

Livy XXIX.14.5–12; Ov., *Fast.* IV.255–344; Pliny VII.34.120; Solin.
I.126.

1. For the arrival of the statue in Rome, see also III.3 above.

LXXVIII. HYPSICRATEA, QUEEN OF PONTUS

Val. Max. IV.6, ext. 2; Oros. VI.5.3–5.

LXXIX. SEMPRONIA, A ROMAN WOMAN

Sallust, *De coniuratione Catilinae* XXV.

1. et miseriam *MS*.: et in miseriam *Zac*

2. modestia<m> *Zac*: modestia *MS*.

a. Sempronia, sister of Tiberius and Gaius Gracchus (chapter LXXVI above).

LXXX. THE WIVES OF THE CIMBRIANS

Val. Max. VI.1, ext. 3; Annaeus Florus, *Epitome de gestis Romanorum* I.38.1–18; Oros. V.16.1–19.

1. <Cymbrorum> *Zac*: theutonorum *erased in MS*.
2. Cimbros *MS*.: Cymbros *Zac*   3. Theutones *Zac*: -tonos (?) *MS*.
4. viros *MS*.: vires *Zac*   5. Cimbre *MS*.: Cymbre *Zac*
6. meliori *Zac*: -ris *MS*.

LXXXI. JULIA, DAUGHTER OF THE DICTATOR JULIUS CAESAR

Val. Max. IV.6.4.

LXXXII. PORTIA, DAUGHTER OF CATO UTICENSIS

Val. Max. III.2.15, IV.6.5.

1. preclara *MS*.: -clare *Zac*   2. eduxisse<n>t *Zac*: -set *MS*.

LXXXIII. CURIA, WIFE OF QUINTUS LUCRETIUS

Val. Max. VI.7.2.

1. <cum> *Zac.*, *om. MS*.   2. ea *MS*.: eo *Zac*   3. qua *MS*.: quo
Zac   4. ancillulam *MS*.: ancillam *Zac*   5. numquid *Zac*

LXXXIV. HORTENSIA, DAUGHTER
OF QUINTUS HORTENSIUS

Val. Max. VIII.3.3.

1. exolvende *MS.*: exsol- *Zac*

LXXXV. SULPICIA, WIFE OF TRUSCELLIO

Val. Max. VI.7.3.

a. This is the proscription, described in chapter LXXXIII.2 above, which also affected Curia's husband.

LXXXVI. CORNIFICIA, A POETESS

Euseb. 159.2–5.

a. Euseb. 159.4–5.

LXXXVII. MARIAMME, QUEEN OF JUDAEA

Joseph. XIV, XV and *De bello iudaico* I.22 ff.; Hegesip. I.22.1, 37.2–3.

1. pulcri- *MS.*: pulchri- *Zac*   2. pulchri- *MS.* (h *added above the line*)
3. Quas *MS.*: Quam *Zac*   4. eodem *Zac*

LXXXVIII. CLEOPATRA, QUEEN OF EGYPT

Luc. X; Pliny IX.58.119–121, XXI.9.12; Suet., *Iul.* I.35, 52, II.17; Macrob. III.17.14–18; Hegesip. I.29–32; Oros. VI.16.1–2, 19.4–18.

1. schapha *MS.*: scapha *Zac*   2. rege *Zac*: regem *MS.*
3. Arthabarza- *MS.*: Arthabaza- *Zac*   4. cum *Zac*   5. ex *MS.*:
e *Zac*

a. The Psyllians, an African tribe, were known for their immunity to snake venom (Pliny VII.2.14) and their care of others who had been bitten (Luc. IX.909–911).

LXXXIX. ANTONIA, DAUGHTER OF ANTONY

Val. Max. IV.3.3.

XC. AGRIPPINA, WIFE OF GERMANICUS

Suet., *Tib.* III.52.3, 53 and *Calig.* IV.23.1.

1. exacerbabatur *Zac*: exarceba- *MS*.   2. posse *Zac*: posset *MS*.

XCI. PAULINA, A ROMAN WOMAN

Hegesip. II.4.

1. ex *Zac, om. MS*.

XCII. AGRIPPINA, MOTHER
OF THE EMPEROR NERO

Suet., *Claud.* V.44 and *Ner.* VI.5.3, 28.2, 34.1–4; Tac. XII.1–10, 64–69, XIV.1–9.

1. materno *MS., om. Zac*   2. formosissima *MS.*: formossima *Zac*
3. Ancio *MS.*: Antio *Zac*   4. obsequiis *corrected in the margin to*
exsequiis *by another hand*   5. sui<s> *Zac*

a. Chapter XC above (Agrippina, Wife of Germanicus).

b. Valeria Messalina (born before A.D. 20) had married her second cousin, the emperor Claudius, in A.D. 39 or 40 and was infamous for her sexual profligacy.

XCIII. EPICHARIS, A FREEDWOMAN

Tac. XV.48, 51, 53, 57.

1. venere *MS.*: deve- *Zac*   2. Puteelos (?) *MS.*: Puteolos *Zac*
3. rata *Zac*: ratam *MS.*   4. conspirantium *MS.*: cospi- *Zac*

a. This proverb first appears in chapter L.5 above.

XCIV. POMPEIA PAULINA, WIFE OF SENECA

Tac. XV.60–61, 63–64.

1. memoriam *Zac*: -ria (?) MS.   2. <per>noctando *Zac*: noctando MS.

XCV. SABINA POPPAEA, WIFE OF NERO

Tac. XIII.45–46, XIV.63–64, XVI.6.

1. consulatu MS.: conso- *Zac*   2. e MS.: ex *Zac*

a. The death of Agrippina, Nero's mother, is described in chapter XCII.16–23 above.

XCVI. TRIARIA, WIFE OF LUCIUS VITELLIUS

Tac., *Historiae* II.63, III.76–77.

1. recuperato oppido *added in the margin of the MS.*   2. Ingentes *Zac*
3. <solent> *Zac, om.* MS.

XCVII. PROBA, WIFE OF ADELPHUS

Isid. I.39.26 and *De viris illustribus* (*De scriptoribus ecclesiasticis*) V.18; Paulinus Minorita (Zaccaria).

1. opus *Zac, om.* MS.   2. <ingenium> *Zac, om.* MS.   3. quam *Zac*: qua MS.

a. The text of Proba's *Cento*, as it appears in the Patrologia latina (vol. 19) and the Corpus scriptorum ecclesiasticorum latinorum (vol. 16.1), ends at the feast of the Ascension, not Pentecost Sunday.

b. It is doubtful that Proba composed a Homeric *cento*; see Zaccaria, p. 546 n. 8.

XCVIII. FAUSTINA AUGUSTA

SHA (Julius Capitolinus, *Marcus Antoninus* XIX.1–9, XXVI.4–5, 7–9, XXIX.1–3).

1. sculpperetur *MS.*: sculpe- *Zac*   2. permaximum *Zac*
3. Antoni\<n\>o *Zac*: Antonio *MS.*   4. scelestis *Zac*: scelestibus *MS.*
5. volens ob *MS.*: volens et ob *Zac*

XCIX. SYMIAMIRA, WOMAN OF EMESA

SHA (Julius Capitolinus, *Opellius Macrinus* IX; Aelius Lampridius, *Antoninus Heliogabalus* I-II, IV, XVII-XVIII).

1. patre *Zac*: tempore *MS.*   2. Anthiochiam *MS.*: Antio- *Zac*
3. Anthiochia *MS.*: Antio- *Zac*   4. ut *MS.*: et *Zac*

a. For the translation of *stiline* as 'sister' and Boccaccio's possible confusion of this word with *scilicet*, see Zaccaria, p. 548 n. 3.

C. ZENOBIA, QUEEN OF PALMYRA

SHA (Trebellius Pollio, *Tyranni triginta* XV, XVI, XXX; Flavius Vopiscus, *Divus Aurelianus* XXII-XXX, XXXIII-XXXIV).

1. \<amores hominum et contubernia spernere\> *Zac, om. MS.*
2. quatuor *MS.*: quattuor *Zac*   3. et ad ingentem *Zac*
4. haud *Zac*: aut *MS.*   5. Aureli\<an\>um *Zac*: Aurelium *MS.*
6. permaximum *MS.*: maxi- *Zac*   7. \<triunphus\> *Zac, om. MS.*

CI. JOAN, AN ENGLISHWOMAN AND POPE

Martinus Polonus, *Chronicon pontificum* (Zaccaria).

1. Iohannes *Zac*: Iohanna *MS.*   2. existimatus *Zac*: extimatus *MS.*
    3. diabolo *MS.*: dya- *Zac*   4. \<actum est\> *Zac*

a. The Rogation Days (also known as the Minor Litanies) are celebrated with penitential processions on each of the three days immediately preceding Ascension Thursday.

b. Literally, "cast her into outer darkness"; the language recalls Matthew XXII:13: "Mittite eum in tenebras exteriores".

CII. IRENE, EMPRESS OF CONSTANTINOPLE

Anastasius Bibliothecarius, *Chronographia tripartita* (Zaccaria).

1. Costantinopolitana *Zac*: Constinopolitana *MS.*   2. humanis
MS.: romanis *Zac*   3. fidentem viribus *MS.*: viribus fidentem *Zac*
4. ten\p/tassentque *MS.*: temptas- *Zac*   5. Constanti<n>um *Zac*:
Constantium *MS.*   6. luminibusque *Zac*: lumibusque *MS.*
7. Nycepharo *MS.*: *more correctly* -phoro *Zac*   8. Sycopeo *MS.*: *more
correctly* Syno- *Zac*   9. ut *MS.*, *om. Zac*   10. ten\p/tasse *MS.*:
temptas- *Zac*

CIII. GUALDRADA, A FLORENTINE MAIDEN

Coppo di Borghese Domenichi (Zaccaria).

1. tum *MS.*: tunc *Zac*

CIV. CONSTANCE, EMPRESS OF ROME
AND QUEEN OF SICILY

Giovanni Villani, *Cronica* V.20, VI.16, VII.1.

a. Constance was the daughter of Roger II of Altavilla and the aunt of
William.

b. Joachim of Fiore (ca. 1135–1202), abbot of Corazzo and author of famous prophetical works.

c. Constance's age is exaggerated throughout this biography; she married
Henry when she was thirty-one years old and could not have been older
than forty when she gave birth to a son.

CV. CAMIOLA, A SIENESE WIDOW

See Zaccaria, pp. 554–55.

1. decore<m> *Zac*: decore *MS.*   2. consce<n>dere *Zac*: conscedere
MS.   3. Goffridianis *MS.*: Goffredi- *Zac*   4. tantum *Zac*:
tamen *MS.*   5. ceterorum captivorum *MS.*: capti- cete- *Zac*
6. es *MS.*: est *Zac*   7. celesti *Zac*: celeste *MS.*

8. exsolvi *MS.*: exol- *Zac*   9. servare *Zac*: -varem *MS.*
10. reiecerit *MS.*: deie- *Zac*

a. For a study of this chapter and the events connected with the battle of Lipari, see S. Tramontana, "Una fonte trecentesca nel 'De rebus siculis' di Tommaso Fazello e la battaglia di Lipari del 1339," *Bullettino dell'Istituto Storico Italiano per il Medio Evo* 74 (1962) 227–55.

b. Zaccaria, p. 555 n. 4 points out that *pro terre fece* (literally 'for the dregs of the earth') seems to be derived from a similar expression in Seneca, *Epistulae ad Lucilium* XC.45; I follow Zaccaria ('a prezzo d'oro') in rendering the phrase as 'for the price of gold'.

CVI. JOANNA, QUEEN OF JERUSALEM AND SICILY

Serv. I.235.

1. clari *MS.*: preclari *Zac*   2. veteri *Zac*: vetere *MS.*   3. miti *MS.*: micti *Zac*   4. Brutii *MS.*: Bruttii *Zac*   5. ierosolomi- *MS.*: ierosolimi- *Zac*   6. Alpesque *Zac*: Alpelque (?) *MS.*
7. exiliumque *MS.*: exilium *Zac*   8. forti *MS.*: forte *Zac*
9. uti *MS.*: ut *Zac*   10. sociam *MS.*: sotiam *Zac*

a. Literally, "no other offspring of the better sex".

b. Zaccaria, p. 556 n. 4 suggests that the curious reading *Vestales* (transmitted by the manuscripts, including the autograph, and previous printed editions) is a slip for *Vestini*.

c. Joanna had four husbands: Andrew of Hungary, Louis of Taranto, James III of Mallorca, and Otto of Brunswick. This allusion to her husbands' 'grim ways' must have been written during the approximately six months of 1362 when she was a widow, i.e., from 26 May (when Louis died) until 14 December (when she married James); consequently it is an important clue for the dating of the *Famous Women*.

CONCLUSION

1. omissas *MS.*: obmissas *Zac*   2. ut *Zac, om. MS.*   3. fatebor *MS.*: fateor *Zac*   4. inadvertente *MS.*: -tenter *Zac*   5. laborantis *Zac*: -tes *MS.*

Bibliography

ᘓᖇᖇᘓ

COMPLETE EDITIONS

Boccaccio, *De mulieribus claris* (Ulm, 1473).

———, *De preclaris mulieribus* [Strassburg, ca. 1474–75].

———, *De preclaris mulieribus* (Louvain, 1487).

———, *De claris mulieribus* (Bern, 1539).

Branca, V., ed., *Tutte le opere di Giovanni Boccaccio,* vol. X: V. Zaccaria, ed., *De mulieribus claris* ([Milan,] 1967; 2nd edition, 1970). (With an Italian translation.)

TRANSLATIONS

DUTCH

Johannes Boccatius van Florentien, poeet ende philosophe, bescrivende van den doorluchtighen, glorioesten ende edelsten vrouwen . . . (Antwerp, 1525).

ENGLISH

Schleich, G., ed., *Die mittelenglische Umdichtung von Boccaccios De claris mulieribus, nebst der lateinischen Vorlage,* Palaestra 144 (Leipzig, 1924).

Wright, H. G., ed., *Forty-Six Lives Translated from Boccaccio's De Claris Mulieribus by Henry Parker, Lord Morley,* Early English Text Society, Original Series 214 (London, 1943). (With the Latin text.)

Guarino, G. A., *Boccaccio, Concerning Famous Women* (New Brunswick, N.J., 1963).

FRENCH

Le liure de Jehan Bocasse De la louenge et vertu des nobles et cleres dames (Paris, 1493).

Le plaisant livre de noble homme Jehan Bocace, poète florentin, auquel il traicte des faictz et gestes des illustres et cleres dames (Paris, 1538).

Boccace. Des Dames de renom, nouvellement traduict d'italien en langage françoys (Lyons, 1551).

Baroin, J. and J. Haffen, Boccace. *"Des cleres et nobles femmes."* Ms. Bibl. Nat. 12420, Annales Littéraires de l'Université de Besançon 498 (*Chap. I-LII*), 556 (*Chap. LIII-fin*) (Paris, 1993–95).

GERMAN

Steinhöwel, Heinrich, *Johannes Boccacius. Von etlichen Frowen* (Ulm, 1473).

——, *Johannes Boccacius. Von ettlichen Frauen* (Augsburg, 1479).

——, *Ein schöne Cronica oder Historibuch von den fürnämlichsten Weybern, so von Adams Zeyten angewesst, was guttes oder böses je durch sy geübt, auch was nachmaln guttes oder böses darauss entstanden. Erstlich durch Joannem Boccatium in Latein beschriben* (Augsburg, 1543).

——, *Historien von allen den fürnembsten Weibern, so von Adams Zeiten angeweszt, was gutes und böses je durch sie geübt, auch was nachmals darausz entstanden* . . . (Frankfurt, 1576).

——, *Boccaccio. De claris mulieribus. Deutsch übersetzt von Stainhöwel*, ed. K. Drescher, Bibliothek des literarischen Vereins zu Stuttgart 205 (Stuttgart, 1895).

ITALIAN

Albanzani, Donato degli, *Volgarizzamento di Maestro Donato da Casentino dell'opera di Messer Boccaccio De claris mulieribus, rinvenuto in un codice del XIV secolo dell'Archivio cassinese*, ed. L. Tosti, 2nd edition, Biblioteca scelta di opere italiane antiche e moderne 426 (Milan, 1841).

——, *Delle donne famose di Giovanni Boccacci*, ed. G. Manzoni, 3rd edition (Bologna, 1881).

Betussi, Giuseppe, *Libro di M. Giovanni Boccaccio delle donne illustri, tradotto per Messer Giuseppe Betussi. Con una additione fatta dal medesimo delle donne famose dal tempo di M. Giouanni fino a i giorni nostri, & alcune altre state per inanzi, con la vita del Boccaccio* . . . (Venice, 1545).

——, *Libro di M. Giovanni Boccaccio delle donne illustri . . . con una giunta fatta dal medesimo* . . . (Venice, 1547).

——, *Libro di M. Giovanni Boccaccio delle donne illustri . . . con una giunta fatta dal medesimo . . . e un'altra nuova giunta fatta per M. Francesco Serdonati d'altre donne illustri, antiche e moderne* . . . (Florence, 1596).

Zaccaria, V.: see above under EDITIONS.

SPANISH

Tractado de Johan Bocacio de las claras, excellentes y mas famosas y señaladas damas (Zaragoza, 1494).

Libro de Juan Bocacio que tracta de las illustres mugeres (Seville, 1528).

Goldberg, H., ed., *Text and Concordance of the Zaragoza 1494 edition of Boccaccio's de la ilustres mujeres en romance*, 3 microfiches (Madison, Wis., 1992).

SECONDARY LITERATURE

INFLUENCE

Galigani, G., ed., *Il Boccaccio nella cultura inglese e anglo-americana. Atti del Convegno di Studi "Il Boccaccio nella cultura inglese e anglo-americana" — Certaldo 14–19 settembre 1970* (Florence, 1974).

Mazzoni, F., *Il Boccaccio nelle culture e letterature nazionali. Atti del Congresso Internazionale "La fortuna del Boccaccio nelle culture e nelle letterature nazionali" — Firenze-Certaldo, 22–25 maggio 1975* (Florence, 1978).

Pellegrini, C., *Il Boccaccio nella cultura francese. Atti del Convegno di Studi "L'opera del Boccaccio nella cultura francese" — Certaldo 2–6 settembre 1968* (Florence, 1971).

VARIA

Boitani, P., "The *Monk's Tale*: Dante and Boccaccio," *Medium aevum* 45 (1976) 50–69.

Branca, V., *Tradizione delle opere di Giovanni Boccaccio*, vol. I: *Un primo elenco dei codici e tre studi*, Storia e letteratura 66 (Rome, 1958), pp. 92–98 (brief listing of 85 extant complete or partial manuscripts of the *De mulieribus claris* and 11 manuscripts cited in inventories or whose location is not presently known); vol. II: *Un secondo elenco di manoscritti e studi sul testo del "Decameron" con due appendici*, Storia e letteratura 175 (Rome, 1991), pp. 57–62 (brief listing of 23 additional surviving manuscripts of the *De mulieribus claris* and 17 manuscripts cited in inventories or sold at auction, with location presently unknown).

———, *Boccaccio medievale e nuovi studi sul Decameron*, 6th rev. and enl. edition (Florence, 1986).

——, ed., *Boccaccio visualizzato. Narrare per parole e per immagini fra Medioevo e Rinascimento*, 3 vols. (Turin, 1999) (extensive bibliography in vol. I, pp. 213–61).

——, and V. Zaccaria, "Un altro codice del 'De mulieribus claris' del Boccaccio," *Studi sul Boccaccio* 24 (1996) 3–6 (Los Angeles, Private Collection, S. N.).

Buettner, B., *Boccaccio's Des cleres et nobles femmes. Systems of Signification in an Illuminated Manuscript*, College Art Association Monographs on the Fine Arts 53 (Seattle–London, 1996).

Jodogne, P., "Lemaire de Belges et Boccace," in *Il Boccaccio nella cultura francese*, pp. 489–504. (For complete bibliographical details, see above, under Pellegrini.)

Jordan, C., "Feminism and the Humanists: The Case of Sir Thomas Elyot's *Defence of Good Women*," *Renaissance Quarterly* 36 (1983) 181–201.

——, "Boccaccio's In-Famous Women: Gender and Civic Virtue in the *De mulieribus claris*," in C. Levin and J. Watson, eds., *Ambiguous Realities: Women in the Middle Ages and Renaissance* (Detroit, 1987), pp. 25–47.

Phillippy, P. A., "Establishing Authority: Boccaccio's *De claris mulieribus* and Christine de Pizan's *Le Livre de la cité des dames*," *Romanic Review* 77 (1986) 167–94.

Ricci, P. G., "Studi sulle opere latine e volgari del Boccaccio," *Rinascimento* 10 (1959) 3–12 ("1. Un autografo del *De mulieribus claris*"), 12–21 ("2. Le fasi redazionali del *De mulieribus claris*"), 21–32 ("3. Per la datazione e il commento della lettera al Rossi"). Reprinted, with some addenda, in P. G. Ricci, *Studi sulla vita e le opere del Boccaccio* (Milan-Naples, 1985), pp. 115–48, nos. VIII–X.

Simpson, J., "The Sacrifice of Lady Rochford: Henry Parker, Lord Morley's Translation of *De claris mulieribus*," in M. Axton and J. P. Carley, eds., *'Triumphs of English.' Henry Parker, Lord Morley: Translator to the Tudor Court. New Essays in Interpretation* (London, 2000), pp. 153–69.

Torretta, L., "Il 'Liber de claris mulieribus' di Giovanni Boccaccio," *Giornale storico della letteratura italiana* 39 (1902) 252–73 ("Parte Prima. Il 'Liber de claris mulieribus'"), 273–92 ("Parte II. I fonti del 'Liber de claris mulieribus'"); 40 (1902) 35–50 ("Parte III. I traduttori del 'Liber

de claris mulieribus'"), 50–65 ("Parte IV. I plagiari, gli imitatori, i continuatori del 'Liber de claris mulieribus'").

Tuve, R., "Spenser's Reading: The *De Claris Mulieribus*," in *Essays by Rosemond Tuve: Spenser, Herbert, Milton* (Princeton, 1970), pp. 83–101.

Zaccaria, V., "Le fasi redazionali del 'De mulieribus claris'," *Studi sul Boccaccio* 1 (1963) 253–332.

——, "Appunti sul latino del Boccaccio nel 'De mulieribus claris' (dall'autografo Laur. Pl. 90 sup. 98^1)," *ibid.* 3 (1965) 229–46.

——, "Boccaccio e Tacito," in G. Tournoy, ed., *Boccaccio in Europe. Proceedings of the Boccaccio Conference, Louvain, December 1975* (Louvain, 1977), pp. 221–37.

——, "I volgarizzamenti del Boccaccio latino a Venezia," *Studi sul Boccaccio* 10 (1977–78) 285–306. Reprinted in V. Branca and G. Padoan, eds., *Boccaccio, Venezia e il Veneto. Atti del Convegno di Studi in occasione del sesto centenario della morte di Giovanni Boccaccio (Venezia, 21–22 novembre 1975)* (Florence, 1979), pp. 131–52.

——, "La fortuna del 'De mulieribus claris' del Boccaccio nel secolo XV: Giovanni Sabbadino degli Arienti, Iacopo Filippo Foresti e le loro biografie femminili (1490–1497)," in F. Mazzoni, ed., *Il Boccaccio nelle culture e letterature nazionali,* pp. 519–45. (For complete bibliographical details see above, under INFLUENCE, Mazzoni.)

Index

❧❦❧

References are to the English translation by chapter and paragraph. Latin forms that differ from the English are cross-referenced and are also given in parentheses after the English version. Additional identifying information is provided in square brackets.